Monetary Economics
theories, evidence and policy

Second edition

To our families

Monetary Economics
theories, evidence and policy

Second edition

David G. Pierce
Peter J. Tysome

Butterworths
London Boston Durban Singapore Sydney Toronto Wellington

First published, 1985

© Butterworth & Co (Publishers) Ltd, 1985

British Library Cataloguing in Publication Data

Pierce, David G.
   Monetary economics – 2nd ed.
   1. Money
   I. Title   II. Tysome, Peter J.
   332.4   HG221

   ISBN 0-408-70953-7

Library of Congress Cataloging in Publication Data

Pierce, David G.
   Monetary economics
   Bibliography: p.
   Includes index.
   1. Money 2. Monetary policy 3. Balance of payments
   I. Tysome, Peter J. II. Title
   HG221.P57 1984   332.4   84-9604

   ISBN 0-408-70953-7

Photoset by Butterworths Litho Preparation Department
Printed in Great Britain at the
University Press, Cambridge

Preface

The preface of the first edition, written in 1971, began: 'Over the last decade or so monetary economics has taken on a remarkable new lease of life. The revival of interest in the importance of money has gained so much momentum that monetary economics has, in this short period of time, moved from relative obscurity to the forefront of modern economic analysis.' In the dozen or so years since that was written, monetary economics has continued to thrive and remain at the forefront of contemporary economics. Moreover, the increasing attention that has been paid to the subject in the academic sphere has been mirrored in the increasing awareness of the importance of money and monetary variables, both by politicians and the general public.

Further impetus to the growing interest in the role of money came from the fact that the 1970s witnessed several developments in the national and international economy which were of great relevance. The decade was the most inflationary of the century, and in addition the inflation was accompanied by historically high levels of unemployment. At the beginning of the decade the Bretton Woods system of fixed exchange rates collapsed, and countries generally moved towards the adoption of floating exchange rates. On the policy front, several changes were made to the way in which monetary policy was operated, with the explicit adoption, in the latter half of the decade, of monetary targets.

The aim of this second edition remains that of the first, but updated a decade, i.e. to provide a basic introduction to the main subject matter and controversies of monetary economics as they existed at the beginning of the 1980s. The changes that have been made in content from the first edition are extensive, reflecting the substantial academic developments that have taken place in the discipline, and the changing institutional environment. Although several sections of the first edition have been retained, the changes that have been made are so substantial that this is perhaps best regarded as a new book. Certainly no useful purpose would be served by itemizing the detailed changes from the first edition. Instead, we can simply state that the changes are designed to:

(1) Reflect major theoretical developments, such as the rational expectations 'revolution'.
(2) Give more emphasis to policy issues and problems.

(3) Alter the treatment of international economics so as to give more explicit attention to the monetary aspects, and to recognize the move to floating exchange rates.

The book is intended primarily as an undergraduate text is monetary economics, although it should also be useful to postgraduates reading monetary theory and policy, undergraduates reading macroeconomics, and undergraduates reading international monetary economics. 'Monetary' economics, perhaps more than most other branches of economics, is taught in a variety of ways, sometimes as a separate subject, sometimes as part of a broader macroeconomics course. As a result no single textbook can structure its material in a way which will coincide with the order in which that material is taught in more than a few courses. The content of this book is therefore organized around a number of 'topics' which commonly feature in monetary economics and related courses. This does, however, result in some overlap of material, e.g. rational expectations 'appears' significantly in Chapters 2, 7, 9, 11. To avoid wasteful duplication, we have made fairly extensive use of cross-referencing. The student is also advised to make full use of the comprehensive index.

We would like to express our gratitude to our colleague Mike Pearson for his useful comments on several chapters. Our thanks go also to editors at Butterworths for their encouragement and understanding, and to Jen, Claire, Liz and Susan who typed from almost totally illegible handwriting. As is usual, all errors and inaccuracies in the text are solely the responsibility of the authors.

David G. Pierce
Peter J. Tysome
Nottingham

Contents

The functions, advantages and definitions of money

The major part of this book is concerned with the role of money in the workings of the macroeconomy, i.e. the relationships that are thought to exist between the stock of money and such macroeconomic variables as the level of, and rates of change of, unemployment, interest rates and prices. As a preliminary to these matters, this first chapter will consider the very basic issues of what money is and why we have it at all. We begin by setting out the traditional functions of money. We then look at the nature of a monetary economy and the advantages to be derived from using money. Next we consider some of the various theoretical and empirical definitions of money which have been suggested by economists, and look at the problems involved in trying to enumerate all those assets which are embraced by the definitions. Finally, we set out the official definitions of money that are employed in the United Kingdom.

The functions of money

The word 'money', as used in economics, has two quite distinct meanings. Firstly, it has an abstract meaning in that it is the unit of account or the measure of exchange value. This simply means that money is a sort of common denominator, in terms of which the exchange value of all other goods and services can be expressed. Money in this sense is simply a unit of measurement, denoting the value in exchange of all goods and services, just as, for example, metres denote length, ohms give electrical resistance, and degrees centigrade give temperature. The use of a unit of account greatly reduces the number of exchange ratios between goods and services. With n commodities, one of which is acting as a unit of account, there will need to be only $n-1$ rates of exchange. Without a unit of account, however, there will be $\frac{1}{2}n(n-1)$ separate rates of exchange. Thus, if there are 1000 goods, one of which is a unit of account, then each of the remaining 999 goods will have an exchange rate in terms of the nth, i.e. there will be 999 exchange rates. With no unit of account, however, there will be a separate exchange rate between each pair of commodities, giving 499,500 separate exchange rates.

Money as a unit of account is an abstract form of money, though it may have a physical counterpart. In primitive societies a tangible object such as a cow or a cowrie shell may act as the unit of account, so that the exchange values of all other commodities are expressed in terms of a quantity or number of cows or cowrie shells. But physical objects such as cows tend themselves to vary in the very quality they are supposed to be a measure of. In other words there is no such thing, for example, as a 'standard' cow. No two cows are exactly alike, so that if it is said that a week's labour services are equal to one cow, there is the added problem of deciding which cow is being used as the standard of measurement. Consequently, in developed monetary systems, physical units of measurement are replaced by abstract ones, which are uniform in the sense that they do not themselves vary in the quality measured. One pound sterling is the same as any other pound sterling, one USA dollar is the same as any other USA dollar etc.

The unit of account may, as we have already suggested, have a physical counterpart. This brings us to the second meaning of the word money; money in its more 'concrete' or tangible form. By 'concrete' it is not meant that the money necessarily exists in a physical form (though it may do so), but that ownership of it is capable of changing hands and that there is a supply of it which, to a greater or lesser extent, is capable of being measured. This is money acting as a means of payment and, as such, money is also a medium of exchange. This means it is an intermediary that comes between final exchanges and thereby obviates the need for establishing a double coincidence of wants (i.e. a situation where both parties to an exchange want what the other has and have what the other wants) before an exchange can take place. The means of payment is accepted in return for goods and services because the recipient knows that it can, in turn, be used in exchange for the goods and services he or she requires. The essential characteristic of the means of payment is that it is generally acceptable.

Shackle (1971) has pointed out that while a means of payment is also a medium of exchange, not all mediums of exchange are means of payment. A medium of exchange is anything that enables a transaction to take place in the absence of a double coincidence of wants. Thus, credit may act as a medium of exchange. A builder, for example, may acquire materials from a builders merchant and have their value debited to his or her account. While it is the credit arrangement that has enabled the transaction to take place, the actual payment will not be made until the account is settled, say at the end of the month. As Shackle (1971, p. 32) says:

> Payment has been made when a sale has been completed. Payment has been made when the creditor has no further claim. Payment is in some sense final.

Whether one should confine the definition of money 'concrete' to the means of payment or to the broader medium of exchange is a matter of debate, and is considered in the next section.

The abstract unit of account may have a physical counterpart in the form of, for example, paper money. The pound note may be regarded as a physical embodiment of the pound sterling. It is really only a piece of paper whose value in exchange is equal to one pound sterling. Corresponding to the distinction between money abstract and money concrete, it is helpful to distinguish between accounting prices and money prices. The accounting price is the price denominated in terms of the unit of account: the money price of a commodity is the value of the means of payment that must be given up for a unit of the commodity. We may also distinguish relative prices which are the prices of commodities in terms of one another.

The means of payment itself, like any other good, will have an accounting price. As has already been indicated, the accounting price of a pound note is one pound sterling. The money price of the means of payment, however, must of course be unity. The relative price of the means of payment can only change if the money prices of all other goods, services and assets change. Because the means of payment represents generalized purchasing power, it may be held until the point in time is reached at which the holder wishes to exercise his or her purchasing power. In this way money is performing the function of acting as a store of value. It is permitting the separation in time of the act of sale from the act of purchase. The existence of a means of payment enables a person to sell a commodity or service without simultaneously having to 'buy' another commodity or service in exchange. Receiving a means of payment in exchange for the commodity sold allows the seller to hold on to it until such time as it is needed to be exchanged for the goods and services he or she requires.

Sometimes a fourth function of money is identified, that of acting as a standard for deterred payments. This simply means that if a good, service or asset is 'bought' today, but payment for which will not be made until some later date, then the amount due for deferred payment can be measured in terms of money. It is fairly common practice, however, to argue that this particular function is embraced by the others and does not require separate consideration.

The advantages of having money: the monetary economy

Having briefly stated the functions that money performs, we can now consider the advantages to be derived from using money. What are the benefits enjoyed by the monetary economy that are not available to the barter economy?

If we lived in a world where everybody was self-sufficient there would be no need for money. If nobody engaged in an exchange transaction with anybody else there would be no need for a means of payment or for a measure of exchange value. Thus a precondition for the existence of money is an exchange economy.

An exchange economy is not, however, a sufficient condition for having money. It is quite possible to devise and establish a social system for the exchange of goods which obviates the need for a means of payment. Families, monasteries and communes are examples of social groups in which the members specialized in the performance of particular tasks and exchange goods and services between themselves without recourse to money. However, as the number of participants and the range of goods and services involved all increase, then the problems of coordinating and controlling the large number of exchanges that would be required are likely to become enormous. Some members of the society may well think that they can get a better deal by making their own arrangements for exchanging goods and services. Once people start entering into transactions on their own initiative, then we have a market system, and it is in relation to such market economies that the advantages of using money arise.

A market economy is not, however, a sufficient reason for having money. It is also necessary that the economy be operating under conditions of uncertainty. To see this, let us assume that perfect certainty prevails throughout the economy. With perfect certainty all economic agents have complete information about everything affecting production and exchange. The qualities of all goods and services are known, the relative prices of everything are known, all price changes are correctly foreseen, the creditworthiness of everybody is known and so on. In such a world, multilateral exchanges of goods and services can take place, even over time, on

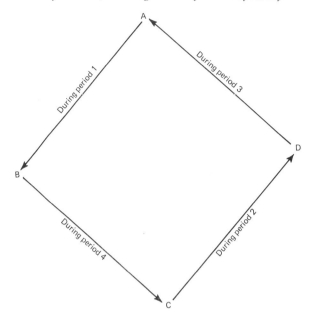

Figure 1.1 Multilateral, intertemporal exchanges of goods in the absence of uncertainy (arrows give the direction of movement of goods and services sold)

terms and conditions which are known at the outset, but which do not require the use of a specialized means of payment. Thus, in *Figure 1.1* individual A may sell goods to person B in period 1 without receiving a money payment from B, because he or she has the full and certain knowledge that he or she will receive goods of an equivalent value from D in period 3. In turn, D knows that he will receive services of an equivalent value from C during period 2, while finally person C receives other services from B during period 4. As Goodhart (1975a, p. 3) has put it

> In such a world of certainty the whole time path of the economy is effectively determined at the outset with both present and all future markets cleared at known relative prices. No one can default on an obligation, or purchase goods and services which over the course of time exceed the value of the goods and services which he can proffer in return, through the employment of his initial endowment of physical and human capital (plus transfer payments). Under these circumstances everyone knows to whom to send his products and where to pick up his own consumable goods in return.

While multilateral exchanges of goods and services can take place in a world of perfect certainty without the use of a specialized means of payment, the factors of time and the desire of economic agents to divorce the act of sale from that of purchase will necessitate the use of a medium of exchange. Credit is one obvious medium of exchange which would enable goods and services to be exchanged now for claims against goods and services at points of time in the future. *Figure 1.1* provides an example of multilateral exchanges based on the use of credit.

Of course, the assumption of perfect certainty is unrealistic and its removal provides us with the *raison d'être* for a means of payment in a market economy. Without perfect certainty there is a lack of complete information. People do not know the characteristics of all goods and services, they do not know the demand and supply schedules for current goods let alone future ones, they do not know the creditworthiness of all other people, and so on. In the absence of perfect certainty people will need to acquire information about all the different things that will influence their decisions on production, consumption and exchange. But the acquisition of such information will incur real costs, and the use of money defined as a specialized means of payment, is seen to derive from its ability to reduce these costs.

Under simple barter anyone wishing to exchange goods and services will have to devote time and effort to (a) seeking out somebody else with whom a double coincidence of wants can be established, and (b) haggling over the rate of exchange between the goods involved. Clower (1969) called these expenditures of time and effort on search and bargaining 'transaction costs'. They will vary directly with the frequency with which exchange expeditions or 'trips to the market' are undertaken. The transactions costs of exchanging any given quantity of goods will be less if they are exchanged in a few large transactions than if they are exchanged in a large number of small transactions. Defining the period between exchange expeditions as the transactions period, then transaction costs per unit of calendar time will vary inversely with the length of the transactions period. Thus, if only one exchange expedition is made every month, then the transactions costs per annum would be lower than if one exchange expedition were made every week. The inverse relationship between transactions costs and the length of the transactions period provides an incentive for people to make as few exchange expeditions as possible per unit period of calendar time.

On the other hand, a second type of cost distinguished by Clower (1969) provides an incentive to increase the frequency of exchange expeditions.

These are the costs, both subjective and objective, of postponing or delaying desired exchanges. The subjective costs will include the loss of satisfaction from having to consume one's own produce rather than exchanging it for a preferred alternative. The objective costs of waiting are the costs of storing goods for the

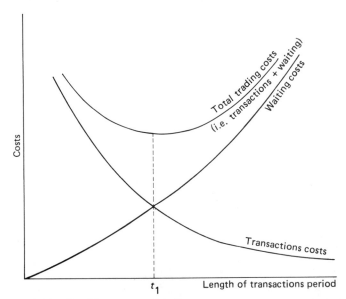

Figure 1.2 The different costs of trading

period between exchanges and the income forgone on earning assets by not acquiring them sooner. These subjective and objective costs of delayed exchange expeditions are called by Clower, 'waiting costs'. Because they arise from delaying transactions they vary directly with the length of the transactions period. Waiting costs per annum will be lower if, for example, exchange expeditions are undertaken every week rather than every month.

Transaction and waiting costs are shown graphically in *Figure 1.2*. The precise shapes and positions of the curves will depend on such things as the individual's time preference for goods in the present rather than in the future and on his initial endowment of resources. Summing the two curves vertically gives us the U-shaped curve depicting total trading costs. The lowest point on this curve gives the optimal transaction period, t_1, which is the transaction period that generates the lowest total trading costs. At t_1 marginal waiting costs are equal to marginal transactions costs, because any lengthening or shortening of the transactions period would add more, either to total waiting or to total transactions costs, than it subtracted from the other.

In an economy which relies on simple isolated barter for the exchanging of goods and services, total trading costs will be exceptionally high. These costs can be lowered by introducing institutional arrangements for the organization of trade. One possibility would be to bring transactors together in a market place, an arrangement usually referred to as fairground barter. The costs of searching out other transactors with whom a double coincidence of wants may be established would be lowered further if the fairground had a number of trading posts, one for each pair of commodities. The number of trading posts required, however, would be very considerable. If there are *n* goods then there would need to be $\frac{1}{2}n(n-1)$ trading posts.

The effect of these institutional arrangements on trading costs is shown in *Figure 1.3*. Fairground barter generates a total trading cost curve which is lower at every point than the isolated barter curve, while trading post barter generates a curve

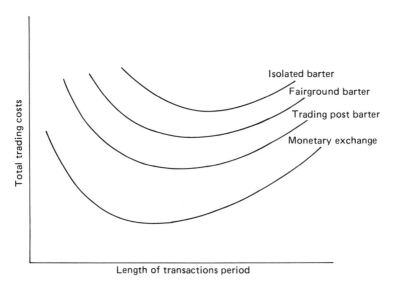

Figure 1.3 The costs of different kinds of trading

which is lower at every point than the fairground barter one. Moreover, because the institutional arrangements affect the transactions costs rather than the waiting costs, the lowest point on successively lower cost curves lies nearer and nearer the cost axis. This means that the optimal transactions period is being reduced and exchange trips are being undertaken more frequently. The three types of barter we have so far considered – isolated, fairground and trading post – have all been examples of simple or direct barter. That is, they have all required a double coincidence of wants to be established before an exchange can take place.

In order to avoid the high costs to which such direct barter gives rise, particularly in the absence of organized markets, people may engage in and develop a system of indirect barter. This simply means that in an exchange people accept as payment goods that they do not want directly, i.e. for their own sake. Thus, if person A wants football boots and is offering in exchange shirts, then rather than try to find somebody else who wants shirts in exchange for football boots, person A may exchange his shirts for flour with person B, the flour for meat with person C and finally the meat for football boots with person D. But such a transaction chain clearly has more 'links' than direct barter. In our example there are three links or exchanges rather than one, and each link will involve person A in the transactions costs of search and bargaining. Why then should anyone engage in indirect barter in preference to direct. One answer is that it is because transactions costs vary not only with the number of transactions but also with the characteristics of the goods being traded. Because of this the total transactions costs of a single direct barter exchange may exceed the total transactions costs of a large number of exchanges involving different goods. The transactions costs of any particular exchange are likely to reflect the extent to which the good received in payment has a wide and stable market. As Brunner and Meltzer (1971, p. 786–787) put it

> Transactors can acquire information most readily and at lowest cost about commodities that are most widely used and best known, so the prices of those commodities have the least dispersion.

In our example above, person A will be willing to accept flour and meat as payment in transactions, because he believes it will make it easier for him to find somebody else prepared to accept them, rather than shirts, in payment for football boots, and at a more predictable rate of exchange. Just as an indirect and longer route between two towns may be quicker than the direct route, so the indirect but longer chain of transactions between two commodities may be cheaper (i.e. have lower transactions costs) than the single direct barter transaction.

We might therefore expect that those goods which have a wide and stable market will come to be frequently used in transactions chains. The costs of acquiring information about them, with regard to their characteristics, disperson of prices and exchange opportunities, will be lower than for goods with narrower markets. But the more widely they are used in transactions the lower still will be the costs of acquiring information about them, making their use in transactions even more extensive. There will therefore be a general tendency to move towards a situation where only a small number of goods are used as a generally accepted means of payment. Thus, according to Brunner and Meltzer (1971, p. 793) money 'results from the opportunities offered by the distribution of incomplete information and the search by potential transactors to develop transaction chains that save resources'.

In terms of the Clower diagram (*Figure 1.3*), the use of one or a small number of commodities as generally accepted means of payment lowers the transactions costs of trading and gives a total trading cost curve which is lower than that for any form of direct barter. This is shown in *Figure 1.3* by the curve labelled 'monetary exchange'. Again the minimum point on the curve lies nearer to the vertical axis than do the minimum points on the direct barter curves, indicating that monetary exchange generates the shortest optimum transactions period.

In summary, the advantage of using money in an exchange economy characterized by uncertainty is that it facilitates exchanges by lowering the costs of acquiring information about exchange opportunities. From this will come other advantages.

To begin with, the resources that in the absence of money would be used up in acquiring information, are now released for production or increased leisure. Moreover, there will be increased opportunities for specialization and the division of labour, resulting in an increased output of goods and services. With the widening of the market there will be increased opportunities for specialists (e.g. insurance brokers) to reduce further the costs of acquiring information. The use of money also influences the allocation of resources over time.

> Deferred payment, borrowing, credit and the payments system expand when a standardised asset with well known properties becomes available. The reason is that transactors become more willing to enter into contracts calling for deferred payment (Brunner and Meltzer 1971, p. 800).

Further gains can be obtained by using as money assets which have certain characteristics. Most obviously the replacement of commodity money by claims and fiat paper money reduces the resources used in making exchanges. With commodity money (e.g. cattle) the value in exchange of the commodity will be derived from its intrinsic value, and while the commodity is being used as money it is not available for use in consumption or production. The use of token money (notes or coins of base metal) means that the value of the money in exchange can considerably exceed the intrinsic consumption or production value of the money. The resource cost of money is reduced further by the use and the development of a fractional reserve system.

In the evolution of monetary systems, all kinds of commodities, assets and claims have been used as money – some privately, some publicly produced – as efforts have been made to reduce both the costs of trading and the costs of providing the means of payment. In addition to having low real costs of production a good money should have certain other characteristics. It should be durable if it is to fulfill its role as a store of value, and it should be divisible if it is to accommodate transactions of different sizes. Clearly the money must be recognizable if it is to be generally acceptable and if it is to facilitate trade over wide geographical areas. The money should be homogeneous, for if it is not, the money that has the lower intrinsic value will continue to function as a means of payment while the money with the higher intrinsic value will disappear into hoards or production/consumption. Finally, the money should have stable supply and demand conditions in order to avoid wild fluctuations in its value.

What is money? Some theoretical and empirical definitions

Having considered the functions of money and the advantages of using it, we turn in this section to a consideration of some of the theoretical and empirical definitions that have been used to identify money within an economy that has a developed financial system. A lack of consensus on what money is has often been a reason for the disagreement amongst economists about the role of money in the economy, and about the aims and limitations of monetary policy. Thus, for example, the interest-elasticity of the demand for money will depend on whether money is defined to include interest bearing assets or not.

There are two interrelated problems in most definitional processes, namely the problems of definition itself and also that of classification. By definition we mean a precise statement of the essential nature of a thing. By classification we mean the detailed enumeration of those items that accord with the definition. Disagreement may exist about both definition and classification, or there may be agreement about one but disagreement about the other.

If we turn now to the definition of money we may begin by asking just what is 'the essential nature' of money? One answer is derived from interpreting nature to mean functions, so that money becomes anything that performs the functions of money. Money abstract, we have already seen, performs the function of acting as a unit of account, while money concrete is usually attributed with two functions, those of acting as a means of payment and as a store of value. Attempts have been made to derive definitions of money from both of these functions, with most emphasis being placed on the means of payment function. We shall consider first, however, definitions derived from the store of value role of money before examining the rather more technical means of payment aspect.

Money defined as a store of value

The means of payment represents generalized purchasing power, so that it may be held and act as a store of value or wealth until the point in time at which the holder wishes to exercise his purchasing power.

But the means of payment is not unique in acting as a store of wealth, for there are a great many assets that could perform this function. The major advantage of the means of payment as a store of value is that it represents immediately realizable purchasing power; wealth held in this form can be spent or converted into other assets with a minimum of inconvenience or delay.

Other assets acting as stores of value can only be 'spent' if they are first exchanged for the means of payment itself, thereby involving two transactions rather than one. How much more inconvenient this is will depend on the characteristics of the assets being held. These characteristics will include:

(1) The period of notice that has to be given or that will elapse before the asset can be converted into the means of payment.
(2) The amount of 'form filling' that is necessary to convert the asset into the means of payment.
(3) Any money costs, such as brokerage fees, involved in the conversion.
(4) Whether the money values of the assets are certain, i.e. whether the holder of the assets knows exactly how much of the means of payment he will get when he makes the conversion.
(5) The inconvenience of the times when the conversions can be made.

Non means of payment assets will offer their own particular advantages as stores of value. These may include the payment of interest or dividends, or a greater real value certainty from that offered by the means of payment.

It is the store of value function which is emphasized by Friedman (1964) in his definition of money. He argues that money is a 'temporary abode of purchasing power' because it enables people to separate the act of purchase from the act of sale. However, the time period to which the term temporary applies is not fixed, and consequently a range of assets, and not merely the means of payment, may act as temporary abodes of purchasing power.

The existence of very-short-term stores of value which are close substitutes for the means of payment has caused some economists to suggest that they should be included in the classification of money, as this may facilitate the analysis of the motives for holding money, and because they may play a part in determining the flow of expenditure on goods and services. The Radcliffe Committee (1959), which reported on the working of the monetary system in the United Kingdom, argued that the high degree of substitutability between a wide range of assets acting as temporary abodes of purchasing power makes it impossible to identify a class of assets that possess a unique monetary quality.

Money defined as a means of payment

This brings us now to a consideration of those definitions of money that are based on its means of payment function. These definitions are based on the view that the existence of assets which are close substitutes for money as stores of value, does not destroy the significant difference between the means of payment and other assets. Probably the most common definition of money is that it is anything that is generally acceptable as a means of payment or in final settlement of a debt.

A means of payment or a medium of exchange?

One difficulty with this definition has already been touched upon earlier and is that of distinguishing between a medium of exchange and a means of payment. Some writers have defined the means of payment to be anything that enables goods and services to be acquired without the need to supply other goods and services in exchange. Thus, Clower (1971, p. 18) has argued:

> The essential issue here is whether the tender of any given financial instrument permits a buyer to take delivery of a commodity from a seller. On this criterion, trade credit qualifies as money – trade credit being interpreted to include credit card and overdraft facilities, department store credit and travellers' cheques, as well as commercial paper and book credits.

As we have seen, however, Shackle (1971) and others have pointed out that the use of credit to effect a transaction still leaves a debt to be settled, and the credit is not therefore a final means of payment and should not be regarded as money.

A similar difference of opinion exists over the monetary status of unused overdraft facilities. Thus, Shackle (1971, p. 33) has argued that:

> a man can just as well make a payment by increasing his overdraft (if he has his bankers' permission to do so) as by reducing a credit balance. Unused overdraft permission, 'lines of credit', ought to be included in the stock of money ... if we are using as our definition of money 'the means of making payments'.

On the other hand, it may be argued that until the overdraft facility is actually used, the means of payment is not brought into existence. In any case, the difficulties of quantifying unused overdraft facilities makes it virtually impossible to include them in statistical measures of the money stock.

Acceptability as a matter of degree: the pragmatic approach

A second difficulty involved in classifying as money anything that is generally acceptable as a means of payment is that such acceptability is very much a matter of degree. There is no obvious or clear dividing line between those assets that have a 'sufficient' degree of acceptability to be classified as money and those that have not. Whatever classification is made it must inevitably be an arbitrary one. The only items that have complete general acceptability are those that are legal tender. In the United Kingdom only Bank of England notes are full legal tender in that the law requires they be accepted in unlimited amounts in payment of debt. Coinage is subsidiary legal tender, which simply means that coins are legal tender only up to specified amounts. Items other than coins and notes can have general acceptability only by virtue of custom and convenience. Of such items, current accounts (or demand deposits) with clearing banks have the greatest degree of acceptability. Such deposits circulate widely because people have confidence in the ability of the banks to meet any claims on them to exchange the bank deposit for legal tender. Should this confidence be undermined, then bank deposits may cease to be generally acceptable, and cease to function as a medium of exchange. Such bank deposits are not universally acceptable, however, because some members of the community do not have bank accounts (perhaps because they do not consider their income sufficient to justify having an account, or perhaps because they do not have confidence in banks, preferring to keep their money in a form they can see and handle). Current accounts with clearing banks do not have perfect acceptability, but in countries with developed financial systems there is widespread agreement amongst economists that they have a sufficient degree of general acceptability to be classified as money. The same is now true of the deposits withdrawable on demand that are held with the other banks in the United Kingdom monetary sector.

There is, however, less agreement about whether time deposits should be included in the classification of money. The difference of opinion arises because in principle cheques cannot be drawn against such deposits, as a period of notice is required before withdrawals can be made. If, however, banks are prepared in practice (and in the United Kingdom they often are) to meet cheques drawn against current accounts that have insufficient funds, provided that they are backed by deposit accounts, then it may be argued that the latter accounts are acting as a means of payment and should be classified as money.

If it can be argued that bank time deposits should be regarded as money, then why not include interest-bearing deposits of the major non-bank deposit-taking financial institutions, particularly building societies? Building societies now have a larger share of the deposits of the personal sector than the banks, and it could be argued that people regard building society deposits as more or less equivalent in their spending decisions. For example, people might regard building societies as performing essentially the same important retail banking function – the deposit and withdrawal of cash ('money to spend') – as the banks; indeed they may consider that building societies offer in this area a better service than the banks as their branches are open for more hours and, in particular, are open for customer business on Saturday mornings.

An obvious argument against the inclusion of building society deposits is that they do not constitute an immediate means of payment. However, if the cost (in terms of inconvenience etc.) of converting building society deposits into a means of payment is considered negligible, perhaps for many people no more than the cost of converting bank deposits into a means of payment (currency), then it can be argued that they posses a sufficient degree of 'moneyness' to be included in the money supply definition; particularly as a few of the major building societies are introducing cheque-book account facilities, thus reducing this particular distinction between bank and building society deposits.

Shackle (1971) has suggested that an additional reason why building society deposits should not be included is because it would involve a substantial element of double counting. Given that building societies hold their reserves as deposits with the banks, a transfer of funds, for example from banks to building societies, would change only the ownership of bank deposits and not their total. Thus adding building society deposits to bank deposits can be seen as double counting. Llewellyn (1979), however, points out several ways in which banks might in fact lose deposits through competition with building societies, and in any case the double counting element can be eliminated by excluding transactions between banks and building societies.

Theoretical approaches to defining the means of payment

Several economists have attempted to develop formal theoretical definitions of money based on its means of payment function. We shall consider four of these proposals, starting with that of Yeager.

Yeager's approach (1968)

Yeager argues that there is an asymmetry in the outcome of changes in the public's asset preference between assets used as means of payment and non-money assets. It is this asymmetry which can be used to distinguish between money and other assets.

Because income is usually received in the form of the means of payment people can adjust their holdings of it simply by altering their payments relative to their income. Should they wish to reduce their holdings of money they need only increase their payments, assuming their income remains unchanged, while if they wish to increase their holdings of it they need only reduce their payments, again assuming their income is unchanged. Thus, the means of payment does not have a specific market of its own, nor a price of its own expressed in terms of only one item. As has already been explained, the means of payment always has a money price of unity, so that its relative price can only change when the money prices of other goods and services change. The relative price of the means of payment is the inverse of the money prices of all other goods and services. As people can individually change their holdings of the means of payment by adjusting their expenditure relative to their income, any general excess demand or supply will be felt as a deficiency of demand or excess of demand respectively, for other goods and services. An excess demand/supply for the means of payment thus has widespread repercussions, affecting all prices in the economy.

With non-money assets, on the other hand, people can only change their holdings by entering the specific market on which that asset is traded and then either purchasing or selling it. In the case of a market-clearing non-money asset market, the main impact of excess demand or supply for the asset would, according to Yeager, be largely confined to that specific asset market, producing a change in price or supply of the asset. In the case of a non-money asset traded in a market which does not clear – as a result, for example, of price controls – the excess demand or supply would be diverted to other markets, but these repercussions are likely to be neither widespread or substantial. Thus, Yeager considers that an excess demand/supply for the means of payment asset has widespread repercussions in a way that an excess demand/supply for anything else does not have.

Yeager's approach, however, does not provide a sharp line of demarcation between a means of payment and other assets. As explained in Chapter 2, portfolio balance theory shows that adjustments to excess demand in one market are bound to have repercussions in other asset markets. So the difference between means of payment and other assets would appear once more to be a matter of degree rather than of kind. Moreover, this view, which continues to define money in terms of its means of payment function, is still confronted with the problem of classification, of enumerating those items which actually are a means of payment. The next three theoretical approaches that we look at all attempt to suggest criteria by which the means of payment can be clearly distinguished from other assets.

The Pesek and Saving approach (1967, 1968)

Pesek and Saving attempt to distinguish between money and other assets by using a net wealth principle. Money consists of items used as means of payment which are assets to their holders but are not a liability to others.

Money, they argue, is a net resource of the community, a constituent part of the net wealth of that community. All money renders services in facilitating the exchange of goods and thereby promoting the division of labour and increasing output and productivity. The services rendered by a unit of money depends on the price per unit of that money, which is the reciprocal of the general price level: hence the total services rendered by money do not depend on the number of physical units of money. Money is not a debt of its issuer, but a service-providing product which is produced and sold by the money and banking industry. The criterion used by Pesek and Saving to establish whether an item is money or just a debt is the absence or presence of interest.

> In any business transaction, if a loan exists, the lender will demand interest from the borrower: if production and sale exist there will be no such payments (1967, p. 173).

State-issued fiat currency, for example, given the large difference between its exchange value and costs of production (seignorage), is clearly part of the community's net wealth: it is an asset to its holders without being a liability to its producers.

In the case of bank deposits, Pesek and Saving argue that there is a clear theoretical difference between the role of banks as producers of demand deposits transferable by cheque and their role as financial intermediaries borrowing funds (e.g. time deposits) at one rate of interest and lending at another. Demand deposits are regarded as a product of the banking industry, sold by the banks for currency, or for financial claims (e.g. government securities), or sold for credit (e.g. bank advances). Bank money, like fiat currency, is seen as being resource-cheap in the sense that the real resources used to produce a unit of bank money are extremely small; in other words, bank money has low costs of production. Because of this bank money cannot be produced under conditions of free entry into the industry. Production is restricted to a limited number of producers so that the price per unit of bank money is kept appreciably above the cost per unit of producing it.

Bank money also has certain advantages over fiat currency. Bank deposits are, for example, of variable denomination so that a user of bank deposits may write a cheque for exactly the amount he or she wishes; there is also less risk of losing bank deposits in the sense of misplacing them. The general acceptability of bank deposits as a substitute for state-issued fiat currency is enhanced by the bank's willingness to exchange deposits for fiat currency at fixed exchange rates. This situation Pesek and Saving call the instant repurchase clause. They argue that bank demand deposits are produced and sold by the banks for cash, credit or certain financial claims, but subject to a guarantee that they (the banks) will purchase the deposits in return for fiat currency. According to Pesek and Saving, the fact that banks do produce and sell demand deposits is quite clear because no interest is given on them.

> If bank money were a debt of the banks and not a product sold by the banks, we would see the borrower (the banks) paying interest to the holders of bank money. If the bank money was purchased for cash we do not see any interest payments: on the contrary, many of us pay service charges to the banks (1968, p. 184).

Time deposits, on the other hand, bear interest and are therefore a debt of the bank and do not add to the community's net wealth. So according to Pesek and Saving there is a clear theoretical demarcation between the means of payment (i.e. money) and other items, the distinction being whether interest is or is not paid. This criteria leads Pesek and Saving to classify coins, notes and bank demand deposits as money. This simple and apparently clear-cut criteria for classifying money has, however, been subjected to considerable criticism.

One problem arising from their approach concerns the case of payment of interest on demand deposits. If demand deposits bear some interest they are considered by Pesek and Saving as joint products, part money and part a liability of the bank issuing them. This would presumably also apply in the case of the United Kingdom banking practice of paying implicit interest rates on demand deposits which partly offset charges to the customer arising from the costs of the money transmission service. What proportion of interest-bearing demand deposits constitute money and what proportion debt depends, according to Pesek and Saving, on the ratio of the demand deposit rate to the market rate of interest. The 'moneyness' of demand deposits declines as the interest rate paid approaches the market rate of interest, until the point when the deposit equals the market rate, whereupon the demand deposit ceases to be money and is wholly debt. The problem here is deciding what market rate of interest to use. There is a whole spectrum of debts and likewise a whole spectrum of interest rates. Pesek and Saving recognize that differences in interest rates between assets may exist because of differences in the services provided by these assets, apart from the service of acting as a means of payment. The 'moneyness' of an asset is then measured by the difference between the rate of interest on it and the market rate – over and above the extent to which this difference represents the value of other services provided by the asset. But some of these other services, such as absence of default risk and variability of denomination of the asset, may be closely associated with the use of the asset as a means of payment and consequently with its degree of 'moneyness'.

Thus, the Pesek–Saving criterion, while seemingly simple and clear-cut, would also appear to give a classification of money which is rather arbitrary. The presence or absence of interest on an asset does not appear to provide a sufficient means of distinguishing between money and other assets, particularly when some items both circulate as means of payment and pay interest, so that the problem is that of deciding the amount of moneyness they comprise.

Friedman and Schwartz (1969) point out that the major problem with the Pesek–Saving analysis is that it confuses price with quantity and marginal with average. Pesek and Saving argue that if bank demand deposits pay interest at the market rate, their value as money must be zero if there is to be equilibrium on the side of demand. That is, the means of payment services provided by the deposits are in effect available as a free good, in the sense that no interest has to be forgone in order to enjoy them: their price is zero. But the value to which they refer must be the *marginal value* of the money services provided by the deposits and not the average or total value. Though the last (marginal) unit of deposits provides no non-pecuniary services, each of the intramarginal units may well do so. As Friedman and Schwartz (1969, p. 5) point out (emphasis theirs):

A zero *price* for the transactions services of demand deposits does not mean that the *quantity* of money in the form of demand deposits is zero. Alternatively, a marginal yield of transactions services of zero does not mean that the *average* yield is zero.

The Newlyn and Bootle (1978) approach

Newlyn and Bootle identify two criteria for distinguishing a means of payment from other assets. An asset used to finance payment is a means of payment if: (i) the payment has no further repercussions on the economy; for example on the market for loans (termed the neutrality condition); and (ii) if the payment leaves the aggregate of the asset unchanged.

On the basis of these two criteria they classify as money currency and bank deposits. Currency is seen as a means of payment according to these criteria since the transfer of currency in an exchange transaction leaves the total unchanged and has no further repercussions, the effects of the exchange are confined only to the payer and payee. Both bank demand and time deposits also qualify as means of payment since the financing of payments using these deposits would only affect the payer's and payee's individual deposit totals; the total of bank deposits would remain the same, and there would be no changes on the assets side of the bank's balance sheet. This does require the assumption, however, that banks observe the same desired reserve ratios for both demand and time deposits (which is normally the situation for United Kingdom banks). A transfer of deposits, for example, from a bank with a high reserve ratio to one with a low reserve ratio, would be likely to lead to an increase in the total of bank deposits.

The deposits of non-bank financial intermediaries do not, according to Newlyn and Bootle, satisfy those criteria. Take as one example the case of an exchange transaction effected by the withdrawal of funds by cheque from a building society. Given that the building society's reserves are held within the banking system, payment would be made by a cheque drawn by the building society on its bank in favour of the payer in the exchange transaction (alternatively, the cheque can be drawn by the society directly for the payee). After the exchange transaction, and assuming the cheque is paid into the payee's bank account, the payee's bank deposits would increase while the building society's bank deposits would fall by the same amount, leaving aggregate bank deposits unchanged. Total building society deposits, however, would have decreased and there would consequently have been a reduction in the aggregate of banks and non-bank deposits. The neutrality condition would also be violated since the loan creating capability of the building society would be affected.

There are, however, problems with Newlyn and Bootle's approach which limit its effectiveness in distinguishing between money and other assets. Suppose the payee in the above example, instead of paying the building society cheque into a bank account, deposits it in a building society account. There would be no change in total building society deposits and bank deposits and no repercussions for the loan market: the Newlyn and Bootle criteria would be satisfied and consequently building society deposits would qualify as a means of payment. Thus, although Newlyn and Bootle regard instances of this kind as insignificant, it would appear that their criteria for classifying non-bank deposits as money or non-money assets depends on what assumptions are made about the reactions of the payee on receiving the cheque. In fact, it is not at all clear if one applies Newlyn and Bootle's neutrality condition that one can even classify currency and bank deposits as money. For example, if a payment is made by drawing on a holding of currency, the payee might decide to deposit the currency in a building society account with consequent repercussions for the loan market.

The Morgan approach (1969)
Finally, we may turn to a classfication of money that is based on responses to excess demand/supply of assets. This view suggests that the essential characteristic of money is that the response to excess supply/demand for it will reveal itself as an excess demand/supply respectively of all other assets which, assuming their prices are flexible, would imply an increase/decrease respectively in the prices of these assets. Morgan suggests that two conditions are necessary for this response to occur. Firstly, the price of the asset must be fixed in terms of the unit of account, so that an excess demand/supply is not reflected simply in a change in the price of that asset. The second condition is that the asset's supply should be exogenous.

> In the sense that the amount issued by any one issuer is not affected by the transactions of any transactor that is not itself an issuer of an asset qualifying as money (1969, p. 242).

Morgan, however, considers these conditions too restrictive since only state-issued currency would fully satisfy them. Bank deposits would be excluded, because the volume of such deposits could be changed by the actions of depositors. In order, therefore, to include bank deposits in a money definition, Morgan is forced to introduce an additional condition: that there exists a mechanism (the actions of the monetary authority) that offsets the effects of actions by depositors on the total of bank deposits. This condition would be met, according to Morgan, only by banks who keep operational reserves with the central bank.

In other words, Morgan's approach requires the controversial assumption that bank deposits can be determined exogenously by the monetary authority. It also assumes, equally controversially, that the monetary authority actually chooses to control bank deposits in this way. The authorities may have other policy aims. These are matters of considerable debate and are considered in detail in Chapters 4 and 9.

Our brief survey of some *a priori* definitions of money leads us to the conclusion that economists have still not found a conceptual definition which permits a clear-cut classification of these assets to be termed money. Consequently, a great deal of effort has been directed to trying to find an empirical definition of money, and several different approaches have been used.

Empirical definitions

One possibility is to use empirical investigation to try and find the best empirical counterpart to a conceptual definition. For example, if money is being defined as a means of payment, and there are a number of assets that perform this function to a greater or lesser degree, then empirical investigation may help to show where the significant gap is in the extent to which these assets act as means of payment.

Instead of starting with a conceptual definition of money, a different approach to the construction of an empirical definition is to start with the monetary problem in which one is interested and then try to find the empirical definition of money that best facilitates the examination and analysis of that problem. We have already seen that Friedman and his followers believe that the basic characteristic of money is that it is a temporary abode of purchasing power, but their classfication is derived from empirical investigation.

> Our aim is to formulate an empirical definition of money that will facilitate, as far as is possible, the separation and analysis of the forces of demand and supply for the country or countries and period or periods being studied ... a definition that will enable us most readily and accurately to predict the consequences for important economic variables of a change in the conditions of demand for or supply of money. (Friedman and Schwartz 1969, p. 16).

The demand for and supply of money has been the focus of attention in many of these empirical studies because of their importance to our understanding of the role of money and monetary policy. Probably the most important single question in monetary economics, at least from a policy point of view, is whether the authorities, by manipulating the money supply, can influence specified variables such as the level of employment, output and prices, in a predictable manner.

Clearly, if the answer to this question is to be in the affirmative then the money supply must be classified so as to consist of a class of assets over which the authorities can exert effective control. In addition, if the effects of changes in the supply of money are to be predictable with reasonable accuracy, then the demand function for money must be 'sufficiently' stable. But, of course, the demand for any class of assets, like the demand for anything, will be highly stable if one includes enough arguments in the demand function. If the demand function is to be of any theoretical or practical use then the variables in it must be restricted to an acceptable number, and as a result its stability be relative rather than absolute. In comparing the stability of different functions a more stable function

> may be taken to be one that requires knowledge of fewer variables and their parameters in order to predict the demand for money with a given degree of accuracy, or which amounts to the same thing, one that yields parameter estimates that are less subject to variation when the same arguments are included in the function and hence enables more accurate predictions of the demand for money to be made (Laidler 1969, p. 517).

The evidence from this type of approach is discussed in Chapter 3, where we will be concerned with various aspects of the demand for money.

A second approach to the formulation of an empirical definition that emphasizes the demand for money is concerned with the extent to which assets are substitutes for one another. Attempts have been made to measure directly the degree of similarity or substitutability among assets. This approach, however, has not led to a clear-cut definition, for different studies have yielded different results as to which assets are considered good substitutes for one another in the eyes of the public.

A third and different approach has been the attempt to define money on the basis of an empirically observed relationship between a group of assets and other relevant macrovariables. Money then becomes that collection of assets which appears to be most closely correlated with the macro variables considered to be significant. This approach raises a number of questions to which there is no clear answer. For example, the class of assets most closely related to the relevant macrovariables may well depend upon the variables chosen. The definition of money then depends upon which macrovariable is taken to be the most significant. Further, which class of assets is most closely related to any given macrovariable may depend upon the time lags considered. It may be, for example, that a definition of money that includes coins, notes and total commercial bank deposits performs best in explaining nominal income after a time lag of six months, but that a definition comprising coins, notes and demand deposits only does better in predicting income with a shorter time lag, say three months. The evidence from this approach is inconclusive and does not provide a definition of money that is acceptable to all.

The empirical approaches considered so far have all attempted to measure the money stock as the aggregate value of a particular class of assets. But this approach assumes that each asset within the class has as much 'moneyness' as every other asset in the class. However, we have already seen that this may not be the case. Many assets are joint products, providing both the services of money and non-money services, with the proportions in which they are provided varying from asset to asset. Consequently, several writers have suggested that when aggregating assets to arrive at a quantitative measure of the money stock, weights should be attached to each asset corresponding to its degree of moneyness. The quantity of money would then be the weighted sum of the aggregate value of all assets specified as money. The major difficulty with this approach is that of deciding on the relative weights. One possibility, which we have already encountered, is that suggested by Pesek and Saving. They argue that the relative 'moneyness' of an asset, and therefore its relative weight, can be ascertained by comparing the interest it pays with the market rate. But from our earlier discussion we know that this criterion is open to a number of criticisms. Several other attempts have been made to suggest criteria for assigning weights, but they too have failed to provide a generally acceptable solution, so that most writers continue to define the money stock as an unweighted aggregate.

What conclusion has our consideration of theoretical and empirical definitions of money led us to? It can only be that from the point of view of both approaches, economists have not yet been able to formulate a definition which commands general approval. The acceptability of definitions of money, like the acceptability of means of payment, is a matter of degree. But perhaps this is not so important as the need to recognize that different definitions do exist, and to make allowance for it in comparing theories and prescribing policies.

United Kingdom definitions of monetary aggregates

In this section we shall briefly describe the various official definitions of money that are employed in the United Kingdom. Reflecting the problems of definition and classification that were considered in the previous section, a number of money measures have been used over the years, and others are likely to be developed in the future. The official definitions in current use (1984) are as follows:

M0

This measure, known as the wide monetary base, comprises notes and coins, both in circulation with the public and held in the tills of banks, together with banks' operational balances with the Bank of England.

M1

This is a narrow measure of money, based on its means of payment function. M1 comprises notes and coins in circulation with the public plus United Kingdom private sector sterling sight deposits with the monetary sector.

Sight deposits are defined as those which are essentially available on demand and include current accounts and deposits which are on call or are placed overnight. Some sight deposits are consequently interest-bearing.

Non-interest bearing M1

This comprises M1 less private sector interest-bearing sterling sight deposits.

M2

This measure was introduced in 1982. According to the Bank of England (1982a, p. 24):

> The object was to design a new measure which could be expected to be more directly related to transactions in goods and services than Sterling M3, and somewhat less sensitive to relative interest rates than M1.

Because a large proportion of M1 is non-interest-bearing, increases in interest rates lead to movements out of it and into other interest-bearing deposits. The movements in M1 are consequently thought to exaggerate the underlying monetary conditions. M1 also includes some balances (large, interest-bearing, overnight deposits) which are more akin to investment than transaction balances.

Thus, the authorities sought a new money supply measure, between M1 and £M3, based on deposits (termed retail deposits) that can most readily be used for transactions purposes. The criterion used for identifying such deposits was whether they could be transferred to third parties on demand or at short notice.

To be specific, M2, the new aggregate, comprises notes and coins in circulation with the public, sterling retail deposits held by the United Kingdom private sector with the monetary sector, shares and deposits with the building societies which are within one month of maturity, and deposits with the National Savings Bank ordinary account.

Sterling retail deposits with the monetary sector consist of

(1) Non-interest bearing sight deposits.
(2) All other deposits on which cheques may be drawn or from which other payments to third parties may be made (e.g. by standing orders).
(3) Other deposits of less than £100,000 with a residual maturity of one month including deposits of less than £100,000 for which less than one month's notice of withdrawal is required.

Sterling M3

This is a broader definition of money reflecting it's store of value function in addition to it's means of payment one. £M3 consists of notes and coins in circulation with the public plus all private sector sterling deposits held with the monetary sector.

Until March 1984 this measure also included all public sector sterling deposits held with the monetary sector. The reasons for now excluding these deposits appear to be that they are a very small part of £M3, though subject to large monthly changes, which themselves are not likely to be related to changes in economic activity. Over longer periods the exclusion of these public sector deposits will probably leave the growth rate of £M3 largely unaffected.

M3

This consists of £M3 plus all deposits held by private sector residents in non-sterling currencies. As with £M3 this measure now excludes public sector deposits.

Since the abolition of exchange controls, United Kingdom private sector residents have sometimes held foreign currency deposits as a temporary store of value, to an extent largely determined by exchange rate movements and interest rate differentials. The Bank of England (1982d, p. 533) however argues that '... changes in foreign currency deposits reflect in large part transactions by the holders in goods and services of other countries rather than those of the UK'.

The Bank recognizes that while these deposits may act as a reserve enabling their holders to maintain a higher-than-otherwise level of expenditure in the UK, any large switch from foreign currency to sterling in order to finance expenditure in the UK would, from the point of view of its effect on the money supply and level of expenditure, be largely offset by consequential exchange rate movements.

In the above definitions, two adjustments are made to the deposits with the monetary sector. Transactions between institutions within the sector are excluded, and 60 per cent of the net value of sterling transit items is deducted from non-interest bearing deposits. This deduction is made to avoid an element of double counting of deposits which can arise, for example, as a result of the delay between the crediting of a payee's account when a cheque received is deposited, and the debiting of the payer's account.

The monetary sector classification was adopted in 1981 to supersede the more narrowly defined 'banking sector'. It consists of all recognized banks and licensed deposit-takers', the National Girobank, the Trustee Savings Bank, the Banking Department of the Bank of England and certain banks in the Channel Islands and the Isle of Man. Licensed deposit-takers (LDTs) are institutions which are licensed to accept deposits from the public and make loans, but which are not officially recognized as banks.

In addition to the various money measures, the Bank of England has also provided since 1979 two measures of private sector liquidity (PSL). PSL_1 includes 'wholesale' liquidity items and the wider PSL_2 also includes 'retail' items.

PSL_1

This measure comprises 'money', other money market instruments and certificates of tax deposit.

'Money' consists of sterling M3, excluding deposits with an original maturity of more than two years. Other money market instruments include Treasury bills, bank bills and deposits with local authorities.

PSL_2

This measure consists essentially of PSL_1 plus savings deposits with the major non-monetary sector institutions (building societies and the National Savings Bank), and National Savings Securities.

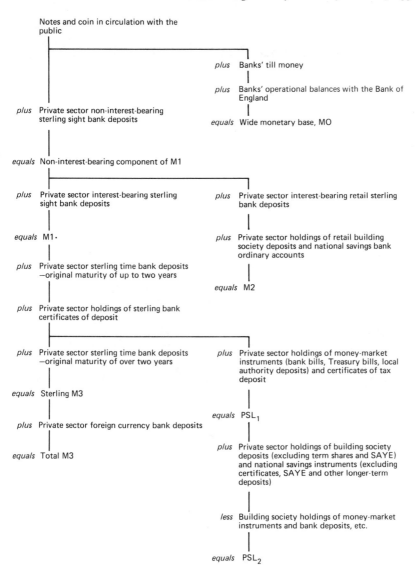

Notes and coin in circulation with the public

plus Banks' till money

plus Banks' operational balances with the Bank of England

plus Private sector non-interest-bearing sterling sight bank deposits

equals Wide monetary base, M0

equals Non-interest-bearing component of M1

plus Private sector interest-bearing sterling sight bank deposits

plus Private sector interest-bearing retail sterling bank deposits

equals M1·

plus Private sector holdings of retail building society deposits and national savings bank ordinary accounts

plus Private sector sterling time bank deposits —original maturity of up to two years

equals M2

plus Private sector holdings of sterling bank certificates of deposit

plus Private sector sterling time bank deposits —original maturity of over two years

plus Private sector holdings of money-market instruments (bank bills, Treasury bills, local authority deposits) and certificates of tax deposit

equals Sterling M3

equals PSL$_1$

plus Private sector foreign currency bank deposits

plus Private sector holdings of building society deposits (excluding term shares and SAYE) and national savings instruments (excluding certificates, SAYE and other longer-term deposits)

equals Total M3

less Building society holdings of money-market instruments and bank deposits, etc.

equals PSL$_2$

Figure 1.4 Relationships among the monetary and liquidity aggregates and their components (reproduced from *Bank of England Quarterly Bulletin*, March 1984, with permission of the Bank of England)

Excluded from building societies savings deposits are term deposits (shares), all SAYE deposits, and shares and deposits held by overseas residents. The savings deposits are net of holdings of 'money' and other money market instruments and net of building societies' deposits with other savings institutions. Also excluded from the measure are certificates of tax deposit holdings by building societies.

The relationship between the monetary and liquidity aggregates is summarized in *Figure 1.4*. In this figure the term bank deposits refers to deposits with all institutions of the monetary sector.

2

Monetary transmission mechanisms and the channels of monetary influence

The purpose of this chapter is to provide an overview of the various mechanisms by which changes in the supply of money are transmitted to the goal variables of prices, output and employment. Some of the ideas presented in this chapter will be taken up again in later chapters where they will be considered in the context of particular models.

The transmission mechanisms differ from one another in the way they see changes in the money supply working through intermediating variables to bring about changes in the goal variables. For a closed economy (or an open economy operating a fixed exchange rate) four transmission mechanisms have received prominent treatment in the literature. In the case of an open economy operating a floating exchange rate it can be argued that the exchange rate itself provides another transmission mechanism. We will consider the floating exchange rate case in the final section of the chapter but first we consider the four 'closed economy' transmission mechanisms. These are:

(1) Money supply – link (a) → Portfolio balance   – link (b) → Prices, output, employment
(2) Money supply – link (a) → Wealth   – link (b) → Prices, output, employment
(3) Money supply – link (a) → Credit availability   – link (b) → Prices, output, employment
(4) Money supply – link (a) → Expectations – link (b) → Prices, output, employment

The efficacy of these causal relationships depends upon whether or not both links in the causal chain are valid. If either link (a) or (b) breaks down or is found to be invalid in any of these four causal connections, then we shall say that the particular monetary transmission mechanism does not operate. If it is link (a) which breaks down it does not automatically follow that the 'intermediating' variable (wealth, credit availability, etc.) is irrelevant to an explanation of the behaviour of economic activity. For example, the link between money supply and the availability of credit may be very tenuous, yet credit may contribute very significantly to the determination of prices, output and employment. In this situation, policy should be directly focused on credit; in this way we can conveniently distinguish 'credit' from monetary policy. If it is link (b) which breaks down we shall say that the particular monetary transmission mechanism is of no 'operational significance' as far as the goal variables of the economy are concerned. We should also distinguish between a monetary transmission mechanism and a channel of monetary influence. The monetary transmission mechanism refers to the general conceptual framework within which the analysis of monetary disturbances may be undertaken, whereas the channel of monetary influence refers to the route through which these monetary disturbances influence the goal variables. It is possible for there to exist a number of channels of monetary influence within the context of the same monetary transmission mechanism. This will become more apparent as we proceed.

The portfolio balance transmission mechanism

Link (a): money and portfolio balance

A portfolio, loosely defined, is an array of assets and debts of differing yields, risks, maturities and other characteristics. Portfolio management theory is concerned with providing explanations of the behaviour of individual and economy-wide portfolios.

Portfolio balance theory contends that the composition of a portfolio will depend upon the characteristics of assets (and debts) – primarily yield, risk and maturity – as well as wealth-holders' preferences. It predicts that changes in 'market conditions', the characteristics of assets, the size of the portfolio, and wealth-holders' preferences, will cause portfolio re-composition and that the interrelationship of the different assets will depend upon the wealth-holders' views of the degree of substitutability and complementarity between assets.

As a monetary transmission mechanism, portfolio balance theory takes as given both the preferences of wealth-holders and the characteristics of assets apart from their yields. Money is seen as one asset amongst many that may feature in the portfolios of wealth-holders. Others would include a wide range of financial assets, such as government bills and bonds, debentures, equities and deposits with building societies and other financial institutions, and real assets, such as producers' goods and consumer durables.

Each asset may be regarded as providing a yield, the nature of which will depend on the particular characteristics of that asset. Yields on financial assets, for example, will reflect not only money yields (e.g. interest payments or dividends) but also such factors as the ease and speed with which they can be converted into money, their capital value certainty, risk of default, etc. Thus the yield from a government bond will differ from the yield on a debenture in a private company not only because of any difference in money rates of interest, but also because there is less risk of the government defaulting on its debt than there is of the private firm defaulting. Real assets of course provide a yield in the form of a flow of services. Thus a house generates a flow of accommodation services, and a bicycle or a car a flow of transportation services. Money is regarded as yielding a flow of services in the form of security and convenience derived from its general acceptability as a means of payment.

The yields obtained from each asset are subject to diminishing returns. The greater the quantity of an asset already held, the smaller will be the yield obtained from an additional unit of that asset. A portfolio will be in balance when the marginal yields are the same on all assets, i.e. when the last pound spent on each asset provides the same return. The demand for any asset will vary directly with its own yield and inversely with the yield on all other assets. Thus the demand for money as a proportion of a total portfolio will rise when the yield on other assets falls, and fall when the yield on other assets rises.

A change in the yield of any one asset will affect the demand to hold all other assets. An increase in the yield on long-term government securities, for example, will influence the demand for short-term government securities, private debts, equities, real capital, as well as the demand for money. How much the demand for any one asset is affected by a change in the yield on another, depends on how close they are as substitutes for one another, i.e. on the yield cross-elasticity of demand between them.

It is on this question of the elasticity of substitution between assets that significant differences are to be found in the ways by which economists see portfolio adjustments influencing aggregate expenditure and through this expenditure the goal variables. Thus, although portfolio balance is generally accepted as the main monetary transmission mechanism, there are different hypotheses as to the precise channel of monetary influence. In other words, while there is widespread agreement that changes in the money stock bring about portfolio adjustments, there are different views as to the precise nature of these adjustments, and the ways in which they bring about changes in employment, prices and output. Let us consider some of them by reference to link (b) of the portfolio balance transmission mechanism.

Link (b): portfolio balance and the goal variables

The portfolio balance transmission mechanism operates through aggregate expenditure. Adjustments to portfolios lead to increased expenditures and through that to employment, prices and output. In this section we are concerned only with the possible ways that portfolio adjustments can affect expenditure. How, and to what extent, these expenditure changes are reflected in changes in the goal variables is discussed in later chapters when specific models are considered.

The simple Keynesian approach

We can begin with the traditional Keynesian analysis as incorporated in the IS/LM model. In this model the economy is categorized into two sectors only – the public and private, and only three kinds of assets are identified – money, government bonds and real assets. There is only one financial rate of interest, that on bonds. The demand for money and the demand for real assets are both taken to be perfectly inelastic with regard to the yield on the other.

If the monetary authorities undertake an open market operation to increase the money supply then bond prices will be bid up and the rate of interest on bonds will fall. This reduces the opportunity cost of investing in real capital assets, raises the size of the optimum capital stock and leads to an increased demand for capital assets, i.e. an increased flow of investment expenditure. This channel of monetary influence, usually known as the cost of capital channel, involves a re-adjustment of portfolios working entirely through the rate of interest on government bonds. There is substitution between money and bonds and between bonds and real assets, but no direct substitution between money and real assets.

Tobin and the Yale School

The extension of the simple Keynesian three asset model to one which incorporates a much wider range of assets and interest rates was made primarily by James Tobin and his associates at Yale. They believe that monetary theory broadly conceived is simply the theory of portfolio management by economic units: households, businesses, financial institutions and governments. It takes as its subject matter stocks of assets and debts (including money proper) and their values and yields: its accounting framework is the balance sheet. It can be distinguished from branches of economic theory which take the income statement as their accounting framework and flows of income, saving, expenditure and production as their subject matter. (Tobin and Hester 1967, pp. v–vi).

They therefore

regard the structure of interest rates, asset yields and credit availabilities rather than the quantity of money as the linkage between monetary and financial institutions on the one hand and the real economy on the other (Tobin, 1963, p. 410).

In the Tobin approach money stands at one end of a continuous spectrum of assets with real assets at the other. An increase in the stock of money will result in portfolio adjustment involving the whole spectrum of assets and asset yields, and resulting eventually in increased expenditure on real assets. An example may help to illustrate some of the major aspects of the approach, though it will inevitably ignore most of the detail. Assume that the central bank decides to increase the quantity of money in circulation by releasing special deposits back to the banking system. The release of these deposits raises the cash reserves of the banks. The banks will not wish to hold the reserves redundant when they can employ them profitably, so they attempt to diversify their portfolios by expanding their earning assets. Banks can increase their earning assets in a number of ways, but for simplicity we shall concentrate on only two of them.

One possibility is to expand loan business. On the assumption that initially the bank loan market was in equilibrium, an increase in the willingness of banks to lend money, will, given the unchanged demand for bank loans, produce a state of excess supply in the bank loan market. This excess will drive down the bank loan rate. The bank loan market will be cleared at a lower equilibrium interest rate and a larger volume of bank loans will be available: consequently the level of bank deposits rises.

Another possibility is to increase the bank's holdings of government bonds by purchasing them from members of the non-bank private sector. The increased demand for bonds, given a fixed stock of bonds in existence will create an excess demand for bonds, an increase in the price of bonds and a reduction in the bond yield. The higher bond prices clear the bond market, as non-bank members of the private sector exchange bonds which they no longer require for bank deposits: consequently the level of bank deposits rises. The increased level of bank deposits spells a commensurate increase in bank money and at an unchanged demand for money an excess supply of it. In fact, it is likely that the demand for money has increased as a result of the drop in the bond yield, i.e. some people are willing holders of the additional bank money so that the excess supply of money is less than the increased supply of bank money. There is still however a state of portfolio imbalance in the economy for two reasons. First, there is still disequilibrium in the money market: the supply of money exceeds the amount people wish to hold. Consequently there will be an attempt to restore portfolio balance by switching out of money and into near-money assets (e.g. building society deposits). Secondly the reduced bond yield will persuade some wealth-holders to substitute for bonds in their portfolios other financial assets which are regarded as close substitutes for bonds and which now offer a relatively higher yield. But in both cases the substitution into other assets (i.e. from money and from bonds) will push up the prices of these other assets and depress their yields. This in turn will initiate a movement out of these assets and into others next along the spectrum with similar consequences. This process has been described by Goodhart (1970, p. 161):

> The effect of a change in the money supply is seen to be like a ripple passing along the range of financial assets, diminishing in amplitude and unpredictability as it proceeds further away from the initial disturbance.

The 'ripple' will eventually reach to the demand for equities, pushing up their price and depressing their yield. In the Tobin approach to portfolio balance it is the increase in equity prices which stimulates the demand for real physical assets. The price of equities is seen as the valuation placed by the market on the existing stock of capital. A rise in equity prices (i.e. a fall in equity yields) is taken as an indication that the market has increased the value that it places on the existing stock of capital. This will make newly produced capital relatively cheaper – compared with the valuation of the existing stock of capital – than it was before. The result will be an increased demand for new capital. Thus if the increase in equity prices means that the existing stock of capital of a firm is now valued at £2m but could be replaced by new capital at a cost of £1½m, then the firm will be encouraged to add to the existing stock of capital, i.e. undertake investment expenditure.

Unlike the simple Keynesian approach Tobin recognizes that changes in the supply of any asset, not just money, would create portfolio imbalance and disturb the whole spectrum of asset prices and asset yields.

Most writers see the Tobin analysis as being an extension of the Keynesian model. An important difference between the two approaches, however, is that in the Keynesian one it is the cost of borrowing which is the crucial channel of influence, while in the Tobin approach borrowing costs are ignored, the major link between money and the goal variables being equity yields. Many Keynesians, while accepting the Tobin approach of widening the range of assets included in portfolios and the idea of a 'ripple effect', would still argue for the importance of debt finance in firms, and continue to attach significance to the cost of borrowing.

Chick (1977) has suggested another difference between the approaches. In Keynes' model the economy is disaggregated into two different sectors – government, firms and householders – which borrow from and lend to one another, perform different economic functions and have differently composed portfolios.

In Tobin's portfolio balance approach however there is no disaggregation of transactors, only of assets.

> People and institutions are replaced by a portfolio of assets ... for which there are demands and supplies. The identity of the demanders, suppliers and owners is unknown. Only the government retains its identity. It conducts policy, changing asset supplies. (Chick 1977, p. 98).

The monetarist approach

The monetarist transmission mechanism is also one of portfolio balance. Monetarists are critical of the Keynes and Tobin versions, however, for concentrating on too narrow a range of capital assets, yields and associated expenditures. This has been stated quite explicitly by Friedman and Meiselman who, using the phrase 'credit-view' to describe the Keynesian position, said:

> the crucial issue that corresponds to the distinction between the 'credit' and 'monetary' effects of monetary policy is not whether changes in the stock of money operates through interest rates but rather, the range of interest rates considered. On the 'credit' view, monetary policy impinges on a narrow and well-defined range of capital assets and a corresponding narrow range of associated expenditures. On the 'monetary' view, monetary policy impinges on a much broader range of capital assets, and correspondingly broader range of associated expenditures. (1963, p. 217).

The term 'interest rates', as used in this quotation, refers not only to those on financial assets but also to the rates of return that the flow of services from any real asset represents on the cost of that asset. Thus consumer durables such as houses, cars, hi-fi equipment and jewellery may all be regarded as providing over time a flow of consumable services which may be seen as a yield or rate of interest on the cost of that particular asset. Of course these rates of return are implicit and unobserved, but that does not make them any the less real or important.

To monetarists, money is a substitute not only for financial assets but for all assets that comprise wealth portfolios. Consequently the cross-elasticity of demand for money with regard to the yield on any one particular asset is likely to be low. The implication of this is that asset-holders who find their portfolios in imbalance because they have surplus money balances are just as likely to switch directly into equities and real physical assets as they are into financial ones.

The monetarist approach is in fact so broad that it virtually embraces all possible chains of substitution. It is often the direct substitution between money and real assets which is identified with the monetarist approach, but much longer Tobin-type chains of substitution are also allowed for. We consider the monetarist transmission mechanism more fully in Chapter 7.

Portfolio adjustment and expenditure on non-durables

So far we have been concerned with the ways in which the substitution effects that may follow from a portfolio imbalance brought about by an increase in the money supply will sooner or later affect the flows of expenditure on new physical assets, both producer and consumer. We now consider how expenditure on non-durables may be affected by portfolio adjustments.

Changes in the flow of expenditure on non-durable consumer goods may result from decisions to add to or to reduce existing portfolios by saving and dissaving respectively. As asset yields are lowered through the process of portfolio adjustment, there will be two influences at work on the saving/dissaving decision. To begin with there will be a substitution effect as the opportunity cost of consuming and dissaving falls. The opportunity cost of consuming now is the present value of the stream of consumption that would be generated by current saving and asset acquisition. A fall in yields means a fall in these discounted present values and therefore a stimulus to current consumption. For similar reasons there will be an increased incentive to run down accumulated assets (i.e. dissave) and also to borrow. However, the change in asset yields and prices will also generate an income effect, which may work in the opposite direction. The fall in interest rates reduces the income flow (and therefore potential future consumption) from any given level of savings. If people feel that they want to maintain the income flow from their assets, then they will have to save out of current income (i.e. not consume) in order to add to their stock of income-earning assets. The net effect on peoples saving-dissaving decisions will therefore depend on whether the income or the substitution effect is the stronger.

There is a second way in which portfolio adjustments may influence consumption expenditure and that is through windfall capital gains. As portfolio adjustments force up asset prices the net wealth of the private sector is increased. If wealth is a determinant of consumption expenditure, then consumption will rise. It may be argued that this particular channel of influence is better regarded as part of the wealth transmission mechanism rather than portfolio balance. In any case it is to the wealth transmission mechanism that we now turn.

The wealth transmission mechanism

Link (a): money and wealth

Prior to the publication of Keynes' *General Theory* very little explicit consideration had been given to the role of wealth in macroeconomic theory. Keynes discussed wealth effects in the *General Theory* but did not integrate them into his general scheme. As we shall see in Chapter 6, Keynes demonstrated the possibility that the economy could be frustrated from attaining a full employment equilibrium position. As a result of this novel and challenging assault upon received classical dogma, a considerable amount of intellectual energy was subsequently expended in trying to show that it rested upon the absence of wealth effects in the economy resulting from the omission of the stock of wealth from the macromodel. Once explicit recognition was given to the existence of these wealth effects, it was argued, unemployment could be eradicated by means of an appropriately chosen monetary policy and the economy would be projected on to its full employment path. Before we investigate the nature of these wealth effects we must first establish a relationship between changes in the money supply and changes in wealth.

Aggregate wealth of the private sector is physical wealth (such as capital equipment, raw materials and human resources), plus financial assets held by the private sector which are not offset by corresponding liabilities. For an item to constitute 'net wealth' it must represent an asset without at the same time representing a corresponding debt to holders of it; nor must it constitute a debt to non-holders of it and, more particularly, issuers of it. In order to see whether money is a component of net wealth we need first to consider the distinction made by Gurley and Shaw (1960) between inside and outside money.

Outside money is money backed by assets that do not represent a claim on members inside the economy, for example, fiat currency backed by government securities, gold or foreign exchange reserves. In all these cases the holding of fiat currency by members of the economy does not impose any offsetting obligations upon them, so that money is a net asset. Inside money is money backed by assets which do represent an equal claim on members inside the economy: for example, fiat currency backed by private bonds issued by firms or, what is more likely, commercial bank deposits backed by investments and loans to the private sector. In these cases the money held by members of the private sector is backed by assets of the banking system that are a corresponding claim on the private sector. As far as the members of the private sector are concerned, so Gurley and Shaw contend, 'inside' money is not a net asset but a debt.

Before we start the analysis proper we must distinguish between two quite separate issues: (i) Is money, however defined, a constituent of net wealth? (ii) Will a change in the stock of inside and outside money change the level of net wealth? This distinction is important because we shall demonstrate that although money may be a constituent of net wealth, variations in its quantity in existence may not necessarily alter aggregate net wealth. Let us consider whether money of the outside variety is a constituent of net wealth. Pesek and Saving (1967) believe that outside money is a net asset because it is an asset to holders of it (members of the private sector) and yet not a debt to issuers of it (the government). Gurley and Shaw (1969) also believe that outside money is a constituent of private net wealth, although essentially such money is a debt (of the government). In order words, according to Gurley and Shaw and others (e.g. Patinkin 1965), money is a debt to issuers of it just as it is an asset to holders of it. They do not, however, believe that there is anything fundamentally inconsistent with the view that on the one hand 'money-is-a-debt' and yet on the other money is a constituent of net wealth. This is because they believe that the government is unconcerned about the level of its own debts. This means, in effect, that when the government increases its indebtedness to the private sector by issuing more money it does not feel 'worse off' when the private sector feels 'better off'. Pesek and Saving criticize the Gurley–Shaw– Patinkin thesis on the grounds that its rationale is an asymmetry of behavioural responses by different sectors of the economy (the private sector feeling 'better off' when its currency holdings have increased and the government not feeling 'worse off' when the level of its outstanding debts have increased), and that such behaviour implies irrationality on the part of the government. However, Gurley and Shaw's standpoint is a tenable one for two reasons. Firstly, there are numerous branches of received economic doctrine whose basis is such an asymmetry of behavioural responses. Secondly, it is quite 'reasonable' to assume that the government is not particularly concerned about the level of its debts because, unlike other debtors, it is under no compelling obligation to repay all of them.

Goodhart has argued that the recognition of asymmetrical behaviour responses should not be confused with 'statistical estimations of net wealth positions'. As far as accounting principles are concerned, it would be misleading to regard an issue of outside money which alters the indebtedness between the public and private sectors as changing wealth. What is important, argues Goodhart, is that even if wealth has not changed in an accounting sense the changed indebtedness between the two sectors leads to different behavioural responses.

> more broadly the effect on total expenditures of an increase in the value of the private sectors financial claims on the public sector, is basically a distributional, or differential response effect, rather than a pure wealth effect (Goodhart 1975a, p. 206).

However, even if outside money is accepted as a constituent of net wealth it does not follow necessarily that changes in the stock of outside money will alter aggregate net wealth. To understand why not requires us to consider the way in which the stock of outside money is expanded. If the government prints and issues more fiat currency via deficit spending then, unambiguously, the level of net wealth in the economy must rise. Consider now the situation if the central bank increases the stock of outside money by purchasing government bonds from the private sector. If government bonds are not a liability of the private sector then open-market purchases of government bonds merely causes an exchange of more of one asset (cash) for less of another (bonds) (i.e. only changes wealth composition), leaving aggregate net wealth unchanged.

It can however be argued that government bonds are not part of the net wealth of the private sector. If the private sector takes into account the increase in taxes required to finance the interest payments on the bonds, and if the capitalized value of the anticipated future stream of tax liabilities equals the present value of the bonds, then the bonds are an asset matched by an offsetting liability and cannot be perceived as adding to the net wealth of the private sector. If this is the case, then an open-market purchase of bonds will raise the aggregate net wealth of the private sector by increasing the supply of outside money, while at the same time extinguishing assets that were also a debt (bonds). It is clear therefore that what is relevant to the relationship between money and wealth is not whether money is a constituent of net wealth but the attitude of the private sector towards government interest-bearing debt.

Whether or not the private sector perceives government bonds as adding to aggregate net wealth is a subject of some controversy (see Tobin 1980 for a review of the theoretical and empirical issues). One argument in favour of treating bonds as part of private sector net wealth is connected with the timing of the tax liabilities. Government issues of long-term bonds, which of course can be refinanced in the future by further bond issues, can effectively defer the tax burden to future generations: the current generation of tax-payers with finite lives are likely to be indifferent to this long-term future tax liability. If this is the case then the relevant time period for the capitalization of the future tax liability will only be the remaining (average) lifetimes of the current taxpayers and will therefore only partly offset the present value of bond issues. This argument, however, is countered by Barro (1974) who develops an 'overlapping generations' model where the utility function of each generation includes the utility of the next generation, thus making the time horizon of each generation effectively infinite. His results support the view that government bonds are not a component of private sector net wealth, although of course his approach does assume (one would like to think realistically) that each tax-paying generation is not indifferent to the living standards of the next generation.

Most monetary economists would probably say that the conclusions of this analysis on 'outside' money are not really important anyway because most of the money in existence nowadays is of the 'inside' variety, i.e. bank money. Let us now, therefore, consider the relationship between 'inside' money and net wealth. The general view is that inside money is not a component of net wealth because while it is an asset to those who hold it, it is a liability to those who issue it. Bank deposits are debts owed by the banks to their customers so that adding the banks and their customers together would mean that the asset status of the deposits to the banks' customers would be exactly offset by their liability status to the banks.

Pesek and Saving (1967) however have argued differently. As we saw in Chapter 1 they visualize money primarily as a 'producer's good', whether it be commodity money (gold), fiat money (currency) or bank money (bank deposits). In respect of bank money, the banks 'produce' money which they then sell to the non-bank private sector for financial assets and other debt instruments, subject to a repurchase clause. If we accept their contention that bank money is 'resource cheap' to produce and in the extreme has zero costs of production, then it follows quite logically that the purchases of bank money by the non-bank private sector raises the stock of financial assets in existence without correspondingly reducing the stock of real assets, so that unequivocally, the total stock of assets in the economy must increase. The net wealth of the economy rises by the full amount of the bank money produced and sold. At the other extreme, where the costs of producing and selling bank money equals the revenue received from its sales, the addition of the stock of financial assets afforded by the purchase of bank money is exactly offset by the reduction in the stock of real assets that are entailed in the production of bank money. Total wealth in the economy remains unchanged and the economy exchanges more financial assets for less real assets, i.e. changes the composition of its portfolio. The crucial issue, therefore, becomes an empirical one, namely the cost of producing bank money in relation to the anticipated revenue from its sale.

To the majority of economists, however, the basic assumption of the Pesek–Saving analysis – that money is produced and sold – is unacceptable and they consequently reject the idea that inside money is part of net wealth.

So far we have only looked at the direct effect of money on wealth, but there is also, as we saw at the end of the last section, an indirect effect arising out of portfolio adjustments. The portfolio adjustments that follow from an increase in the money supply depress asset yields and force up asset prices. These increased asset prices confer capital gains on the asset holders (i.e. increase the market value of their wealth). This particular wealth effect has come to be known as the 'Keynes windfall effect'.

Link (b): wealth and the goal variables

The wealth transmission mechanism, like the portfolio balance one, influences the goal variables through the flow of expenditure. In this section we shall be concentrating on the link between wealth and aggregate expenditure by looking at the possible effects of increased wealth on the money market, the assets market, and the market for goods and services.

The money market

If the community feels better off when the money supply rises, some members may decide to indulge in a higher level of liquidity by hoarding some part of the increase in the money supply. The money market wealth effect leaves the market for goods, services and assets undisturbed because the increased money in circulation is absorbed into idle cash balances, and is not, therefore, transmitted to ultimate spending units. In the extreme, should the community decide to hoard all the additional wealth as money then there will be no operational effects in the economy at all. In this situation, of course, there would be a zero relationship between wealth and aggregate expenditure despite the existence of a wealth effect (in the money market).

The asset market

On the demand side households may use part of the increase in their money balances to acquire additional earning assets. In the simple Keynesian model the only alternative financial asset to money is bonds, but in the Tobin and monetarist models there are a larger number of assets which compete for inclusion in households' portfolios, so that this wealth effect is likely to occur in a broad range of asset markets.

As far as the supply side is concerned, if firms and financial institutions as well as households share in the additional money in circulation, then they too can be expected to feel better off and to alter their lending and borrowing behaviour accordingly. For example, financial institutions with additions to their cash base may be expected to increase their supply of loans.

These two wealth effects, one operating on the demand and the other on the supply side of the assets and loanable funds markets, will affect the extent to which operational effects can take place in the final goods market. In some asset markets, wealth-induced changes in demand and supply will alter the availability of assets and loans, and any consequential effects on expenditure in the goods market are known as availability effects: these are discussed in the next section. In other asset markets, changing supply and demand conditions will alter asset prices and asset yields. The effects of such changes on expenditure in the goods market were discussed in the section on portfolio adjustment.

The goods market

We must now consider the direct effects that increased wealth may have on expenditure. Two possible channels of influence can be identified. Firstly, the proportions in which a person divides his current income between consumption and saving (i.e. adding to wealth) may well depend on the consumer's existing level of wealth. The usual view is that more wealth one already has, the smaller the percentage of current income one will devote to further saving. An increase in wealth might therefore be expected to increase the level of aggregate consumption expenditure. In this channel there is no dissaving, only a change in the rate of current consumption and saving.

The second effect is whether the increased money balances are actually drawn on to provide the finance for increased consumption expenditure. The underlying assumption here is that there is a desired level of real cash balances which consumers wish to hold. Any increase of actual balances over the desired level will then be reflected in increased expenditures on goods, financed by drawing on these surplus balances.

The credit availability transmission mechanism

Link (a): money stock and credit availability

The Radcliffe Report (1959) emphasized that it is the 'overall liquidity of the economy rather than the stock of money in existence' which is the centrepiece of monetary action. The Report was very conscious of the crucial role played by the availability of credit to ultimate spending units in the formulation of expenditure decisions. One thing seems to be fairly apparent from the Report, and this is that the market for loans in general, and bank loans in particular, is very imperfect and that more attention should be directed to the supply side of the loanable funds market, particularly to lenders' preferences and the interest-sensitivity of the supply of loanable funds. The main reasoning behind this was the belief in the existence of an 'unsatisfied fringe of borrowers' whose demand for loanable funds was relatively inelastic with respect to the loan rate, and certainly less interest-elastic than the supply curve of loanable funds. As far as borrowers are concerned, so the argument goes, it is not the cost of credit but its availability which matters.

> While the cost of borrowing money can only affect total demand in a limited manner ... the monetary authorities may bring to bear another influence which is altogether more peremptory. This is the availability of funds to borrow ... [If] the money for financing the project cannot be got on any tolerable terms at all, that is the end of the matter. (Radcliffe 1959, p. 387),

Bank and other loan markets function imperfectly because, basically, loan rates are 'administered prices' and therefore are likely to adjust, if at all, only with a time lag, in response to changes in credit market-conditions. Even where loan rates are free to vary, time lags in adjustment are still a real possibility. If we assume the existence of an excess demand for, say, bank loans and 'stickiness' in bank loan rates, then it follows that the banks will be forced to ration credit, some loan requests being completely turned down and others being scaled down. The argument can be illustrated with the aid of a simple diagram *Figure 2.1*.

If the current 'sticky' bank loan rate i_0 lies below that necessary to clear the loan market of all willing borrowers q_1, then there will be an excess demand for bank loans of distance $b-a$. For as long as (i) the loan rate remains at i_0; (ii) the demand schedule for loanable funds remains unchanged; and (iii) the supply schedule of loanable funds remains unchanged, there will be an excess demand for bank loans and banks will be forced to ration credit to q_0.

The relationship between the availability of bank credit and the money supply can also be shown within the context of this simple model of the loanable funds market. Let us consider the effect on the availability of bank credit of an increase in the money supply brought about through an open-market purchase of government bonds from private portfolios. Such a transaction tends to influence the supply of bank loans in two quite specific ways, analogous to an 'income' and a 'substitution' effect. First, the increase in the cash reserves of the banking system resulting from the open-market operation creates excess cash reserves and enables the banks to expand their holding of all assets, including loans. Secondly, the open-market operation will have lowered the yield on government bonds held by the banking system relative to the fixed bank loan rate and will have persuaded the banks to substitute loans for securities in their portfolios. The result of these two effects is an increase in bank loans which shifts the supply schedule of loanable funds to the right (SL_o to SL_1). An additional volume of loanable funds of distance q_2-q_0 is made available to ultimate spending units. An increase in the quantity of money serves partially to eliminate the 'unsatisfied fringe' of borrowers.

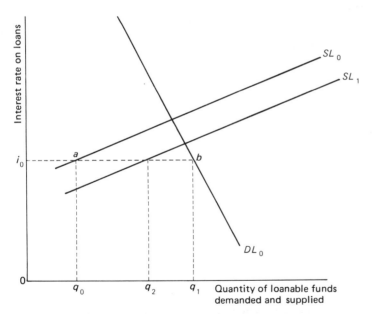

Figure 2.1 Credit rationing and increases in the quantity of money

We may have established a possible connection between changes in the money supply and the volume of bank credit in existence, but we cannot then argue that we have also established a connection between the money supply and total credit in the economy. Bank credit is just one component of the total amount of credit in the economy. To argue from bank credit to total credit requires us to make some assumptions about the behaviour of non-bank credit when the availability of bank credit rises in response to an increase in the money supply. There are three possibilities we can consider. First, we can postulate that non-bank credit is unrelated to bank credit so that when the latter rises so too does total credit in the economy. Secondly, we can postulate than non-bank credit is complementary to bank credit so that when the latter rises so too does the former so that, unambiguously, total credit in the economy rises. This could happen if, during the expansion of bank deposits, some of the newly created funds flow to the non-banks, enabling these institutions to expand their loans as well. Thirdly, we can postulate that non-bank credit is a substitute for bank credit so that when the latter rises the former falls and the total stock of credit rises only slightly, falls, or remains unchanged. This could happen in our model if there were a marked preference for bank over non-bank credit, because the former was cheaper than the latter. In this situation an increase in the supply of bank credit would reduce the demand for non-bank credit so that the net effect upon total credit would be zero. Clearly, the validity of the relationship between the money supply and the total volume of credit in the economy is an empirical question.

Link (b): credit availability and the goal variables

As with the two previous transmission mechanisms that we have considered, credit availability affects the goal variables through aggregate expenditure.

Assuming that an increase in the money supply does in fact raise the total stock of credit in existence, then the credit transmission mechanism is an operationally signficant one. This follows from the fact that credit is almost exclusively made available to ultimate spending units. Borrowers do not usually raise money to hoard it or purchase financial assets; they raise money so that they may spend it. There is no major endogenous component of aggregate expenditure that is not related in a meaningful way to the volume of credit in existence. We shall say that such operational effects are 'availability' effects.

The expectations transmission mechanism

Link (a): the money supply and expectations

Changes in the money supply, or in its rate of growth, may have an effect on many kinds of expectations. We shall concentrate our attention in this section on just two of these effects: price expectations and business confidence.

Price expectations

The price expectations channel of influence postulates a relationship between changes in the quantity of money in circulation, and the views of various economic agents, such as consumers, trade unions and employers, about the likely course of price movements in the future. How, if at all, economic agents are likely to revise their price expectations as a result of a change in the money supply depends on how those agents form their expectations. Let us consider two possibilities. The first of these is that they believe, on the basis of past experience, that increases in the money supply result in increases in the level of prices. Thus whenever the money supply is observed to rise, economic agents immediately revise upwards their price level expectations.

The alternative approach that we consider is that price level expectations are formed on the basis of experience of current and possibly recent price levels. Price level expectations are then revised only after actual changes in the price level have been experienced. If these actual changes are the consequence, through some other transmission mechanism, of prior changes in the money supply, then it may be argued, somewhat tenuously, that revised price level expectations are a secondary response to changes in the money supply.

The distinction we have made between these two ways of forming price expectations is essentially that between what is called in the literature 'rational expectations' and 'adaptive expectations'. (The distinction is made more formally and fully on pp. 204–206.)

Business confidence

It is difficult to know exactly how businessmen might react to the news that the money supply has expanded, but we can put forward a few tentative suggestions. An increase in the money supply may be interpreted as either that more money will be available for investment purposes (or, negatively, that banks are not going to recall loans, thereby easing any liquidity problems which firms may have), or that money will be available more cheaply, or both. It may also be taken as a sign that the monetary authorities are firm in their resolve to raise the level of economic activity. Additionally, firms may expect that more money available for household expenditure will stimulate a consumer boom. On the other hand, if demand is already at a fairly high level, an expansion in the money supply might indicate to businessmen the possibility that attempts will shortly be made to restrain the level of demand by means of fiscal contraction. Clearly the impact on business confidence of an increase in the money supply could go either way.

Link (b): expectations and the goal variables

Price expectations

Revised price expectations, just like the other transmission mechanisms, may influence the goal variables via aggregate expenditure, but may also have a more direct effect on them through wage and price setting behaviour. If we consider the expenditure channel first, revised price expectations may affect both the flow of consumption expenditure and of investment expenditure. As far as consumption is concerned two opposite effects may be distinguished. On the one hand, if prices are expected to be higher in the future than they currently are, this may cause an acceleration in consumer expenditure. On the other, the expectation of having to pay higher prices in the future may encourage some consumers to save more now, in order to be able to keep up future consumption levels in the face of higher prices. The net effect on consumption depends on which of these two opposing pulls is the stronger.

The impact on investment expenditure is likely to be small. This is because although the supply price of capital equipment is expected to rise in the future, so too are the prices of goods and services produced by the capital equipment, so that the marginal efficiency of investment is likely to remain unchanged.

We turn now to the more direct channels by which revised price expectations may influence the goal variables. One possibility is that expectations of higher prices may result in larger wage claims as workers try to protect their real standards of living. To the extent that these claims are conceded and passed on there will be a further upward push to the general level of prices.

Another possibility is that producers fix their own prices in the light of their expectations as to what other producers will charge. If then these expectations are raised, producers will increase their own prices. If all producers behave in the same way the result will be an increase in the general level of prices (see pp. 201–202).

Business confidence and the goal variables

An improvement (deterioration) in business confidence will obviously have an effect on the desired flow of investment expenditure by raising (lowering) the marginal efficiency of investment.

The open economy

So far our consideration of the possible monetary transmission mechanisms has been confined to a closed economy. With the widespread adoption of floating exchange rates in the 1970s, however, increasing attention has been paid to the determination of exchange rates and to their importance in influencing the major goals of policy. In this section, therefore, we shall briefly consider the role of the foreign exchange rate as a monetary transmission mechanism. There are in fact some considerable differences of view on this issue of the determination and role of exchange rates, and we shall be considering some of them further in Chapter 10.

With fixed exchange rates any increase in the money supply of a country, which results in increased purchases by domestic residents of foreign goods, services and assets, would tend to deteriorate the balance of payments. To maintain the fixed exchange rate the authorities must purchase the excess currency coming onto the foreign exchange market, paying with foreign currencies. The implication of this is that with fixed exchange rates, the domestic authorities cannot control their own money supplies (see pp. 223–224). Under such conditions, it is fairly generally agreed that domestic expansion of the money supply will have no permanent effect on aggregate demand, and the major domestic macrovariables will be unaffected.

In the context of floating exchange rates, however, the picture is very different. As with our previous discussion of the transmission mechanisms we will divide our consideration of the role of the foreign exchange rate into two parts. First, we may ask how a monetary expansion is transmitted to the exchange rate, and secondly, we can consider how any change in the exchange rate influences the major macrovariables.

Link (a): money to the exchange rate

The variety of ways by which changes in the money supply can be transmitted to the exchange rate can be seen as particular channels of influence within the transmission mechanisms that we have already identified. Particularly important are the portfolio adjustment and expectations transmission mechanisms.

In considering portfolio adjustments we need to recognize that in an open economy, wealth portfolios include not only domestic assets, but foreign ones as well. Thus when an expansion of the money supply triggers off a series of portfolio adjustments, these adjustments at some stage will involve an increased demand for foreign assets. This will increase the demand for foreign currency, either as an asset to hold in its own right, or as a pre-requisite for the purchase of other foreign assets, whether financial or real. For example, an open market operation by the domestic authorities which increases the money supply will push down domestic interest rates, both absolutely and relatively to interest rates on foreign assets. This is likely to increase the demand for such assets and thereby increase the demand for foreign currency and depreciate the foreign exchange rate. Within this broad senario there is clearly scope for differences of opinion as to the stage at which portfolio adjustments will involve moving into foreign assets. At one extreme is the view that the exchange rate is essentially the relative price of two moneys so that, assuming an initial position of equilibrium, an increased supply of the domestic one will have its immediate impact in an attempt to exchange part of the surplus for the foreign money. The result would be immediate depreciation of the exchange rate.

Another view, as we have already seen, is that portfolio adjustments involving foreign assets come into force as a response to changes in interest rates on domestic financial assets.

A third view sees foreign assets and the exchange rate being involved only when portfolio adjustments have pushed up domestic prices of real goods and services.

The three views considered above are obviously not exhaustive of all possibilities, but they emphasize that there is no consensus on the question of how soon, within the process of portfolio adjustment, the foreign exchange rate becomes involved. Thus, on the third view just considered, many economists argue that the foreign exchange rate is a more flexible price than the domestic prices of goods and services, and is therefore more likely to adjust before them, to attempts by portfolio holders to purchase goods and services.

The expectations transmission mechanism also embraces the exchange rate in a number of ways. If, for example, people expect interest rates to fall and prices to rise when they observe an increase in the money supply, then they may adjust their portfolios in accordance with these expectations, rather than waiting for interest rates and prices to actually change. Similarly, if people expect the domestic currency to depreciate whenever the money supply increases, then observing such an increase is likely to lead to an immediate movement out of that currency, forcing down its foreign exchange value. The expectation of a depreciating currency initiates action which actually depreciates it.

Link (b): the exchange rate to macrovariables

A number of channels may be identified whereby a fall in the foreign exchange rate may influence output and prices. Let us consider first the possible effects on prices.

The depreciation of the domestic currency will raise the domestic prices of imports. Some of these imports will be finished goods, both consumer and producer, and the increase in their prices will feed directly into the general level of prices.

Secondly there will be a cost-push impetus to prices coming through as a result of the increased cost of imported raw materials and semi-finished goods.

The depreciation lowers the foreign currency price of exports at unchanged domestic prices. This increases the competitiveness of those goods, and the produces may decide to absorb some of that greater competitiveness in increased profit margins achieved by charging higher prices. Similarly the depreciation makes domestically produced import substitutes relatively cheaper and will stimulate an increased demand for them and possibly pull up their prices.

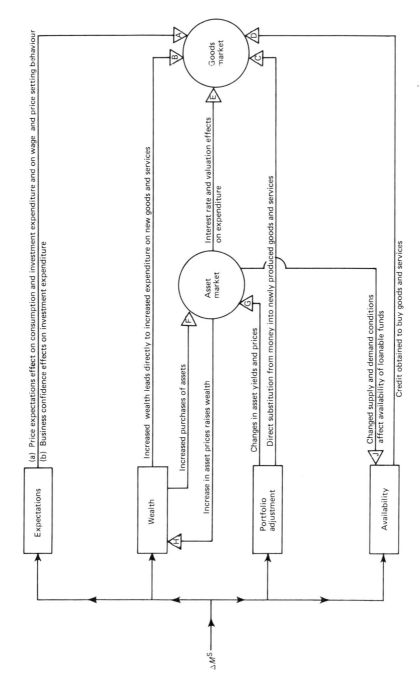

Figure 2.2 Major transmission mechanisms in a closed economy

The effects considered above will tend to raise the general level of prices and/or the profitability of producers. This may well stimulate trade unions to seek compensating increases in wages, which may well be conceded because of the increased profitability of production. To the extent that they are conceded, this will provide a further increase in costs with subsequent cost-push effects on prices.

We turn now to the effects of the depreciation on output. To a large extent these will vary inversely with the effects on prices. The greater the effect of the depreciation on prices, the smaller will be the effect on competitiveness and subsequently on output.

The role of the exchange rate in the monetary transmission mechanisms is still very much one of controversy. This was clearly reflected for example, in the replies to the question on a Treasury and Civil Service Committee questionnaire which asked whether the principal 'transmission mechanism' between monetary policy actions and the ultimate target is via changes in the exchange rate. Thus at one extreme Friedman replied:

> I strongly disagree. Monetary policy actions affect asset portfolios in the first instance, spending decisions in the second, which translate into effects on output and then on prices. The changes in exchange rates are in turn mostly a response to these effects of home policy and of similar policy abroad ... Floating exchange rates are necessary in order for a monetary policy proper to be possible. They are a facilitating mechanism not a 'transmission mechanism'. (1980, p. 61).

At the other extreme of responses was, for example, that of Artis who replied:

> Yes. There are of course other channels of the transmission mechanism – expectations and interest rate-demand channels. The evidence on these is not powerful. (1980, p. 44).

Summary and conclusion

The major transmission mechanisms that we considered for a closed economy are summarized in *Figure 2.2*. An important point to emerge from the figure, and from the discussion in the text, is that while all four mechanisms can exert direct influences on the goods market (channels A, B, C, D, in *Figure 2.2*), there are also some important interrelationships between them via their effects on the assets market. For example, portfolio adjustments, that bring about increases in asset prices (G), generate a wealth effect (H). Similarly, wealth-induced purchases of assets (F) may increase the availability of credit (J).

One can thus conceive of a quite generalized and integrated transmission process which takes account of the repercussions of 'disturbances' in the assets market (portfolio or wealth-induced) on asset values, asset yields and the availability of loanable funds. It is for this reason that by the beginning of the 1970s portfolio adjustment came to be accepted as the dominant monetary transmission mechanism, operating through asset imbalances and subsequent re-adjustments.

The last decade, however, has seen increasing attention paid to the role of expectations and of the exchange rate in the transmission process. As far as expectations are concerned the major development has been the 'rational expectations revolution' with its major policy implications. This controversial concept is considered more fully in Chapters 7, 9 and 13. The significance of the exchange rate in the transmission process is, as we have already pointed out, an issue of considerable debate. We have argued that the exchange rate is best regarded as one channel of influence to be set within the broad portfolio balance and expectations mechanisms, along with such other channels as 'cost of capital', 'valuation' and 'availability'.

3

The demand for money

In this chapter we shall be looking at the various explanations that have been put forward as to why people demand money, and also at the factors that influence the amount they demand. The determinants and stability of the demand for money are of vital importance to an understanding of how, if at all, changes in the supply of money affect real and nominal variables. The question of stability is of course an empirical one, and is probably one of the most thoroughly researched issues in the whole of monetary economics. We consider the empirical evidence in the last section of the chapter, but first we trace out the variety of theoretical approaches to the demand for money.

The classical approach

The transactions balance version

The classical economists' analysis of the demand for money was based on the view that money was simply a medium of exchange and as such was held only to facilitate exchanges. Money had no intrinsic utility which made it desirable for its own sake. No one really desired to hold money, but people were obliged to do so because of a lack of synchronization between monetary receipts and payments. The existence of a time lag between receiving payments from the sale of goods and services (e.g. a weekly wage), and then making payments for goods and services purchased, necessitated the holding of cash balances during the intervening period. In the classical approach, all money held is in transactions balances, kept in order to finance future transactions. This approach to the demand for money is, for fairly obvious reasons, usually called the 'transactions balance' approach. In the classical system there was no analysis of the factors that determined the size of transactions balances, i.e. of the amount of money people had to hold.

The amount of money held in transactions balances both by individuals and the community as a whole depended very largely on institutional arrangements within the economy. Turning first to individuals, some major influences can be shown with the aid of some simple diagrams. In *Figure 3.1* the continuous line on the graph refers to an individual who receives an income of say, £300, every 30 days, and proceeds to spend $\frac{1}{30}$ of it on each of the succeeding 30 days; at the end of the 30 days the money balance is zero. The individual then receives an income for the next

30 days and proceeds to spend it in the same manner. During each period
£300-worth of transactions are undertaken. At the beginning of each 30-day period
the individual's cash balance is £300, while at the end of the period it is zero: the
average cash balance is £150.

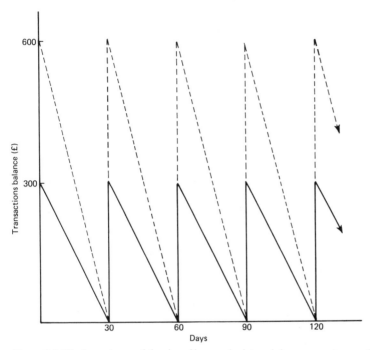

Figure 3.1 The importance of the size of income in determining average transactions balances

The broken line in *Figure 3.1* refers to an individual who also receives income
every 30 days, but whose income is £600 per period. The individual also spends it at
the rate of ¹⁄₃₀ per day, being left at the end of the period with a balance of zero.
During the 30-day period £600-worth of transactions are undertaken. The average
cash balance of this individual is £300. It can be seen therefore that the size of a
person's income (which, on the assumption that all income is spent, is the same as
the value of transactions undertaken by the individual) is a major influence on the
size of individual cash balances.

Figure 3.2 shows the importance of a second factor, the frequency with which
income is received. The continuous line refers to a person who is paid £280 every 28
days and who, spending uniformly over the period, has a cash balance of zero at the
end of the period and an average cash balance of £140.

The broken line refers to an individual who has the equivalent income of the first
person but receives it as £70 every 7 days. The recipient also spends it uniformly
over time and has a balance of zero at the end of the period; therefore, the average
cash balance is £35. It is clear that the frequency with which income is received is
another influence on the size of individual's cash balances.

A third influence is the expenditure pattern of the individual. This is illustrated in
Figure 3.3. Clearly, the individual whose expenditure pattern is reflected in the

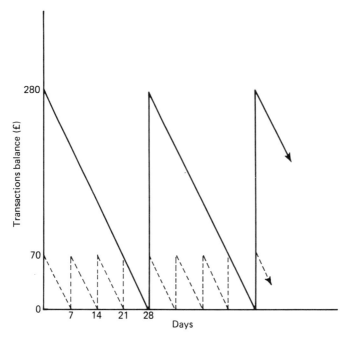

Figure 3.2 The importance of the frequency with which income is received for determining average transactions balances

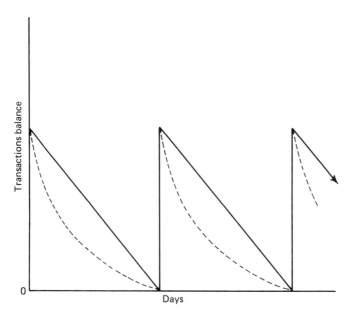

Figure 3.3 The importance of expenditure patterns in determining average transactions balances

solid lines has an average cash balance greater than that of the individual whose expenditure pattern is reflected in the dotted lines.

When we turn to the community as a whole, then other influences on the size of transactions balances emerge. These include the timing of the payments made by the various economic units, and the extent to which they overlap, the amount of integration in industry, and the extent to which credit is used. We shall say no more about these factors here except to point out that they are largely concerned with institutional arrangements. Thus it would appear that if money is held only to finance transactions, then the amount held for this purpose depends on the level of transactions to be financed and on certain institutional arrangements surrounding those transactions.

If it is assumed that the institutional arrangements are given, then the amount of transactions balances required will depend upon the nominal value of transactions. If, on the other hand, we assume a given level of transactions, then the transactions balance requirements will depend upon the institutional arrangements, so that if these arrangements change, the amount of money required to finance any given level of transactions will also change. The ratio of the level of transactions to the money stock is called the transactions velocity of money. The classical economists assumed that the institutional factors influencing the transactions balance requirements of the community were more or less fixed in the short run and changed only slowly in the long run. They were therefore able to assert that the transactions velocity of circulation of money was virtually constant. Let us represent these views symbolically.

Let M be the stock of money in transactions balances and, because transactions balances are the only balances held, M is also the total money stock. Let T be the number of transactions undertaken during the period, and P the average price level of those transactions. Finally, let V be the transactions velocity of the money stock. Then:

$$V = \frac{PT}{M}$$

which may be rewritten as

$$MV = PT$$

This is the familiar equation of exchange of Irving Fisher. Both 'equations' are in fact identities. In the first case V is defined as the ratio of the money value of transactions to the money stock. The two sides are identical by definition. In the second case we have two sides of the same thing. The stock of money multiplied by the average number of times each unit of that money changed hands in financing transactions is simply the money value of expenditure on transactions during the period. This must be equal to the number of transactions multiplied by the average price of those transactions, because this latter product is simply the money value of receipts from all transactions that took place during the period. In other words, one side represents expenditure on transactions and the other receipts from those same transactions.

We have seen that of the four variables M, V, P and T, the classical economists believed that V would tend to be constant, depending as they thought it did on institutional factors which could be taken as given. They also took T to be constant, believing that output would correspond to the full employment level which their macroeconomic theory led them to believe was the normal state of affairs, and on the assumption that the ratio of transactions to output was constant. M, the quantity of money, was determined independently of the other three. This left only P as the dependent variable, whose value would be determined by the interaction of M, V and T. Further, as V and T were assumed constant it meant that P would vary proportionately with any change in M. This last proposition is the classical Quantity Theory of Money which may be summarized as

$$P = \frac{M\bar{V}}{\bar{T}} \text{ or } M\bar{V} = \bar{P}$$

where the bars denote constants.

The classical economists approached the demand for money, then, from the point of view of the velocity of money rather than the motives for holding money. One can of course, though the classical economists did not, express their views in terms of a demand for money function.

$$\text{If } M\bar{V} = P\bar{T} \text{ then } M = \frac{P\bar{T}}{\bar{V}} \text{ or } M = \frac{1}{\bar{V}} P\bar{T}$$

If we let $1/\bar{V}$ be denoted by k then we have

$$M = kP\bar{T}$$

All this says, of course, is that the money requirements (i.e. money demanded) of the community, being equal to an institutionally determined constant fraction of the value of transactions, will depend upon the value of the transactions to be undertaken within the economy.

The cash balance approach

The Cambridge 'cash balance' approach, associated particularly with Marshall and Pigou, starts from the assumption that people *want* to hold money and attempts to analyse the demand for it by asking just what are the factors that determine the amount of money individuals desire to hold. As Marshall (1924, p. 43) said,

> The total value of a country's currency, multiplied into the average number of times of its changing hands for business purposes in a year, is, of course, equal to the total amount of business transacted in that country by direct payments of currency in that year. But this identical statement does not indicate the causes that govern the rapidity of circulation of currency: to discover them we must look to the amounts of purchasing power which the people of that country elect to keep in the form of currency.

With the Cambridge approach the analysis of the demand for money thus turned away from the institutionally determined needs of the community to the choice-determined behaviour of the individual.

According to the Cambridge approach individuals desire to hold money because it provides certain services. Because it is immediately realizable purchasing power it provides the service of convenience to its holders. In addition, ownership of it enables people to buy on favourable terms, should the opportunity arise, and also to be prepared for other future contingencies: in this sense money may be seen as providing the service of security.

But other goods and assets for which money could be exchanged also provide services, but of a different nature. The problem for the individual is to balance out the different services available. As Marshall (1924, p. 39) said,

But currency held in hand yields no income: therefore everyone balances (more or less automatically and instinctively) the benefits which he would get by exchanging his stock of currency in the hand, against those which he would get by investing some of it either in a commodity – say a coat or a piano, from which he would derive a direct benefit: or in some business plant or stock exchange security, which would yield him a money income.

The amount of money an individual holds depends then on the convenience derived from holding it, the feeling of security that holding it gives, the expectations of the individual, the variety of opportunity costs involved in holding it, the individual's total 'resources' and so on. However, while this approach sets out many of the influences acting on a person's demand for money, it did not go very far in analysing just how these motives were interrelated or in discussing their relative importance. While indicating the path along which much later analysis was to proceed, the cash balance approach did not itself travel very far along it.

The balancing by each individual of the advantages and disadvantages of holding money would determine the proportion of his or her income that each individual would keep in the form of money, so that for

every state of society there is some fraction of their income which people find it worthwhile to keep in the form of currency: it may be a fifth, or a tenth or a twentieth (Marshall 1924, p. 45).

For the community as a whole the proportion of its income that it desires to hold in the form of money would also be influenced by the kinds of institutional factors that were important in the Fisher analysis.

Marshall himself never attempted to express his cash balance approach in the form of an equation, but later expositors of his views have often found it useful to do so. If PY represents the money income of the individual, and k the proportion of his nominal income that the individual desires to hold in the form of nominal money balances, then the individual's demand for money function may be written

$$M^d = kPY$$

It may be argued that this equation is simply the transactions balance equation in modern dress. Certainly the Fisher equation can be reformulated in terms of the level of money income simply by multiplying price by output rather than by the number of transactions. V would then become the income velocity of money rather than the transactions velocity. If the Fisher equation were further recast in terms of a demand for money function we would have:

$$M^d = \frac{1}{V} PY \text{ or } M = kPY$$

Put this way the transactions balance approach and the cash balance approach would appear identical. But this would be misleading. Recasting the transactions balance approach in terms of a demand for money function hides the fact that the proponents of that view made no attempt to analyse the motives for demanding money: they were concerned simply with the determinants of velocity. It was the Cambridge school who actually directed attention to the demand for money and the factors that influence it.

The Keynesian analysis

In this section we will be concerned with the analysis of the demand for money expounded by Keynes in his *General Theory of Employment, Interest and Money* (1936).

Keynes distinguished three main motives for holding money, namely the transactions, precautionary and speculative motives: it is the last of these three motives, and Keynes' analysis of it, which is his major contribution to the analysis of the demand for money. The transactions and precautionary motives are derived from money's use in facilitating exchanges, while the speculative motive is derived from money's use as an asset, as a store of value.

The transactions and precautionary motives

Keynes's treatment of the transactions and precautionary motives adds nothing particularly new to the analysis developed by the Cambridge school, but rather develops that earlier analysis a little further. The transactions demand is simply the demand for money that is necessary to carry out normal current transactions, i.e. those which are routine and predictable. These transactions are carried out both by private persons and businesses so that Keynes divided his transactions motive into an income motive and a business motive. The income motive is the transactions motive applied to private persons, a motive arising out of the absence of perfect synchronization of personal payments and receipts. The strength of this motive depends, according to Keynes, largely on the size of incomes and the length of time between the receipt of income and its being paid out. The business motive refers to the desire on the part of businesses to hold cash in order to bridge the interval between the incurring of costs and the receipt of the proceeds from sales. The strength of this motive depends on 'the value of current output (and hence on current income) and on the numbers of hands through which output passes' (Keynes 1936, pp. 195–6).

While Keynes' treatment of the transactions motives may be regarded as an elaboration of the Cambridge 'convenience' motive, his analysis of the precautionary motive may be regarded as a straightforward restatement of the Cambridge 'security' motive. To Keynes the precautionary motive was

> to provide for contingencies requiring sudden expenditure and for unforseen opportunities and advantageous purchases and also to hold an asset of which the value is fixed in terms of money to meet a subsequent liability fixed in terms of money (Keynes 1936, p. 196).

The demand for money to satisfy this motive would also appear to depend on the level of income.

These three motives (the income, business and precautionary) were also regarded by Keynes as being influenced by two other factors. First, there is the cost of and the ability to obtain money at the point in time when it is actually required to be spent; if a person is certain that he can borrow money cheaply at the point in time in the future when he knows he will be incurring expenditure, he may prefer to do this rather than 'carry' a cash balance for the intervening time period. Secondly, there is the opportunity cost (Keynes called it the relative cost) of holding money.

> If the cash can only be retained by forgoing the purchase of a profitable asset, this increases the cost and thus weakens the motive towards holding a given amount of cash .... It may, however, be that this is likely to be a minor factor except where large changes in the cost of holding cash are in question. (Keynes 1936, p. 196).

But if the rate of interest has only a minor role to play in the transactions and precautionary motives it has a role of major significance in Keynes' speculative motive.

The speculative motive

People want to hold money, Keynes said, not only for transacting current business but also as a store of value or wealth. But why, assuming there is a positive rate of interest, should anyone want to keep their wealth in the form of non-interest-bearing money rather than in assets that do bear interest? The reason, or necessary condition, 'failing which the existence of a liquidity preference for money as a means of holding wealth could not exist' (Keynes 1936, p. 168), is the existence of uncertainty: uncertainty as to the future of the rate of interest. Once the future rate of interest is uncertain people have the opportunity to speculate in the hope of 'securing profit from knowing better than the market what the future will bring forth' (Keynes 1936, p. 170).

By 'uncertainty' Keynes did not appear to mean uncertainty on the part of any individual as to what the future rate of interest would be, but differences of opinion between individuals as to the future course of the rate of interest. Each individual is seen as being quite clear in his or her own mind as to what is going to happen to the rate of interest, but individual views will differ from person to person. If there were no differences of opinion, then nobody would be able to profit from knowing better than the market what the future will bring forth: nobody's view would differ from the market view.

In his analysis of the speculative motive, Keynes considered only one alternative to money as a store of value, namely bonds. A bond is an asset which provides its owner with a fixed annual money income, so that its yield and market value vary inversely to one another. For a bond-holder there are two sources of return, the interest income and the capital gain or loss (the loss being a negative return). A bond-holder expecting the rate of interest to rise, anticipates a capital loss on the bond which must be set against the interest income from the bond. In some cases the capital loss will more than wipe out the interest income, in others it will be less than the interest income, while in yet other cases it will exactly equal the interest income: in the first case bond-holding would offer a negative income, in the second a positive income, and in the third a zero income.

On the other hand, holding money provides no interest income, neither is its value affected by changes in the rate of interest. In cases where bond holding offers a positive income it will be preferred to money as a store of wealth, while in cases where it offers a negative income, money will be the preferred store: in the case where bond-holding offers a zero income the person will be indifferent as between bonds and money as stores of wealth.

It is what people think is going to happen to the rate of interest which will determine whether they store their wealth in bonds or money. If a person does not think that the rate of interest is going to change, then no capital gain or loss is anticipated, so the interest income from bond-holding will induce the individual to hold bonds. If an individual thinks that the rate of interest is going to fall, then a capital gain is anticipated which reinforces the desire to hold bonds. If, however, the individual expects the rate of interest to rise, then a capital loss is anticipated which will reduce, perhaps even outweigh, the interest incentive effect to hold bonds.

What a person thinks is going to happen to the rate of interest will depend upon the relationship of the current rate of interest to the rate that the person thinks is the normal one. Every person is thought to have in mind an idea as to what is the safe or normal level for the rate of interest. This normal rate will vary from person to person. Any person who believes that the normal rate is above the current rate therefore expects the current rate to rise, and would expect it to fall when the market rate is above the normal level. The following exposition is based on that given by Tobin in his classic 1958 article (Tobin 1958). For any individual who has given expectations as to the future level of the rate of interest, there will be a level of the current rate such that a capital loss is anticipated from holding bonds and is of such magnitude that it exactly offsets the interest income from bond-holding. This particular level of the current rate is the speculator's critical rate. Let the current rate be denoted by i, and let the normal rate, to which the speculator expects the current rate will return by the end of the year, be i_e. The capital gain or loss, denoted by g, from holding bonds is

$$g = \frac{i}{i_e} - 1$$

Thus if $i > i_e$, the speculator anticipates a positive capital gain, while if $i < i_e$ he anticipates a negative one (i.e. a capital loss). The critical rate for the individual is where

$$i + g = 0$$

Substituting, $i + g = i + \dfrac{i}{i_e} - 1 = 0$

Simplifying $i = \dfrac{i_e}{i_e + 1}$

Let us denote this critical value of i (where $i + g = 0$) by i_c.

This analysis implies that speculators will put the whole of their speculative balances either into money or into bonds. The choice between money and bonds is an all-or-nothing one – all bonds and no money or all money and no bonds. At current rates above the critical one, bond-holding will offer a positive return $(i + g > 0)$ and so all speculative balances will go into bonds: at current rates of interest below the critical level, bond-holding offers a negative return $(i + g < 0)$ and all speculative balances go into money. Diagrammatically this means that the individual's speculative demand for money curve is a discontinuous step function as in *Figure 3.4*, where M^{SP} is the individual's total resources available for holding either in speculative balances or in bonds.

Different individuals will, however, have different views as to what is the normal rate of interest, and consequently will have different critical values of the current rate. At any level of the current rate, all those people whose critical rate is below it will put their speculative balances into bonds, while all those people whose critical rate is above it will all put their balances into money. With any given distribution of critical rates, the higher is the current rate, the greater will be the number of people who have critical rates below it and the smaller will be the amount of money going into speculative balances. Similarly, with any given distribution of critical rates there must be a maximum critical rate, the highest held by anybody.

At current rates above the maximum critical rate, everybody will put the whole of their speculative balances into bonds and no money will be held at all. Equally there will be a minimum critical value, the lowest one held by anybody, so that at current rates below it, everybody holds all of their balances in money.

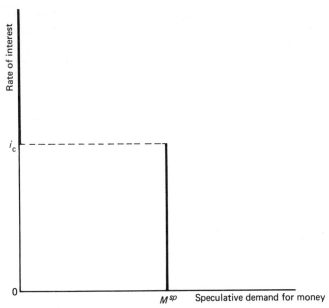

Figure 3.4 The speculative demand for money by an individual

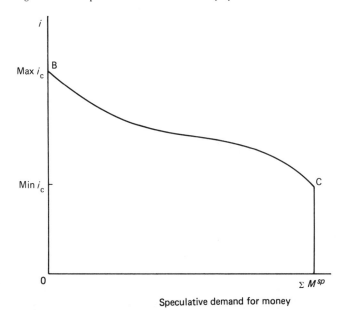

Speculative demand for money

Figure 3.5 The speculative demand for money by the community

Diagrammatically, the community's speculative demand curve will look something like that in *Figure 3.5*.

At current rates above max i_c all speculative balances go into bonds, below min i_c all speculative balances (denoted by ΣM^{SP}) go into money. The shape of the curve between B and C will depend upon the numbers of people associated with each critical rate, and the distribution of speculative balances between those individuals. The curve in *Figure 3.5* is in fact drawn on the assumption of a normal distribution of speculative balances between critical rates.

The discussion so far has assumed that individuals have fixed levels of speculative balances, but if wealth consists partly of bonds, then a change in *i*, by changing the market value of those bonds, alters the total value of wealth that could be held in speculative balances.

An increase in the rate of interest, by lowering capital values of bonds, reduces the value of wealth available for holding as speculative balances. For the individual, the total value of such wealth might be depicted by a curve such as EGF in *Figure 3.6*. Suppose the current rate of interest is above i_c; then the individual is holding all

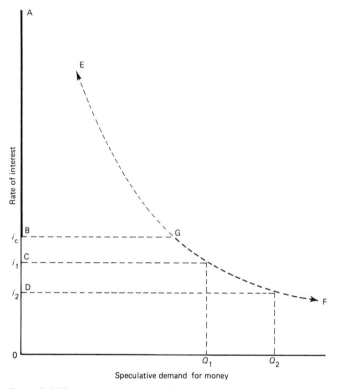

Figure 3.6 The speculative demand for money of an individual with variable speculative balances

of his speculative balance in bonds. If the current rate of interest now falls to say, i_1 then the individual would move out of bonds into cash. At the current rate i_1, the market value of the person's bond-holding is greater than it was when the current rate was above i_c. The encashment of his bonds at the rate i_1 enables him to hold $0Q_1$ money. If the current rate had fallen to i_2 rather than i_1, then the individual would be able to encash his bonds for $0Q_2$ money, which would be his speculative demand at that current rate. Thus the individual's speculative demand for money would appear to be ABGF. This explanation needs qualifying, however. Suppose that the current rate of interest is marginally above the individual's critical rate, so that his speculative balances are held wholly in bonds. If the current rate now falls to a level marginally below the person's critical rate he will move all of his speculative balance into cash. Once all his speculative balance is held in cash, however, its size becomes invariant to the rate of interest: the speculative demand curve becomes, in other words, perfectly inelastic at the rate of interest at which the individual's speculative balance is held wholly in cash. If, for example, the current rate were i_1 with the individual holding all of his balance in money, then a fall in the current rate to i_2 would not increase the individual's speculative demand for money to $0Q_2$.

Similarly, for the community as a whole, the demand curve for speculative balances which allows for wealth effects will be flatter than one which does not. This will be demonstrated in *Figure 3.7* where we consider the consequences of increasing the money supply. Before that, however, we must recognize that Keynes introduced a theoretical limiting case into his analysis of the speculative motive, namely absolute liquidity preference or, as it is more usually known – the liquidity trap. As we have seen, the lower the current rate of interest, the more people there are who will want to hold all of their speculative balances in the form of money, believing that the interest rate is going to rise sufficiently rapidly to cause a capital loss that will wipe out the interest income from bond-holding. There will therefore be some low level of the current rate – the minimum critical rate of the community – at which everybody desires to hold cash; the demand for cash at this rate of interest is perfectly elastic in the sense that whatever the amount of money available for the speculative motive, it will all be demanded and disappear into idle speculative hoards.

In *Figure 3.7* we can consider the effect of an increase in the quantity of money on the community's speculative demand for money. In the figure the curves labelled BE, BF and BG are three aggregate speculative demand curves each drawn on the assumption of a given level of aggregate wealth. If now the money

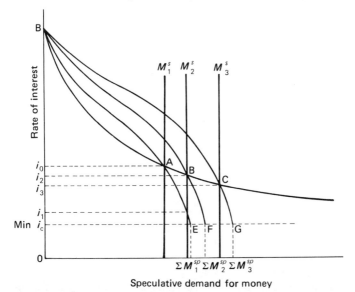

Figure 3.7 The speculative demand for money by the community with total speculative balances a function of the rate of interest

supply is depicted by the curve M_1^s, and the relevant demand curve is BE then the equilibrium position is at A and the rate of interest is i_0. Suppose now the money supply is increased to M_2^s. With an unchanged demand curve the interest rate would fall to i_1. But the fall in the interest rate increases aggregate wealth and shifts the demand curve to the right to position BF, where a new equilibrium position is given by point B with interest rate i_2. Similarly a further increase in the money supply to M_3^s again depresses interest rates, thereby shifting the demand curve to BG and establishing a new equilibrium position at C, with interest rate i_3. If points of equilibrium like those of A, B and C are joined up, we derive the demand curve for speculative balances that allows for interest rate and wealth effects. Such a curve will approach minimum i_c asymptotically becoming flatter and flatter as i falls, and thus having the shape traditionally assigned to the demand for money curve.

The basis of Keynes' speculative motive, then, is uncertainty, uncertainty in the sense that different people will hold different views as to what is going to happen to the current rate of interest. Each person will believe that it is going to move towards what he regards as the normal rate. But, of course, people's views as to what constitutes a normal rate may change as their expectations change, expectations being subject to a very large number of influences. Keynes (1936, p. 198) himself said,

> Changes in the liquidity function itself, due to a change in the news which causes revision of expectations, will often be discontinuous and will, therefore, give rise to a corresponding discontinuity of change in the rate of interest.

In other words, the rate of interest may change either as the result of a movement of the whole liquidity preference curve or as a result of a movement along a given curve.

> In dealing with the speculative motive it is, however, important to distinguish between the changes in the rate of interest which are due to changes in the supply of money available to satisfy the speculative motive, without there having been any change in the liquidity function, and those which are primarily due to changes in expectations affecting the liquidity function itself. Open-market operations may, indeed, influence the rate of interest through both channels; since they may not only change the volume of money, but may also give rise to changed expectations concerning the future policy of the Central Bank or of the Government. (Keynes 1936, pp. 197–8).

The instability of the speculative demand curve has prompted Shackle (1967, p. 217) to say that it

> must be looked upon as a thread floating in a gusty wind, continually liable to change its form not only because of 'the news', but even because of a change in the total quantity of money itself.

We have now looked at each of Keynes' three motives for holding money. The amount of money for the transactions and precautionary motives he denoted by the symbol M_1; the amount held for the speculative motive by M_2. Corresponding to this division there are two liquidity functions L_1 and L_2. L_1 depends mainly on the level of income, L_2 mainly on the rate of interest and expectations. Thus:

$$M = M_1 + M_2 = L_1(Y) + L_2(i)$$

Keynes' analysis of the demand for money is clearly, therefore, divided into two parts, one part approaching money simply as a means of payment, the other as an asset. Individuals, according to this view, are seen to hold some money for transactions purposes and some for its use as a store of wealth. According to Johnson (1962, p. 90) this approach is

> a rather awkward hybrid of two theoretically inconsistent approaches, with the transactions demand being regarded as technologically determined, and the assets demand being treated as a matter of economic choice.

Certainly most post-Keynesian writing has attempted to aggregate the demand for money rather than continue the Keynesian distinction.

The significant innovation of Keynes' analysis was to show that the demand for money was interest-elastic and that at some low rate of interest it might become perfectly so. The rationale for this was the existence of a speculative motive based on the existence of a gap between what individual speculators regard as the normal level of the rate of interest and the actual current level. There have, however, been several criticisms of these views. For example, it has been suggested that the gap between the normal and current interest rates would disappear as investors learned from experience. Any rate, if it persists long enough, will come to be accepted as normal. In equilibrium the demand for money for the speculative motive would be zero. Another suggestion is that in quantitative terms speculative balances may be relatively unimportant thereby minimizing the interest elasticity of the aggregate demand for money. It has also been pointed out that the particular meaning Keynes attached to 'uncertainty' and the all-or-nothing bond/money choice derived from it do not appear to accord with the real world.

Keynes' analysis of the demand for money then, suggested several areas for fruitful empirical research and subsequent theorizing, and it is to some of the subsequent theorizing that we must now turn, taking up the whole question of empirical testing in the last section of the chapter.

Post-Keynesian developments

Interest-elasticity of the transactions demand

It will be recalled that in the Keynes analysis the major influences on the transactions demand for money were the level of income and certain institutional or mechanistic factors. Although Keynes stated that the rate of interest might be another influence, he considered it to be of only minor importance. Later writers, using an inventory theory approach (notably Baumol 1952 and Tobin 1956) have provided reasons why the transactions demand for money might be significantly interest-elastic.

Transactions balances may be regarded as a sort of inventory, which the holders keep in order to be prepared to finance transactions (usually predictable and often routine) as and when they arise. Money is held in transactions balances because it is convenient to do so. But holding transactions balances also involves cost, particularly in income that is forgone by not putting the money held in transactions balances into some form of income-bearing investment. Following Baumol's approach we can analyse the demand for cash as an inventory in two stages. The first and simplest stage is where the transactor converts his income into interest-bearing assets (e.g. bonds) at time zero. He then has to decide only the magnitude and timing of subsequent encashments. Let us take as an illustrative example a person who converts his income into bonds as soon as he receives it. In *Figure 3.8* the person's income is measured along the vertical axis of the top diagram, so that at the beginning of each income period he receives 0A. Let us further assume that the person spends the income at a known uniform rate over time so that at the end of the four week period his income is zero. During the first week he will spend AB, during the second BC and so on. The spender must decide what is the best timing and size of encashment from his bonds given this pattern of expenditure and the cost of encashments. The cost is made up of two parts. Firstly there is the interest-opportunity cost of holding money, i.e. the interest forgone by cashing the bonds. Secondly there are the costs, both pecuniary and subjective, of making the encashment. The pecuniary costs will include items such as brokerage fees and stamp duties. The subjective costs will include factors such as the time and trouble of filling in forms etc. For the present we will assume that only sufficient encashments are made at the beginning of each week to finance that week's expenditure. Then the transactions balance of the individual would appear as in the lower half of *Figure 3.8*. Different assumptions about the timing and size of encashments would give a different pattern for the transactions balance of the individual. The problem for the individual is to find the optimum size of encashment that would minimize the costs involved.

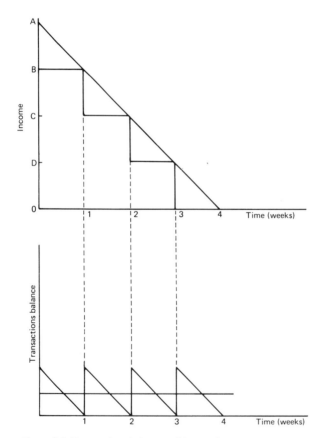

Figure 3.8 Transactions balances with encashments once a week

To solve this cost minimization problem, we first set out the total costs for the transactions period. We will assume that the costs of making each encashment (the 'brokerage' costs) consist of a fixed element and an element which varies with the amount of encashment. The brokerage cost for each encashment can therefore be represented by $(a + bE)$, where a is the fixed cost, b the proportional cost, and E the value of cash withdrawn in equal amounts. If we let T be the total of the known, uniform stream of transactions per given transactions period (= total income), and i the interest rate forgone by holding money, then the total cost (C) is given by

$$C = \frac{T(a+bE)}{E} + \frac{iE}{2} = \frac{aT}{E} + \frac{bT}{2} + \frac{iE}{2}$$
(3.1)

where $E/2$ is the average money holding, given the assumption that money holdings are run down evenly to zero after each encashment. The optimum value of E which minimizes total costs is obtained by differentiating (3.1) with respect to E and setting the result equal to zero:

$$-\frac{aT}{E^2} + \frac{i}{2} = 0$$
(3.2)

Therefore $E = \sqrt{\frac{2aT}{i}}$
(3.3)

This is the so-called 'square root rule' for the transactions demand for money. Note that with this simple model, the variable brokerage costs component does not affect the optimum size of encashment. Since the average money holding is $E/2$, the (average) transactions demand for money (M^d) is

$$M^d = \frac{E}{2} = \sqrt{\frac{aT}{2i}}$$
(3.4)

According to this result therefore, transactions money demand is an inverse function of the rate of interest and an increasing function of income. In particular, the 'square root rule' result shows that the demand for money rises less than in proportion to the volume of transactions, i.e. there are economies of scale in the use of cash for transactions purposes.

This result has two important implications. First, the way income is distributed is of importance in determining the demand for money. If, for example, there is a redistribution of income away from high income earners towards low income earners, the aggregate demand for money would, according to this theory, rise. The second important implication is that the effects of an increase in the money supply under less than full employment conditions will differ from those that would result if the demand for cash balances was proportional to the level of transactions. In the latter case an increase in the money supply would result in an equivalent proportional increase in the volume of transactions. But if the demand for money increases less than in proportion to the volume of transactions, then an increase in the money supply would result in a more than proportional increase in the volume of transactions. Thus the model suggests that monetary policy has a greater influence on economic activity than would be the case for a simple linear functional relationship between money and income. We will see, however, that the economies of scale prediction of this simple model is substantially altered when the analysis is modified to allow for a more rational investment strategy at the start of the transactions period.

If we now turn to the second stage of the analysis we can recognize that the individual may not put all of his income into bonds as soon as he receives it. It would be more realistic to assume that the individual will retain some of that income as cash, and therefore there is the additional problem of deciding how much of the initial cash receipts (income) should be retained as cash and how much to put into bonds. In addition we also need to recognize that the individual will incur brokerage costs involved in purchasing bonds as well as the costs of encashing bonds and, as a simplification, the brokerage costs $(a + b)$ will be used to represent both types of cost.

It is therefore necessary to consider two parts of the total transactions period: the first part of the period when expenditures are financed by the initial retention of cash balances (R), and the rest of the period when expenditures are financed by the encashments of the initial balance invested in bonds (I). Thus

$$T = R + I \tag{3.5}$$

The first part of the transactions period financed by R will be equal to $(T - I)/T$ and the average cash balances for this fraction of the transactions period equals $(T - I)/2$. The holding of R involves a cost in the form of interest forgone, equal to

$$\frac{(T - I)}{2} \, i \, \frac{(T - I)}{T} \tag{3.6}$$

Clearly, the smaller the size of the cash balance the smaller will be the interest forgone. But in order to reduce the size of the cash balance a bigger proportion of the initial cash receipts must be invested in bonds, and the brokerage costs incurred would therefore increase. The total combined costs are

$$\frac{(T - I)}{2} \, i \, \frac{(T - I)}{T} + a + bI \tag{3.7}$$

During the remaining part of the transactions period (I/T), the amount I will have to be wholly encashed by a number of encashments, each of size E and the interest cost involved will be

$$\frac{E}{2} \, i \, \frac{I}{T} \tag{3.8}$$

Brokerage costs will also, of course, be incurred, and if these costs are added to the interest costs, the total cost of financing transactions in the second part of the transactions period will be

$$\frac{E}{2} \, i \, \frac{I}{T} + (a + bE)\frac{I}{E} \tag{3.9}$$

where I/E is the number of encashments. Adding (3.9) to (3.7) therefore gives the total costs (TC) for the whole transactions period;

$$TC = \frac{(T - I)}{2} \, i \, \frac{(T - I)}{T} + a + bI + \frac{E}{2} \, i \, \frac{I}{T} + (a + bE)\frac{I}{E} \tag{3.10}$$

In order to find the values of I and E which minimize the total costs, we take the partial derivatives of (3.10) with respect to I and E and set the derivatives equal to zero. For E we obtain

$$\frac{iI}{2T} - \frac{Ia}{E^2} = 0 \tag{3.11}$$

therefore $\quad E = \sqrt{\dfrac{2aT}{i}}$

(3.12) gives us the optimal size of the encashments from the initial investment in bonds and is the same result as the 'square root rule' derived in the first stage model (3.3)

For I we obtain

$$\frac{(-T + I)i}{T} + 2b + \frac{Ei}{2T} + \frac{a}{E} = 0 \tag{3.13}$$

Solving for I and using (3.12) we can obtain

$$I = T - E - \frac{2bT}{i} \tag{3.14}$$

and therefore

$$R = T - I = E + \frac{2bT}{i} \tag{3.15}$$

The optimum average transactions demand for money (M^d) for the whole of the transactions period is

$$M^d = \frac{R}{2}\left(\frac{T - I}{T}\right) + \frac{E}{2}\left(\frac{I}{T}\right) \tag{3.16}$$

i.e. the weighted average of the optimum average cash balances for both parts of the transactions period.

Substituting for R and E in (3.16) using (3.15) and (3.12) we can obtain

$$M^d = \sqrt{\frac{aT}{2i}}\left(1 + \frac{2b}{i}\right) + 2T\left(\frac{b}{i}\right)^2 \tag{3.17}$$

In contrast to the simple model (3.4) obtained in the first stage of the analysis, (3.17) shows that the variable cost component is an important determinant of the transactions demand for money. If b were zero, (3.17) would of course reduce to expression (3.4). Thus the simple 'square root rule' is replaced by a more complex relationship between transactions money demand and the volume of transactions, and consequently the economies of scale prediction of the simple model is substantially modified. As Brunner and Meltzer (1967) explain, the elasticity of transactions money demand with respect to the volume of transactions will vary with the size of the volume of transactions. Scale economies become less (i.e. transactions-elasticity approaches unity) as the volume of transactions increases. This modification does not, however, change the main result of the inventory theory approach, that, in contrast with Keynes' approach, the rate of interest is, in theory at least, an important determinant of the transactions demand for money.

One additional interesting implication of the inventory approach is that if all brokerage costs were zero, there would be no demand for money for transactions purposes, i.e. there would be perfect synchronization of asset sales with every expenditure. Now in our examination in Chapter 1 of the fundamental reasons for using money we argued that the existence of money depends on uncertainty. Given that the approach effectively assumes away uncertainty (it assumes a known future income and expenditure pattern), it would appear that the analysis identifies an additional reason for using and holding money, namely the presence of brokerage costs (which includes of course the subjective costs involved in converting an asset into a means of payment). Of course the fact that the approach excludes uncertainty means that it has only very limited application to the real uncertain world, and more recent models have extended the analysis to allow for uncertain transactions patterns (see, for example, Orr 1970). Such models, however, may be considered more relevant to an examination of the precautionary motive for holding money.

Some developments in the analysis of liquidity preference

In our earlier discussion we saw that Keynes based his analysis of the speculative demand for money on the presence of uncertainty. But the uncertainty with which Keynes was concerned was a diversity of opinions as to the future course of the rate of interest, and was not uncertainty in the mind of any individual as to its future: indeed quite the opposite, for each individual was thought to be firmly convinced as to what the future rate would be. The implication of this was that for the individual the rational decision would be to hold either all bonds or all cash.

This does not accord with the real world, where people do hold combinations of both bonds and money, and where they have diversified portfolios. A theoretical analysis to explain this observation was provided by Tobin (1958). Tobin attempts to show how people's desire to hold money may be derived from their attitude towards the risk involved in holding bonds. His analysis is also based on uncertainty, but this time the uncertainty exists in the mind of the individual. People are no longer convinced about what the rate of interest is going to be.

Uncertainty as to the future rate of interest also means uncertainty as to the future capital value of bonds. People holding bonds are consequently unsure whether they will make a capital gain or capital loss: there is risk involved in bond-holding.

For most people the prospect of money income is desirable, while risk is undesirable. Suppose a person is offered the choice between a perfectly safe £100 or the 50–50 chance of either £50 or £150. Which will be choose? If he chooses the risky option he will have an equal chance of making £50 more or £50 less than the safe option. But if we assume diminishing marginal utility of money income then the extra utility derived from the last £50 of the £150 would be less than the utility lost on the £50 by which the less desirable outcome of the risky option falls short of the safe choice. In terms of utility therefore, the possibility of making £50 more than the 'safe' choice does not compensate for the risk of the e٫ual chance of making £50 less than the 'safe' choice. Most people confronted by this choice would probably choose the safe £100. But of course not everybody would do so: some people, the gamblers amongst us, would be attracted by the possibility of the large gain, and would prefer a choice involving this possibility to the more certain but lower income. It is these basic ideas that Tobin has developed into a fairly sophisticated theory of choice under conditions of uncertainty.

Let us assume that an individual has a savings balance which he can keep in the form of money or invested in bonds. If he keeps it in the form of money, then on the assumption of a stable price level there is no risk attached: his savings will retain their nominal and real value over time. But while there is no risk attached to money holding there is no possibility of an income either.

If the individual invests his savings balance in bonds, then he does have a money income in the form of the interest the bonds will earn him. There may also be income in the form of a capital gain should the rate of interest fall while he is holding the bonds. But if the rate of interest rises he will incur a capital loss. If the individual is uncertain in his own mind whether the rate of interest will rise or fall then he is uncertain whether he will make a capital gain or loss, and the possibility of making the loss is a risk attached to the holding of bonds. With bond-holding, therefore, one has the atttraction of a return in the form of a money income, but the risk that the income may turn out to be negative if the bond has to be sold for a capital loss which more than wipes out the interest income. The problem for the individual is in the balancing of the risk and return elements in bond-holding. The problem can be illustrated with some indifference curve diagrams. To construct these diagrams we will need measures of risk and return. Let us take return first. The individual has, we have said, a savings portfolio which he wishes to divide between cash and bonds; the proportion of the portfolio held in bonds we denote by F_2 and the proportion in cash by F_1. As cash provides no return, the return from the total portfolio (denoted by R) will depend on the fraction held in bonds. The return itself will contain two elements, the interest income and the capital gain (which will be negative in the case of a capital loss). Thus we have

$$R = F_2(i + g)$$

where i is the rate of interest and g the capital gain.

But g, we have said, is uncertain because the individual is uncertain what is going to happen to the rate of interest. There will be a number of possible values for g, but the mean value of these possibilities provides a useful single measure. If we take the mean value of g, then of course we are also taking the mean value of the total possible return, so we have

$$R_e = \mu R = F_2(i + \mu g)$$

where R_e = the expected return, μR = mean value of the return, and μg = mean value of capital gains/losses.

The expression can be simplified if we make the assumption that the individual thinks there is an equal chance of a capital gain and loss of the same size so that $\mu g = 0$. We then have

$$\mu R = F_2 i.$$

As the measure of the risk involved in bond-holding, Tobin takes the standard deviation of the return, σR, which is a statistical measure of possible returns around the mean value μR. A high standard deviation means roughly that there is a high probability of large deviations, both positive and negative, from the mean, while a low standard deviation means a low probability of high deviations from the mean. Because no risk is attached to holding money, the risk surrounding the total return depends, of course, on the risk surrounding the capital gain/loss from bond-holding, and the proportion of the total portfolio held in risk-bearing bonds. Thus

$$\sigma R = F_2 \sigma g$$

The expected return and the risk are both dependent on the proportion of the total balance held in bonds. As this proportion increases, both the return and the risk attached to the total portfolio increase. In other words, in order to enjoy a greater expected return the portfolio holder must also assume more risk. The relationship between expected return and risk can be found from simple manipulation of the expressions already derived. As

$$\sigma R = F_2 \sigma g$$
$$F_2 = \frac{\sigma R}{\sigma g}$$

Substituting into $\mu R = F_2 i$

We get $\mu R = \dfrac{\sigma R}{\sigma g} \, i$

This expression enables us to draw in *Figure 3.9* the opportunity curve 0B, which traces out the various combinations of return and risk that will be associated with different combinations of money and bonds.

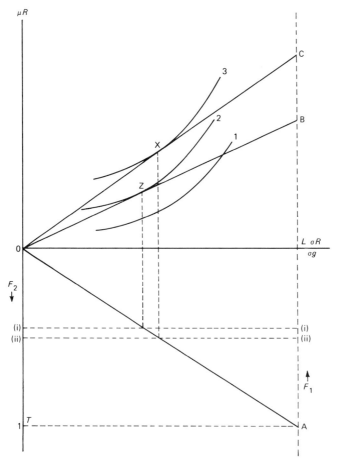

Figure 3.9 Liquidity preferences as behaviour towards risk and the effect of a change in the rate of interest on the demand for money

In the top half of *Figure 3.9* risk, in the form of the standard deviation of total returns and of capital gains, is measured along the horizontal axis, while the mean values of expected returns are measured along the vertical axis upwards from the origin. As we have seen, the line 0B is the opportunity curve, tracing the combinations of risk and expected return available to the investor, and is derived from the expression $\mu R = (\sigma R/\sigma g)i$ so that its slope is $i/\sigma g$.

From the expression $\sigma R = F_2 \sigma g$ it is clear that if $F_2 = 1$ (i.e. all of the investor's portfolio is put into bonds) then the standard deviation of the total return will be equal to the standard deviation of the capital gains so that $\sigma R/\sigma g = 1$. When $F_2 = 1$ the expression $\mu R = (\sigma R/\sigma g)i$ reduces to $\mu R = i$. So when all of a portfolio is invested in bonds, the risk will be σg, and the return will be equal to i. In *Figure 3.9* σg is equal to 0L when $F_2 = 1$ and LB is the mean value of the expected return and is equal to the rate of interest. The slope of the opportunity line 0B is LB/0L which equals $i/\sigma g$.

In the lower half of *Figure 3.9* the proportion of the total portfolio invested in bonds is measured down the vertical axis from the origin. The line 0A traces out the relationship between the proportion of the portfolio held in bonds and the risk attached to the portfolio; i.e. it traces out the relationship $\sigma R = F\sigma g$. When all of the portfolio is held in bonds (when $F_2 = 1$) then, as we have seen, $\sigma R = \sigma g$. In *Figure 3.9* $\sigma g = 0$L when $F_2 = 1 = 0$T $=$ AL. The slope of the line 0A is therefore LA/0L $= 1/\sigma g$.

In the upper half of the figure an indifference curve map has been superimposed on the opportunity line 0B. Each indifference curve joins up the various combinations of risk and return between which the portfolio-holder is indifferent. The slope of the indifference curves will depend upon the portfolio-holder's attitude towards risk. If we assume the individual is a risk-averter, somebody who

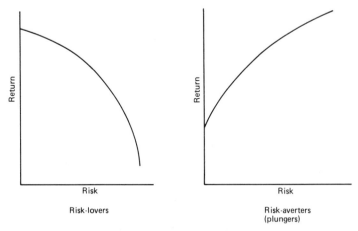

Figure 3.10 The risk-return indifference curves of 'risk-lovers' and 'risk-averters'

finds risk unattractive, then he will only assume more risk if at the same time it increases his expected return. For such an individual the indifference curves will slope upwards from left to right. Further, we may assume that the greater the risk already assumed, the more undesirable becomes any further incremental increase in risk, while the greater the expected return the smaller will be the extra satisfaction derived from further incremental increases in expected return.

Consequently, incremental increases in risk will require bigger and bigger increases in expected return to leave the individual indifferent between the various combinations, making the indifference curves convex downwards. Moving upwards to the left, successively higher indifference curves represent higher and higher levels of satisfaction because combinations containing, say, the same amount of risk will, on higher indifference curves, contain more expected return and, presumably, offer a higher level of satisfaction.

The indifference curves of gamblers, the risk-lovers, will however be negatively sloped. Such individuals are prepared to accept a lower expected return in order to have the chance of unusually high capital gains associated with a high σR. Diagrammatically their indifference curves would look like the downward-sloping curve in *Figure 3.10*. Tobin also discusses the possibility of risk-averters who are also plungers. Their indifference curves will slope upwards from left to right but will be linear or convex upwards.

The portfolio-holder will try to reach the highest indifference curve available to him. In *Figure 3.9* this will be indifference curve 2, the one which is tangenital to the opportunity curve at point Z. By reading down to the horizontal axis it can be seen how much risk this combination includes: from the curve 0A can then be found the proportion of the total portfolio held in bonds that gives this amount of risk. In *Figure 3.9* the preferred combination Z is made up of proportion $OF_2(i)$ bonds and $AF_1(i)$ money. Clearly this individual has diversified his portfolio, holding some money and some bonds.

For risk-lovers and risk-averter plungers the picture is rather different. The risk-lover will not diversify his portfolio, but will hold all of his portfolio in bonds, being attracted by the possibility of large capital gains. His preferred combination will always be a corner one as in *Figure 3.11*, panel 1. The risk-averter plunger will

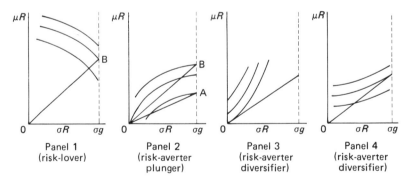

Figure 3.11 The 'all money' or 'all bonds' choice of risk-lovers and risk-averters

also seek a corner maximum, but it may be an all money or all bonds one. In panel 2, for example, if the opportunity line is 0A then the preferred position is at 0, while if the opportunity line is 0B the preferred position is at B. Even for a risk-averter diversifier it is possible for the preferred position to consist of all bonds or all money as panels 3 and 4 show.

What now would be the effect on such portfolios of a change in the rate of interest? Let us take first the case of the risk-averter diversifier and assume an increase in i. This would alter the slope of the opportunity line because for any given level of risk a greater return can be expected. The line 0B will therefore become steeper, moving say, to 0C (*Figure 3.9*). The opportunity line has become tangential to a new higher indifference curve, indifference curve 3 at point X.

Reading down through the horizontal axis to the lower diagram it can be seen that the combination at point X consists of proportion OF_2(ii) bonds and AF_1(ii) money. The increase in the rate of interest has increased the proportion of the portfolio held in bonds and reduced the proportion held in money. This is, of course, only one possibility. A different positioning of the indifference curves would give points of tangency lying further and further to the left at higher and higher rates of interest, while yet another possibility is that points of tangency will lie vertically above one another. The reason for this variety of possible outcomes is to be found in the income and substitution effects of a change in the rate of interest. At higher rates of interest the return from holding bonds is increased, making them relatively more attractive and there will be a tendency to substitute them for money: this is the substitution effect. The income effect may work either way, however: a higher level of interest enables the investor to have the same income for less risk, or to enjoy some more of both. Some investors would prefer to 'divide the expansion of opportunity' provided by the higher interest rate largely in favour of security, others would divide largely in favour of expected return, while yet others would divide fairly evenly. In cases where the income effect is positive (i.e. where it induces a tendency to take more risk), it will reinforce the substitution effect: where it is negative but weak it will reduce, but not completely offset, the substitution effect: while finally, where it is negative and strong, it will outweigh the substitution effect and reduce the amount of risk taken and consequently reduce the proportion of a portfolio held in bonds at higher rates of interest.

Diagrammatically the income and substitution effects can be illustrated as in *Figure 3.12*. When the rate of interest rises, shifting the opportunity line from 0B to 0A, the preferred combination changes from X to Y. This change is the consequence of both income and substitution effects. The effects can be isolated by drawing a new opportunity line WT parallel to 0A but tangential to the lower indifference curve 1 at Z. This new opportunity line, as compared with the original line 0B, does not allow a greater level of satisfaction to be enjoyed; more expected return can only be obtained at the expense of assuming greater risk. The movement from X to Z is the substitution effect, bonds having been substituted for money. The parallel upwards shift of the opportunity line from WT to 0A reflects the fact that the increase in the rate of interest enables the investor to enjoy greater expected return from the same risk. The movement from Z to Y is the income effect, the effect of being able to enjoy both more expected return and more security (less risk) at the same time. The position of Y relative to both X and Z depends on the direction and strength of the income effect. If expected return and security are 'normal' goods in that they are subject to positive income effects, Y will lie to the right of X if the substitution effect is stronger than the income effect, but to the left of it if the income effect is the stronger.

Clearly, whether *Figure 3.12* shows a direct or inverse relationship between the rate of interest and the proportion of the portfolio held in bonds depends on the positioning of the indifference curves, which in turn depends on the assumptions one makes in constructing them. Empirically the possibility of an inverse relationship may be important for, as Tobin (1965, p. 51) said, 'strong income effects have been detected by market observers who refer to some portfolio managers as "reaching for income" at times of generally reduced yields; i.e.

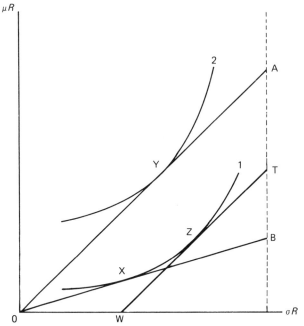

Figure 3.12 The income and substitution effects of a change in the rate of interest

increasing equity investments at the expense of bonds in order to maintain the average portfolio return'.

For the risk-lover a change in the rate of interest and the slope of the opportunity line will not cause him to change his holding of bonds or cash, as he will continue to hold all bonds, but will enjoy a greater level of satisfaction from them. For the risk-averter plunger, an increase in the rate of interest may cause him to shift his entire portfolio from cash to bonds, and a fall in the rate of interest cause him to shift from bonds to cash as in *Figure 3.13* panel 2. For the risk-averter diversifier there may also be possibilities other than those discussed in the text. He may move from a corner maximum to a diversified one, and vice versa when the rate falls as in panel 3. Another possibility is that he will remain at a corner maximum as in panel 4. Whether the opportunity line is 0A or 0B the preferred position is a corner one containing all bonds.

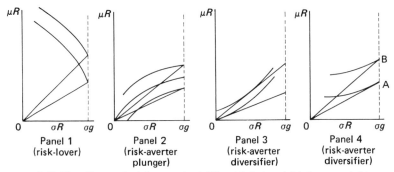

Figure 3.13 The effect on the 'all money' or 'all bonds' choice of risk-lovers and risk-averters of an increase in the rate of interest

The theory of risk-avoiding behaviour appears to have several advantages over the Keynesian analysis of liquidity preference. It can provide an explanation of the interest-elasticity of demand for money that does not rest upon speculators being certain in their own minds about what is going to happen to the rate of interest. It can also explain why some people might have a positive relationship between their demand for money and the rate of interest, at least over some ranges of the interest rate. The theory also provides an explanation of why portfolios are usually diversified, containing both bonds and cash; at the same time the theory can account for non-diversified portfolios, be they all cash or all bonds.

However, the theory as it has been described above is incomplete. In our exposition of the theory we assumed only one alternative to holding cash, namely bonds. But there are, of course, a variety of forms in which wealth can be held, and recognition of this fact has been a significant post-Keynesian development. One distinction between assets is according to maturities; e.g. a simple distinction between short-term and long-term securities. Speculators concerned about the possibility of a capital loss may move from long-term assets to short-term assets in general, rather than to one particular asset – money. The Keynesian speculative motive would then be a speculative demand for short-term assets rather than a speculative demand for money.

Maturity is, of course, only one difference between assets; there are other differences based upon degree of risk, convenience of encashment and so on. Recognizing and allowing for a variety of differences between assets is necessary in the construction of a general theory of asset-holding. In such a theory, money would be only one of several forms in which wealth could be held. Alternatives would include:

(1) Fixed-interest bearing assets whose capital value would fluctuate with the current rate of interest, i.e. bonds.
(2) Fixed-interest bearing assets whose capital value is fixed in nominal terms, i.e. deposits with financial intermediaries.
(3) Equities, which provide a variable return.
(4) Real physical assets such as durable consumer goods, productive equipment, buildings and land.

Within each of these groups, of course, there will be a number of assets all differentiated from each other in various ways. For example, deposits with building societies and deposits with hire-purchase finance houses are both included in category (2), both beng fixed-interest bearing assets with fixed nominal values: they are, however, differentiated from one another in other respects. The extent to which assets are substitutes or complements in the portfolios of wealth-holders and the composition of such portfolios will depend upon the characteristics of the assets themselves and of the wealth-holders.

> Among the relevant properties with which the theory must deal are: costs of asset exchanges; predictability of real and money asset values at various future dates; correlations-positive, negative or zero – among asset prospects; liquidity – the time it takes to realize full value of an asset; reversibility – possibility and cost of simultaneously buying and selling an asset; the timing and predictability of investors' expected needs for wealth. (Tobin 1961, p. 28).

This, in fact, is the approach of Professor Tobin and his followers at Yale, an approach usually labelled 'portfolio balance theory'. As differences in the degree of risk attached to assets is an important characteristic differentiating assets one from another, the Tobin theory of investor behaviour towards risk, outlined above, is an important part of their portfolio balance theory. But, as we have pointed out, our exposition of it was over-simplified in assuming only one alternative to cash, but the analysis and conclusions are

> not essentially changed however if F₁ is taken to be the aggregate share invested in a variety of non-cash assets, e.g. bonds and other debt instruments differing in maturity, debtor and other features. The return R and the risk σ on consols will then represent the average return and risk on a composite of these assets.' (Tobin 1958, p. 82).

What we have said, then, is that the risk aversion theory we have outlined is part of a broader portfolio balance theory and although our analysis was of a simple two-asset model, the analysis can be applied to models containing more than two assets.

The model is, however, also over-simplified in assuming that cash is riskless. Once the price level is allowed to change, then holding cash is no longer riskless. But again the analysis can be modified to make allowances for expectations of price changes, but then becomes more complicated:

> the present analysis has been deliberately limited to choices among monetary assets. Among these assets cash is relatively riskless even though in the wider context of portfolio selection, the risk of changes in purchasing power, which all monetary assets share, may be relevant to many investors. Breaking down the portfolio selection problem into stages at different levels of aggregation – allocation first, among, and then within asset categories seems to be a permissible and perhaps even an indispensable simplification both for the theorist and the investor himself. (Tobin 1958, p. 85).

However, with the growth of large institutional investors offering to wealth-holders assets that are fixed in money value, and encashable at very short notice or even on demand, it is arguable whether even among monetary assets cash is relatively riskless. Deposits with institutions like building societies are also virtually riskless. An aversion to risk on the part of a wealth-holder does not therefore necessarily lead him to hold cash. It may lead him to choose some other riskless asset. Liquidity preference based on aversion towards risk is a preference for riskless assets in general rather than a preference for one particular asset.

It has also been suggested that the theory is concerned only with individual financial behaviour and is not applicable to instutional investors, whose portfolio decisions may depend upon very different considerations: for example, they may be almost entirely concerned with the interest income of assets, intending to hold them until maturity, or very nearly so. Indeed there may be some individuals who act on these lines.

Next we may note that our outline of the Tobin theory was based on the assumption that the wealth elasticity of the demand for money was unity. The division of the wealth portfolio between money and other assets was regarded as independent of the level of wealth, so that changes in wealth which followed from changes in the rate of interest were not thought to have any effect on the relative shares of money and other assets in that wealth. But this need not be the case. The demand for money might increase in greater or lesser proportion than any increase in wealth. In fact the role of wealth on the demand for money has been another area of much post-Keynesian discussion.

Finally we may note the suggestion that the theory is at the same time both involved and incomplete. As an explanation of investor behaviour it has been suggested that the theory is too involved in that it requires investors to make a lot of calculations in order to derive mean expected returns and standard deviations. On the other hand it has been suggested that the theory is incomplete because it does not contain a theory of the formation of expectations.

The monetarist approach

We conclude our survey of the major theories of the demand for money with a discussion of the monetarist approach, and in particular the classic statement of that approach by Milton Friedman (1956).

Monetarists look at the demand for money from the point of view of money as an asset, as one of a whole menu of assets that might feature in any balance sheet or portfolio of assets. To the monetarist, the demand for money can be treated as part of capital or wealth theory. Friedman distinguishes two types of money 'demander'. Firstly, there are the ultimate wealth-holders, who demand money as one way in which to hold their wealth. Secondly, there are business enterprises who demand money as a productive resource, just like plant and machinery or any other asset that contributes towards production.

Demand by ultimate wealth holders

The analysis of the demand for money by ultimate wealth-holders is made on similar lines to the analysis of the demand of consumers for consumption goods. In the analysis of consumer choice there are three major sets of factors to be considered:

(1) The consumer's income, which acts as a constraint on his ability to demand.
(2) The price of the good being demanded, and the prices of other goods and services.
(3) The consumer's tastes and preferences.

If money is regarded as an asset that features in wealth portfolios then the total wealth of the individual becomes the constraint on his demand for money. Further, as money is only one form in which wealth can be held, the demand for it will depend upon the wealth-holder's tastes and preferences and upon the return to be obtained from holding money compared with that to be obtained from holding all other assets that could feature in wealth portfolios. Let us take each of these factors separately.

We have already noted in our discussion of the portfolio balance approach to the demand for money that recognition of wealth as an influence on the demand for money has been a significant post-Keynesian development. There has not, however, been complete agreement amongst economists as to what is the relevant concept of wealth. To the modern quantity theorist total wealth includes all sources of consumable services. A major source of income for most people is, of course, the productive capacity of their own bodies, the simple fact that they can use their own bodies to produce goods and services in return for some form of income. Human wealth is one form in which wealth can be held.

Wealth in this sense is a stock, a collection of assets providing income and consumable services. The income and consumable services are, on the other hand, a flow emanating from ownership of the assets. The relationship between the stock, wealth, and the flow, income, is given by 'the' rate of interest. Income is the yield on wealth and wealth is the present value of the discounted flow of income. If Y is the total flow of income, W is the stock of wealth and i 'the' rate of interest, then

$$W = \frac{Y}{i}$$

In this approach, income enters as an influence on the demand for money only in its role as an alternative to wealth, and not as a measure of the 'work' to be done by money. According to Friedman this is probably the main difference between his own and earlier formulations of the quantity theory.

Income to Friedman and his followers is not income as measured by the statisticians, because that income they consider an unsatisfactory index of wealth being, as it is, subject to erratic year-to-year fluctuations. The income they consider more useful is the concept of 'permanent income' originally developed by Friedman in connection with his theory of the consumption function.

Within the total of wealth, special consideration is given to human wealth. The reason for this is primarily that all other forms of wealth can be bought and sold on markets, while human wealth cannot. An individual wealth-holder can consequently adjust his or her holdings of non-human wealth by appropriate purchase and sales. For example, if a wealth-holder wishes to increase the proportion of building society deposits and reduce the share of government bonds in his or her wealth portfolio, then he can do so by selling the government bonds on the Stock Exchange and putting the proceeds into the required building society deposits. The individual cannot, however, so easily adjust his holdings of human wealth. What he can do is invest in his own education in order to increase his future income and thereby increase the present value of his human wealth. The limited ability of wealth-holders to substitute human wealth for other forms of wealth, and vice versa, has led many economists to argue that non-human wealth is a better index of the constraint upon the demand for money to hold, than is wealth defined to include human wealth. If the wealth-holder does not have the opportunity to convert the whole of his human wealth into money whenever he wishes to do so, then human wealth should not be part of the constraint on his ability to demand money.

Friedman's view is something of a compromise. He uses a comprehensive definition of wealth in his demand for money function, but in order to make some allowance for the absence of a market in human wealth includes the ratio of human to non-human wealth as a separate variable in the function: the higher is the proportion of human wealth in the total of wealth, the greater is likely to be the demand for money rather than other non-human assets in order to compensate for the low marketability of human wealth. Let us denote the total of wealth by (Y/i) and the ratio of human to non-human wealth as h.

The second group of factors affecting the demand for money are the returns to be had from holding money and from holding other assets. Friedman distinguishes five assets that may feature in wealth portfolios: money, bonds, equities, physical non-human goods, and human capital.

Whether or not money provides a nominal return in money depends on the form the money takes. Currency provides no monetary return to its holder, while time deposits (which Friedman includes in his definition of money) do; on the other hand current accounts, because of the bank charge levied on them, can be regarded as providing a negative return. Apart from any monetary return, money provides its owner with a return in kind, in the form of convenience and security etc., derived from its generalized purchasing power. The amount of security and convenience that is provided by a nominal unit of money (e.g. £1) depends on the quantity of goods and services that unit of money is capable of purchasing. This in turn depends on the general level of prices. The real return per nominal unit of money is a function of the general price level. The same is true of course with regard to the real return obtainable on a 'pound's worth' of each of the other forms of wealth. The price level, which we denote by P, affects the real return obtainable on all forms of wealth.

A bond entitles its holder to a regular money income, fixed in nominal terms, for a specified period of time (in the case of a consol, i.e. an irredeemable bond, in perpetuity). But, of course, while a bond is being held its market price can change, so that the money return from holding a bond, as we saw in our discussion of Keynes' speculative motive, consists of two parts: the interest income, fixed in a nominal amount, and also any capital gain or loss that may occur. The market price of the bonds varies inversely with the current rate of interest, so that the percentage rate of change in the rate of interest can be taken as a measure of the percentage rate of capital gain or loss. When a wealth-holder is considering whether or not to hold bonds in his portfolio, it is anticipated capital gains and losses which he must take into account, and therefore it is expected rates of change in the rate of interest which matter to him. Let us denote the interest income from holding bonds as i_b and the expected capital gain/loss from holding bonds by $-((1/i)(di_b/dt))$. The total return from holding bonds therefore is $i_b - ((1/i_b)(di_b/dt))$.

Equities are similar to bonds except that they provide an income stream which is fixed in real terms, i.e. the nominal income stream has a purchasing power escalator clause, so that when prices rise the nominal income stream is increased in step, thereby maintaining its real value; similarly a fall in prices would be matched by a fall in the nominal income stream, leaving its real value unchanged. The return from an equity therefore comprises three parts. Firstly, there is the constant nominal return which would be received in the absence of any inflation or deflation: we denote this by i_e. Secondly there is the addition or subtraction from this amount to compensate for price level changes, denoted by $(1/P)(dP/dt)$. Thirdly, there is any anticipated capital gain or loss arising from a change in the nominal price of the equity. Analogously with the anticipated capital gain or loss on bonds we can write the anticipated change in the nominal price of the equity as $-((1/i_e)(di_e/dt))$. The total return from equity is therefore

$$i_e + \frac{1}{P}\frac{dP}{dt} - \frac{1}{i_e}\frac{di_e}{dt}$$

Physical goods are similar to equities except that the return they provide to their owners is in kind rather than in money. The nominal value of this return depends on what is happening to prices. Clearly the increase in prices that has occurred in the post-war period has raised the nominal value that may be attached to the flow of services in kind emanating, say, from ownership of a house, even though the real value of the services has not changed. Additionally, and again like equities, physical goods provide a nominal return in the form of any appreciation/depreciation in nominal value (e.g. change in the market price of a house). This is given by the expression $(1/P)(dP/dt)$.

The final group of factors affecting the demand for money may be termed tastes and preferences. These are factors other than those already discussed that will influence the utility attached by wealth-holders to the services provided by money and to those provided by other assets. Friedman includes in such factors the level of real wealth or income,

since the services rendered by money may in principle, be regarded by wealth-holders as a 'necessity' like bread, the consumption of which increases less than in proportion to any increase in income, or as a 'luxury', like recreation, the consumption of which increases more than in proportion. (Friedman 1970a, p. 203).

Other factors included by Friedman in this category are: the degree of economic stability (more value placed on services of money when uncertainty is great), the amount of geographical movement by wealth-holders (more moving about likely to mean greater demand for money), and the volume of capital transfers relative to income.

> The higher the turnover of capital assets, the higher the fraction of total assets people may find useful to hold as cash. This variable corresponds to the class of transactions neglected in going from the transactions version of the quantity equation to the income version. (Friedman 1970a, p. 204).

Let us denote the tastes and preferences by the symbol u. Combining all these variables gives the following demand for money function

$$M^d = f\left(P, i_b - \frac{1}{i_b}\frac{di_b}{dt}, i_e + \frac{1}{P}\frac{dP}{dt} - \frac{1}{i_e}\frac{di_e}{dt}, \frac{1}{P}\frac{dP}{dt}, h, \frac{Y}{i}, u\right) \tag{3.18}$$

The equation contains three explicit rates of interest, i_e, i_b and i. The last of these is a general rate, a composite of i_e and i_b and the rates on human wealth and physical capital. If we assume that the last two implicit rates vary systematically with the first two explicit ones, then the influence of i is accounted for by the inclusion of i_e and i_b and may be dropped from the equation.

By making the further assumption that i_e and i_b are stable over time, and noting that $(1/P)(dP/dt)$ occurs separately in the equation anyway, Friedman is able to replace the cumbersome terms denoting the return on bonds and equities by the simpler i_b and i_e respectively.

Thus the function may be simplified to

$$M^d = f\left(P, i_b, i_e \cdot \frac{1}{P}\frac{dP}{dt}, h, Y, u\right) \tag{3.19}$$

The function is assumed to be homogenous of degree one in prices and money income, for the 'demand equations must be considered independent in any essential way of the nominal units used to measure money variables' (Friedman 1956, p. 10). Thus if prices and money income change by X per cent, all other independent variables remaining unchanged, then the demand for nominal money balances will change by X per cent. Thus equation (3.19) may be written in two other ways.

$$\frac{M^d}{P} = f\left(i_b, i_e, \frac{1}{P} \cdot \frac{dP}{dt}, h, \frac{Y}{P}, u\right) \tag{3.20}$$

$$\frac{M^d}{Y} = f\left(i_b, i_e, \frac{1}{P} \cdot \frac{dP}{dt}, h, \frac{P}{Y}, u\right) \tag{3.21}$$

Equation (3.21) can now be used to derive a velocity function. The desired income velocity of circulation of money (denoted by V^d) may be identified as the ratio of income to the stock of money that people wish to hold:

$$V^d = \frac{Y}{M^d}$$

Therefore $\dfrac{1}{V^d} = \dfrac{M^d}{Y} = f\left(i_b, i_e, \dfrac{1}{P} \cdot \dfrac{dP}{dt}, h\dfrac{P}{Y}, u\right)$

$$\tag{3.22}$$

or $$V^d = f \left(i_b, i_e, \ \frac{1}{P} \cdot \frac{dP}{dt}, \ h, \ \frac{Y}{P}, u \right)$$ (3.23)

The velocity of circulation is therefore a function of the same variables as the demand for money, though as can be seen from equation (3.23) the form of the functional relationship is different. Thus a stable demand for money implies a stable velocity. Hence the importance given by modern monetarism to the stability of the demand for money in contrast to the classical quantity theory, where velocity is regarded as a institutionally determined constant.

The demand for money function discussed so far is that of an individual wealth-holder. In deriving a function for the economy as a whole certain problems will be encountered, particularly the distribution problem – the possibility that the aggregate demand for money may depend not only upon the aggregate value but also upon the distribution of such variables as wealth and the ratio of human wealth to total wealth.

Demand by business enterprises

We can approach the analysis of the demand for money on the part of business enterprises by asking to what extent, if at all, is the demand for money function of the ultimate wealth-holder, already derived, applicable to the business unit? Let us take each of the terms in the function in turn. Y/i, the wealth constraint, has no counterpart for the business unit, because the business has the opportunity of varying the amount of capital it owns by recourse to the capital market. Nevertheless, the 'size' or 'scale' of the enterprise must have some influence on its demand for money, since larger firms are almost certainly likely to 'need' larger cash balances than will smaller firms. 'This is more nearly in line with the earlier transactions approach emphasising the "work" to be done by money.' (Friedman 1970a, p. 205). Friedman argues that it is not obvious what the appropriate index or 'scale' is; but be it total output, value added, or some other concept let us denote it by the symbol Y.

For business units, the division of wealth between human and non-human types, is of no particular importance, so the variable h will have no place in their demand for money function. The rates of return on money and other assets will, however, be of considerable importance to business units, though the relative importance of the various rates of return is likely to be different for businesses compared with ultimate wealth-holders. Finally, tastes and preferences will also be relevant to the demand of business units for money, covering factors such as expectations about economic stability, and certain conditions of production such as the amount of vertical integration within the enterprise.

With the omission of the variable h it would appear that the demand for money on the part of business units can be represented by a function similar to that used to symbolize the demand for money of ultimate wealth-holders, and therefore the equation (3.19) inclusive of h can represent the aggregate demand for money of the economy as a whole.

The empirical evidence

The various theories of the demand for money which were surveyed in the last section, all contain hypotheses which can be, and to a greater or lesser extent have been, subjected to empirical testing. The Keynesian analysis, for example, predicts that the demand for money is interest-elastic, and that at some low rate it is infinitely so. The more modern theories of the transactions demand for cash predict that the demand for money will increase less than proportionately to increases in income, while the risk-aversion analysis suggests that changes in the riskiness of bond-holding will affect the demand for money at given interest rates. The monetarist approach says that the demand for money is a stable function of a small number of variables and that wealth rather than current income is the relevant constraint.

Very simply, the typical demand for money study has involved a relationship in which the demand for nominal money balances is a function of (i) real income or wealth; (ii) a measure of the opportunity cost of holding money; and (iii) the price level. Sometimes the demand for money is assumed to be unit elastic with respect to the price level, and a relationship used in which the demand for real money balances is a function of (i) and (ii) above. Thus an equation typical of demand for money studies would be

$$M^d = \alpha \cdot Y^{\beta_1} \cdot i^{\beta_2} \tag{3.24}$$

where M^d is the demand for nominal money balances, Y the nominal level of the income or wealth constraint, i the appropriate rate of interest, and β_1 and β_2 the income and interest elasticities respectively. In logarithms equation (3.24) is linear, giving

$$\text{Log } M^d = \text{Log } \alpha + \beta_1 \text{Log } Y + \beta_2 \text{Log } i \tag{3.25}$$

The logarithmic form has the advantage that the coefficients β_1 and β_2 are direct estimates of the income and interest elasticities respectively. As it stands however, equation (3.25) does not allow for time lags in the adjustment of actual money balances to their desired levels. It assumes that actual holdings of money adjust to desired levels within the time period to which the study relates. The shorter the time period taken, the less likely is this to be true. Consequently, short-run demand for money functions, which are usually based on quarterly data, often allow for adjustment lags by using a two equation approach:

$$\text{Log } M_t^{d*} = \text{Log } \alpha + \beta_1 \text{Log } Y_t + \beta_2 \text{Log } i_t \tag{3.26}$$

where M^{d*} is desired money balances and

$$\text{Log } M_t^d - \text{Log } M_{t-1}^d = \lambda (\text{Log } M_t^{d*} - \text{Log } M_{t-1}^d) \tag{3.27}$$

Equation (3.27) makes the assumption that the lag of actual money holdings adjusts to the gap between the log of desired holdings and the log of actual holdings of the previous period. λ is the constant coefficient of adjustment, and has a value between 0 and 1.

Substituting into (3.27) gives

$$\text{Log } M_t^d - \text{Log } M_{t-1}^d = \lambda (\text{Log } \alpha + \beta_1 \text{Log } Y_t + \beta_2 \text{Log } i_t - \text{Log } M_{t-1}^d) \tag{3.28}$$

$$\text{Log } M_t^d = \lambda \text{Log } \alpha + \lambda \beta_1 \text{Log } Y_t + \lambda \beta_2 \text{Log } i_t + (1 - \lambda) \text{Log } M_{t-1}^d \tag{3.29}$$

The coefficients $\lambda \beta_1$ and $\lambda \beta_2$ are the short-run elasticities. The long-run elasticities β_1 and β_2 are given by dividing $\lambda \beta_1$ and $\lambda \beta_2$ by λ. λ itself is not estimated directly but can be obtained from

$$\lambda = 1 - (1 - \lambda)$$

because $(1 - \lambda)$ is estimated directly. Thus

$$\beta_1 = \frac{\lambda\beta_1}{1 - (1 - \lambda)} \text{ and } \beta_2 = \frac{\lambda\beta_2}{1 - (1 - \lambda)}$$

So far the only lag that we have considered is that which arises because actual money holdings adjust only partially, rather than fully and instantaneously to their desired levels. There is a second kind of lag that may feature in demand for money equations, a lag associated with the formation of expectations.

Expectations may be important because desired money holdings may be a function of the expected values of the relevant variables, rather than their current values. Suppose, for example, that the demand for money is assumed to be a function of permanent rather than current measured income. Permanent income cannot be observed directly but may be proxied by expected income. But of course people's expectations of income are not directly measurable either, so in order to obtain data on expected income, the researcher must have a theory of how expectations are formed. This means however that any test of the hypothesis that the demand for money is a function of permanent income is also a test of the particular hypothesis about expectations-formation that is incorporated in the test.

Let us illustrate, by taking the assumption frequently made in empirical work of this kind, that expectations are extrapolated from the past. Specifically we shall assume an 'adaptive' expectations' mechanism whereby people adjust their current expectations in the light of expectations errors made in previous periods. Thus current expectations of permanent income (Y_t^p) may be revised from last year's expectations of permanent income (Y_{t-1}^p) by a constant fraction $(0<\eta<1)$ of the amount by which actual current income (Y_t) differs from the expectations of permanent income held last year (i.e. Y_{t-1}^p). This may be written as

$$Y_t^p = Y_{t-1}^p + \eta(Y_t - Y_{t-1}^p) \tag{3.30}$$

Re-arranging (3.30) gives

$$Y_t^p = \eta Y_t + (1 - \eta)Y_{t-1}^p \tag{3.31}$$

It is implicit from (3.31) that

$$Y_{t-1}^p = \eta Y_{t-1} + (1 - \eta)Y_{t-2}^p \tag{3.32}$$

Substituting (3.32) into (3.31) gives

$$Y_t^p = \eta Y_t + \eta(1 - \eta)Y_{t-1} + (1 - \eta)^2 Y_{t-2}^p$$

Continual substitution in this way for Y_{t-2}^p, Y_{t-3}^p etc. gives

$$Y_t^p = \eta[Y_t + (1 - \eta)Y_{t-1} + (1 - \eta)^2 Y_{t-2} \ldots \quad] \tag{3.33}$$

Equation (3.33) says that Y_t^p is a geometrically weighted average of past values of Y.

This could now be incorporated into a demand for money function which has permanent income as the constraint variable. To illustrate let us take the simplest possible case

$$M_t^d = \alpha Y_t^p \tag{3.34}$$

Substituting (3.33) into the above gives

$$M_t^d = \alpha\eta[Y_t + (1 - \eta)Y_{t-1} + (1 - \eta)^2 Y_{t-2} + \ldots \quad] \qquad (3.35)$$

Now clearly this equation incorporates two separate hypothesis, namely: (i) the demand for money is a function of permanent income and (ii) permanent incomes can be proxied by expected income, which is itself a geometrically weighted average of past values of actual income. Thus if equation (3.35) does not provide a good fit to the data, then we don't know whether it is because permanent income is not the most appropriate constraint on the demand for money or whether the hypothesis about the formation of expectations is wrong.

But there is a further complication. Even if equation (3.35) does fit the data well, this does not necessarily mean that the two hypotheses incorporated in it are supported by the data. The reason for this is that equation (3.35) can be derived from an entirely different hypothesis about the demand for money.

To illustrate, let us assume that the demand for money is a simple function of current income

$$M_t^{d*} = \varepsilon Y_t \qquad (3.36)$$

Let us further assume following our earlier discussion, that there is a lag in the adjustment of actual money holdings $(M^d)/(M^{d*})$ to their desired levels, so that

$$M_t^d = M_{t-1}^d + \pi(M_t^{d*} - M_{t-1}^d) \text{ where } 0 < \pi < 1 \qquad (3.37)$$

Re-arranging gives

$$M_t^d = \pi M_t^{d*} + (1 - \pi)M_{t-1}^d \qquad (3.38)$$

If we follow the same process of lagging and substituting back, that we did with equation (3.31) then (3.38) becomes

$$M_t^d = \pi[M_t^{d*} + (1 - \pi)M_{t-1}^{d*} + (1 - \pi)M_{t-2}^{d*} \ldots \quad] \qquad (3.39)$$

so that the actual stock of money held is a weighted average of past desired stocks. Substituting (3.36) into (3.30) gives

$$M_t^d = \varepsilon\pi[Y_t + (1 - \pi)Y_{t-1} + (1 - \pi)^2 Y_{t-2} + \ldots \quad] \qquad (3.40)$$

Now (3.40) is formally identical to (3.35) even though the two equations are derived from entirely different hypotheses about the demand for money. Equation (3.40) is obtained from the hypotheses that the demand for money is a function of current income and that there is a lag in the adjustment of actual to desired money balances, while equation (3.35) is derived from the hypothesis that the demand for money is a function of permanent income with no adjustment lags between actual and desired money holdings. Of course one can combine the two kinds of lags that we have considered, i.e. lags in adjustment and lags in the formation of expectations, and some studies have in fact done so (Coghlan 1978; Laidler and Parkin 1970).

Before turning to a consideration of the results of demand for money studies there are some further problems of empirical work in this field that we must consider. To begin with there is the so-called 'identification problem', which arises because one cannot observe the demand for money directly. All that one can observe or measure is the quantity supplied. To infer that the amount supplied is also the amount demanded it is necessary to assume equilibrium in the money market. Moreover, when different observations of the money supply are made and related to specified variables, one cannot be certain that what is being measured is the demand function rather than the supply function or some combination of the two. The problem is illustrated in *Figure 3.14*. In all panels we have a demand for money curve which shows greater amounts of money being demanded at lower rates of interest, and an increasing supply of money being supplied at higher rates of interest. Only in panel 1 would the observations a, b, c, trace out the demand curve: in panel 2 they would trace out the supply curve, while in panel 3 the observations trace neither the demand nor the supply curve.

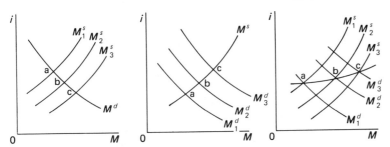

Figure 3.14 The identification problem

It is only when the different observations are the result of supply curve shifts that they do in fact trace out the demand curve. Some studies have tried to take account of this problem by fitting supply and demand functions simultaneously. The use of non-simultaneous estimation procedures will also mean that if all of the variables on the right-hand side of the estimating equation are not truly exogenous, but are determined simultaneously with the money supply, then the result obtained will be biased and increase the likelihood that the demand relationship will not be accurately estimated.

The final problem that we shall mention is that of choosing the appropriate empirical counterparts to the variables specified in the demand for money equation. Consider first the money supply itself. Does it matter which definition of money (M1, M2, etc.) is used in empirical work? Certainly some studies have been based on the view that there is a general specification of the demand for money which is essentially independent of the definition of money used. On the other hand, it may be argued that the specification should depend on whether a narrow or broad definition of money is being employed. For example, the demand for narrow money (M1) is primarily a demand for transactions balances and we might therefore expect short rates rather than long to be the appropriate measure of its opportunity cost. The use of a broad definition however would appear to require the specification of a function which reflects the demand for money as an asset, and hence long rates of interest and wealth would appear to be important arguments.

The choice of the appropriate income constraint rests primarily between current measured income and permanent income. If the choice is current measured income there are again a number of alternative measures, including GNP and personal disposable income. If it is permanent income that is used then there are a number of ways in which it could be specified.

The range of interest rates is, of course, enormous. The basic choice is between short and long rates, but once this decision has been made there is still the problem of picking the rate that best reflects that choice.

The results

We shall confine our attention in this section to the results of demand for money studies made on UK data. We consider first the evidence on the basic question of the stability of the demand for money. It will be useful to divide this evidence into that obtained from studies made on pre-1971 data and that obtained from studies incorporating data from the post-1971 period.

The earliest studies of the demand for money in the UK were those of Brown (1939) and Khusro (1952). Both studies, like the early American ones, attempted to separate idle balances from total money in order to test for the influence of interest rates on the demand for the former. However, the methods used and, consequently, the results obtained in these pioneering studies are not now regarded as satisfactory. Instead it is on the basis of studies made in the 1960s and 1970s that any conclusions on the stability of the demand for money pre-1971 must be reached. Amongst the early studies were those of Kavanagh and Walters (1966), Fisher (1968), Goodhart and Crockett (1970) and Laidler and Parkin (1970).

Between them the studies embraced a wide range of definitions of money (including the old M2 as well as the more conventional M1 and M3), income and wealth measures, interest rates, lag structures, and estimation periods.

On the basis of the goodness of fit statistics and the plausibility of the coefficients that were obtained, these studies are generally regarded as providing strong evidence of a stable demand for money in the UK before 1971. As Laidler put it

> Now this evidence for Britain certainly points to the existence of a stable demand for money function in that economy ... For the United States the evidence is overwhelming, and for Britain it is at the very least highly suggestive. (Laidler 1971, p. 99).

Laidler and others have pointed out, however, that the British results differed significantly from the American ones in that they were sensitive to quite small changes in the specification of the demand function. Kavanagh and Walters also found that the stability of the function was reduced when they used changes in, rather than levels of, data. This has been interpreted as suggesting that the long-run stability of the functions may be the consequence of strong trends in the variables concerned.

The generally held view at the start of the 1970s – that the evidence supported the existence of a stable demand for money – was challenged by the results of studies based on post-1971 data. The demand for money functions that had been estimated from pre-1971 data failed to forecast at all accurately in the years following the introduction of Competition and Credit Control in 1971 (see Chapter 13). The evidence has not been entirely consistent however, and has given rise to two particular debates: (i) whether the break-down of the demand function applies to M1 as well as to M3 and (ii) whether the stability of the demand function was re-established in the later years of the 1970s.

As far as (i) is concerned, Artis and Lewis (1981) in particular have argued that there was a break-down in the demand for narrow money (i.e. M1) in the immediate post-1971 period. They claim that this view is based not only on the evidence provided by their own researches, but also on that provided by Hamburger (1977), Boughton (1979), and Rowan and Miller (1979). Artis and Lewis (1981) also emphasize that there are 'disturbing differences' in the estimates made in the various studies of both income and interest rate elasticities.

Coghlan (1980), on the other hand, believes that there is sufficient evidence to justify the view that the M1 equation has remained stable. His own 1978 study of

1964–76 data, employed a more flexible lag structure than the simpler distributed lags of conventional models, and appeared to provide evidence for a stable M1 demand function. The forecasting performances of his flexible lags model was considerably better than that of models incorporating only the simpler distributed lags, and it satisfied fairly rigorous tests for stability. Some support for Coghlan's views is provided by Hacche (1974), Mills (1978) and Laumas (1978). Artis and Lewis (1981) provide evidence obtained from equations that contain the same explanatory variables as Coghlan's, but are estimated for later periods. These equations generate income and interest rate elasticities similar to those obtained by Coghlan. This is interpreted by Artis and Lewis (1981, p. 20) as being 'suggestive of reasonable stability in the M1 function after 1971'. On the other hand they argue that the equations are far less successful in predicting short-run changes in M1.

We turn now to the stability of the demand for broad money. Most studies made in the 1970s suggest that the demand for M3 became unstable in the early years of that decade. Artis and Lewis (1981, p. 22) draw the following conclusion from their survey of the available evidence

> The breakdown is much the same for all M3 equations irrespective of whether the dependent variable is in nominal terms or expressed as real or real per capita balances: the same is found to be true for functions which incorporate as arguments short-term rates, long-term rates, foreign rates, dividend yields, and measures of the variance of bond yields. Even equations with generalized functional forms or more sophisticated lags fail after 1971.

Laumas (1978), however, using a varying parameter technique on data from the two periods 1964–71 and 1971–76, came to a different conclusion. His view was that for the latter period stable demand equations did exist for M3 as well as M1 and for both short and long rates of interest. The short-run income and interest elasticities were, however, both lower in the latter period than in the former and Laumas suggests that there was a major shift in the demand for money relationship between the two periods.

Artis and Lewis (1981) have also provided some evidence for the long-run stability of the demand for money. They used an M2 definition (currency in circulation outside the banks plus sterling deposits of the London clearing banks), assumed a unitary income elasticity of demand for money, and then using an equation of the form

$$\frac{M}{Y} = \alpha i^{\beta} \text{ or } \text{Log} \frac{M}{Y} = \text{Log } \alpha + \beta \text{Log } i$$

fitted a regression line to annual data for the years 1920–57. They then compared data for the period 1957-79 with the curve that had been fitted. Data points for each year of 1960–72 lie very close to the regression line, but those for 1973–6 lie well above it. The data points for 1977–9 then return almost exactly to the curve. Artis and Lewis conclude that 'this evidence is suggestive of a considerable extent of long-run stability in the demand for this definition of money' (1981, p. 29).

Artis and Lewis also fit a simple trend line to quarterly data on the income velocity of £M3 for the period 1963–71, and then project it forward. There is a very noticeable fall in velocity below trend after 1971, but a return to it around 1976. Artis and Lewis conclude that, 'All of our tests point to there being some underlying longer run stability of the demand for broad money (1981, p. 32).'

It would appear then that the first half of the 1970s were in some way 'abnormal' and several different explanations have been put forward as to why the demand for broad money did not fit during this period.

The first point to note is that the apparent breakdown in the early 1970s of demand for money equations derived from pre-1971 data may, of course, be a purely statistical problem. As Coghlan points out, the 'breakdown ... refers only to the estimation of single-equation demand functions and does not exclude the possibility that a stable but unidentified demand function actually existed' (1980, p. 132).

The introduction of Competition and Credit Control in 1971 abolished the clearing banks' interest rate cartel, and extended the new reserve asset ratio to the non-clearing banks. The result was increased competition between the banks to attract deposits. Such competition was not only between the clearing banks themselves, but also between the banks and the parallel money markets for 'wholesale' deposits. Interest rates on bank deposits were consequently bid up and money became a more attractive asset to hold. Moreover, the loan rates charged by banks rose less rapidly than deposit rates so that it became profitable for companies to borrow from banks and re-invest in money market assets including certificates of deposit, a process known as 'round-tripping'. Some writers have argued that under such circumstances the own rate of interest on money had become a significant argument in the money demand function, and the estimating equations that did not include it were therefore mis-specified.

This argument would suggest a differential effect on the demand for narrow and broad money. M1 balances, being essentially transactions balances, might be expected to remain largely unaffected by these developments, while M3 comprising a larger 'idle balances' component might be expected to be more affected. Some early support for this kind of argument was obtained by Hacche (1974). Artis and Lewis (1976) also allowed for the 'own rate' on money, but while recognizing the statistical problems of measuring it, came to the conclusion that 'equations which include measures of the own rate of money still do not provide satisfactory explanations of the 1971–3 experience' (Artis and Lewis 1981, p. 23).

A very different explanation of the apparent breakdown of money-demand equations in the early 1970s has been provided by Artis and Lewis (1976, 1981). They do not accept that the demand for money is necessarily equal to the supply, and argue that the early 1970s were in fact characterized by an excess supply of money. A combination of factors, including the relaxation of bank lending controls in 1971 and the size of the budget deficit in 1972 and 1973, resulted in an increase in the money supply that was not demand determined, and which generated a disequilibrium situation ($M^s > M^d$). Evidence that the demand for narrow money remained stable during this period is not necessarily inconsistent with their argument, because there are good reasons for believing that M1 is demand determined even if M3 is not.

Finally, we can consider the argument that the apparent breakdown of the demand for money equations may be due to an inability to identify and include the appropriate interest rate variable. While most studies have used domestic rates, a few (Hamburger 1977; Rowan and Miller 1979) have used the three-month eurodollar rate. The reasoning is that national capital markets have become more integrated, increasing the sustitutability between domestic and foreign assets. The authors found that for M1 balances, the three-month eurodollar rate performed better statistically, at least up to 1971, but then broke down. The explanation may be that the change to flexible exchange rates increased the risk attached to dealings in foreign assets, reduced the substitutability between the latter and domestic assets, and thereby diminished the appropriateness of the eurodollar rate as the measure of the opportunity cost of holding money.

What conclusions about the stability of the demand for money does our brief survey of the evidence lead us to? Certainly there is less agreement now than there was when Laidler expressed the view quoted on page 76. There is clearly a need for more empirical evidence, using more recent data. Nevertheless, we will conclude by tentatively suggesting that

(1) There is a stable demand for M1 balances.
(2) The long-run demand for broad money is also stable.
(3) The early 1970s witnessed a temporary disturbance to the stability of the demand for money affecting broad money rather than narrow, and due probably to a combination of factors.

To complete our survey of empirical evidence on the demand for money we shall briefly consider results on elasticity estimates and on the most appropriate choice of variable. Estimates of income-elasticity vary considerably. Hacche, for example, looking at data for the period 1963–71, obtained elasticities of under 0.5 for both M1 and M3 though they did rise appreciably when the data period was extended to the end of 1972. Artis and Lewis, on the other hand, have found for the period 1963(QII) to 1973(QI) that the income elasticity exceeds 1 for both narrow and broad definitions of money. The evidence certainly does not present a clear picture, with the result that reviewers of it have derived very different conclusions. Thus while some writers (e.g. Dennis 1981, p. 170) believe that the evidence shows the income elasticity to be less than one, others would not agree (e.g. Artis and Lewis 1981, p. 29).

Almost all studies have found interest rates to be statistically significant though a notable exception was the 1970 Laidler and Parkin study which used the Treasury bill rate rather than the more customary three-months local authority rate. Elasticity estimates again vary considerably, reflecting in part the varying data periods and equation specifications employed. The estimates obtained, have, with one or two exceptions, been within the range -0.07 to -0.8, and indeed most of them have been between -0.25 and -0.6. Studies that used a broad definition of money and a long rate of interest usually obtained estimates within the range -0.2 to -0.5. Those using a broad definition with a short interest rate generated estimates between -0.09 and -0.36. Studies employing a narrow definition of money obtained estimates for long and short rates that were normally within the ranges -0.1 to -11.0 and -0.06 to -1.2 respectively. There is no evidence to support the existence of a liquidity trap; indeed there is virtually no evidence to suggest that elasticity increases as the rate of interest falls.

Most studies have assumed a price elasticity of unity, but those that have tested for it (e.g. Coghlan, 1978; Courakis, 1978; Rowan and Miller 1979), have in fact found it to be less than 1. Not much work has been done in the UK on the importance of price expectations as a determinant of the demand for money. Evidence from other countries suggests that price expectations are important in times of very rapid or hyperinflation but not in mild inflation. Rowan and Miller did include the expected rate of change of prices in their M1 study but found it to have only a minor role in determining the demand for M1 balances. They estimated the elasticity to be approximately 0.7.

On the question of the most appropriate constraint on money holdings, there has not been a great deal of testing of the various alternative measures of wealth and income in the UK. What evidence there is however indicates that permanent income performs better than current measured income, a conclusion which is supported by the more numerous studies of USA data.

4

Financial intermediaries and the supply of money

The purpose of this chapter is threefold. Firstly to outline the nature and functions of financial intermediaries in general. Secondly to examine the way in which the money supply is determined, and in so doing to pay particular attention to the banks as suppliers of money. Thirdly to consider the importance of the non-bank financial intermediaries (NBFIs), both for the total flow of credit and for the volume of bank deposits.

The nature and functions of financial intermediaries

Financial intermediaries are economic units whose primary function is 'to purchase primary securities from ultimate borrowers and to issue indirect debt for the portfolios of ultimate lenders' (Gurley and Shaw, 1960). Ultimate borrowers are individuals or institutions who wish to spend on real resources in excess of their income (sometimes called deficit spenders) and who intend to finance the additional expenditure by borrowing. Such borrowings may be for a variety of purposes and may be undertaken either by persons or by institutions. Individuals borrow, for example, in order to finance the purchase of consumer durables, and to finance the purchase of a house. Firms borrow to finance purchases of capital equipment, while governments borrow to finance a variety of capital expenditures. When such borrowings are made the borrower will usually have to provide some form of security and enter some form of contract to repay the sum borrowed, usually over some specified period of time. In effect they may be regarded as providing a claim upon themselves in return for the money borrowed. It is convenient to regard these claims, which we call primary securities, as being sold. Indeed in some cases they clearly are. A firm issuing equities in order to raise funds to finance capital expenditure is actually selling the equities, being under no obligation to 'buy' them back: it is not borrowing the money for a specified period but acquiring it for permanent use. Redeemable bonds, on the other hand, do have maturity dates, at which the money borrowed has to be repaid. Similarly, money borrowed on a mortgage, or on hire-purchase, also has to be repaid, so that the primary securities are not actually sold in the everyday meaning of that word. It is convenient, however, to regard them as being sold, but subject to a repurchase clause.

Ultimate lenders are individuals or institutions who do not spend all their income and are prepared to lend all or part of the surplus. Just as we called ultimate borrowers 'deficit spenders', so we can call ultimate lenders 'surplus spenders' because they have a surplus of their income over their expenditure.

Indirect securities (sometimes called secondary securities) are the claims upon themselves issued by the financial intermediaries; they are issued in return for the savings placed with them by ultimate lenders. The ultimate lender will place either currency or bank deposits with the financial intermediary and receive in return the indirect security of the intermediary. The particular form the indirect security takes will depend on the nature of the financial intermediary concerned, for each financial intermediary will provide an indirect security which is differentiated to a greater or lesser extent, from the indirect securities of other intermediaries. The indirect securities of the commercial banks, for example, are their deposits, the main distinguishing characteristic of which is their general acceptability. The indirect securities of building societies are their shares and deposits. These are not generally acceptable as a means of payment but they do bear interest which is taxed in an unusual way, and they are encashable (i.e. they can be sold back to the building society) at fairly short notice. The shares or units of investment and unit trusts are examples of yet another kind of indirect security. As a final example, we can take the indirect securities of insurance companies. These are mainly the insurance policies or cover that they give in return for the regular payment of premiums. Their differentiating characteristic is the protection they afford against future contingencies such as accidents and premature death. All other financial intermediaries, be they hire-purchase finance houses, pension funds, merchant banks or any other, will offer similar but differentiated indirect securities in return for receipt of currency or bank deposits. Of course most financial intermediaries will offer more than one kind of indirect security, which will not only be differentiated from the indirect securities of other financial intermediaries but will also be differentiated from each other. Commerical banks, for example, provide both current accounts and deposit accounts, building societies offer share and deposit accounts, while insurance companies provide a wide range of insurance and endowment policies.

So far we have been looking at the nature of the instruments in which financial intermediaries deal and at the individuals and institutions with whom they deal. But why have such intermediaries at all? Clearly they can exist only in a society in which there are both deficit and surplus spending units. If there were no surplus spenders, if nobody wished to spend less than their current income, then clearly there would be no savings to be put at the disposal of deficit spenders who wish to spend in excess of their current income. If there are no savings to be transmitted from ultimate lenders to ultimate borrowers, then financial intermediaries can play no part in transmitting them. Clearly then, financial intermediaries will exist only when some income recipients wish to spend less than their income, while other income units wish to spend more; that is, when the distribution of expenditure in the economy does not coincide with the distribution of income.

But this is only a necessary and not a sufficient condition for the existence of financial intermediaries. Even though there are both ultimate lenders and ultimate borrowers in our economy, financial intermediaries need not exist if the ultimate borrowers and lenders deal directly with one another. If ultimate lenders who have saved part of their income put it directly at the disposal of ultimate borrowers wishing to spend in excess of their income, then it is the ultimate lenders who acquire the primary securities of the ultimate borrowers. But if ultimate borrowers and lenders have to deal directly with one another, then there will be the same kinds of difficulties that characterize the direct exchanges of the barter economy. Thus financial intermediaries exist for much the same reasons that money is used – to lower transactions costs and reduce the problems associated with uncertainty. The intermediaries are able to provide financial services more efficiently than ultimate borrowers and lenders could provide them for themselves. This they are able to do because they enjoy such benefits as economies of scale in trading, and advantages in the acquisition of information. They consequently increase the efficiency of markets and raise the level of lending and borrowing. Let us consider some examples of the benefits that NBFIs can bring to both ultimate lenders and ultimate borrowers.

To begin with, the terms on which the ultimate lenders are prepared to lend may not be acceptable to the ultimate borrowers, while the terms on which the ultimate borrowers wish to borrow may not be acceptable to the ultimate lenders. In a situation such as this the financial intermediaries will reconcile the conflicting portfolio requrements of the lenders and borrowers. Lenders are likely to want to be able to get their money back at very short notice, while borrowers will want to know that they will not be required to repay the sum outstanding for much longer periods, if at all. It is these sorts of conflicting requirements that financial intermediaries try to reconcile. Thus they accept savings from ultimate lenders, giving in return their own indirect securities which they usually promise to buy back at very short notice, or even on demand. The period of notice that has to be given before an indirect security can be sold (exchanged) for currency or bank deposits will vary from one financial intermediary to another and between the different indirect securities offered by each intermediary. Usually the longer the period of notice the higher is the interest paid on the security. By varying the combinations of interest, period of withdrawal notice and other characteristics, the various preferences of ultimate lenders can be catered for.

The financial intermediary will also purchase primary securities from ultimate borrowers on terms which are fairly convenient to such borrowers. Building societies, for example, will make large sums available for the purchase of houses and spread the repayments over periods of up to 35 years. Other intermediaries such as hire-purchase finance houses and merchant banks will make funds available for the purchase of consumer durables on terms convenient for the borrowing consumer.

In these ways, then, the financial intermediaries satisfy simultaneously the conflicting portfolio requirements of ultimate borrowers and ultimate lenders. The indirect securities they provide for the ultimate lenders in return for currency or bank deposits are liabilities of the intermediaries but assets to their holders, the ultimate lenders. The primary securities which the intermediaries purchase from the ultimate borrowers are assets to the intermediaries but liabilities to the borrowers.

By reconciling the conflicting requirements of lenders and borrowers, financial intermediaries probably increase the amount of saving that takes place and which flows to borrowers who wish to spend in excess of their current incomes. Whether this leads to an increase in aggregate expenditure, however, is another question, which we take up later in this chapter.

Why are financial intermediaries able to reconcile the conflicting portfolio requirements of lenders and borrowers? The reason is primarily that they enjoy certain economies of scale. By dealing with large numbers of lenders and borrowers they are able to pool the risk involved. By having large numbers of depositors to whom they have sold indirect securities the intermediaries are able to predict far more accurately what total withdrawals will be, because as some depositors are making withdrawals others will be paying in, and the greater the number of individual transactions making up the total, the more likely are random variations in individual magnitudes likely to cancel one another out, leaving the total more stable per unit period of time. Similarly the intermediaries can more accurately predict the number of borrowers who are likely to default than could a small-scale lender lending to only a few borrowers. Financial intermediaries will also enjoy administrative economies and managerial economies, being able to employ specialist staff in a wide range of activities. Their size, too, plus in some cases the fact that they are subject to government regulation and supervision, may make them appear less risky investments to ultimate lenders, who, as a result, may be prepared to lend to them at lower rates of interest than they would be prepared to lend to ultimate borrowers.

A rather different kind of intermediation with related benefits is provided by institutions like investment trusts, unit trusts, and in some respects pension funds. These institutions, along with others, 'alleviate the market imperfections caused by economies of scale in transactions in financial markets and also in information gathering and portfolio management' (Goodhart 1975a, p. 104). Economies of scale in brokerage and management enable the intermediaries to offer diversified portfolios to investors more cheaply than they could acquire them for themselves. Similarly these intermediaries may, through specialization and size, enjoy advantages of expertise, information and marketing that enable them to arrange such things as new share issues for companies in more favoured large blocks rather than numerous small ones.

Finally we have the example of the insurance companies who, through their ability to pool risks and enjoy other economies of scale and information advantages, are able to meet the insurance requirements of people much more cheaply than would otherwise be the case.

In this section we have sought to outline the essential characteristics of financial intermediaries, characteristics shared by all such intermediaries such as banks, hire-purchase finance houses, building societies, etc. Traditionally, however, a distinction has been drawn between the commercial banks on the one hand and non-bank financial intermediaries on the other. The rationale of this distinction was that the banks were regarded as being unique in that the indirect securities they issue (their deposits) are a means of payment and are therefore money, while the indirect securities of all other intermediaries are not generally acceptable as a means of payment and are therefore not money. Indeed it has been argued that the banks, by getting their indirect securities accepted as the main form of money have, in fact, ceased to perform an intermediary function to any significant degree. This is because a decision by ultimate lenders to save through a bank will normally take the form of allowing bank balances to accumulate. But this does not increase the ability of the banks to increase their own lending to ultimate borrowers: they can only do that if the additional savings placed with them are in the form of cash.

This traditional view of the uniqueness of banks has been criticized by supporters of the 'new view' of financial intermediaries, which emerged in the 1960s. According to the new view all financial intermediaries are unique in the sense of offering differentiated indirect securities, but all are subject to the same economic constraints of costs and revenues and in varying degrees are in competition with one another. In the next section we shall therefore consider the traditional and new view of banks in the context of a discussion of the determinants of the money supply. In the final section of the chapter we shall return to the non-bank financial intermediaries and consider if and how they influence the total of bank deposits and credit flows.

The supply of money

In this section we will be looking at two main theories of money supply determination, the money supply multiplier approach and the portfolio or structural approach. We shall be particularly interested in trying to find out the extent to which the money supply is exogenous or endogenous.[1] Exogenous in this chapter means that the money supply is actively determined by the monetary authorities, while endogenous means that it is determined within the private sector. The exogenity/endogeneity of the money supply is of the greatest importance in analyzing the role of money in the macroeconomy – in trying to discover whether and how the money supply influences such variables as output, prices and interest rates. Those who claim that the money supply is in fact exogenous are asserting both that the monetary authorities are able to control the money supply and that they actively do control it as a matter of policy, rather than passively allowing it to adjust to changes in the demand for it. We shall consider the question of the passivity of the authorities in Chapters 9 and 13 and will mainly concentrate in this chapter on the ability of the authorities to control the money supply. We begin by setting out the traditional monetary base model.

The money supply multiplier approach – the monetary base model

The monetary base model, which, in one form or another, has become the standard textbook model of money supply determination, can be seen as a simple extension of the traditional bank deposit multiplier approach to deposit creation.

If a profit seeking commercial bank receives additional cash reserves it will seek to increase its revenue by purchasing securities, or making new loans, and in so doing it will expand the volume of its deposits. This deposit creation process, however, is constrained by the need to hold a certain proportion of deposits as cash in order to meet deposit withdrawals and to settle inter-bank debt. Thus the bank has to strike a balance between its desire for profits and its need for liquidity (i.e. cash reserves). Moreover the authorities may impose a cash ratio on the banks independently of any ratio that the banks, as a matter of prudence, may impose upon themselves.

In order to illustrate the deposit creation process, we will assume that banks maintain a ratio (r) of cash reserves (R) to deposits (D) of say 10% (a figure chosen only for its arithmetical simplicity). Cash reserves are assumed to consist of till currency (cash in hand) and balances at the central bank. We will also assume initially that the non-bank private sector's demand for cash is constant and therefore there is no leakage of cash from the banks to the public. Suppose one bank (A) now receives an increase in reserves of £100. Given the assumed reserve requirement of 10% the maximum the bank can lend is £90, i.e. $(1 - r)$ times the additional cash received. Assume the borrower spends the amount of the loan, and the cheque is deposited by the seller in another bank (B). After cheque clearing and inter-bank debt settlement (by a transfer of balances of £90 at the central bank), bank A has lost cash reserves equivalent to the loan and its final balance sheet position shows a deposit expansion of £100 matched on the assets side by loans of £90 and extra cash reserves of £10. Thus the bank's cash reserve ratio is maintained at the required 10%. Bank B is now in a position to make additional loans, having had an equal increase in cash reserves and deposits of £90. It can 'afford' to lend out an extra £81 and still satisfy its 10% cash reserve ratio. Thus the initial increase in reserves of £100 results in a first round increase in deposits of £100, a second round increase of $£100(1 - 0.1)$, a third round increase of $£100(1 - 0.1)(1 - 0.1)$ and so on. The sum of this series if £1000, so the deposits have risen by ten times the initial increase in cash reserves. In notational form the total deposit expansion for the banking system (ΔD) maybe represented by a geometric progression.

$$\Delta D = \Delta R + \Delta R(1 - r) + \Delta R(1 - r)^2 \ldots + \Delta R(1 - r)^n \tag{4.1}$$

Multiplying by $(1 - r)$ gives

$$(1 - r)\Delta D = \Delta R(1 - r) + \Delta R(1 - r)^2 \ldots + \Delta R(1 - r)^{n + 1} \tag{4.2}$$

Substracting (4.2) from (4.1)

$$\Delta D - (1 - r)\Delta D = \Delta R - \Delta R(1 - r)^{n + 1}$$

Therefore

$$\Delta D = \frac{\Delta R - \Delta R(1 - r)^{n + 1}}{r} \tag{4.3}$$

As n approaches infinity (4.3) reduces to

$$\Delta D = \frac{\Delta R}{r} \tag{4.4}$$

This is the traditional bank deposit multiplier formula. Thus for the banking system as a whole the total volume of deposits is equal to a multiple $(1/r)$ of the system's cash reserves.

$$D = \left(\frac{1}{r}\right)R \tag{4.5}$$

Now the cash reserves (R) constitute only part of the total amount of cash potentially available to the banks. The total quantity available is referred to as the monetary base (B) and consists of the cash reserves held by the banks (R) plus currency in circulation outside the banks (C_p). Hence

$$B = C_p + R \tag{4.6}$$

The monetary base comprises the monetary liabilities of the central bank and is assumed in this approach to be determined by the monetary authorities. For a given size of the base, the amount of reserves available to the banks depends on the demand for cash by the non-bank private sector.

In order to derive the simple deposit multiplier we assumed that the public's holding of cash remained constant. We can now relax that assumption and instead make the more realistic one that the demand for cash will rise with an expansion of deposits. More precisely we will assume that the non-bank private sector maintains a fixed ratio (c) of cash to deposits. Thus

$$c = \frac{C_p}{D}$$

(4.7)

We can now derive the standard monetary base model which generates a multiple relationship between the money supply (defined generally as bank deposits plus currency in circulation), and the monetary base.

$$M = C_p + D$$

(4.8)

$$B = C_p + R$$

(4.9)

$$D = \left(\frac{1}{r}\right)R$$

(4.10)

$$c = \frac{C_p}{D}$$

(4.11)

Dividing (4.8) by (4.9)

$$\frac{M}{B} = \frac{C_p + D}{C_p + R}$$

(4.12)

Re-arranging (4.10) and (4.11) and then substituting into (4.12) gives

$$\frac{M}{B} = \frac{cD + D}{cD + rD} = \frac{c + 1}{c + r}$$

Hence[2] $M = \left(\frac{c + 1}{c + r}\right)B$

(4.13)

If we denote the expression in brackets by m then (4.13) may be rewritten as

$$M = mB$$

(4.14)

In this model the money supply is seen as a multiple (m) of the monetary base, with m usually referred to as the money supply multiplier. Due to this multiplier relationship the monetary base (B) is often referred to as high powered money. According to this approach, therefore, money supply determination depends on three factors: (i) the banks' cash reserve ratio; (ii) the non-bank private sectors cash ratio; and (iii) the monetary base.

Whether or not this model provides an adequate or useful description of the money supply determination process is an issue of some debate. Thus for example, Goodhart (1973) has argued that equation (4.13) can be derived from the money supply and monetary base identities, and is therefore essentially an identity itself, lacking in behavioural content. On the other hand it underlies the proposal for monetary base control of the money supply advocated by many economists (see pp. 259–264).

The model, as we have presented it so far, is in fact the simplest, naive version. If the two ratios are fixed, and if the authorities can control the monetary base, then they can control the total money supply. The proponents of this approach recognize, however, that the ratios can only be considered fixed if the factors influencing them are assumed constant. In other words the ratios are behavioural variables and therefore the model can be extended to incorporate the factors influencing the ratios. Critics of the approach argue that not only does variability of the two ratios create 'slippage' between control of the base and control of the money supply, but that in any case the authorities cannot control the base itself. We shall now consider the variability of the ratios and then move on to examine the controllability of the monetary base.

The determinants of the money supply multiplier ratios

We shall consider first the factors likely to determine the public's cash ratio, then consider the determinants of the banks cash reserve ratio and finally, briefly review the empirical evidence on the variability of the two ratios.

The public's cash ratio
The size of this ratio is likely to depend on a number of variables. An important one is likely to be the level of real national income (Y/P). As the level of real national income rises, the public's demand for both currency and bank deposits is likely to increase. However, the demand for bank deposits is likely to increase by a greater proportion than is the demand for currency, because the rise in real national income is likely to lead to a relatively bigger increase in the number of transactions financed by cheque than in transactions requiring payment in currency.

Another factor influencing the c ratio might be changes in the price level of those goods and services normally purchased with currency relative to changes in the price level of goods and services normally purchased with cheques (P_{cu}/P_{ch}). Thus if the price of food rises relative to the price of consumer durables, then this is likely to increase the public's desired currency/deposits ratio.

It has also been suggested that the ratio of armed service personnel to the total population may be important, in influencing the c ratio (Crouch 1968) while Cagan (1958) found that the ratio of taxes to income (T/Y) was useful in explaining the demand for currency in the US. A possible rationale for this latter influence is that the bigger the ratio of taxes to income the greater the incentive to evade tax payments, with tax evaders being likely to conduct a greater proportion of their transactions in currency.

Other factors that may influence the c ratio include the extent to which bank and other credit cards are used, the incidence of wage and salary payments by cheque and uncertainties about general economic and political stability. Finally, it is likely that the public's desired currency/deposits ratio will be influenced by the interest offered by the banks on deposits (i_d). The higher the interest offered by the banks on deposit accounts and the lower the level of bank charges on current accounts, the greater the incentive for the public to economize on their holdings of currency and to hold bank deposits instead. Thus the publics currency ratio may be written:

$$C_p = f(Y/P, P_{cu}/P_{ch}, i_d, T/Y, u) \tag{4.15}$$

where u embraces all influences on C_p not separately specified.

The banks' reserve ratio
In the simple deposit creation example outlined above, there is an implicit assumption that banks are always fully loaned up. That is, banks will always expand their assets and liabilities to the limit allowed by the increase in cash reserves and the required cash ratio. We now consider one possible reason why the banks in fact

may not always operate with a reserve ratio at the absolute minimum considered necessary to meet the cash demands of customers and possible indebtedness at the clearing house. Banks will maximize their profits when the marginal rate of return on each of the assets they hold is the same. The holding of assets will involve varying degrees of risk, so that the relevant marginal rates of return are those that have been adjusted for risk. If then, the rate of interest on loans and securities rises, (i_L), the risk-adjusted marginal rate of return from such assets increases and banks will be induced to make a marginal movement out of cash and into loans and securities, thereby lowering their cash to deposits ratio. If, on the other hand, the interest to be earned on loans and securities falls, then given the risk attached to holding them, their attractiveness is reduced and there will be a marginal movement out of such assets, thereby raising the cash-to-deposits ratio.

However, it is possible that the banks' desired cash/deposits ratio may be directly related to the rate of interest. A comparison may be drawn between the banks' demand for cash and the demand of non-bank institutions for money. In our discussion of Tobin's risk-aversion theory of liquidity preference we saw that strong income effects might induce some institutions to 'reach for income' in times of generally reduced yields: the same might be true of banks who may prefer to operate with an above minimum cash reserve ratio when interest rates are high, but depress it to the minimum so as to maintain their income when yields are low. However those who argue that the reserve ratio of the banks is variable, usually assert that it is inversely related to the rate of interest on loans and securities. This is illustrated graphically in *Figure 4.1* where 'the' rate of interest on primary securities (loans and investments of the bank) is measured along the vertical axis and the quantity of deposits along the horizontal. The supply curve of bank

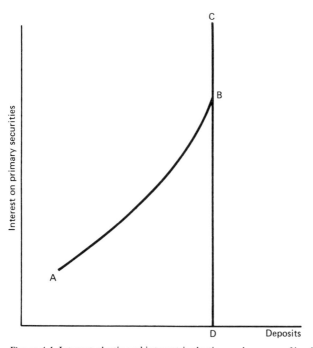

Figure 4.1 Interest-elastic and interest-inelastic supply curves of bank deposits

deposits (ABC) then slopes upwards from left to right as higher interest rates induce the banks to depress their cash reserve ratios and expand their loans and investments. On the assumption that there is some absolute minimum reserve ratio that the banks must observe as a matter of prudence (r^*), then the supply curve would eventually become vertical. The curve is drawn on the assumption of a given level of cash reserves in the banks. An increase in the banks' reserve base would be expected to move the supply curve to the right, with banks making a greater volume of loans and investments at given rates of interest. In contrast, the curve labelled DBC in *Figure 4.1* shows the traditional, 'fully loaned-up' approach, where the interest rate on primary securities has no effect on the banks' cash reserve ratio and consequently the supply curve of deposits is vertical at a quantity of deposits determined by the banks reserves and its fixed reserve ratio.

The banks reserve ratio may therefore be written

$$r = f(r^*, i_L) \tag{4.16}$$

Substituting equation (4.15) and equation (4.16) into equation (4.13) gives

$$M = \left(\frac{1 + c(Y/P, P_{cu}/P_{ch}, i_d, T/Y, u)}{r(r^*, i_L) + c(Y/P, P_{cu}/P_{ch}, i_d, T/Y, u)} \right) B \tag{4.17}$$

Clearly this is a more elaborate version of the monetary base model and represents a loosening of the relationship between the money supply and the monetary base. It acknowledges that the behaviour of the banks and the public as well as the actions of the authorities have a part to play in the determination of the money stock.

According to this more elaborate version of the money supply multiplier approach, the ability of the monetary authorities to control the money supply depends upon the stability and predictability of the two cash ratios. If the ratios and hence the money supply multiplier are reasonably stable, as assumed by the supporters of this approach, then there will be a strong link between the money supply and the monetary base. Under these circumstances the monetary authorities will be able to control the money supply by varying the monetary base. Any variations in the ratios could be predicted and offset by appropriate action on the monetary base. What then is the empirical evidence on the stability of these two ratios?

Empirical evidence
The c ratio has large seasonal variations, though they are prevented from effecting the banks reserves by the authorities taking offsetting action on the monetary base. Studies of the longer run stability of the ratio also indicates some variability. Crouch (1967) found several instances during the period 1945–65 when changes in the currency ratio more than offset changes in the monetary base. For example, during the UK monetary contraction of 1954–6, the increase in the monetary base would, *ceteris paribus*, have led to a 6½% expansion in the money supply; however the currency ratio changed to such an extent that the money supply decreased by 1.36%. Crouch concludes that the authorities ignore the c ratio 'at their peril'. Sheppard (1971) looking at data for a longer period (1880–1962) found that the c ratio varied between 0.3 and 0.14, but only between 0.16 and 0.21 in the post Second World War data period.

Empirical evidence on the stability of the *r* ratio is somewhat inconclusive. Sheppard (1971), looking at the period 1881–1962, found that it varied between 0.06 and 0.17, though in the post Second World War period it remained much more stable around the 0.08 level. Crouch also found that the ratio remained very stable during the 1950s and early 1960s, and argued that clearing banks have no reason to hold reserves over and above what they are required to hold, because liquid assets are virtually riskless, cheap to move into and out of, and therefore preferable to hold even at low rates of interest, compared with cash.

In addition to testing for the stability of the *c* and *r* ratios that enter into the money supply multiplier, some studies have sought directly to test for the stability of the money supply multiplier itself. As we have already indicated Crouch found several examples of short-run instability in the relationship between changes in the base and changes in the money supply, but over his whole data period changes in bank reserves were capable of explaining most of the fluctuations in bank deposits. Sheppard found that for the period 1881–1962 approximately 92% of changes in the money stock could be explained by changes in high powered money. Black (1975), looking at data for the 1960s, also found that changes in the monetary base dominated changes in the total money supply.

The tentative conclusion that seems to emerge from these studies is that there is significant short-run instability in the relationship between the monetary base and the money supply (probably due more to the variability of the publics currency ratio than to the variability of the bank's cash reserve ratio), but that over the longer run changes in the monetary base dominate changes in the total money stock.

The determinants and controllability of the monetary base

In order to assess the ability of the authorities to control the monetary base we must set out the factors determining the size of that base. These determinants can be ascertained from an examination of the public sector budget constraint which shows how public sector borrowing is financed. Essentially, if this borrowing requirement is not financed by sales of government debt to non-banks or by sales of foreign exchange reserves, it has to be financed by borrowing from the banking system, a procedure which can result in an increase in the monetary base. The banking system acts, in effect, as a residual source of public sector finance.

The budget financing constraint can be written as

$$\text{PSBR} + \text{MAT} = \text{MGD} + \text{NMGD} + \text{FE} + \Delta\text{B}$$

The public sector borrowing requirement (PSBR), and the additional finance required to repay maturing debt (MAT), represent the borrowing requirement of the public sector. This requirement is met by sales of marketable government debt (MGD), sales of non-marketable government debt (NMGD), sales of foreign exchange reserves (FE), and monetary base expansion (ΔB).

This expression can be re-arranged to show the sources of change in the monetary base

$$\Delta\text{B} = (\text{PSBR} + \text{MAT}) - (\text{MGD} + \text{NMGD}) - \text{FE}$$

This shows that there are a number of important factors which influence the size of the monetary base. To what extent the authorities can effectively control the monetary base depends, therefore, on their degree of control of these individual influences.

PSBR

The public sector borrowing requirement is the borrowing requirement resulting from any excess of public sector spending (including loans) over current revenue (mainly taxation). Changes in government spending and taxation are normally associated with fiscal policy and, certainly in the past, the monetary implications of fiscal policy were of secondary consideration compared with fiscal policy objectives. In recent years, however, with the adoption in the UK of money supply targets, far more attention has been paid by the authorities to the monetary implications of the PSBR, and changes have been made in the PSBR (for example, by cutting public sector spending) for monetary control reasons. In principle, therefore, the authorities can alter the PSBR to influence the monetary base. The borrowing requirement, however, is subject to substantial short-term variations which cannot be easily predicted and, therefore, it is not feasible to vary the PSBR to maintain short-run control of the monetary base.

MAT

The amount of government debt maturing at any particular time depends, of course, on sales of debt in previous years and is not therefore under the immediate control of the monetary authorities. This is a particular problem in the UK because of both the size of the national debt and the rapid expansion in public borrowing in the 1970s.

MGD

The financing requirement arising from the PSBR and maturing securities is largely met by sales of marketable government debt to the private sector. If the authorities were not concerned about the monetary implications, the borrowing requirement could in principle be financed by borrowing from the Bank of England. If the Bank purchases securities issued by the government this increases the government's deposits at the Bank which can then be used by the government to finance its spending. This is the modern equivalent of 'printing money' to finance government spending. If, however, the authorities wish to avoid 'printing money', then government securities must be sold on the open market to the private sector.

Suppose, for example, the authorities sell longer-term debt (government bonds) to the non-bank private sector. The buyers (typically financial institutions such as insurance companies) will pay for the securities by means of cheques drawn on their bank accounts, and made payable to the Bank of England. This will result in a fall in the buyer's bank deposits and a transfer of funds from the bank's balances to the government's account at the Bank. Thus open-market sales of government bonds to the non-bank private sector will reduce bank deposits and the banks cash reserves.

The amount of bonds the authorities can sell depends, of course, on the demand for them, which will depend, *inter alia*, on the yield offered, which varies inversely with the price of bonds and expectations about the level of future rates. In order therefore to persuade potential purchasers to buy more bonds, the price of the bonds must be lowered and therefore interest rates would have to increase. Thus, if the authorities want to sell a given quantity of bonds, they will have to accept the level of interest rates dictated by the market's demand for bonds. In other words the authorities can determine either the quantity of bonds sold or the level of interest rates, but not both. In practice, there may not always be such a stable relationship between the price of bonds and demand, and the market could on occasions be determined by unstable speculation which would considerably complicate open-market operations by the authorities.

NMGD

The borrowing requirement is also met by tapping the savings of the personal sector by issuing non-market debt such as national savings certificates. The demand for these securities depends on the rate of return offered. In recent years, these rates have been increased from time to time to make them more attractive.

The rate of return on these securities are however unlikely to vary as freely as interest rates on marketable debt and therefore it's not feasible to obtain close control of this influence on the monetary base.

FE

The influence of foreign exchange on the monetary base depends crucially on the authorities exchange rate policy. In the absence of official operations in the foreign exchange market, the sterling exchange rate will be determined by the forces of supply and demand for sterling. The demand for sterling essentially arises from foreign residents demand for UK exports and assets, and the supply of sterling from UK residents wishing to exchange sterling for foreign currencies with which to purchase imports and foreign assets.

If there is an excess of sterling on the market arising from, say, an excess of imports over exports, in the absence of official intervention the sterling exchange rate would depreciate. Suppose the authorities now intervene in the market in order to prevent the fall in the exchange rate. This could be achieved by selling foreign exchange from the official foreign exchange reserves and purchasing the excess surplus of sterling, which represents an additional source of sterling to finance the borrowing requirement. This is sometimes referred to as 'external financing of the public sector', and would tend to reduce the size of the monetary base.

If there were an excess demand for sterling and the authorities wished to prevent an appreciation of the exchange rate, they would sell sterling and purchase foreign exchange on the market and this would tend to expand the monetary base. The authorities could attempt to 'sterilize' or 'neutralize' this impact on the monetary base by sales of debt to the private sector. However, as explained above, in order to sell more securities, interest rates would have to increase and, if international capital flows are sensitive to interest rate changes, this will attract capital inflows, increasing the demand for sterling and necessitating further sales of sterling by the authorities and therefore increasing the expansive pressure on the monetary base.

This could result in a vicious circle of increased demand for sterling, higher interest rates, further sales of sterling, upward pressures on the monetary base, more sales of securities, higher interest rates and so on. It would seem therefore that such sterilization operations would be largely self-defeating.

Thus, if the authorities aim to stabilize the rate of exchange, the monetary base will be affected by balance of payments flows which are largely outside the control of the authorities. If, however, there is no official intervention to influence the exchange rate, balance of payments flows will have no effect on the monetary base. It is not possible, therefore, for the authorities to control both the monetary base (and hence the money supply) and the rate of exchange.

It would seem clear from the above analysis that the assumption in the monetary base model, that the monetary base is exogenously determined by the authorities, is an oversimplification of reality. A more comprehensive and realistic model of money supply determination should ideally incorporate the main determinants of the monetary base which the authorities have to take into account in order to control the money supply. As Goodhart (1973, p. 246) points out,

fluctuations in certain elements, which affect the level of [the monetary base], for example foreign exchange inflows and government budget deficits, have in the UK during recent years at least posed a far more difficult problem for the monetary authorities in trying to achieve their objectives than have the variations in the reserve ratios or the currency/deposit ratios.

This is not to say, however, that the authorities cannot control the monetary base should they wish so to do. In principle, if the authorities allow interest rates and the exchange rate to be determined by market forces, then the monetary base can be controlled. Control would, however, be considerably complicated by the existence of a large PSBR and the consequent need to sell large quantities of debt instruments.

It is also clear from the examination of the monetary base determinants that the monetary base is functionally related to market interest rates. Given that the two ratios in the monetary base model are also likely to be functions of interest rates it would appear that the three determinants of the money supply in the model are interdependent. Any attempt therefore by the authorities to offset variations in the two ratios by changing the monetary base, in order to achieve a desired level of money supply, are likely to cause further variations in the ratios. Considerable 'slippage' therefore exists between the money supply and monetary base, and this calls into question the usefulness of this model of money supply determination.

The new view and the portfolio approach to money supply determination

In the simple monetary base model, the behaviour of the banks and the public is represented by the cash ratios in the money supply multiplier formula. The stock of money is taken as being determined only by the size of the money supply multiplier and the exogenously determined monetary base. Consequently the approach has been criticized as being a far too simplistic and misleading account of the money supply determination process. In particular, it is argued that such an approach obscures the major role of the private sector in the determination of the money supply. For example, Goodhart (1973, pp. 248–9) argues that the monetary base multiplier approach

often leads pedagogues to explain changes in the quantity of money in terms of a mechanical multiplier, in which high-powered money gets passed from hand to hand like a hot potato. The portfolio adjustments of the banks in this description apparently play no role in this process, except in so far as they may seek to alter their reserve ratios. The public's asset preferences are seemingly irrelevant to the determination of the stock of money except in so far as they seek to alter their cash/deposit ratios.

The major alternative to the monetary base model is the so-called portfolio approach. This is based on the view that 'the determination of the money stock involves a process of general portfolio adjustment in response to relative interest rate changes.' (Goodhart 1973, p. 264).

This portfolio adjustment approach stems from the neo-Keynesian 'New View' of money, banks and other financial intermediaries which was initiated in the early 1960s. The 'new view' blurs the sharp distinction traditionally made between money and other assets and between commerical banks and other financial institutions. All financial institutions have liabilities which are differentiated in some way or other from those of the other institutions: banks are not unique in this respect. Conseqeuntly there is a wide range of institutions which compete with one another for the acquisition of primary securities and the issue of indirect ones. Such competition is partly reflected in the price of primary securities (e.g. rates of interest charged on loans) and in the interest offered on indirect securities. All financial institutions are regarded as engaging in portfolio adjustments so as to maximize their utility functions, subject to any constraints that may apply to them (e.g. authority imposed reserve requirements). Thus in considering the money supply Tobin argues

> there is more to the determination of the volume of bank deposits than the arithmetic of reserve supplies and reserve ratios. The redundant reserves of the thirties are a dramatic reminder that economic opportunities sometimes prevail over reserve calculations. The significance of that experience is not correctly appreciated if it is regarded simply as an aberration from a normal state of affairs in which banks are fully loaned up, and total deposits are tightly linked to the volume of reserves. The thirties exemplify in extreme form a phenonenon which is always in some degree present. The use to which the commercial banks put the reserves available to the system is an economic variable depending on lending opportunites and interest rates (1963, p. 416).

Banks, along with other financial institutions, are constantly having to compare the marginal cost of acquiring additional reserves against the marginal revenue of making additional loans and investments. Moreover the marginal cost and marginal revenue schedules that they face reflect the preferences and portfolio decisions of ultimate lenders and spenders. We have already noted that the public's demand for currency relative to bank deposits will probably be affected by the rate of interest on bank deposits. In other words the willingness of the public to supply the banks with cash reserves is directly related to the rate of interest paid on bank deposits. The demand for bank deposits is also likely to be related to the price of primary securities. If the banks are to increase the money supply, then they must purchase more primary securities from the non-bank public. Some of these securities will already be in existence; others will be newly created. The non-bank public are of course doing the reverse of the banks: they are selling primary securities in return for the indirect debt of the banks – bank deposits. Their willingness to sell securities to the banks, which is the same as their demand for bank deposits, will depend on the price of the primary securities. Thus the lower the rate of interest on bank credit, the more willing will the public be to borrow from the banks. Thus it seems likely that the demand for bank deposits will be directly related to the price of primary securities. The position of the demand curve at any given rate of interest on bank loans and investments will depend upon a number of other factors. The new view particularly emphasizes the importance of competition from other financial intermediaries. Thus a deficit spender may have the opportunity of borrowing from a wide range of potential lenders. If the rate of interest at which loans can be obtained from non-bank lenders falls, then the demand for loans from such institutions is likely to rise, while the demand for loans from banks is likely to fall. Again the position of the demand curve will depend upon the economic climate. A period of general prosperity with business keen to expand and consumers keen to spend in anticipation of rising incomes is likely to mean a high demand for bank loans.

These ideas are illustrated in *Figure 4.2*. The supply curve of deposits is shown as a direct function of the rate of interest on loans and investments, with the position and slope of the curve reflecting the costs of attracting reserves. The demand curve is an inverse function of the same interest rates. The quantity of deposits will be

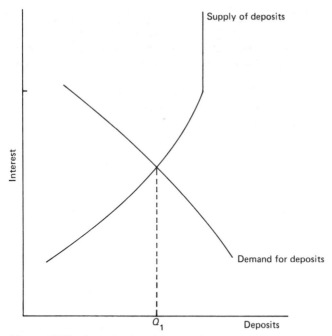

Supply of deposits

Interest

Demand for deposits

Q_1 Deposits

Figure 4.2 The determination of the quantity of deposits

determined by the intersection of the two curves, and will therefore be Q_1. To expand deposits beyond Q_1, the banks would have to persuade the public to borrow more from them or sell them securities. But they would only do this if they were prepared to lower the interest they were charging on loans and the interest they were earning on their investments (i.e. to pay higher prices for primary securities). But this would mean that 'the marginal returns on lending and investing, account taken of the risks and administrative costs involved, will not exceed the marginal cost to the banks of attracting and holding additional deposits' (Tobin 1963, p. 414). Thus according to the 'new view', a complete theory of the money supply determination process must start from the point that: Marshall's scissors of supply and demand apply to the output of the banking industry no less than to other financial and non-financial industries' (Tobin 1963, p. 418).

The portfolio approach, which has developed out of these ideas, views the money supply as essentially an endogenous variable reflecting the portfolio behaviour and the objectives of the banks and other economic agents in the private sector. To provide an adequate behavioural theory of money supply determination it is necessary, according to this approach, to set out a detailed structural model of the monetary system, incorporating behavioural equations showing how banks and the rest of the private sector allocate their wealth portfolios among various assets in response to changes in relative interest rates (see, for example, Tobin 1969b).

It would be beyond the scope of this book to attempt to set out a fully specified structural model of sufficient size to do justice to this approach. We will attempt, however, following Goodhart (1973), to illustrate the flavour of this approach by setting out a highly simplistic (closed economy) model of private sector portfolio adjustment, distinguishing between the banking sector and the non-bank private sector.

The portfolio preferences of the two sectors are represented in the model by their respective balance sheet constraints and behavioural equations showing how total funds available for each sector are distributed among various assets in response to relative rates of return on the assets (for an assumed given level of risk associated with each asset).

Abstracting from real expenditure decisions, we will assume that the non-bank private sector's net financial wealth (W) is distributed among three assets, currency (C_p), government securities (S_p), bank deposits (D), and one liability, bank loans (L). This sector's balance sheet constraint is therefore,

$$W = C_p + S_p + D - L$$

Asset demands are assumed to be a function of relative rates of return on available assets and the sector's net financial wealth.

$$C_p = C_p \overset{- \quad - \quad - \quad +}{(i_S, \; i_D, \; i_L, \; W)} \tag{4.19}$$

$$S_p = S_p \overset{+ \quad - \quad - \quad +}{(i_S, \; i_D, \; i_L, \; W)} \tag{4.20}$$

$$D = D \overset{- \quad + \quad - \quad +}{(i_S, \; i_D, \; i_L, \; W)} \tag{4.21}$$

$$L = L \overset{+ \quad + \quad - \quad +}{(i_S, \; i_D, \; i_L, \; W)} \tag{4.22}$$

Where i_S and i_D are the rates of return on government securities and deposits respectively, and i_L the rate charged on bank loans. The signs above the variables show the direction of their effects on asset demands.

The set of behavioural equations for the non-bank private sector illustrate an important feature of the portfolio approach – that the asset markets are interrelated; that is, it is not possible to consider the demand for any particular asset in isolation from other assets or debts. A change in demand for an asset must result in adjustment of the demand for the remaining assets since the sector is constrained by its balance sheet identity. Thus a change in an asset rate of return will cause a substitution between all the assets in the sector's portfolio and will of course have repercussions for the portfolio choice of the other sectors.

Ignoring non-deposit liabilities (bank equity), the banking sector's balance sheet constraint is shown as

$$D = R + S_b + L \tag{4.23}$$

where R = bank cash reserves, S_b = banks' holdings of government securities, and L = bank loans.

In the non-bank private sector, economic agents are assumed to be price-takers, allocating their wealth across a portfolio of assets according to the market-determined relative rates of return. However, because of the oligopolistic nature of the UK banking system, banks are in a position to act as 'price-setters' with regard to their deposit and loan rates. For example, the abolition of the banks' interest rate cartel in 1971 considerably increased the practice of 'liability management' whereby banks actively bid for funds to finance their lending. We need therefore to incorporate this important rate setting feature of bank behaviour in the model.

There will be, in practice, a number of factors taken into account by the banks in their rate setting decisions, including, for example, the competitive nature of the market, the banks' liquidity and capital position, and expected loan demand. In the interests of simplicity we will assume that deposit and loan rates will depend primarily on the returns on the assets held by the banks and their cash reserve positions.

$$i_D = i_D \overset{+}{(}i_L, \overset{+}{i_S}, \overset{-}{R})$$ (4.24)

$$i_L = i_L \overset{+}{(}i_D, \overset{+}{i_S}, \overset{-}{R})$$ (4.25)

The rate offered on deposits is included in the loan rate function on the assumption that banks are likely to take into account the cost of obtaining funds in their loan rate setting decisions.[3] With this 'administered rate' feature built into the model, banks can compete for additional reserves in order to meet loan demand, until constrained by profit-maximizing considerations (i.e. where the marginal cost of attracting additional funds equals the marginal revenue from additional loans).

With the loan and deposit rates set by the banks, deposits and loans will be determined by the portfolio behaviour of the non-bank private sector (equations 4.19–4.22). The banks' demand for the remaining assets in their portfolio (securities and cash reserves) are taken to be a function of the relative rates of return on assets held and total funds available.

$$S_b = S_b \overset{+}{(}i_S, \overset{-}{i_L}, \overset{+}{D})$$ (4.26)

$$R = R \overset{-}{(}i_S, \overset{-}{i_L}, \overset{+}{D})$$ (4.27)

Thus in the model, bank deposits (the main component of course of the money stock) are an endogenous quantity determined along with other variables in the model, by the interaction of the portfolio preferences of the banking and non-banking sectors. Having sketched out a simplified model of private sector portfolio behaviour, we can now examine the effects of monetary policy intervention by the authorities. For the purposes of this exercise we will assume that the authorities' monetary policy actions take the form of open-market sales of securities. The authorities could in principle set the price of securities at a sufficiently attractive level (i.e. raise i_S) and supply the resultant demand, or alternatively, increase the supply, allowing the return to vary in accordance with market demand. In practice the effect of these alternative approaches will depend, *inter alia*, on the stability of the securities market in a world of uncertainty about further possible capital gains or losses. We will, however, ignore these complications and assume that open-market sales cause private sector portfolio adjustments, with the non-bank private sector substituting securities for deposits, thus putting pressure on the banks' cash reserves.

In the simple money supply multiplier-type models, a fall in cash reserves will result in a multiple reduction in loans and deposits. In practice however, banks, with extensive loan commitments, are unlikely to react in this way. Instead, as suggested by the portfolio model, they will respond to an outflow of reserves by engaging in liability management, bidding for additional reserves by increasing the rate paid on deposits. In addition to this measure, banks can also rebuild reserves by selling securities from their asset portfolios. As suggested by the loan rate setting equation (4.25), both of these responses by the banks to reserve outflows will cause the banks to increase the loan rate (to maintain profitability). With the banks selling securities, putting further upward pressures on i_S, there is likely to be additional substitution of securities for deposits by the non-bank private sector, which will in turn put further pressure on the banks' cash reserve position. Banks can respond to this by bidding for more deposits, putting more upward pressure on the loan rate. Given that the banks can counter attempts to reduce their reserves by bidding for more deposits, the ultimate effect of open-market sales on the banks' liabilities and loans will depend on the repercussions of loan demand to the cost of loans (i.e. the interest elasticity of loan demand). The more interest inelastic the demand for loans, the less the impact on deposits and loans for a given open-market intervention by the authorities.

Although we have not spelt out in this simple illustrative model an explicit utility-maximizing function for the banks, the underlying behavioural assumption is that bank behaviour is characterized by profit-maximization. Banks may, however, on occasions, have different short-term objectives, depending on the nature of the market. They may be more interested, for example, in preserving their share of the loan market and may in consequence be reluctant to pass on fully to bank borrowers, through an increased loan rate, the cost of obtaining additional funds. In other words, banks may be willing to take a loss on marginal loan business to preserve market shares, particularly as, in practice, a large component of their liabilities are non-interest bearing deposits (current accounts) and banks can therefore obtain 'endownment profits' when the returns are rising on their earning assets. It therefore follows that the effect of monetary policy actions on money creation is likely to depend on the exact nature of the utility-maximizing behaviour of the banks.

Although highly simplistic, the above model of the monetary system does serve to illustrate the real world complexities of the money supply determination process and suggests, at least to the followers of the portfolio approach to money supply determination, that an adequate money supply theory requires a detailed structural model setting out the asset-choice behaviour and objectives of the banks and the non-bank private sector. There are, however, considerable technical problems in the construction and estimation of a model of sufficient size to approximate a real world financial system. Such a model would contain a large number of behavioural equations, some of which may exhibit non-linear properties which would add to the estimation difficulties. Further considerable estimation problems would arise if the structure of the financial system to be modelled changed overtime. This could occur, for example, if (as mentioned above) banking objectives changed or if private sector behaviour was influenced and altered by policy intervention.

Given these formidable problems, the followers of the multiplier approach would suggest that one might just as well use the simple monetary base model, which has the virtue of being able to explain money supply changes in terms of only three determinants. This simplicity, however, is obtained at the cost of considerable loss of information about the portfolio adjustments involved in the money creation process in the real world. However, as we have shown above, the simple monetary base model can be extended to incorporate some behavioural content, although at the risk of the loss of simplicity of the simple version.

It can be argued that which approach is to be preferred depends on the particular problems being investigated. For example, the simple monetary base model may be useful if the intention is just to predict changes in the money supply for a given change in the monetary base. On the other hand, the more general structural model would be essential when the aim is to explain the channels that link monetary policy actions and money creation. Following this argument the two approaches can therefore be considered not as mutually exclusive but as being complementary; the monetary base model shows the *result* of policy changes on the money stock. The structural approach explains *how* policy actions influence money creation.

In the context of the UK economy, however, the main weakness of the monetary base model is the assumption that the monetary base is an exogenously determined variable controlled by the authorities. Given that in the UK (in common with many other countries) the authorities do not attempt to control directly the monetary base, this assumption is clearly invalid and therefore the monetary base model does not provide an accurate description of the money supply determination process in the UK. Certainly the UK monetary authorities favour the more general structural approach and the Treasury has recently developed an operational large-scale portfolio model of the monetary system to evaluate the money supply determination process (Spencer and Mowl 1978).

Non-bank financial intermediaries

The period since the end of the Second World War has seen a considerable growth in the size of the non-bank financial intermediaries, both absolutely and relatively to the commercial banks. Accompanying this growth of the NBFIs there has been considerable debate over the significance of these intermediaries in the financial system, and the extent to which they are capable of offsetting a restrictive monetary policy.

Let us begin our discussion of these controversies by taking a closer look at the extent to which, and the way in which, these non-bank intermediaries create credit. What do we mean by the term 'create credit'? While it is easy to think of specific examples of credit and of institutions that provide it, it is not so easy to provide a general definition. For example, some shops provide credit when they allow customers to buy goods, payment for which will be made later. Similarly, hire-purchase finance houses provide credit when they enable consumer-durable goods to be bought on hire-purchase. Firms may provide credit to one another by means of trade credit, while banks and other financial institutions provide credit when they make loans.

In all of these cases, purchases are made for which the purchaser does not pay out of his own income or wealth until later. The purchase is paid for either by persuading the seller to wait for payment (in which case we can regard the buyer as 'borrowing' the purchase price from the seller), or by borrowing from a third party (e.g. a bank). In general we may say that an economic unit provides credit whenever it enables a deficit spender to purchase goods or services in excess of their current income. We use the term 'provide credit' advisedly, because we now wish to distinguish between the 'creation' and the 'transmission' of credit. We would regard an economic unit as creating credit when it adds to the total flow of credit available, while we would regard an economic unit as transmitting credit when it simply 'passes on' credit – when it acts as a pure intermediary in the transmission of credit from one economic unit to another. For example, if firm A receives trade credit from a supplier of materials, firm B, and as a result is then able to give credit of an equivalent amount to its own customers, then A has added nothing to the total flow of credit. It has simply 'passed on' the credit that had been given to it. To add the credit given by A to C to the credit received by A from B would be double-counting.

Commercial banks are regarded as creating credit because the credit they provide takes the form of loans, which are in money created by the banks themselves. The banks, because of their ability to create money, are able to create the commodity which they lend out. The banks are collectively able to lend out more than has been loaned to them. In one sense, of course, not even the banks can create credit in as far as they create something out of nothing. Unless cash is first deposited with banks they are unable to have any deposits at all. But once currency has been deposited with them, the banks are able, within limits, to expand deposits by making appropriate book entries. In so doing the banks are adding to the total supply of credit.

But what of non-bank financial intermediaries? Do they create credit or merely transmit it from ultimate lenders to ultimate borrowers? Clearly they would be able to create credit if, like the banks, their own indirect securities were regarded as money, for then again like the banks, they would be able, within limits, to 'write up' their liabilities. We have already seen in Chapter 1 that the indirect securities of some non-bank financial intermediaries do circulate to a limited extent as a means of payment but, as of yet, not to a sufficient degree to enable these institutions to be regarded as creators of money. Thus when they make loans to deficit spenders these NBFIs cannot make them in the form of claims upon themselves, but only in the form of currency or claims upon a bank account. Thus it is often said that the non-bank intermediaries act as dealers in the commodity (money) which has been produced by the banking system. Thus these intermediaries cannot create credit by adding to the total stock of the means of payment in the economy. They can only lend out the money that others have previously loaned to them.

Whether they are able to create credit simply by lending out what others have loaned to them depends on what use the money loaned to them would otherwise have been put to. Clearly there are four possibilities: (i) the money could have been left idle; (ii) it could have been actively used to purchase goods and services; (iii) it could have been held in public sector debt; or (iv) it could have been lent out to some other person or institution. Taking this last possibility first, it should be fairly obvious that by attracting such funds the intermediary is having no effect on the total size of the flow of credit, but only on the directions in which it is flowing. Suppose, for example, that an ultimate saver/lender was going to put £100 of his current savings into the purchase of newly issued ordinary shares in a manufacturing company, but as a result of an increase in the rate of interest on building society deposits decides instead to put the £100 into a building society. The building society in turn will lend out most of the £100 (some being kept back as reserves) to potential house purchasers. Thus £100 less has flowed to manufacturing while nearly £100 more has flowed into housebuilding. The total savings and credit has not changed but the distribution has.

However, when the financial intermediaries attract funds that would otherwise have been idle or would have been used to purchase goods and services or held in public sector debt, they can alter the total flow of credit. Again suppose that an individual A, has a deposit account with a commercial bank which he regards as a savings account and consequently leaves idle. Now building society interest rates rise and our individual is persuaded to transfer £100 from his idle deposit account at a clearing bank to a deposit with a building society. The building society will open a deposit account for the customer and credit it with the £100, and put the £100 received into its own commercial bank current account. Thus the building society's total assets (via money at the bank) and liabilities (via deposits) have increased by the same absolute amount. As for the banking system, nothing has happened in total, but there has been a redistribution in ownership of deposits. Individual A now has £100 less in his deposit account with the banking system while the building society has £100 more in its current account. Clearly the total of bank deposits is unchanged. As long as the banks observe the same reserve ratios for current and deposit accounts there is no need for them to react at all to this redistribution of total deposit liabilities. The totals of bank deposits and bank lending are unchanged. But the building society has got an extra £100, most of which they will proceed to lend out to potential house purchasers. In so doing they will be adding to the total supply of credit, because their increased lending is not offset by reduced lending anywhere else. The same would apply, of course, if the idle funds attracted into the non-bank financial intermediaries were funds that would have been kept under a mattress, up a chimney or at the bottom of a garden. As long as they would not otherwise have been lent elsewhere but kept idle, then the reactivating of such balances by the NBFIs will add to the total flow of credit.

In similar vein, if the intermediaries succeed in attracting to themselves funds that would otherwise have been used to purchase goods and services, then they have increased the total amount of saving in the economy and by making it available to ultimate borrowers they have added to the total flow of credit.

Finally if the intermediaries attract funds that would otherwise have been held in public sector debt, then there will be an increased flow of credit to the private sector.

Thus it can be argued that NBFIs can add to the total flow of credit in the economy if they are able to activate idle money balances, or to persuade some economic units to economize on their active money balances and to become, or increase the extent to which they are already, ultimate savers/lenders.

There are, however, important distinctions between these channels by which NBFIs can increase the total flow of credit. If they do it by activating previously idle money balances, then what they are doing is increasing the velocity of circulation of the given money stock. In so doing not only are they adding to the total flow of credit, but they are also adding to the total flow of expenditure as well. Again, if the intermediaries attract funds that would otherwise have gone in loans to the public sector, then the Exchequer will have to increase its residual borrowing through the banking system and thereby increase the volume of bank deposits. However, if the intermediaries simply persuade some economic units to economize on active money balances, then they will have no effect on the velocity of circulation of the total money stock and no effect on the total flow of expenditure.

These distinctions are important in discussing the extent to which NBFIs are capable of engaging in a multiple expansion of credit. If the NBFIs have added to the total flow of expenditure, they will increase the level of incomes. These additional incomes will of course, generate additional savings, some of which will be placed with the NBFIs. This will then enable the NBFIs to engage in a second round of credit creation, which will give a further impetus to expenditure, incomes and savings. There will then follow a third round of credit creation and so on until the sums involved become so small as to be of no consequence. In this sense the NBFIs can be said to have engaged in a process of multiple creation similar in some respects to the multiple expansion of deposits generated by the banking system.

However, if the NBFIs create credit by persuading people to economize on active money balances and to save more, then they will not generate any additional expenditure, or income, or savings, and will be incapable of generating a multiple expansion of credit.

If we compare the multiple creation of credit by NBFIs with that by commercial banks some significant differences in the two processes appear. For example, the multiplier process of the NBFIs is subject to much bigger leakages than that of the banks. The expansion of credit by the NBFIs relies on some of the additional savings that result from the additional income being placed with themselves. If none of the additional savings were placed with NBFIs then clearly the expansionary process in which the NBFIs engaged would end after the first round. The bigger the proportion of the additional savings placed with the NBFIs, the bigger the total expansion of credit in which they play a part. In practice this proportion is likely to be quite small, most of the additional savings flowing into other channels. With the bank multiplier process, however, the leakages in each round are likely to be quite small, being in fact the loss of cash to the public as deposits expand. Thus the size of the bank credit multiplier is likely to be much bigger than that of the NBFI credit multiplier.

The time periods involved in the multiplier processes may also be different. As far as the banks are concerned the time interval involved in each round of expansion depends upon the characteristics of the payments mechanism which determines what W. L. Smith (1959) calls the 'payment-turnover' period. This is the 'average time that elapses between the receipt of excess reserves by one bank and the receipt by other banks of that portion of the excess reserves that is transmitted to them as a result of the first bank's lending'. This period may well be only a matter of days.

With the NBFIs, however, each round in the expansionary process depends on what Smith calls the 'income-turnover' period, which is 'the average period that elapses between successive receipts of income in the income expenditure process'. This time period is likely to be much longer than that for the bank multiplier.

So far in this section we have suggested that NBFIs are not able to create money but are able to influence its velocity of circulation. However, in our earlier discussion of the new views on money supply we suggested that the ability of the banks to create money was influenced by competition from NBFIs. In other words, while the NBFIs may not be able to create money themselves they may be in a positions to influence the amount of money created by the banks, as well as influencing its velocity of circulation.

Several routes have been suggested by which NBFIs can affect the volume of bank money. To begin with, we have already pointed out one way in which the activities of NBFIs can increase bank deposits. This was when their success in attracting funds that would otherwise have been held in public sector debt resulted in increased public sector borrowing from the banks. To the extent that the NBFIs themselves use their extra funds to acquire public sector debt, this effect will of course be prevented from occurring. Llewellyn (1979) has suggested two other ways by which the activities of NBFIs may lead to increased bank deposits: (i) where the demand for such deposits rises as a result of an NBFI induced increase in total credit and national income; and (ii) where the funds attracted by the NBFIs would otherwise have been held as notes and coins by people without bank accounts, so that when the increased loans of the intermediaries enter the banking system there will be an increase in bank deposits. We must now consider the ways in which the activities of NBFIs can reduce bank deposits. Suppose, for example, that NBFIs succeed in attracting deposits away from commercial banks. This, of course, will not initially reduce the total of commercial bank deposits because the NBFIs are themselves customers of the banks. Ownership of bank deposits changes but the total does not. If the funds newly deposited with the NBFIs would otherwise have been idle, the lending out of these funds by the NBFIs will lead to a multiple expansion of credit, expenditure and income. If this expansion of aggregate demand gives rise to inflationary pressures, then the authorities may be forced to intervene and to try to remove the inflationary pressure by reducing the volume of bank deposits. Thus the volume of bank deposits may be forced below what they would otherwise have been because of the expansionary process initiated by the NBFIs attracting idle deposits away from the banks. The links in this chain may be summarized thus:

$\uparrow$ in NBFI deposits $\rightarrow$ $\uparrow$ supply of credit $\rightarrow$ $\uparrow$ aggregate demand $\rightarrow$ inflationary pressure $\rightarrow$ official measures to reduce bank lending and volume of bank deposits

A second possible mechanism runs along the following lines. Suppose again that the NBFIs attract deposits away from the commerical banks and generate a multiple expansion of credit, income and expenditure. As income rises so do savings and, as we have seen, it is the placing of part of the additional savings with NBFIs that enables the NBFIs credit multiplier to proceed. But it is also likely that part of the additional savings will be placed in government debt. Having obtained more funds from the non-bank private sector, the authorities will now need to borrow less from the banks, leading to downward pressure on bank deposits. Thus the main links are:

$\uparrow$ in NBFI deposits $\rightarrow$ $\uparrow$ supply of credit $\rightarrow$ $\uparrow$ aggregate demand $\uparrow$ income and savings $\rightarrow$ $\uparrow$ non-bank purchases of government debt $\downarrow$ government borrowing from banks $\rightarrow$ $\downarrow$ volume of bank deposits

A third possible route we can mention is rather different from the first two. Assume NBFIs again attract deposits away from banks and proceed to lend these deposits out, initiating a multiple expansion of credit. It may be that somewhere in the expansionary process the circulating deposits come into the possession of people or institutions with bank overdrafts, which they repay with the newly acquired deposits. The repayment of bank loans will reduce the volume of bank deposits, but leave the banks with the power to restore them by making new loans or investments. But there may not be a fringe of unsatisfied borrowers at prevailing rates on bank loans, or willing sellers of securities at prevailing yields. Thus if the banks are to restore the volume of deposits by making new loans or new investments they may only be able to do so if they are prepared to lower the interest they charge on their loans and/or pay a higher price for their investments. And this, as we discussed earlier, they might not be prepared to do. According to this mechanism, then, the raising by the NBFIs of the velocity of circulation of the money stock has the consequence of reducing the size of that stock. In summary:

$\uparrow$ in NBFI deposits $\rightarrow$ $\downarrow$ stock of idle balances $\rightarrow$ $\uparrow$ velocity of circulation $\rightarrow$ repayment of bank loans $\rightarrow$ reduced bank deposits

A fourth possibility is that the NBFIs will use part of any new funds they acquire to invest in public sector debt. To the extent that they do, this will reduce the government's residual borrowing from the banks and in so doing reduce the level of bank deposits. In summary:

↑ in NBFI deposits → ↓ in NBFI purchases of public sector debt → ↓ in government borrowing from banks → ↓ bank deposits

So far in our discussion of NBFIs we have been concerned primarily with examining their influence on the supply of money and credit, and have given no attention to the demand to hold the indirect securities of the NBFIs or to the demand for NBFI credit. However, the response of 'demanders' is important when considering the ways in which the NBFIs may influence the effectiveness of monetary policy, assuming that the policy does not embrace the NBFIs themselves. One view is that the indirect securities and credit of NBFIs are substitutes for bank deposits and bank credit, and there is therefore competition between the banks and NBFIs to attract deposits and make loans. Policy which tries to reduce the volume of bank deposits and bank credit is then likely to lead to an increase in the demand for the indirect securities and credit of non-bank intermediaries, with the consequences for credit, income and expenditure that we have already discussed.

A different view is that the indirect securities of non-bank intermediaries are not close substitutes for bank money. Thus it is possible that when the authorities raise interest rates in an attempt to reduce the supply of money this does not increase the demand for non-bank deposits but reduces it. This would happen if people whose money balances had been depleted by the actions of the authorities tried to rebuild their balances by cashing some of their near-money holdings. In other words, there would be a fall in the demand for near-moneys which, if it were big enough, could more than offset the extension in the demand for such assets due to the higher rate of interest. In this case the reduced money supply would be accompanied by reduced and not increased holdings of near-moneys. It would appear then that there are still very different views held as to whether NBFIs can and do offset restrictive monetary policies. Certainly they have grown very considerably during the last two decades, and have developed facilities designed to bring them increasingly into competition with the banks. Evidence on whether NBFIs do frustrate monetary policy has been obtained using a number of methodological approaches, but remains inconclusive. At one extreme is the multi-sector disaggregated portfolio choice model (Clayton *et al*, 1974); at the other are those studies that test for the effect of NBFIs on the velocity of circulation of money, by conducting tests of the stability and elasticity of the demand for money. To the extent that there exists a stable money demand function, this implies there is a stable velocity, and is therefore evidence that NBFIs have not significantly frustrated monetary policy (see evidence in Chapter 3). In Chapter 1 we saw that an increasing range of NBFIs have had their deposits included in various measures of the money supply, while in Chapter 13 we shall consider some of the effects of NBFIs further in the context of post-war UK monetary policy.

Notes

1. Chick (1977) has pointed out that the use of the term exogenous in this context is unfortunate. In its technical sense, whether or not a variable is exogenous can be decided only by reference to a particular model. According to Chick (1977, p. 85):

The debate among monetary theorists, however, plainly is not about exogeneity in the technical sense, since no model is given. If one were specified, there could be no debate, it takes little technical expertise to identify exogenous variables in an explicit model. The debate is about how the money stock is determined in the real world, where the term exogenous is not defined.

2. A slightly different money multiplier formula can be derived by assuming that $C_p = cM$ rather than $C_p = cD$

The formula is $\dfrac{1}{r(1 - c) + c}$, so that

$$M = \frac{1}{r(1 - c) + c} B$$

3. Goodhart (1973, p. 265) points out (following Monti 1971) that the banks' portfolio asset choice depends on the relative yields on the assets and not on the deposit rate. However, since the rate offered on deposits represents the cost of obtaining funds to meet loan demand, the major component of the banks' asset portfolio, the rate charged on loans will need to reflect the deposit rate in order to maintain profitability. In the Treasury model of the monetary sector, for example, loan rate setting behaviour is modelled by a simple mark-up relationship with loan rates determined essentially by the cost of money market funds plus a mark-up factor (Spencer and Mowl 1978).

5

The classical system and the neutrality of money

In this chapter we shall set out the main features of the classical system and the role played within it by monetary variables, and then consider the meaning of, and conditions for, the neutrality of money. The 'classical system' cannot be attributed to the work of any one particular economist. It is in fact a synthetic summary of the various ideas and propositions formulated by a large group of economists from the middle of the eighteenth century to the 1930s.

We must now define what we mean by the 'role of money' as contained in the question 'does money matter'? Money matters if variations in the money stock exert a systematic effect upon macrovariables that economists feel are important for some reason or another. Broadly speaking there are two categories of macrovariables, 'real' and 'monetary'; the former comprises variables such as the level of output, employment, real wages and real rates of interest, while examples of the latter are money wages, prices and nominal interest rates. Some economists feel that the criterion by which money is viewed to be of importance is whether it is capable of influencing the real equilibrium profile of the economy or not. They argue that if variations in the money stock have no effect on the real system, then money is 'neutral' and 'money does not matter'. Other economists would argue that both monetary and real variables are of importance to policy-makers who have the responsibility of controlling the behaviour of both, e.g. high and stable levels of employment and reasonable price stability. On this interpretation, money could be said to matter if its behaviour were capable of influencing either real or monetary variables or both. It is this latter criterion that we shall be using in this chapter.

We can also distinguish between the proposition that 'money does or does not matter' and the proposition that 'monetary variables do or do not matter'. Although variations in the money stock may not be capable of exerting systematic effects upon key macrovariables, other monetary variables such as the 'structure of interest rates' or the 'availability of credit' may. An evaluation of the role and importance of money along these line will enable us to draw some conclusions about the effectiveness of monetary policy as an anti-depression, anti-inflation control device.

The classical system

We shall begin our construction of the classical system with one of its central pillars – Say's Law. This is a proposition which states that 'supply creates its own demand'. In a barter economy it is easy to see why this is the case. A person offering product(s) for barter (i.e. for sale) does so with the intention of exchanging those products for others which he desires. An offer to barter is contemporaneously and equivalently an addition to total demand. In a barter economy aggregate supply of goods and services is always equal to the aggregate demand for them. This is not to deny, however, the possibility of relative 'over-supplies' of some goods and services and 'under-supplies' of others. For example, suppliers of some goods might be unable to find suppliers of other goods prepared to supply enough of their goods at a rate of exchange that would justify the continued production of the first type of good at its current level. Under such circumstances the supply of 'over-supplied' goods would contract while that of 'undersupplied' goods would probably expand. Thus in a barter economy Say's Law implies that whatever the level of output it will be assured of a market despite changes in the composition of that output.

But does Say's Law apply to a money-using economy as well as a barter economy? If it does, and aggregate demand (AD) and aggregate supply (AS) are always necessarily equal then money is merely a 'veil' which covers the underlying 'real' forces in the economy. For Say's Law to be valid in a money-using economy two conditions must be fulfilled. Firstly, the aggregate cost of producing the economy's total output must be equal to the value of the aggregate factor incomes generated in the process of production. Secondly, the aggregate value of factor incomes so generated must be equal to the level of aggregate expenditure (demand) in the economy. The first equality holds in general in static equilibrium, provided one is prepared to accept the thesis that all profits are 'paid out' in the process of production just as all other factor incomes are. However, this equality cannot hold during periods of expanding levels of output, for the simple reason that profits cannot accrue in advance of sales. Consequently, a discrepancy is bound to occur between the aggregate costs of production incurred and the aggregate of factor incomes received. We may, however, assume for the sake of argument that any discrepancy between the two is made good by temporary bank credit or government loans; such financial assistance being made available in the knowledge that additional profits will be forthcoming in the near future.

The second condition, that aggregate expenditure be equal to aggregate income, is valid as long as *ex ante* current surpluses of households, namely planned savings, are equal to *ex ante* current deficits of firms, namely planned investment. If all income is not consumed, then for aggregate Y to be equal to AE there must be intentional (planned) I expenditure equal in amount to the shortfall of aggregate C from current Y, that is, planned I must equal planned S. The classical economists believed that this was in fact the case, for they held the view that the rate of interest would act as a mechanism for ensuring that whatever the level of output, planned S and I would always be equal. Any tendency for planned S (the supply of loanable funds) to exceed planned I (the demand for loanable funds), i.e. $AE<Y$, would exert a downward pressure on the interest rate to clear the market of all willing lenders, stimulating i and inhibiting S, the rate of interest continuing to fall until it reached a level at which planned S and I were once again equal. A similar equilibrating mechanism was presumed to exist in the opposite direction as well (i.e. $I>S; i\uparrow$). The classical economists presumed that the interest rate adjusted instantaneously to discrepancies between planned S and I so that disturbances to goods market equilibrium were both minimal and transitory and could therefore largely be ignored. Armed, therefore, with this belief in the equilibrating function of i the classical economists were able to assert that Say's Law was just as valid for a money-using economy as for a barter economy.

The operation of Say's Law ensures that whatever the quantity of output it will all be demanded. It does not, however, guarantee that that level of output corresponds to full employment. The tendency towards full employment in the classical system rests upon their second major building block, that of perfect competition in the labour market and the associated flexibility of money wages. The demand for labour in the classical system is seen as a function of the level of real wages alone, i.e. W/P where W = the money wage rate and P some index of the general level of prices. According to classical marginal productivity theory employers will go on hiring labour for as long as each additional unit of labour employed adds more to revenue than it does to costs. Assuming perfect competition in the labour market each additional unit of labour employed will add to costs a sum equal to the money wage received. By assuming perfect competition in the goods market each additonal unit of labour employed will add to revenue a sum equal to the marginal physical product of labour (MPP_L) multiplied by the price per unit at which output is currently selling. Therefore, in symbols, employers will hire labour until:

$$W = MPP_L \times P$$

and after rearrangement

$$MPP_L = \frac{W}{P}$$

which says that labour will be employed (demanded) for as long as the MPP_L is equal to its real wage.

The law of diminishing returns ensures that with a given stock of at least one other factor input, the employment of more and more workers will sooner or later reduce the MPP_L. With a declining MPP_L, the real wage of labour will have to fall for an increasing number of workers to be employed. In *Figure 5.1* the curve MPP_L is, in effect, the demand curve for labour (N^d). It purports to show how many units

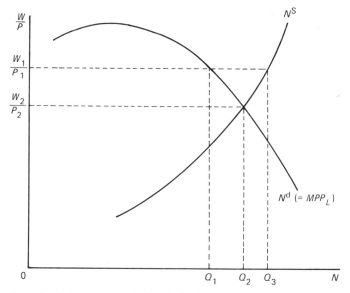

Figure 5.1 Labour market relations in the classical system

of labour will be demanded at various levels of real wages. Thus, for example, at a real wage of W_1/P_1 a quantity of labour equal to $0Q_1$ will be employed because this is the quantity which equates MPP_L with its W/P. The supply of labour (N^s) was also regarded by the classical economists as being a function of W/P and functionally related in such a way that at higher and higher levels of the W/P more and more labour would be willing to offer their services for hire. This relation is depicted by the upward-sloping N^s schedule in *Figure 5.1*. The equilibrium level of employment and real wages will be determined by the intersection of $N^d(=MPP_L)$, the demand for labour, and N^s. Suppose, by way of illustration, that the real wage is W_1/P_1 in *Figure 5.1* where the supply of labour $0Q_3$ exceeds the demand $0Q_1$. As long as this real wage rate W_1/P_1 prevails there will be $0Q_3 - 0Q_1$ units of labour 'involuntarily' unemployed in the sense that there will be that number of workers willing to work at W_1/P_1 who are not being employed. Will the real wage rate remain at this level? The classical economists' answer is no, the reason being that competition amongst the unemployed for employment will bid the money wage rate down. But a falling money wage rate will not, of itself, necessarily raise the level of employment; for there to be an increase in the level of employment the real wage and not the money wage must fall. Quite obviously the drop in W will cause an immediate drop in W/P but not necessarily a permanent fall in W/P if P subsequently falls by the same amount. Is it not likely that P will fall commensurately with W as the drop in W causes income and expenditure to drop? If this is the case then a drop in W will have no influence at all upon the level of employment. The unemployed will bid the money wage down further and there will follow an endless downward spiral of money wages and prices. This possibility was ruled out by the classical economists who argued that a fall in W would be accompanied by a fall in W/P. Their argument was based upon their acceptance of the Quantity Theory of Money.

It will be recalled from Chapter 3 that the classical economists believed that money was held only for the purpose of financing transactions, so that nobody willingly accumulated idle money balances. Thus the velocity of circulation of money is a fixed datum determined by institutional factors such as the frequency and coincidence of payments and receipts. In the 'income' elaboration of the Fisher equation:

$$MV = Py$$

as long as M is constant, the institutionally determined constancy of V ensures that Py, the money value of final output, is also constant. Starting, therefore, from a position of involuntary unemployment in the labour market, the money wage falls under the pressure of competition from the unemployed. If the price level were now to fall proportionately the real wage would be unchanged, so too would be the level of employment and the level of real output (y, in the above equation). Thus P would be falling at the same rate as W and so too would the product Py. But according to the Fisher identity a falling Py must mean a falling MV of the same proportion. But this is impossible if both M and V are assumed to be constant. Consequently, the classical economists maintained that a fall in W would bring about a less than proportionate fall in P as the involuntary accumulation of idle cash balances was spent on goods and services, so resisting a proportionate reduction in expenditure. The reduction in W/P would raise the level of employment and output so that in terms of the Fisher identity y rose by the same proportion that P fell maintaining the product Py unchanged. The process of falling money and real wages and rising employment and output would continue until full employment was reached. In terms of *Figure 5.1* this occurs when the real wage has fallen from W_1/P_1 to W_2/P_2 and the level of employment has risen from $0Q_1$ to $0Q_2$. Full employment is defined not in relation to any short-run capacity limit on output, but merely in terms of the equality between the number of those who are willing to work at the going real wage rate and the number who are being demanded. Schematically, the classical macrosystem can be summarized as in *Figure 5.2*.

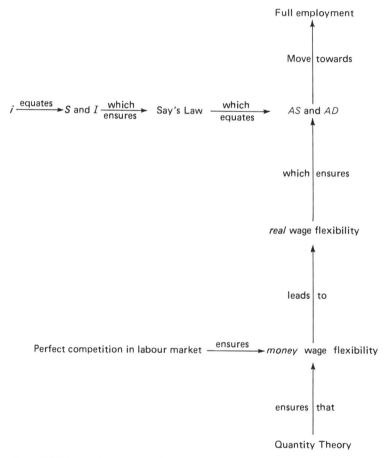

Figure 5.2 The classical macro system

The complete classical model can be represented in terms of a multi-sector diagram as shown in *Figure 5.3*.

Panel 1 represents the labour market where MPP_L varies inversely with N and N^s positively with W/P.

Panel 2 represents the economy's production function which traces the relationship between the level of employment (N) and the level of real output (y) given the state of technology. The slope of the production function flattens out at

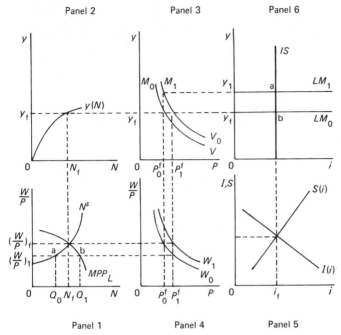

Figure 5.3 The impact of an increase in the money stock in the classical system

higher levels of employment, depicting the phenomena of economy-wide diminishing returns to the variable factor labour.

Panel 3 portrays the classical Quantity Theory. Real output is plotted along the vertical axis and some index of the general level of final goods prices on the horizontal axis. With a given M and V then from the identity $MV = Py$ we can obtain a value for the product Py. A given value of the product Py is consistent with an infinite number of different values of P and y. With a given MV and therefore a given value of Py we can plot a curve which depicts all possible combinations of P and y consistent with this value. The resulting curve, which is a rectangular hyperbola, is in fact the aggregate demand curve for the economy. It shows the total amount of purchasing that takes place in the economy given M and V. A change in the individual values of M and/or V which altered the value of their product MV would mean a new location for the MV curve. An increase in MV would shift the rectangular hyperbola to the right and a decrease in MV would shift it to the left.

Panel 4 shows the money wage–real wage relationship. Real wages are plotted along the vertical axis and the absolute price level along the horizontal axis. For a given value of the money wage one can draw a curve which traces out the relationship between the real wage and the price level. For a given money wage a higher real wage will mean a lower price level while a lower real wage will mean a higher price level. The money wage curve is also a rectangular hyperbola indicating that the total surface area contained within any pair of co-ordinate rays to the axes (the money wage) is constant.

Panel 5 shows the savings/investment relations and is to be regarded as already implicit in the MV schedule of panel 3.

Panel 6 depects the *IS/LM* goods market/money market equilibrium curves. We notice that in the classical system the IS schedule is vertical[1] indicating that S and I could be equal at any level of income, given the equilibrium rate of interest. The *LM* schedule on the other hand is horizontal depicting its presumed interest-insensitivity and it will emanate from the vertical axis at a point denoting the fixed full employment level of income (= output).

Let us trace out the causal interconnections in the classical macrosystem as contained in these six panels. Starting with panel 1 we see that full employment is associated with a real wage of $(W/P)_f$. Reading vertically upwards to panel 2 we notice that full employment generates a level of real output equal to y_f. Reading horizontally to panel 3 and given $M_0 V_0$, the money stock and the velocity of circulation, we can determine the equilibrium price level P_0^f. Next we read vertically down to panel 4 and see that with a price level of P_0^f and a real wage of $(W/P)_f$ the money wage must be equal to W_0. The I and S relations in panel 5 determine the equilibrium rate of interest, i.e. that interest rate which equates ex ante I and S at a full employment level of real output. The *LM* and *IS* schedules in panel 6 intersect at the full employment level of real income and the rate of interest obtained from panel 5.

What then is the role of money in this model? Clearly it is only to determine the money wage rate, money income and the price level. All the real variables of the system – real income, the real wage rate, employment and the interest rate – are determined independently of these monetary variables. In technical language we say that the classical system is 'dichotomized' into a 'real' and a 'monetary' sub-system. As evidence of this dichotomy and as proof of the 'neutrality of money' in the classical system let us examine the consequences of an increase in the quantity of money in circulation. In terms of *Figure 5.3* an increase in the money stock from M_0 to M_1 raises the value of the product MV and shifts the MV schedule in panel 3 to the right as indicated. At an unchanged level of real output the increased level of money expenditure (MV) raises P and money income equiproportionately. As can be seen in panel 4 the increase in P from P_0^f to P_1^f, with an unchanged money wage rate W_0, lowers the real wage, thus creating an excess demand for labour in panel 1 of horizontal distance $b - a$.

Competition in the labour market for scarce labour pushes up the money wage ($W_0 \rightarrow W_1$ in panel 4) which continues to rise until MPP_L and N^S are equated at $(W/P)^f$. Thus the final outcome of an increase in the money supply from M_0 to M_1 is an equiproportionate increase in P and W and no change in y, N, W/P and i. 'Money does not matter', influencing only the 'nominal' values leaving the 'real' variables unchanged.

The classical dichotomy however has been the subject of much debate, and stimulated attempts to integrate value (or microeconomic price theory) with monetary theory. Lange (1942) pointed out an inconsistency in the classical dichotomy, which was taken up by other writers and given its fullest treatment and reconciliation in the work of Patinkin (1956).

Why is the classical dichotomy inconsistent? Simply because the Quantity Theory of Money and Say's Law together are inconsistent with Walras' Law which states that if all markets are aggregated together, the sum of the excess demands will equal the sum of the excess supplies, i.e. when the excess demands are added to the excess supplies they sum to zero. Consequently if money is one of n goods, then if $n-1$ goods markets are in equilibrium, the money market must also be in equilibrium. Say's law, on the other hand, says that there can never be an excess supply of goods in aggregate, i.e. the sum of the excess supplies of individual goods is zero. The important distinction between Walras' Law and Say's Law is that the former refers to all markets including the money market, while Say's Law refers only to commodity markets.

We can now demonstrate why a model containing Walras' Law, Say's Law and the Quantity Theory is internally inconsistent. Starting from a position of equilibrium in all markets, suppose there is then an increase in the supply of money. Say's Law ensures that this disturbance to the money market will have no effect on the zero excess demand for the goods markets as a whole. But if the excess demands in the $(n-1)$ goods markets sum to zero then according to Walras' Law the nth market (money) must also have zero excess demand. The Quantity Theory however says that the increase in the supply of money will create an excess supply in the money market. Thus Say's Law and Walras' Law together imply a zero excess supply while the Quantity Theory generates a 'positive' excess supply. Thus the dichotomy of the real and monetary sectors in the classical system is seemingly inconsistent.

Patinkin (1965) attempted to integrate monetary and value theory by including the value of real balances as a determinant of the demand for every good, including money. Thus with Patinkin's real balance effect, the demands for goods and real money balances are functions of relative prices and the real value of money balances. The relationship between demands and real balances is assumed to be positive.

If the demands (and of course excess demands) are functions of the value of real money balances, then they depend also on the absolute price level. An increase in prices, with given nominal money balances, reduces the real value of those balances and thereby reduces the demand for goods. Introducing real money balances as an argument in the demand functions for goods effectively destroys Say's Law. If the goods markets are initially in equilibrium, then an increase in absolute prices which reduces the value of real balances will induce a fall in the demand for all goods and create an excess supply of them. But of course the existence of excess supplies is inconsistent with Say's Law. Hence the inclusion of a real balance effect in the model denies the existence of Say's Law and in so doing provides for internal consistency in the model.

This internal consistency however depends on the real balance effect applying to the money market as well as to the goods market. Imagine an individual with given real income and stock of idle cash balances. Assume now that all prices in the economy double, then from the identity $Y \equiv Py$, money income also doubles. Is our individual's wealth position unchanged as a result? Clearly it is not, because although his or her real income is unchanged the purchasing power of his stock of idle cash balances has been reduced. Patinkin argued that this deterioration in the relative wealth position of owners of cash balances, will, by causing the actual level of real cash balances to fall below the desired level, prompt some action to restore the real value of these balances. If neither goods nor real cash balances are 'inferior', then the demand for both will drop when P rises, so that although the individual attempts to rebuild his now deficient stock of real balances he stops somewhat short of the original level. In this respect the real balance effect is analogous to the 'income' effect of a price increase which causes expenditure on all goods 'consumed' to fall. The operation of the real balance effect leads to the conclusion that the demand for real cash balances is inversely related to P. When P doubles the aggregate demand for nominal money balances less than doubles so that the demand for nominal money balances with respect to a change in the value of money is of less than unit elasticity. It is for this reason that Patinkin includes the outstanding stock of real cash balances in the nominal demand for money function.

Patinkin's representation of the operation of the real balance effect in the money market is presented in *Figure 5.4* where the vertical money supply curve intersects the less than unit elastic money demand curve at P_0. Assume now that the nominal quantity of money in circulation doubles, shifting the vertical line $M_0 \to 2M_0$. As M_0/P appears as an argument in the demand function for nominal money balances, an increase in M_0 raises, initially, the actual stock of real cash balances above the desired stock and, because of their increased wealth, will cause individuals to increase their demand for nominal cash balances. Because of the operation of this real balance effect in the money market the M_0^d schedule shifts over to the right to M_1^d, $b - a$ measuring the amount of additional nominal cash balances demanded as a result of the improved net wealth position of households and firms. This still

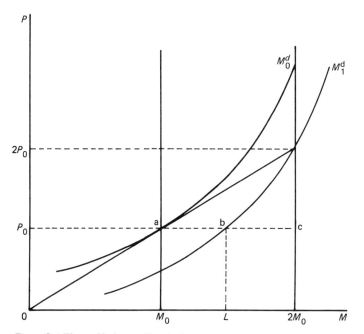

Figure 5.4 The real balance effect in the money market

leaves an excess supply of money of $c - b$, i.e. at an unchanged price level P_0 the actual stock of real cash balances $2M_0/P_0$ exceeds the desired stock L/P_0, and consequently the community will attempt to rid itself of the unwanted cash balances by increasing its level of current expenditure. This is consistent with the position in the goods markets, because the increase in real balances generates an excess demand for all goods. The increased expenditure will raise the general level of prices until a new equilibrium is reached with zero excess demand both in the goods markets and the money market. The new equilibrium position in the money market is shown in *Figure 5.4* as the intersection of M_1^d and $2M_0$, and will be at a doubled price level. Prices must double to eliminate the excess demand in the goods markets, for only then will the doubling of the nominal money supply leave the real value of money balances unchanged, and so too the real demand for goods. Similarly in the money market, if at an initial price level and an initial endowment of nominal cash, a specific amount of nominal cash is demanded, then at a doubled price level and a doubled endowment of nominal cash there must be double the demand for nominal cash balances: the money market will be in equilibrium. In *Figure 5.4* the locus of points of intersection of M^d and M_0 for all levels of the nominal money supply lie along a straight line emanating from the origin. This 'market-equilibrium' curve, i.e. the combinations of P and M_0 that will produce money-market equilibrium is of unitary elasticity, but it is not to be confused with the 'demand curve for money', for this, as we have seen, is of less than unitary elasticity and is derived from enquiring how M^d behaves when P changes, *ceteris paribus*. Thus a doubling of the money supply has resulted in a doubling of the absolute price level, but no change in real variables, i.e. real money balances, relative prices, real demands, output and employment. Money in this model is neutral. Thus Johnson (1971, p. 112) argues that:

> Patinkin's positive contribution was to show that this logical inconsistency in contemporary monetary theory could be resolved by introducing the real balance effect as a bridge between the money and the real systems. This had the effect of destroying the dichotomy while preserving the essential neutrality characteristic of money in the classical system.

A number of criticisms were made of Patinkin's early work by, amongst others, Archibald and Lipsey (1958) and Lloyd (1962), and the interested reader is referred to Harris (1981) and Johnson (1971) for useful summaries and assessments.

We shall now move on to give rather fuller consideration to the concept of neutrality and to the conditions upon which it depends. The term neutrality, as applied to the role of money, is somewhat ambiguous. One interpretation is that money is neutral if it simply acts as a 'veil' over the workings of the 'real' economy. If it is, then this would suggest that a 'real' barter economy functions in much the same way as a monetary economy. However, as we saw in Chapter 1, the existence of money helps to reduce the inefficiencies of barter and thereby brings about higher levels of output etc. From this point of view money is clearly not neutral. Consequently the discussion of neutrality is now conducted in the context of a money-using economy. Money is said to be neutral when starting from a position of equilibrium; an increase in the supply of money results in a new position of equilibrium being reached at which only nominal values have changed, all real variables retaining the values they had before the increase in the money supply. In this sense neutrality is assessed on the basis of comparative static analysis and long-run equilibrium characteristics. At least two other interpretations of neutrality may be mentioned. One considers whether changes in the rate of growth of the money supply has any effect on the equilibrium growth path of the economy and if it does not, money is said to be superneutral. No further consideration will be given to this interpretation as we shall not be discussing growth models. The other interpretation is usually considered in the context of discussions of stabilization policy, and considers whether systematic policy-induced changes in the money supply can have any effect on real variables, even in the short run. If it cannot then again, rather confusingly, money is said to be superneutral. We will be considering this interpretation of neutrality in Chapters 7 and 11. For the remainder of this chapter, however, we wish to consider more fully the conditions necessary for neutrality in the sense we used it in our discussion of the real balance effect. It was in fact Patinkin who developed these 'neutrality conditions' most fully in the context of his four market (labour, goods, money, bonds) general equilibrium neoclassical system, and our exposition is based on his work.

The neutrality conditions

Patinkin sets out six conditions that must be satisfied if money is to be neutral, in the sense that changes in the supply of it have no effect on the equilibrium real profile of the economy. These conditions are:

(1) There must be perfect wage-price flexibility.
(2) There must be an absence of money illusion.
(3) There must be an absence of distribution effects.
(4) Price and interest rate expectations must be of unitary elasticity.
(5) There must be an absence of government interest-bearing debt.
(6) There must be an absence of a combination of inside and outside money.

Patinkin examines what significance each of these six conditions has for the neutrality theorem by investigating the behaviour of a monetary economy when they are not satisfied.

Perfect wage–price flexibility

This first condition enables one to postulate that if there is a determinate solution of a system of general equilibrium equations it will correspond to a full employment level of real output (income). This condition therefore precludes the possibility of a determinate solution that corresponds to a less than full employment level of real output and directs our attention to the behaviour of a monetary economy that is in a state of continuous full employment. If this condition is not satisfied then changes in the money supply can influence the real wage (W/P) and, through that, influence other real variables such as employment and output.

Absence of money illusion

'Money illusion' is said to exist whenever the excess demand functions for goods, services, money, assets and factor inputs are influenced by the nominal rather than the real values of economic variables. Money illusion is absent from an economic system whenever the behaviour of all endogenous economic units is solely determined by real cash balances, real bond-holdings, real income, the real rate of interest, real wages and relative prices.

Money illusion in the commodity market

This can exist either (1) directly in consumption or (2) indirectly in consumption through the tax bracket.

(1) Assume an equiproportionate increase in all money prices and hence everybody's money income, with real income constant. If households base their expenditure plans upon nominal rather than real income, then C can change even though real income is constant, whenever money income changes. It may well be

that when Y increases, and Y/P is unchanged, households feel this signifies an improvement in their real living standards. The illusion that households are better off when, in fact, they are not, may not be rational but it may be consistent. The illusion can be explained along any of the following lines: not all consumers consume everything all the time, so that information about price changes is likely to be imperfect and available only after a time lag; if price changes are small and discrete some people may disregard them whilst others may remain totally ignorant of them; some people may be aware of price rises but, because they are accompanied by a new presentation of products and services, may feel that the quality of the product has improved commensurately so that the increase in P does not represent any deterioration in their real living standards. Of the three the last is likely to be the most potent source of money illusion in modern capitalist economies. The point about money illusion in C is that real expenditure out of real income can change whenever P and thus Y changes, with repercussions on the real economic profile of the economy. For example, if when prices increase, real consumption increases, then equilibrium at full employment requires a reduction in investment, i.e. an increase in the equilibrium rate of interest.

(2) In most advanced industralized economies direct taxes on households' income are levied on money and not real income through a progressive tax structure. This means that whenever Y and P rise at full employment the private sector is pushed into a higher income tax bracket and will therefore pay a larger proportion of its real income in tax. Thus, during an inflationary situation, real private disposable income declines and, *pro rata*, so does real consumption expenditure. Initially, therefore, money illusion in the tax bracket can influence full employment real expenditure; but does it ultimately? The increase in real tax revenue, holding real government transfers constant, will create a budget surplus. If the government is committed to a balanced budget, then the additional real tax revenue will be returned to the private sector so that there will be no net effect upon the absolute level of full employment real expenditure. Money, therefore, would still be neutral in its effects upon the economy. Some economists have challenged this conclusion by pointing out that the neutrality theorem can only be vindicated provided the return of income to the private sector is 'neutral', i.e. is given back to the individual members in the same proportion as they were taxed. For example, if the government took the proceeds of the direct taxes on households and gave tax relief to firms in the form of more generous investment allowances, then C/P might fall and I/P rise within an unchanged aggregate level of real expenditure. This would not disturb the current static equilibrium real profile of the economy, but it would, by influencing the rate of capital formation, disturb the future rate of growth of real income. In a dynamic economy, such a redistribution of real expenditure, springing initially from money illusion in the tax bracket, could disturb its equilibrium real profile.

Money illusion in the labour market

If the supply of labour is determined by money rather than real wage rates, then an increase in the supply of money will increase employment and output and therefore be non-neutral. Money illusion in the labour market is illustrated in *Figure 5.5*. Money wages are plotted on the vertical axis and the supply of labour is shown as a direct function of the money wage. The demand for labour is shown as an inverse

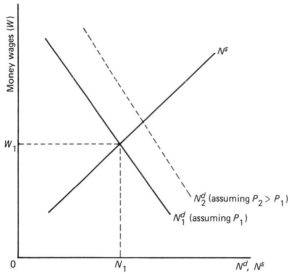

Figure 5.5 Money illusion in the labour market

function of the money wage, for any *given* price level, but will change its position whenever the price level changes, moving to the right when prices rise and to the left when they fall. Suppose the demand curve is initially in the position depicted by the solid line, with money wages of W_1 and prices P_1. If now the money supply doubles, prices will start to rise, lowering the real wage and shifting the demand for labour curve to the right, say to the position of the broken line. Clearly employment increases, and so too does output. There will be an increase in real demand both because prices do not increase in proportion to the money supply thereby increasing real wealth, and because interest rates fall, stimulating investment.

Money illusion in the money market

Such money illusion would exist if, for example, the demand for money was of the form:

$$M^d = P \cdot L_1(y) + L_2(i)$$

Money market equilibrium is given by:

$$M^s = P \cdot L_1(y) + L_2(i)$$

If the money supply, say, doubled, then a doubling of the price level would not be sufficient to keep the money market in equilibrium, because it would not alter $L_2(i)$.

If, however, the demand for money was of the form

$$M^d = P \cdot L_1(y) + P \cdot L_2(i)$$

then the total demand for money is a demand for real money balances, and a doubling of the price level would, in the face of a doubling of the money supply, be sufficient to keep the money market in equilibrium.

Patinkin demonstrates that a doubled money stock and price level will disturb the neutrality of money, if there is money illusion in the money demand function, because the equilibrium interest rate will fall to absorb the doubled money stock. Consider *Figure 5.6*, with initial equilibrium at point B, where $E = y_0$ at $(M_0/P_0, i_0, y_0)$. Considering now a doubling of the money stock which all flows into transactions balances to finance a higher level of expenditure. This causes the E schedule to shift upwards to E_1, denoting the fact that at an unchanged i and y and doubled M_0 the level of real expenditure is higher. This creates an inflationary gap of $A - B$ and prices begin to rise. Let us assume that the price level more than

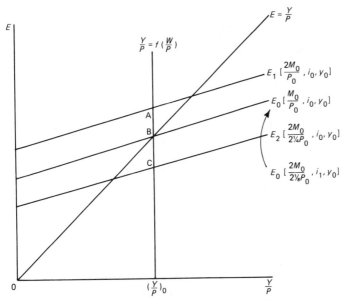

Figure 5.6 Money illusion in the money market and neutrality

doubles by an amount sufficient to absorb all the additional cash in transactions cash balances, (say $2\frac{1}{4}P_0$). This means that the value of real cash balances $2M_0/2\frac{1}{4}P_0$ drops below its initial level, and at an unchanged i and y implies that real expenditure will fall below its equilibrium level (E_2 in *Figure 5.6*). This creates a deflationary gap of $B - C$ pushing prices downwards and depressing the interest rate. A full employment level of real expenditure (E_0) is restored at a lower interest rate and a more than doubled price level: for example, $2\frac{1}{8}P_0, i_1, y_0$. If there was no real balance effect in the goods market, then the price level could rise to a level that enabled all the additional cash in circulation to be absorbed into active cash balances, with no subsequent fall in i. This would still mean however that a real variable, in the form of real balances (M/P) would have been affected by the increase in the money supply, and money would still be non neutral.

Absence of distribution effects

A third condition for the neutrality of money is the absence of 'distribution' effects. Such effects occur whenever economic behaviour is influenced by the distribution of wealth and real income rather than just their aggregate values. Distribution effects manifest themselves ultimately in the commodity market, although they can originate in any other market of the economy. In a closed economy we can usefully identify four possible redistribution effects:

(1) A redistribution of Y/P away from (or towards) wage-earners and towards (or away from) profit-earners (shareholders) may alter the average marginal propensity to consume of the economy and thus aggregate consumption, if the marginal propensity to consume of these two income groups differ. If wage-earners are subject to short period money illusion money wages may lag behind money profits, and there will be a redistribution of income away from wage-earners to profit-earners.

(2) A redistribution of real income between fixed and variable income groups. During a period of rising prices those sections of the community on fixed incomes, such as pensioners, students, etc., will suffer at the expense of those sections that can defend themselves: their defence being achieved either through wage recontracting or through existing contracts which link wages to a purchasing power escalator clause.

(3) A redistribution of income amongst creditors and debtors. During a period of rising prices, the real value of debts falls, so debtors benefit and creditors lose. Even though, in the aggregate, an unanticipated inflation leaves the real wealth of the private sector unchanged, if debtors and creditors react asymmetrically to their changed relative wealth positions, then a redistribution effect will occur, causing aggregate expenditure to depart from its full employment level, requiring some adjustment in interest rates and investment for full employment expenditure to be restored.

In the three situations considered above the change in AE came about through a price-induced distribution effect. There are, however, other channels through which distribution effects associated with changes in M_0 can come about.

(4) It has been tacitly assumed throughout the analysis that any monetary increase does not affect the debtor (the government) but does affect the creditor (the private sector). Indeed this asymmetry of behavioural responses provides the main justification for the existence of Patinkin's real balance effect. To quote Patinkin (1965, p. 28) 'for our money is the debt of the Government, and if the Government were to react to changes in the real value of this debt, as do households and firms to theirs, there could be no real balance effect in the economy as a whole. Any, say, decrease in the price level would generate a positive real balance effect for firms and households and an exactly offsetting negative one for the Government.' However, as we have already seen, Patinkin needs the real balance effect to validate the neoclassical neutrality theorem.

Price and interest rate expectations

The fourth neutrality condition relates to the nature of price and interest rate expectations. Thus if changes in the supply of money cause prices to rise, then neutrality requires that economic agents do not interpret this increase in prices in such a way as to cause them to expect further increases in prices. If they do then they are likely to alter their behaviour in such ways as adding to or running down their money balances, and altering their expenditures, which in turn will affect real variables in the economy.

Absence of government interest bearing debts

On these first four neutrality conditions there seems to be general agreement with Patinkin's analysis. When it comes to the existence of government bonds there seems to be less agreement, mainly because of the assumptions made about the private sector's attitude towards outstanding government interest-bearing debt. The main aspects of the debate have already been considered in Chapter 2 so we shall only be concerned here with the implications of that debate for our neutrality discussions. If government bonds are a net asset of the private sector, then the real stock of bonds as well as the real stock of cash balances should be included in the excess demand functions of the different markets. Let us focus our attention upon the goods market. The inclusion of the real stock of bonds as an argument in the demand function for goods means that the wealth effect associated with a change in the level of prices no longer coincides with the real balance effect. In addition, there is now a 'net financial assets' effect operating through the public's holding of government bonds exerting a depressing influence upon aggregate demand. Let us now demonstrate how the existence of government bonds disturbs the neutrality of money. Imagine a doubling of both the money supply and the level of prices, the increase in the money supply having been brought about by a means other than open-market operations. A doubled money supply and price level leaves the real value of money balances unchanged but reduces the real value of government bonds. With an unchanged rate of interest and real income, but a lower real value of bonds, the level of aggregate demand must be lower than it was initially, because of the net financial assets effect. A full employment volume of real demand can only be restored by a drop in the equilibrium interest rate. The fall in interest will raise investment directly and consumption indirectly by raising the real stock of bonds. Thus the existence of a stock of interest-bearing assets whose real value varies inversely with the price level makes money non-neutral. Neutrality can be preserved if the rate of yield on government bonds is tied to the price level so that an increase of say 5% in prices would raise the annual interest payment by 5%. The inclusion of such a purchasing power escalator clause has the effect of making the real value of bonds invariant to changes in the price level.

However, this neutrality condition is invalidated when the money stock is expanded by means of an open-market purchase of bonds by the monetary authority. Even the existence of an indexed bond cannot fully compensate for the drop in the real value of the stock of bonds that accompanies an open market induced expansion in the money supply. For in addition to the fall in the real value of the stock of bonds resulting from a higher level of prices (which can be compensated for) there is a further fall resulting from the lower quantity of bonds in existence. Clearly the rate of interest must fall to a new lower equilibrium level to stimulate a full employment level of real demand. Money is no longer neutral.

We conclude this section by asking ourselves how alternative assumptions about the nature of government bonds alters the conclusions of the previous section. If bonds are a debt, then the real stock of bonds must be excluded altogether from the real excess demand functions of the economy. This has the effect of producing a system identical to the one we presented initially in which only real money balances enter and which, as we have already shown, is neutral in response to equiproportionate increases in the money supply and the price level.

An absence of a combination of inside and outside money

On the basis of the foregoing discussion it is quite easy to see how a combination of both inside and outside money may disturb the neutrality of money when one of the types is expanded, the other held constant. Let us imagine an economy in which outside money (M^{OA}) is backed by gold, and inside money (M^{OB}) by private bonds held by the banking system. Since the private bonds held by the banks cancel out the inside money in the consolidated balance sheet of the private sector, the net real financial wealth of that sector consists only of the outside money. Let us assume that the stock of outside money doubles and as a result the price level doubles. This will return the net real financial wealth of the community to its initial equilibrium level. However, the real value of total money balances has fallen

$$\frac{2M^{OA}}{2P} + \frac{M^{OB}}{2P} < \frac{M^{OA}}{P} + \frac{M^{OB}}{P}$$

Consequently a real balance effect will come into operation, depressing real expenditure below its full employment level and necessitating a drop in the equilibrium interest rate to restore real expenditure to its original level. Only if the nominal stock of inside money increases in the same proportion to that of outside money will the real variables of the system remain unchanged for only then will the ratio of real assets to liabilities be the same as it was in the original position.

Notes

1. In *Figure 5.3* the labelling of the axes in panel 6 is the reverse of that usually shown on *IS–LM* diagrams. Thus while the *IS* schedule is vertical in *Figure 5.3*, it is, with the more conventional labelling of the axes, shown as horizontal.

6

The Keynesian system

The first section of this chapter considers the role of money in the 'Keynesian model', which is the name given to the model distilled from Keynes writings by his early disciples, and which has featured in macroeconomics textbooks under the label of Keynesian ever since. In the second section of the chapter we will extend the Keynesian model to an open economy. The final section of the chapter will be devoted to a consideration of the re-interpretation of Keynes' writings made by Clower (1965) and Leijonhufvud (1968) in the late 1960s: a reinterpretation which came to be known as the 'economics of Keynes' in order to distinguish it from the traditional 'Keynesian economics'.

Keynesian economics

In this section we will formalize the Keynesian system in the same way as we did the classical system, and then analyze what effect changes in monetary variables have upon the real variables under differing assumptions about the behavioural responses of the economy and structural properties of the monetary sector. We shall see that this allows us to interpret the role of money in the Keynesian system in a number of different ways each with its own specific implication for the conduct and performance of monetary policy. We shall be concerned with four such interpretations:

(1) Cost of capital effect strong.
(2) Cost of capital effect weak.
(3) Inside money, outside money and wealth effects.
(4) Endogeneity of the money stock and the availability of credit.

The Keynesian System differs from the classical system in three important respects. Firstly it rejects the quantity theory of money by recognizing that decision units might voluntarily hold idle cash balances even if only for precautionary purposes. For this reason money expenditure will not necessarily rise in proportion to an increase in the money stock as some of the additional money will be withdrawn from 'active' circulation and held 'idle'. Secondly the system rejects the notion of perfect competition in the labour market by recognizing the existence of 'monopoly' elements in the labour market which will have the effect of reducing the flexibility of money wages in the downward direction. Thirdly the system rejects Say's Law that 'supply creates its own demand' by recognizing the possibility that as savings and investment decisions are made by different people and for different reasons, it is merely coincidental if the two happen to be equal. Moreover, the system rejects the view that savings and therefore consumption are determined by the rate of interest by recognizing that they are both primarily determined by the level of household's income, and that the rate of interest determines not the absolute level of savings but the distribution of these savings betwen idle money balances on the one hand and loanable funds on the other. With the introduction of (i) rigid money wages in the downward direction, (ii) a consumption function, and (iii) a liquidity preference schedule, the Keynesian system is able to demonstrate (i) that the causal link between expenditure and output runs from the former to the latter rather than the other way around as suggested by Say's law, (ii) that expenditure can exceed, equal or fall short of output in the short run, causing the level of output to rise, remain unchanged or fall, and (iii) that there is no reason why the level of output determined by the schedule of effective demand should correspond to full employment.

We assume that the reader is familiar with the Keynesian consumption function and liquidity preference function (for the latter see Chapter 3, pp. 46–53), so we shall concentrate here on the employment–output–price subset of the Keynesian system, preparatory to its integration into the *IS–LM* framework of analysis. The demand for labour in the Keynesian system is determined by the MPP_L as in the classical system. The supply of labour is not determined by independent negotiation between employee and employer as suggested in the classical system, but by collective negotiation between trade unions and employers (and employers'

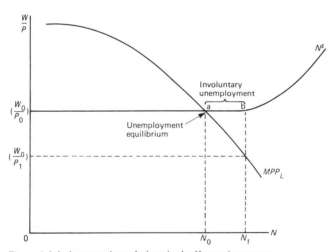

Figure 6.1 Labour market relations in the Keynesian system

associations). In *Figure 6.1* a collectively negotiated money wage is fixed at which $0N_f$ units of labour are willing to work. Assuming, for the moment the price level to be given, the fixing of a money wage renders the supply of labour infinitely elastic at the prevailing real wage rate (W_0/P_0) up to the quantity of labour $0N_f$. It is presumed, perhaps artificially, that nobody is prepared and/or attempts to work for a money wage lower than W_0. If employers would like to engage more than $0N_f$

units of labour they will have to offer a money wage higher than W_0 so that to the right of $0N$ the supply of labour becomes an increasing function of the real wage rate. Full employment is said to exist when $0N_f$ units of labour have been offered employment. With these particular labour market relations equality between MPP_L and N^s does not necessarily define a situation of full employment. In *Figure 6.1* the point of intersection of the MPP_L schedule with the N^s schedule depicts an equilibrium situation in which $b - a$, units of labour are involuntarily unemployed, i.e. who would be willing to work at (W_0/P_0) but who cannot find employment. Thus point a in *Figure 6.1* corresponds to a situation of 'unemployment equilibrium'. Only if the real wage rate drops to (W_0/P_1) as a result of an increase in P will full employment equilibrium be restored. Once the equilibrium level of N is determined it becomes a simple matter to calculate from the aggregate production function, the associated level of real output.

Before we can present a formal Keynesian macrosystem we need to know how the equilibrium price level is determined. It will be recalled that in the classical system, the price level is determined solely by the nominal quantity of money in circulation. In the Keynesian system however, the absolute price level is fixed by the interaction of the joint forces of aggregate demand (AD) and aggregate supply (AS). The AS curve describes the relationship between the price level and the supply of goods and services in the economy, and the AD curve the relationship between the price level and the total demand for goods and services. Let us derive the AD and AS schedules each in turn, starting with the AS curve. Using conventional symbols, the following sequence of events is likely to proceed from an upward departure of the price level from its assumed (imaginary) equilibrium position in the AD subset of the Keynesian system:

$$\uparrow P; \quad \downarrow W/P; \quad \uparrow N^d; \quad \uparrow N; \quad \uparrow Y/P; \quad \uparrow AS$$

The increased price level lowers the real wage rate, raises the demand for labour, and assuming initial unemployment equilibrium, increases the level of employment and real output. Thus the relationship between AS and P is (positive) until full employment is reached whence it becomes zero. The AS schedule slopes upwards from left to right until full employment is reached whence it becomes vertical (as shown in *Figure 6.2*). The AD schedule is derived accordingly:

$$\uparrow P; \quad \uparrow Py; \quad \uparrow M^t; \quad \uparrow M^d; \quad M^d > M^0; \quad \downarrow B^d; \quad B^d < B^s; \quad \downarrow P^B; \quad \uparrow i; \quad \downarrow I; \quad \downarrow AD.$$

We see that an increase in P raises money income and the transactions demand for cash, and creates an excess demand for money. The excess demand for money has a counterpart in the bond market, bonds being presumed the only substitute for money in private portfolios, in the form of an excess supply of bonds. The price of bonds falls, the interest rate rises, investment and/or consumption falls and so too, *ceteris paribus*, aggregate demand. The relationship between AD and P is inverse and consequently the AD schedule in *Figure 6.2* slopes downwards from left to right. The intersection of AD and AS determines the equilibrium level of prices as well as the equilibrium quantity of goods and services in the economy (real output). At a price level above P_0 there will be an excess of AS over AD, in other words a deflationary situation which will tend to push the price level back to its equilibrium position, and at a price level below P_0 there is an excess of AD over AS etc. Throughout the succeeding analysis it will be assumed that prices respond sensitively to changes in market conditions.

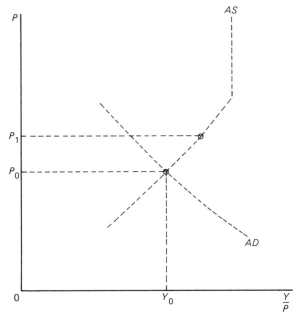

Figure 6.2 The determination of the general level of prices

We can now bring together the *IS–LM* analysis with that of the *AD–AS* synthesis to present a generalized four-market macromodel with the money wage and the stock of money given and the level of employment, output, interest rate, real wage rate and prices to be determined (see *Figure 6.3*). Panel 1 depicts the *IS–LM* relations with $(Y/P)_f$ the level of full employment real output. Intersection of *IS* and *LM* to the left of this vertical line signifies an unemployment equilibrium position. Panel 2 depicts the *AD–AS* relations. Panel 3 depicts the economy's production function. Panel 4 the labour market situation, and panel 5 the money-real wage relation. All markets and sectors of the economy are interrelated and disturbances in one sector or market will have repercussions on all others. The equilibrium values of all endogenous variables are simultaneously determined.

With the aid of this model we shall now investigate the role of money and in particular the impact on 'real' variables of changes in the quantity of money in circulation.

Interpretation 1: cost of capital effect strong

In the Keynesian system the supply and demand for money collectively determines the nominal rate of interest. The rate of interest has a crucial function to fulfil as the intermediary link between the money and the goods markets. By influencing *I* and/or *C* the rate of interest transmits developments in the monetary sector to the expenditure sector and ultimately the production and employment sectors. If *ex ante S = ex ante I* (goods market equilibrium) but $M^d \neq M^s$ then the rate of interest will adjust to equate the two directly, by influencing the demand for idle balances and indirectly, by altering *I* and *C*, *AE*, $(=Py)$ and hence the demand for active cash balances. This causal link running from M^s to Y/P is as follows:

$\uparrow M^s$; $M^s > M^d$; $\uparrow B^d$; $\downarrow B^S$; $\uparrow P^B$; $\downarrow i$; $\uparrow I$; $\uparrow AD$; $AD > AS$;

$\uparrow P$
   (a) $\downarrow W/P$; $\uparrow N^d$; $\uparrow N$; $\uparrow Y/P$ ...

   (b) $\uparrow M^t$; $\uparrow M^d$; $M^d > M^s$; $\downarrow B^d$; $\downarrow P^B$; $\uparrow i$; $\downarrow I$; $\downarrow AD$,
   etc.

It rests crucially upon the interest-elasticity of the demand for money, for this will determine by how much i falls when M^s is expanded (the slope of the *LM* schedule), and the interest-elasticity of aggregate demand, for this will determine by how much *AD* rises when i falls (the slope of the *IS* schedule). When $\Delta M^d/\Delta i$ is low so that i falls considerably under the influence of $M^s > M^d$ and $\Delta AD/\Delta i$ is high so that *AD* rises considerably under the influence of a fall in i, the cost of capital effect is strong and monetary policy can be expected to exert a significant effect upon Y/P, (assuming the economy is operating at a level of output significantly below full employment). As the causal sequence above illustrates and as the tracing out of the impact of ΔM^s in *Figure 6.3* shows, after the impact of ΔM^s has worked its way through to *P* there will be a reverse feedback effect upon *AD* and thus Y/P

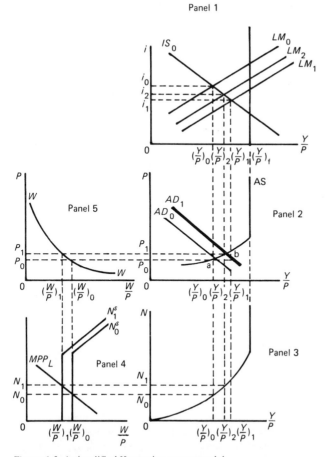

Figure 6.3 A simplified Keynesian macro model

operating through the causal sequence (b) and it corresponds to the movement back up the AD under the influence of a rising price level.

Diagrammatically, the sequence of events following from an expansion in the stock of money is as follows: in panel 1 the increase in M^s shifts the LM schedule to the right from LM_0 to LM_1 depressing the rate of interest to i_1 and stimulating an expansion of demand of horizontal distance $(Y/P)_1 - (Y/P)_0$. In panel 2 the increase in demand at an unchanged price of P_0 creates an excess demand of horizontal distance $b - a$. Under the pressure of this excess demand the price level begins to rise. The higher price level lowers the real wage in panels 5 and 4, increases the level of employment and output in panels 4 and 3, and shifts the LM schedule part way back to its original position in panel 1, $(LM_1 \rightarrow LM_2)$, through the reverse feedback mechanism (b) as indicated earlier. The equilibrium price level P_1 that clears the goods market in conjunction with the interest i_2 and real output (income) level $(Y/P)_2$ produces money market equilibrium, and the lowered W/P rate to the accompaniment of a leftward shift of the N^s schedule in panel 4, clears the labour market. The final comparative static outcome of the monetary expansion operating through the 'strong' cost of capital effect is a lower i and W/P and a higher $Y/P,N$ and P. Under these circumstances monetary policy is provided with plenty of scope for influencing the real economic variables of the system. As L. S. Ritter (1963, p. 140) points out, 'In the Keynesian approach ... money also plays a role in the determination of real output. For the first time money becomes more than merely a veil and a monetary economy is seen as behaving very differently from a barter economy.'

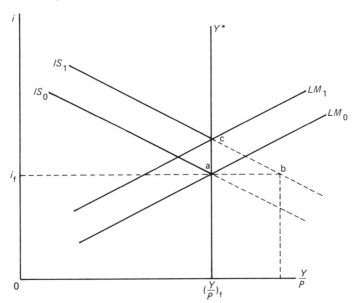

Figure 6.4 Inflation and monetary policy in the Keynesian system

Not only is monetary policy useful as an anti-depression device, i.e. counteracting the effects of a drop in autonomous expenditure and as a device for positively stimulating the level of economic activity; it also has the same strategic role to perform as an anti-inflation device as it has in the traditional classical macrosystem (see also pp. 112–156). If the economy is already situated at full employment as depicted in *Figure 6.4* and for some reason there is a spontaneous increase in autonomous expenditure in the economy pushing the *IS* schedule to the right ($IS_0 \rightarrow IS_1$), this automatically generates, at the initial rate of interest, an excess of money demand (distance $b - a$) over current full employment output. This puts an upward pressure on the general level of prices, presenting the monetary authorities with two possible policy strategies. First of all, they can do nothing and let the 'reverse feedback' mechanism, described earlier operating through increased *P* and higher *i*, remove the excess demand (shifting *LM* back to LM_1 intersecting IS_1 at c). There are, however, two disadvantages attaching to this 'passive' strategy. First, it entails placing the whole of the burden of adjustment upon the price level and price increases which, particularly if they are unanticipated, may have undesirable 'welfare' consequences. Second, there is the danger that excessive increases in the *P* level may trigger off destabilizing expectations of future price changes which may serve to exacerbate and not to remedy the current inflationary situation. The foregoing suggests that there is scope for a more 'active' policy strategy. Alternatively they can contract the money supply as soon as evidence of the excess demand or impending excess demand becomes available (again shifting *LM* to the left), removing the excess demand with a minimum of disturbance to the price level. In the first interpretation of the Keynesian system where the cost of capital effect is strong 'money does matter' in the sense of influencing real economic variables, and there is plenty of scope for monetary policy both as an anti-depression as well as an anti-inflation device.

Interpretation 2: cost of capital effect weak

This second interpretation of the role of money in the Keynesian system is much more pessimistic in outlook than the previous one and suggests that the effectiveness of, and therefore scope for, monetary policy is likely to be very limited. Supporters of this interpretation draw attention to certain crucial 'weak' links in the cost of capital channel of a portfolio transmission mechanism reproduced, for convenience, below:

$$\uparrow M^s; \quad M^s > M^d; \quad \| \uparrow B^d; \quad B^d > B^s; \quad \uparrow P^B; \quad \downarrow i; \quad \uparrow C + I \|$$

and cite three instances in which some or all of the response mechanisms bounded by the two sets of vertical lines may fail to come into operation. The first 'weak' link relates to the possible existence of a 'liquidity trap'. We may recall from Chapter 3 that Keynes posited the possibility of some low (+) rate of interest at which the demand for speculative balances might become infinitely elastic. This would be the rate at which the investing public as a whole believed that no further movement downward could be expected on the basis of past market experience. As a result (as *Figure 6.5* shows) any attempts to depress the interest rate further by increasing the money supply will be frustrated as all the additional money disappears into idle hoards. If the liquidity trap rate lies above that necessary to produce a level of *I* capable of sustaining a full employment level of output, then there will be a continuing state of unemployment which will be intractable as far as monetary policy is concerned.

Some economists hold the view that by its very nature a liquidity trap can be nothing more than a transitory phenomena because its basic rationale is one of inelastic interest rate expectations. Traditional comparative static equilibrium analysis tacitly assumes that changes in 'market expectations' are of a 'second order of magnitude' in relation to the relevant short-run time period and can therefore be ignored. But this, as Mundell (1965) has pointed out, need not necessarily be the case. Market expectations are dynamic economic forces continuously changing over time and are dimensionally equivalent to changes in interest rates. For this

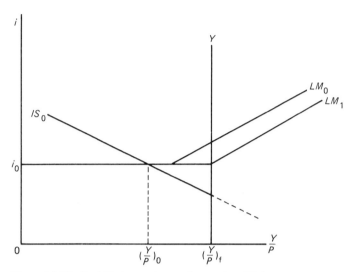

Figure 6.5 The liquidity trap and unemployment equilibrium

reason they should not be omitted from the determination of short-run macro-static equilibrium. The argument is that the current level of the interest rate must enter the speculator's formation model of interest rate expectations causing him continuously to revise upwards and downwards his concept of the 'normal' rate in the light of the current level and the duration of the current level. Consequently the positioning of the horizontal section of the *LM* schedule will be subject to variation over time as interest rate expectations change, and this will inevitably have repercussions on money and goods market equilibrium. Because the expected interest rate (i_e) will not be independent of the current rate (i) and changes in it, the gap between i_e and the liquidity trap rate will narrow and the minimum critical rate (min i_c) may fall. This can be verified by considering again the expression for i_c from Chapter 3 (p. 48):

$$i_c = \frac{i_e}{1 + i_e}$$

The longer the liquidity trap rate prevails the greater the likelihood that the investing public will revise downwards their estimate of i_e in the light of a continuingly low current rate. Some investors with i_e close to the current liquidity trap rate will come to view min i_c as the normal rate around which fluctuations in the actual rate are to be expected. As a result of an assumed uniform downward revision of i_e, min i_c will fall, as can be verified by comparing $i_e/(1 + i_e)$ with ($i_e + \Delta i_e)/(1 + i_e + \Delta i_e)$, i.e. if

$$i_{c_0} = \frac{0.10}{1 + 0.10} = \frac{1}{11}$$

and if the average expected rate of interest drops from 10 to 5% then

$$i_{c_1} = \frac{0.05}{1 + 0.05} = \frac{1}{21} \quad \text{clearly} \quad \frac{1}{21} < \frac{1}{11}$$

so that both critical rates will fall. As *Figure 6.6(a)* shows, the reduction in i_c reduces the demand for idle balances and increases the demand for bonds.

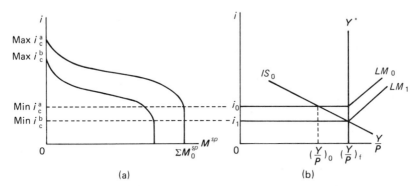

Figure 6.6 The effect on the *LM* curve of revised views of the 'normal' rate of interest

As speculators attempt to acquire additional bonds upon which a positive return is still to be earned, $P_B \uparrow$, $i \downarrow$, $I \uparrow$ etc. and AE rises towards its full employment value. Under these circumstances a change in the demand for money will influence the real variables of the system so that 'money does matter'. However, it is not clear what interpretation one should place on the role of monetary policy in this situation. There is little that monetary policy can actively do to alter interest rate expectations, for this occurs spontaneously as a by-product of time. However, in the sense that the monetary authorites can determine the terms on which they supply bonds to the market, they have an important part to play in the determination of the nominal interest rate. The conclusion we must draw on this first 'weak' link is that as a liquidity trap is only likely to be at most a short-run phenomenon in a dynamic economy it does not impose any real limitations on the influence of M^d and M_0 upon Y/P.

The second weak link in the causal chain is the interest-sensitivity of AE. Some economists are of the opinion, and they claim that the empirical evidence supports this, that Δi has a negligibly small impact upon I and C. In terms of our *IS–LM* diagrams it means that the *IS* schedule can be assumed vertical. If the *IS* schedule is situated to the left of $(Y/P)_f$, then no increase in M_0 will influence real expenditure and the interest rate will fall to a level at which all the additional cash is held idle. Monetary policy is ineffective and to all intents and purposes money does not matter. This is a much more serious limitation on the scope and effectiveness of monetary policy than that of the 'liquidity trap'. Consider, for example, the implications of an interest-inelastic *IS* schedule for combating demand-pull inflation. Imagine that autonomous expenditure has risen to an extent that shifts the vertical *IS* schedule to the right of full employment. Neither the inflationary consequences of the excess demand on M^t and i nor a contraction in M^s will eliminate the disequilibrium situation, only a fall in autonomous expenditure will succeed in doing that. Thus monetary policy loses its potency both as an anti-recession and an anti-inflation device when AE is interest-inelastic. Unless one is prepared to make some additional assumptions about the private sector's response to an excess or deficiency of cash balances, or about the responsiveness of AE to different levels of i, or about its responsiveness to a different concept of i from the one being employed here, changes in M^s and M^d will have no effect upon either the equilibrium profile of the real variables nor the behaviour of money national expenditure and P.

The third weak link in the cost of capital channel of monetary influence revolves around a possible 'inconsistency' between S and I. It may well be that in economic systems where I opportunities are low and the community is very thrifty that I and full employment S can only be equated at a $(-)$ rate of interest, i.e. at all positive interest rates full employment S exceeds I and there is a chronic deficiency of demand in the economy. This possibility is depicted in *Figure 6.7*, where $-i_f$ is the rate of interest which would be needed to produce a level of I commensurate with a full employment level of S. Although conceptually distinct from the previous two

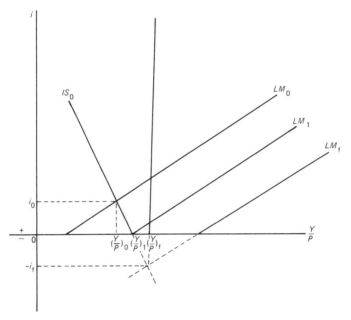

Figure 6.7 Deficient demand and the inconsistency between S and I

cases there is, nevertheless, likely to be a $(+)$ floor level to the interest rate determined by the trade-off between the sacrifice of convenience against the cost of holding money balances idle. In effect the intervention of a liquidity trap (i_0 in *Figure 6.7*) in the short run will determine the level of real output as $(Y/P)_0$ and in the longer run, after interest rate expectations and monetary expansion have depressed the rate to zero (where, by definition, the cost of holding money is zero and no further downward movement of the interest rate is conceivable), the level of real output will reach its maximum at $(Y/P)_1$, where $(Y/P)_1 < (Y/P)_f$. Unless the IS schedule can be made to move to the right by monetary action, monetary policy will become completely ineffective in influencing Y/P when the quantity of money in circulation has reached a value depicted by the LM_1 schedule. As in the previous case where AE is interest-inelastic, 'money does not matter' when there is an inconsistency between S and I.

Interpretation 3: 'inside' money, 'outside' money and wealth effects

These first two interpretations of the role of money have focused attention upon one channel of influence operating through a portfolio-balance transmission mechanism, namely the cost of capital and its effectiveness in influencing the 'real' and monetary variables in the economy. An alternative interpretation of the role of money in the Keynesian macrosystem is one which investigates the impact of changes in the quantity of money on the real behaviour of the economy operating through a wealth-transmission mechanism. Some economists believe that a distinction between 'inside' and 'outside' monetary systems is a useful one in this context because only in the case of an 'outside' money system will an operationally significant wealth effect occur. Other economists however (notably Pesek–Saving) have argued that such a distinction is artificial and that in both types of monetary regime monetary variables are capable of transmitting impulses to real expenditure through wealth effects. Irrespective of which camp one decides to side with on this issue one thing seems to have emerged quite forcefully from the debate concerning it; that one is seriously in error, at least at an abstract level, if one omits from an analysis of the role of money the possibility of 'wealth' influences on AE. It is to a consideration of these that we must now turn.

Two types of wealth effect associated with an expansion of the stock of inside and/or outside money can be distinguished: a real balance and an interest-induced wealth effect.[9]

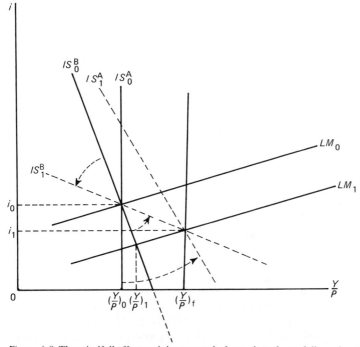

Figure 6.8 The windfall effect and the removal of two obstacles to full employment

The interest-induced or 'Keynes' windfall' effect is the influence upon AE of changes in the current market valuation of financial assets, namely bonds, reflecting changes in market interest rates. This wealth effect is of direct relevance to two of the three cases we have looked at in which monetary stimulation fails to raise the level of economic activity: the i-elastic IS schedule and the inconsistency between S and I. If I is relatively insensitive to Δi but S is not, because of the operation of a strong windfall effect, then this will have the effect of tilting the IS schedule and giving it a non-vertical slope (see *Figure 6.8*, i.e. $(IS_0^A \rightarrow IS_1^A)$,   so making it possible for a monetary expansion to get a grip on real expenditure via the interest rate. Moreover an interest-induced wealth effect may be able to eradicate the inconsistency between I and S if it can influence I directly. It may well be that firms (like households) who do hold bonds in their portfolios may feel psychologically 'better off' as a result of a strengthened balance sheet when the interest rate on the bonds they are holding falls so that they may feel more inclined to finance new I projects from internal sources. If this is the case then the IS schedule will rotate counterclockwise (as in *Figure 6.8*) enabling it, perhaps, to intersect LM on (Y/P) at a positive interest rate $(IS_0^B \rightarrow IS_1^B)$. In the case of a liquidity trap where by definition, in the short-term, no change in i is possible in response to an increase in M^s, there can be no windfall effect and consequently no change in AE.

The 'real balance effect' is the effect of a change in the stock of real cash balances (nominal cash balances deflated by some index of the general level of prices) upon the demand for commodities. According to Patinkin it follows as a matter of logic that

an increase in the quantity of money, other things being held constant, influences the demand for a commodity just like any other increase in wealth: if the commodity is a normal ... one the amount demanded will increase; if inferior it will decrease (1965, p. 20).

To incorporate this effect into our analysis entails respecification of the S function in the IS relation. S is no longer a function solely of Y/P but of M^s/P as well, where M^s/P is the real stock of cash balances. The real balance effect suggests that shifts in the LM schedule associated with expansions in M^s will no longer leave the IS schedule unaffected because it will increase M^s/P, raise private wealth and increase expenditure on goods and services. It can then be presumed that there exists some level of private wealth (some quantity of real cash balances) that is capable of generating a volume of real expenditure of sufficient magnitude to absorb a full employment level of output, $(Y/P)_f$. Because the real balance effect by-passes the cost of capital channel of influence and operates directly upon AE, then interest-inelasticities of AE, an inconsistency between S and I and infinite interest-elasticity of the demand for speculative balances, do not frustrate the stimulatory effect of a monetary expansion upon output and N. In recognizing the theoretical existence of a real balance effect it is possible to reinstate the role and effectiveness of monetary action even when the cost of capital effect does not operate.

We suggested at the beginning of this section that the distinction between inside and outside money could be largely ignored in a discussion of the role of wealth effects in the Keynesian system because it was possible on analytical grounds to justify the existence of such wealth effects under both types of monetary regime. Some economists would probably not agree with this interpretation and would point out that a distinction between 'inside' and 'outside' money systems has important implications for the role of money within the context of a wealth transmission mechanism. Recall again the Gurley-Shaw distinction between inside and outside money. Outside money is government demand debt (currency) backed by government securities. If the government is unconcerned about the level of its debts outstanding and assuming the private sector does feel that the ownership of government interest-bearing debt (securities) is a claim on them in the form of future tax liabilities to finance the interest on this debt, then an increase in the quantity of outside money will have a real balance effect on C by raising the level of private wealth. We have already seen that a real balance effect will shift the *IS* schedule upwards and to the right raising the level of Y/P, even when the cost of capital effect is non-existent. In the case of inside money which is government demand debt/bank money backed by private debt either business bonds and/or bank advances etc., an increase in its stock in circulation will leave private wealth unchanged by expanding the assets of and claims on the private sector commensurately, and with no change in private wealth the real balance effect in the goods market will be absent. If there is no real balance effect and the cost of capital effect is weak or non-existent as well, then only the operation of an interest-induced effect can save the economy from chronic demand deficiency. We have already seen that theoretically an interest-induced wealth effect can cope with two of the three obstacles to full employment, an interest-elastic *IS* schedule and the inconsistency between *S* and *I*. However, it is powerless to extricate the economy from a liquidity trap and it is because under one type of monetary regime (outside money) full employment is theoretically attainable through monetary action via a real balance effect, whereas under another (inside money) this is not necessarily so, that economists feel an analytical distinction between inside and outside money systems is necessary.

However, it can be demonstrated that although an interpretation of the Keynesian system as an inside money system leads one to the conclusion that interest-induced wealth effects associated with monetary expansion are not capable of attaining full employment because of the existence of a liquidity trap there are certain features of an inside money system which make the existence of a liquidity trap doubtful anyway. In a liquidity trap the demand for idle balances is infinite and the demand for bonds zero. At the liquidity trap rate, that rate which lies infinitesimally below the min i_c of the investing public, it is to be presumed that the monetary authority is holding the total stock of outstanding bonds, and the private sector none. If we interpret the Keynesian system as an outside money system then the bonds being held by the monetary authority are government bonds. Because nothing will induce the private sector to hold such bonds (holding interest rate expectations constant) there is no point in continuing to offer bonds to members of the private sector and therefore there is no possibility of influencing i. If, on the other hand, we interpret the Keynesian system as an inside money system then the stock of bonds, although fixed at any point in time, will be subject to continuous variation over time. If firms issue bonds to finance their current account deficits (net I) the stock of bonds in existence will undergo secular expansion provided there is continuing positive net I in the economy. Although households in the private sector may not be prepared to hold such bonds for fear of capital losses, the government might. The monetary authority acting on behalf of the government can enter the bond market and dictate the terms upon which it is prepared to purchase new issues of bonds from the business firms. They can stimulate business investment directly by raising the price (lowering the rate of interest) at which they are willing to purchase bonds. In this way they can depress the interest rate below the liquidity trap rate, induce an incentive to invest and provide the necessary finance. Presumably the authorities can continue with this exercise until they have persuaded business firms to undertake a full employment volume of investment. In an inside money system therefore the concept of a liquidity trap becomes clouded and loses meaning. For this reason a distinction between inside and outside money systems is useful only for indicating the type of wealth effects through which a monetary expansion will operate to raise the level of economic activity. It cannot legitimately be used to enumerate the circumstances in which monetary expansion may or may not raise the level of economic activity because it can do so under either system.

Interpretation 4: endogeneity of the money supply and the availability of credit

It has been tacitly assumed throughout the foregoing that the supply of money in the Keynesian macrosystem is fixed by the monetary authorities and is uninfluenced by the behaviour of endogenous variables; to use the terminology of Chapter 4 the supply of money is exogenous. Recognition of the possibility that the money supply may be partly, if not wholly, determined endogenously offers us the opportunity of another interpretation of the role of money in the Keynesian macrosystem. It will be pointed out in Chapter 13 that for large periods of the 1950s and 1960s the UK monetary authorities were striving to maintain 'orderly conditions in the gilt-edged market' by pegging interest rates and thus allowing the money supply to adjust passively to the demand for money as determined by the

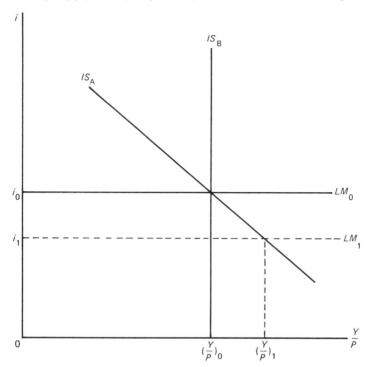

Figure 6.9 Pegged interest rate, variable money stock

level of income etc. Diagrammatically such a policy strategy would entail an infinitely elastic *LM* schedule throughout its entire length (see *Figure 6.9*).

Given the pegged interest rate i_0, the demand for idle cash balances and the volume of *I* expenditure would be fixed. In this situation changes in the money supply could only come about through changes in the transactions demand for cash (M^t). Now the M^t demand for cash is a function primarily of real income, and real income is determined by *AE*. With *I* assumed constant by definition in this model, Y/P is determined by the level of autonomous expenditure in the economy, i.e. the position of the *IS* schedule. As it is only through *i* that changes in M^s and M^d can influence the real variables of the system, and because *i* is assumed constant, the cost of capital effect and the windfall effects are non-operative and 'money does not matter'. This is true, however, only if the pegged rate of interest prevails indefinitely. But stability of an interest rate does not necessarily mean fixity. From time to time the authorities may feel it expedient to alter the level at which they are pegging the interest rate, say, in the interests of long-term growth. If the authorities feel that in order to raise the rate of capital accumulation a lower i is desired, then they can raise the price at which they are prepared to purchase bonds from the private sector thereby shifting bodily downwards the *LM* schedule in *Figure 6.9* from $LM_0 \rightarrow LM_1$. Provided *AE* is *i*-elastic (IS_A) then a shift down of the *LM* schedule will stimulate additional *I* expenditure in the familiar way. However, as depicted in *Figure 6.9* this policy will fail through a conventional cost of capital channel of monetary influence if the *IS* schedule is vertical so that 'monetary variables do not matter'.

However, if we apply a Radcliffe view of monetary action to this type of situation, if offers the opportunity of interpreting the role of monetary variables in a more optimistic light. Although *AE* may be *i*-inelastic, changing the money supply or manipulating interest rates may have repercussions on the availability of loanable funds, and through this have an effect on expenditure. The possible links between the money supply, the availability of bank and total credit, and expenditure, were considered on pp. 32–34. We confine our attention here to a particular link between interest rates and credit availability which gained fairly wide currency in academic and official circles during the 1950s. This is the so-called 'locking-in effect'. The idea is that for a given level of bank loan rates, an authority induced increase in the pegged interest rate on gilt-edged stock (i.e. lowering the market prices of the stock) will deter holders (e.g. banks) from liquidating government bonds in order to finance additional loans. Such potentially loanable funds will be 'locked-in' to government bonds. Lowering interest rates on government bonds will 'unlock' loanable funds and increase their supply, reducing any previously existing market shortage, and stimulating expenditure (shifting the *IS* curve to the right). Thus a fifth interpretation of the role of money and monetary variables in the Keynesian system is to see them influencing expenditure through their effects on the availability of loanable funds.

The Keynesian model in the open economy

In this section we extend the Keynesian model to an open economy. In doing so, however, we shall make the simplifying assumptions that the price level is fixed and unemployment is less than full: hence variations in aggregate demand will be reflected in changes in real output. Keynesian models of inflation in an open economy will be considered in Chapter 9.

The approach adopted in this section was originally developed by Fleming (1962) and Mundell (1963) in the early 1960s essentially for the purpose of analysing the role of monetary and fiscal policies in the context of an open economy: thus it is sometimes referred to as the Fleming–Mundell analysis. The approach nevertheless is essentially Keynesian and has entered the textbooks as the standard open-economy Keynesian model.

Essentially we shall be adding to the conventional *IS–LM* analysis, a balance of payments constraint, so that the goods market, the money market, and the balance of payments are all interdependent. No one of these three can maintain a position of equilibrium unless it is simultaneously a position of equilibrium for the other two.

For an economy engaging in international trade, injections include exports while leakages include imports. Goods market equilibrium prevails when total injections (investment + government expenditure + exports) are equal to total leakages (savings, + taxes + imports). We will assume that exports are a function of two main variables: the level of real incomes in the rest of the world and the price competitiveness of exports (i.e. the ratio of the prices of export substitutes in the rest of the world to the prices of exports). This price ratio depends not only on the own-currency prices of the goods but also on the rate of exchange between currencies. For example UK exports could become more price competitive either because of a fall in their sterling price, or because of a rise in the foreign currency price of competing goods produced in the rest of the world, or because of a depreciation of the pound sterling on the foreign exchange market. We will take imports to be a function of national income and the price competiveness of domestically produced import substitutes *vis-a-vis* imports. This again depends on the own currency price of the goods and services concerned and the rate of exchange between the currencies.

In the money market, the only modification that is necessary to the closed economy analysis in order to take account of international trade is to recognize that the money supply depends not only on domestically produced money (DCE) but also on any addition or subtraction to it arising out of inflows/outflows across the foreign exchanges. Thus with a balance of payments deficit there would be a net outflow of money resulting in a fall in the money supply: with a balance of payments surplus there would be an expansion of the money supply.

We now turn to the balance of payments and derive a curve which traces out the various combinations of interest and income that keep the balance of payments in equilibrium. Assume that initially we have such a combination, so that the balance of payments is in balance in the sense that the total currency flow sums to zero, as also therefore does the official settlements balance. If now, there is an increase in the level of income, then more imports will be sucked into the economy, to an extent determined by the marginal propensity to import. The current account of the balance of payments will deteriorate and the total currency flow will move into deficit. To restore equilibrium the increased outflow on the current account must be offset by an increased inflow on the capital account. Net capital movements into a country are assumed to be directly related to interest rates in that country, given constant foeign rates of interest. Domestic interest rates will therefore need to rise in order to generate the required capital inflow. Thus higher levels of income must be accompanied by higher rates of interest if the balance of payments is to remain in balance. The curve tracing out the different combinations of income and interest thus slopes upwards from left to right. Such a curve is drawn in *Figure 6.10* and labelled *BP*. The slope of the curve depends on the marginal propensity to import and the interest sensitivity of capital flows. A special case would be where capital movements are perfectly interest elastic, giving a horizontal *BP* curve. All points to the northwest of the *BP* curve represent combinations of interest and income that generate a balance of payments surplus, while all points to the southeast of it are combinations of interest and income that give rise to a balance of payments deficit.

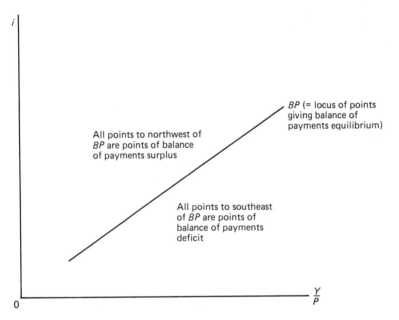

Figure 6.10 The *BP* curve

Figure 6.11 combines the *IS*, *LM* and *BP* curves. The point where all three curves intersect is one of simultaneous equilibrium in the goods market, the money market, and the balance of payments. At any other point there must be disequilibrium in at least one of the two markets and/or on the external account.

Before moving on to look at the role of money in this open economy model, we must distinguish between fixed and floating exchange rate systems. With a fixed exchange rate the authorities will intervene on the foreign exchange market, buying and selling sterling as appropriate, in order to maintain the exchange rate at its fixed level. Under such a system a balance of payments deficit will give rise to a net outflow of money across the foreign exchanges and a resulting fall in the country's money supply: the opposite would arise from a balance of payments surplus. With a floating system, the rate of exchange itself acts as the equilibrating mechanism which keeps the demand for and supply of the country's currency on the foreign exchange market in balance, with no net inflows or outflows of money to augment or reduce the country's DCE.

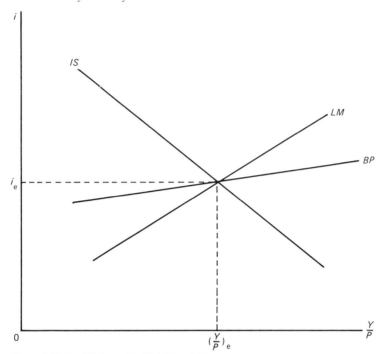

Figure 6.11 Equilibrium with *IS*, *LM* and *BP* curves

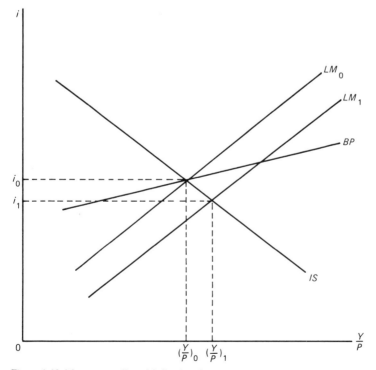

Figure 6.12 Monetary policy with fixed exchange rates

Monetary policy with fixed exchange rates

We can now consider the affects of monetary policy under fixed exchange rates. This is done in *Figure 6.12*. We start from a position of general equilibrium with interest of i_0 and income of $(Y/P)_0$. If now the authorities expand the money supply it will shift the *LM* curve to the right to, say, the position labelled LM_1. This intersects the *IS* curve at a lower rate of interest (i_1), and higher level of income $(Y/P)_1$. But this is a combination of interest and income that would generate a balance of payments deficit, with higher imports (because of the higher Y/P) and lower capital inflows (because of the lower i). The deficit will generate a fall in the money supply and the *LM* curve will shift in a northwesterly direction. As it does so it intersects the *IS* curve at higher interest rates and lower levels of income, thereby reducing the balance of payments deficit. Eventually the *LM* curve would return to its original position, where the balance of payments will be in equilibrium and there will be no further contraction in the money supply. Interest and income too will be back at their original positions and general equilibrium will prevail. The only change that has taken place is that the money supply has a larger domestic component in it and a smaller foreign exchange component. Thus the monetary expansion will have had no permanent effect on the rate of interest or the level of real income.

The above analysis needs to be amended to the extent that the authorities try to neutralize or sterilize the effects of the balance of payments deficit on the money supply. If the authorities continually expand the DCE component of the money supply in an attempt to offset the net outflow across the foreign exchanges so as to keep the new higher level of income, then there will be no leftward movement of the *LM* curve away from its new position of LM_1. However, such steralization cannot be maintained indefinitely because it depletes the country's foreign exchange reserves, and would eventually completely exhaust them.

Monetary policy under floating exchange rates

The effects of an expansionary monetary policy under floating exchange rates is illustrated in *Figure 6.13*. Again the initial position of triple equilibrium is given by the point A, comprising interest of i_0 and income of $(Y/P)_0$. An expansion of the money supply would shift the *LM* curve to the right to the position LM_1. Now, because the exchange rate is free to float it will move so as to keep the balance of payments in balance with no net inflow or outflow of money. This means that the *LM* curve will not shift from its new position LM_1. Conseqeuntly, if equilibrium is to be restored it must lie somewhere along the new LM_1 curve. The shift of the *LM* schedule to LM_1 gives a new point of intersection with the *IS* curve at point B, comprising a lower rate of interest (i_1) and a higher level of income $(Y/P)_1$. This will expand the demand for imports and reduce the net inflow of capital. As a result the exchange rate will depreciate. As it does so it will lower the price of exports and raise import prices. Exports will then rise and imports fall, shifting the *IS* curve to the right, say to position IS_1. Assuming that the improved price competitiveness of exports and the reduced price attractiveness of imports raises the value of net exports, then the *BP* curve will also shift downwards to the right. In this way a new position of general equilibrium is reached at point C where all three curves intersect. The result of the monetary expansion has therefore been an increase in real income, a fall in the rate of interest and a lower external value of the currency.

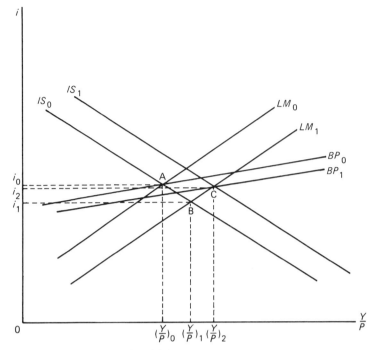

Figure 6.13 Monetary policy with floating exchange rates

The re-interpretation of Keynes

The last two decades have seen a number of related developments in economics which, although going under different names, have all basically been concerned with the problem of how a complex market economy coordinates the activities of transactors under conditions of uncertainty and in the absence of free information. These developments have usually recognized that many transactions take place out of equilibrium, and they have therefore been primarily concerned with disequilibrium analysis in contrast to the comparative static analysis of conventional macroeconomics. In this section we are going to consider how these developments have lead to a re-interpretation and re-appraisal of the work of Keynes.

In a market economy, the coordination of the activites of the various economic agents, each of whom is pursuing his own self-interest, is traditionally seen as being achieved through the workings of the price mechanism. To do this effectively, prices must perform two functions simultaneously. Firstly they must convey information to transactors about the opportunities open to them, and secondly they must provide the incentive for transactors to harmonize their activities so that they are consistent in the aggregate.

Thus if there exists a vector of prices that would clear all markets, and if this vector is known to all transactors, and if the transactors harmonize their transactions accordingly, then resources will be fully employed. If, however, the market-clearing vector of prices is not known, or if it is known but transactors do not adjust their behaviour accordingly, then unemployment of resources may persist.

In the re-interpretation of his work, Keynes is regarded as accepting that prices provide effective incentives for transactors but as denying that they provide, at least in the short run, the information necessary to generate the transcations that guarantee full employment. Before examining this argument further it will be helpful if we first consider the views of the classical economists on the dissemination of information. Specifically we shall consider the Walrasian process of *tâtonnement*.

In this process there is a fictional auctioneer who calls out a random vector of prices and receives offers to buy and sell from all the transactors. If there is an excess supply or excess demand in any market, then no transactions are allowed to take place at all. Instead, the auctioneer calls out another set of prices and receives revised offers to buy and sell. This continues until the auctioneer has groped his way to the vector of prices that clears all markets. Then and only then are transactions actually allowed to take place. Trading therefore only takes place in a situation of static general equilibrium.

If saving and investment are taking place in the economy, then there are added problems of an intertemporal nature. A decision to save is a decision to postpone consumption until future periods. Similarly a decision to invest is a decision to abstain from producing consumer goods in the current period in order to be able to produce more in future periods. The Walrasian auctioneer must now discover and announce the vector of intertemporal prices which clears not only present but also future markets.

With *tâtonnement* it is difficult to see a role for money except as a numéraire or common denominator for measuring exchange values. As we saw in Chapter 1 if there are neither uncertainty nor transactions costs then there is no need for money as a means of payment or store of value. Both of these criteria for avoiding the need for money appear to be met with *tâtonnement*, for all economic agents know that the vector of prices at which they are allowed to trade by the auctioneer is a vector of the best prices obtainable for both buyers and sellers and a vector that guarantees they can buy or sell as much as they want of each and every good. According to Laidler (1974, p. 28) with *tâtonnement*

> It is difficult to apply ... the usual arguments about the greater costs of direct barter, most of which stem from the costs of finding the appropriate set of trading partners; but even if some such artificiality as uncertainty about the precise timing of meetings between pairs of traders during the market period is introduced, this only opens up the possibility of intermediate trades taking place; it stops far short of explaining why it is sensible to hold inventories of any good, and money in particular, between market periods. It only makes sense to do this if the individual sees some chance of his receipts in the market not being equal to his outgoings, and this possibility does not arise when all trades are taking place and are known to be taking place, at equilibrium prices. Only if individuals come to market uncertain of the prices at which they are going to trade or uncertain about the likelihood of expenditures and receipts balancing does it become sensible to hold inventories of goods and money between visits to the market.

According to the re-interpretation of his views, Keynes was concerned to analyse the behaviour of quantities and prices in the absence of the benevolent auctioneer. In this way his theory was more general than that of the classical economists. Keynes was not so much questioning whether there existed a vector of market-clearing prices as asking how in the absence of the auctioneer such a vector would become established and made known to all transactors.

In the real world situation, which was what concerned him, Keynes argued that prices adjust slowly to changing supply and demand conditions in contrast to the perfect price flexibility of *tâtonnement*. Trading takes place at non-equilibrium prices, and transactors are required to make decisions not only on quantities but also on prices. Let us consider three different kinds of transactors – an asset-holder, an employee and an employer. All of them are assumed to have inelastic price expectations.

Consider first the asset-holder and specifically a bond-holder. He cannot know, in the absence of *tâtonnement*, what the future course of bond prices will be. But he will have, according to Keynes's liquidity preference theory, a conception of the normal rate of interest. If bond prices rise above the normal level the bond-holder will sell in anticipation of buying the bonds back again when their prices fall back to normal. Similarly bonds would be bought when their prices fell below normal. If this is the typical response of bond-holders, then bond prices will not diverge much from their normal level.

Consider now a worker who is made redundant. Should he accept a cut in money wages in order to get new employment quickly? Not necessarily, because he does not know whether the decline in the demand for his services is a temporary one, or whether it is localized or general. Until he has information to the contrary the worker may well believe that he can find another job at his previous wage and will therefore remain unemployed while he searches for information about job opportunities. Like the bond-holder, the worker may have inelastic expectations about wages. Even if he realizes that the decline in demand for his services is permanent and general it will still not mean his necessarily accepting the first job offer he receives. Searching for information about job opportunities generates both costs and benefits. It will pay the worker to undertake a further period of search as long as the benefits of doing so exceed the costs. The benefits are the present value of the extra wages that the worker expects to discover during the period of search: the cost is the best wage so far offered minus unemployment benefit.

Finally consider the position of a producer–employer who is confronted with a fall in the demand for his product. How is he likely to respond? He does not know initially whether the fall in demand is specific to his product or is more general, and he does not know whether it is temporary or permanent. He has less than perfect information and must himself try to search out the information he needs. While he does so it may be quite rational behaviour on his part to leave his price unaltered. Until he has information to the contrary the employer may well believe that the fall in demand is temporary and the prevailing price the 'right' one. He will therefore keep to that price until he has information that leads him to the conclusion that it needs lowering. Like the asset-holder and the worker, the employer is regarded by Keynes as having inelastic expectations.

We must now ask what effects this assumed behaviour on the part of transactors has for the response of aggregate output and employment to an exogenous disturbance. Let us use *Figure 6.14* to trace through the consequences of a more pessimistic revision of businessmen's expectations. Assume that initially there is a vector of prices that clears all markets so that we have general equilibrium. A more pessimistic revision of businessmen's expectations is shown in panel 1 as a shift of the *IS* curve from IS_0 to IS_1. The initial response of producer–employers is, according to the analysis above, to leave prices unchanged and adjust quantities. A reduction in output will result, via the production function of panel 3 in a fall in the demand for labour. But this does not mean that the demand for labour curve shifts in panel 4. Instead the employers' actual demand for labour lies off the demand curve. Thus if output fell to $(Y/P)_1$ in panel 1, only N_1 workers would be demanded in panel 4. As there has been no change in goods prices or wages the real wage remains at its original level $(W/P)_0$. The employment position in the labour market is then given by the position A.

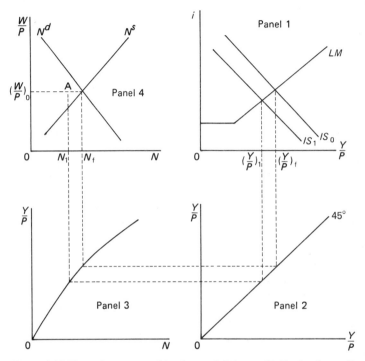

Figure 6.14 Unemployment resulting from a deficiency of 'effective demand'

This is an example of the distinction made by Clower between notional and effective demands. Notional demands are those which would be exercised at equilibrium prices, and unconstrained by an inability to buy or sell at the prevailing prices in any other market. Effective demands on the other hand are actual demands backed up by an ability to pay. The demand for labour curve in panel 4 is a notional demand curve. It is the profit-maximizing demand for labour unconstrained by an inability to sell what the labour makes. The effective demand for labour, given the output $(Y/P)_1$, is only N_1. Only when there is general equilibrium will notional and effective demands be the same.

It is only effective demands that constitute market signals. An unemployed person, for example, has no way of conveying to suppliers of goods the information that he would buy more if only he could gain employment, i.e. supply more labour services. Similarly producer–employers cannot inform households that they would employ more workers if they could sell more goods. In a monetary economy that is not in general equilibrium the price system does not provide the information necessary to re-establish the vector of market clearing prices.

A disturbance to general equilibrium will in fact initiate a cumulative movement away through a multiplier process. People who are made unemployed will find their effective demands for goods constrained by their now reduced incomes. This fall in the effective demand for goods will further constrain the effective demand for labour and lead to more unemployment. Leijonhufvud however argues that these multiplier effects will only occur on a significant scale when the economy has been squeezed of its liquidity. Until that point is reached the unemployed may maintain their effective demands at their notional level by drawing on money balances and other liquid assets. In Leijonhufvud's view:

> In a very general sense at least, quantity theorists and Keynesians should be able to agree on one thing – how great disasters are fashioned. On one view or the other, the system becomes prone to them only when it has first been squeezed dry of 'liquidity'. (1969, p. 45).

The persistence of unemployment is then, according to this analysis, a consequence of the failure by the price system to communicate to transactors the information that would enable them to coordinate their activities in such a way as to restore full employment quickly.

The emergence of unemployment is a consequence of the breakdown in the consistency of inter-temporal plans on consumption and investment. In considering such breakdowns Keynes concentrated on three kinds of disturbance that might act as triggers: (i) a change in the long-run expectations of businessmen; (ii) a change in the propensity to save/consume; and (iii) a change in the community's liquidity preference.

If consumers decide to save more it means they have decided to consume less today in order to be able to consume more tomorrow. To maintain full employment this increased saving should be matched by producers' switching resources from the production of goods for current consumption into the production of the means of producing the extra consumption goods when they are wanted, i.e. into investment.

The required increase in investment however is not likely to take place for two reasons. First, producers will not receive the necessary market signals that will tell in what kinds of goods they should invest. This is because an act of saving is often intended to increase the saver's future command over goods and services in general. Consequently savers do not communicate to producers their future demands for specific goods. Future demands, which are implicit in current acts of saving, are not effective demands. Thus while the current fall in demand for consumption is communicated to producers they are not informed as to where they should re-employ the factors of production no longer required to produce consumption goods.

However the increase in investment required to maintain full employment could still be achieved provided there is a sufficient rise in the demand price of capital relative to its supply price. The demand price of capital (what producers are prepared to pay for capital) depends on the future stream of income and on the rate of interest used to discount it. The rate of interest is likely to fall, thereby increasing the demand price of capital, because consumers who are saving more will demand more financial assets, bidding up their prices and depressing interest rates.

At this point, however, we have the second reason why investment may not increase enough to generate full employment. It is the inelastic expectations of asset-holders as incorporated in Keynes's theory of liquidity preference. Falling yields will induce 'bear' speculators to sell bonds and hold money instead. In so doing they prevent interest rates from falling by the amount required to stimulate the necessary investment.

The same analysis applies when the initial trigger is a more pessimistic revision of businessmen's expectations, which causes an inconsistency of saving and investment plans at full employment.

Thus unemployment emerges because of 'wrong' relative prices. The demand price of capital goods is too low *vis-à-vis* other prices (including, of course, money wages) to equate savings and investment plans at full employment.

If, because of inelastic expectations, interest rates are prevented from falling to the level that would equate savings and investment at full employment, they can still be forced down to this 'natural' level by increasing the money supply. Leijonhufvud's view is that

> in the neighbourhood of full employment equilibrium where the problem is to keep market rates of interest in the near neighbourhood of the 'natural rate', Keynes would keep close to time-honoured British tradition in stabilization policy and rely on monetary measures (1969, p. 41).

If however the economy moves into a severe depression with the 'ineffective' consumption demands of the unemployed and consequential multiplier effects depressing entrepreneurial expectations, then the more appropriate policy is a fiscal one which 'stimulates' expectations and triggers off a multiplier process back towards full employment.

As we have already seen however, Leijonhufvud argues that money balances and other liquid assets act as buffers preventing the cumulative movement of the economy into severe depression until it has been sequeezed dry of liquidity. In the reinterpretation of Keynes, money and monetary policy would appear to matter a great deal.

Notes

1. In fact several different wealth effects have been discussed in the context of the Keynesian model, and confusingly the same term is sometimes used to describe quite different effects. This note simply describes some of the more common usages.

   (1) *The Pigou effect* This is the term given to the wealth effect described by A. C. Pigou (1943) to show that as long as wages and prices are flexible, the Keynesian system, like the classical, would have an automatic tendency to move to a position of full employment, even in the face of interest-inelastic expenditures and liquidity traps. Pigou pointed out that as long as they are flexible, wages and prices would fall in the face of unemployment. But if prices fall, then the real value of wealth, as measured by its purchasing power over goods and services in general, would rise. If the community feels wealthier then it will have less incentive to save to accumulate wealth and will therefore raise its expenditure until eventually a level of expenditure sufficient to generate full employment is reached. The Pigou effect as we have described it does not depend on an expansion of the money supply, but only on a fall in the general level of prices.

   (2) *The real balance effect* This is as described in the main text, and is the effect on expenditure of increases in real money balances, where those balances have risen because of an increase in the nominal supply of money. This particular effect is also sometimes known as the Patinkin effect. A rather

broader interpretation of the real balance effect is to see it as a combination of the Pigou effect and the Keynes effect.

(3) *The Keynes effect* This is the mechanism by which unemployment-induced falls in wages and prices increase the real value of the money stock, which in turn increases the demand for bonds, depresses interest rates and stimulates expenditure on goods and services. In the face of interest inelastic expenditure and/or a liquidity trap the Keynes effect on its own will not ensure full employment.

(4) *Keynes windfall effect* This is as described in the text. A fall in interest rates will increase the market valuation of assets, increase the wealth of asset holders and generate a wealth-induced increase in expenditure.

7

Monetarism

One of the most signficant and controversial developments in monetary economics during the last two decades has been the rise of 'monetarism'. It has generated some widely accepted advances in our knowledge of macroeconomics, while at the same time giving rise to some very considerable academic, public and political debates. Yet there is no general agreement on what exactly is meant by monetarism, or on the major issues separating it from non-monetarism. The term means different things to different people. Indeed many economists may find themselves being labelled sometimes monetarist, sometimes Keynesian, depending on which definition of monetarism is being used. There is, for example, a difference between the British and American usage of the term, such that some economists who would be regarded as Keynesians in America would be regarded as monetarists in the United Kingdom. There is no clear dividing line between monetarism and non-monetarism; there is no unique set of 'monetarist' propositions which all monetarists would accept and all non-monetarists reject.[1] At most there is 'a set of propositions held to a greater or lesser extent by a group of economists who are far from forming a monolithic school' (Mayer 1978, p. 2). In some instances the differences between monetarists themselves may be as great as between monetarists and non-monetarists. Some writers have therefore suggested that the term 'monetarism' has ceased to be a useful label, while others emphasize that the similarities between schools of thought are often more important than the differences.

Our aim in this chapter is simply to set out some of the more widely discussed monetarist propositions and views, and to indicate some of the major differences of viewpoint that exist both within monetarism and between it and non-monetarist schools of thought. Some of the views and ideas considered in this chapter inevitably occur elsewhere in the book, and sometimes it is in the other chapters that the fuller discussion of the arguments is to be found. Whenever this is the case appropriate chapter references are given.

The quantity theory

Probably the most basic characteristic of monetarism is its view that changes in the nominal stock of money are the dominant cause of changes in nominal income. This view is often referred to as the Quantity Theory of Money. The classical version of this theory, expressed in the equation $MV = Py$, was considered in Chapter 5. We saw there that the classical quantity theorists believed that V and y were fixed so that changes in M would be proportionately reflected in P.

The early attempts by monetarists to rehabilitate the Quantity Theory concentrated on the demand for money. Indeed, in his classic restatement of the Quantity Theory approach, Friedman (1956, p. 4) defined the Quantity Theory as 'in the first instance a theory of the *demand* for money. It is not a theory of output or of money income, or of the price level.' The monetarist view is that the demand for money is a stable function of a limited number of variables and has a low interest elasticity. This stability of the demand for money is an essential precondition for the monetarist view that changes in the supply of money are the dominant cause of changes in nominal income. If the demand for money is unstable then changes in the supply of money may be offset by changes in the demand for it, with no consequential effects on spending, output or prices. In the opinion of Johnson (1978, p. 127), '... it is the proposition that there is a stable demand for money that differentiates monetarism from the classical quantity theory of money tradition and 'monetarism' from its Keynesian rival'. If the community has a stable demand for money, then disturbances to expenditure, output and prices are unlikely to be the result of frequent and significant changes in the amount of money that people wish to hold. On the other hand, exogenous changes in the money supply will require a change in the quantity of money demanded if the new money stock is to become willingly held. Given the low interest-elasticity of the monetarist demand for money function, an increase in the supply of money will not disappear into idle hoards, but will be reflected in increased expenditure, as holders of surplus cash balances try to unload them and restore their real cash balances to their desired levels. But one man's expenditure is another man's income, so individuals can only reduce their cash balances if other individuals are prepared to increase theirs. All individuals together cannot reduce their real cash balances just by reducing the number of pounds they hold. They do so instead by reducing the real value of each of the individual nominal pounds held. This comes about because their attempts to reduce the number of nominal pounds they are holding will raise the level of expenditure and push up prices. As prices rise the real value of cash balances will fall, and the process will continue until actual real cash balances are equal to desired real cash balances. Thus Friedman (1970a, p. 225) has written

> the key insight of the quantity theory approach is that such a discrepancy [between the demand for and supply of money] will be manifested primarily in attempted spending, thence in the rate of change in nominal income.

But just how do monetarists see a surplus of money balances becoming manifested in an increase in attempted spending? The answer is to be found in the monetarist transmission mechanism, and it is to a consideration of this that we now turn.

The transmission mechanism

The monetarist transmission mechanism is in fact complex, has much in common with the transmission mechanisms of other schools of thought, and is one within which different monetarists would place different emphasis. We shall find it helpful to consider the transmission mechanism in two stages. In the first stage we shall concentrate on the mechanism by which changes in the supply of money lead to changes in nominal income. This will involve a detailed consideration of the way in which holders of surplus cash balances attempt to reduce those balances to their desired levels. In the second stage we shall be concerned with the division of nominal income changes between changes in prices and changes in output (i.e. real income).

Stage I: the effect of money supply changes on nominal income

Portfolio adjustments

The transmission mechanism whereby surplus money balances become manifested in attempted spending, is one of portfolio adjustment. Money is seen as just one in a spectrum of assets comprising the wealth portfolios of individuals and firms. As such, money is seen by monetarists as being generally substitutable for all other assets, and not just for a small range of financial ones.

Traditionally this has been regarded as the essential difference between the monetarist transmission mechanism and the Keynesian one. Typical of this viewpoint is the following quotation from Goodhart (1970, p. 165):

> The crucial distinction between the monetarists and the Keynesians resides in their widely differing view of the degree to which certain alternative financial assets may be close substitutes for money balances; and in particular whether there is a signficantly greater degree of substitution between money balances and such financial assets than between money balances and real assets.

There is now a widely held view, however, that this traditional distinction is no longer valid when comparing monetarism with the views of contemporary Keynesians. In order to consider this viewpoint we must first consider the essential features of the monetarist portfolio adjustment mechanism.

We begin by assuming that the wealth portfolios of individuals and firms are in equilibrium, and that there then occurs an increase in the money supply. This will lower the marginal rate of return on money balances, and asset holders will attempt to switch from money into other assets, offering higher marginal rates of return. Because wealth-holders have different tastes and preferences they may attach different marginal rates of return to incremental increases in each of the variety of assets within their portfolios and consequently respond in different ways to the fall in the marginal rate of return on money. Let us look at some of the possibilities. Assume the authorities increase the money supply by undertaking an open market purchase of securities. In order to induce wealth-holders to sell securities the authorities must push up the price of the securities and depress their yields. When the bonds are sold to the authorities the vendors receive money in return. But this does not mean that they are willing holders of the money, but simply that they have to hold it temporarily before rearranging their portfolios in the desired manner following the fall in the relative attractiveness of holding bonds.

Of course, the exchange of money for bonds is only the first step in the expansion of the money supply. Whether the bonds were purchased from the banks or the non-bank public, the banks' cash reserves will expand and enable them to engage in a multiple expansion of deposits. The banks will seek to diversify their holdings of earning assets (i.e. to diversify their portfolios) and in so doing will depress yields on those assets they acquire (e.g. investments and advances). Individuals and institutions who sold bonds to the authorities (and also those who sold them to the banks), finding themselves with larger proportions of money in their portfolios than they desire, will attempt to adjust the composition of their portfolios by exchanging some of their surplus money for other assets.

In the traditional Keynesian analysis the exchange would be from money into financial assets regarded as very close substitutes for money. Because of the close substitutability, interest rates on the financial assets would not fall very far before equilibrium in asset-holding was re-established. The fall in the rate of interest would then lead, in so far as they are interest sensitive, to an increase in investment and in aggregate demand. But this mechanism by which money supply changes are transmitted to expenditure is regarded by monetarists as only one possible route, and they are critical of it because it implies that the increased money supply will be willingly held at the lower rate of interest.

Monetarists agree that it is likely that some of the holders of surplus money will at first try to substitute from that money into securities similar to those they have just sold, and that their attempts to do so will raise the prices of such securities and lower their yields. But this, in turn, will reduce their attractiveness relative to other assets and so portfolio-holders, including now some who were not originally involved, will try to substitute into assets further along the spectrum. The increased demand for these other assets will raise their prices and depress their yields. Thus, there will be a 'shunting' effect along the spectrum of assets comprising wealth portfolios and a generalized pushing up of asset prices and pushing down of rates of return.

> Some of these rates of return are observable interest rates on securities, set by specialist dealers in response to supply and demand conditions in organized markets, some are observable borrowing and lending rates set by financial intermediaries of one sort or another, and others are implicit, non-observable, rates of return on assets such as consumer durables. (Laidler, 1978a, pp. 154–5).

Eventually, the shunting effect will influence the demand for and supply of durable goods, both producer and consumer, and also the demand for non-durable consumption goods. As far as durable goods are concerned, Brunner and Meltzer (1972) have suggested a threefold classification. Type I assets have separate market prices for existing and new stock. When the shunting effect pushes up security prices this effectively means that the market value of existing stock rises above the supply price of new stock and stimulates investment in such assets. Type II durable goods have a single price for existing and similar new stock (e.g. houses). Again the shunting effect will eventually result in an increase in the price of the existing assets, which raises the optimum capital stock and leads to increased production of new assets. Type III durable goods have no market for existing stock so that prices exist only for new stock (e.g. some kinds of consumer durables). Here the shunting effect implies that a decline in marginal rates of return on assets immediately preceding these type III assets in the chain of substitution, will lead directly to an increase in the demand for new assets of the type III variety without working through the prices of the existing stock.

With regard to non-durable consumer goods there may well be an increase in demand here too, because the price of current consumption has fallen in terms of future consumption forgone (see p. 27).

So far we have considered only one possible chain of events that might follow from an open-market purchase of securities by the monetary authorities. In that chain the initial holders of surplus money balances attempted to exchange them for financial assets, setting off a shunting effect along the spectrum of assets, altering rates of return and relative prices and eventually affecting the demand for new output.

But not all portfolio-holders will react to the initial surplus money and subsequent asset price changes in the same way. Monetarists emphasize the general substitutability of money for all other assets so that some of those who were involved in the original open-market sale of securities to the authorities will use their additional (surplus) money balances to acquire real goods and services directly: particularly likely in this respect would be increased purchases of consumer durables. Others may put part of their surplus balances into building society deposits, which will increase lending by these societies to potential house purchasers and therefore increase expenditure on physical assets fairly directly and quickly. And, in so far as building society interest rates are sticky, the increased flow of funds into the societies may not affect their interest rates, so that the increased expenditure on physical assets that they help generate is independent of interest rate changes.

Yet another possibility is that some of the additional money balances will be invested in human capital, for as we have seen, monetarists regard human capital as a component of individual wealth portfolios. Such an investment could be achieved by spending the additional money balances on education and training.

By a variety of routes then, the increased money supply will lead eventually to increased expenditure on newly constructed assets. Some of these routes will be fairly short while others will work through a much wider spectrum of financial assets before affecting the demand for newly produced physical assets. The rising demand for newly produced assets will in turn raise the demand for productive services and set off a multiplier process. Similarly, any increase in the demand for non-durable consumer goods and services would increase the demand for factor services, adding further to the generation of income.

It may be that in some cases the prices of factors of production will rise before the prices of the final goods. This would be the case, for example, if the producers of final goods based their prices on average costs of production plus a profit mark-up. Then the sequence of events would be: increased demand for newly constructed products → increased demand for factors of production → increased factor prices → increased costs of production → increased product prices.

In the monetarist transmission mechanism, money is seen as a stock in a portfolio of assets, similar to stocks of paper assets, real assets, etc. The effect of changes in the money supply is consequently to affect stocks, first of money itself, then of other assets. But the attempts to adjust stocks alters flows of expenditure.

> The stocks serve as buffers or shock absorbers of initial changes in rates of flow by expanding or contracting from their 'normal' or 'natural' or 'desired' state, and then slowly alter other flows as holders try to regain that state. (Friedman and Schwarz, 1963b, p. 63).

There is also, however, a wealth effect in the monetarist transmission mechanism. As the prices of existing assets are driven up via portfolio adjustment, the holders of such assets experience a capital gain and as a result are likely to increase their expenditures.

According to the transmission mechanism we have just outlined there will be a general increase in output and prices. The prices of financial assets, existing physical assets, new physical assets, current services and factors of production will all rise. But the rise in prices means that the real value of the money stock is falling. Thus in order to maintain the real value of their money balances, individuals and firms must hold increased amounts of nominal money balances. Eventually, all of the increase in the nominal money stock generated by the initial open-market operations, will be willingly held in portfolios in order to maintain real money balances at their desired level in the face of the increased level of prices.

We may now reconsider the question of how this transmission mechanism differs from those of non-monetarist schools of thought. To begin with we must note that different branches of the monetarist camp would emphasize different aspects of the mechanism. In comparing the monetarist transmission mechanism with the traditional Keynesian one it has, as we have seen, been usual to argue that the monetarist mechanism involves a much wider range of assets than the Keynesian, with the latter's emphasis on the substitution between money and bonds and the cost of capital effect on expenditure. But we saw in Chapter 2 that a portfolio adjustment transmission mechanism is the consensus model, capable of accommodating the differences of emphasis and detail that may exist in the views of most economists. Many writers now argue, therefore, that there is no essential difference between the monetarist portfolio adjustment mechanism and that of other schools of thought. Thus, Purvis (1980, p. 100) argues '... that the extension of the asset menu is a complete 'red-herring' in attempting to define the issues which separate monetarists and Keynesians', while Laidler (1981b, p. 2) states that 'there is no essential difference between it [the monetarist transmission mechanism] and that analzsed for example by James Tobin and his associates'.

The importance of price expectations

Our discussion of the transmission mechanism has so far implicitly assumed no change in the expectations held by economic agents about future prices. We must now consider the possibility that the increase in actual prices which portfolio adjustment would bring about may cause people to revise upwards their price expectations. If this happens there will be additional effects on variables involved in the transmission mechanism. One of these effects will be on wage and price setting behaviour and this is considered in the next section. Here we shall consider the effects of revised price expectations on two variables involved in the portfolio adjustment mechanism outlined above, namely interest rates and the demand for money. We consider them separately, taking first the demand for money.

The 'security' and 'convenience' yield obtained from holding a given nominal amount of money must clearly fall in real terms as the quantity of goods and services which that nominal amount of money is capable of buying falls. Consequently, if people come to expect an increase in the rate at which prices are rising then they must be anticipating an increase in the rate at which the real return from holding money is falling. In other words the opportunity cost of holding money is rising. It is quite likely, therefore, that the real demand for money will fall as it becomes a relatively less attractive asset to hold compared with those assets whose real return is rising or is at least unchanged. For example, if people previously thought that prices were going to rise at 15% p.a., but now think that they will rise at 20% p.a., the increased relative unattractiveness of holding money will lead to a fall in the demand for it. But once the demand has fallen there will be no reason for it to fall any further as long as people continue to believe that prices will rise at 20% p.a. Should they revise their expectations further, thinking prices will rise, say, at 25% p.a., then this increases the relative unattractiveness of holding money even further, and will induce another fall in the demand for it. In other words, there is, *ceteris paribus*, a given demand for money for every state of expectations about the future rate of change of prices. If the demand for money is to continue falling because of price expectations, then people must be continually revising upwards their estimates of the rate at which they think prices will rise. It is probable that equal additions to the expected rate of change of prices will lead to successively smaller and smaller reductions in the demand for money. This will be because equal reductions in the amount of money held are likely to mean bigger and bigger sacrifices by the holder. As long as money is used for the finance of transactions, then of course a minimum amount must be held, so that demand for it cannot go on falling indefinitely.

By reducing the demand for real money balances, inflation expectations aggravate the portfolio disequilibrium that set off stage I of the transmission mechanism. This means that an even higher rate of inflation will be required before equilibrium is re-established, with the demand for money once more equal to the supply. The path to equilibrium is also likely to be 'cyclical' in nature, involving 'overshooting' of the new equilibrium. One reason for this is that money holders will initially over-react to their surplus money holdings. They will evaluate their nominal money balances in real terms at the level of prices they expect to prevail in the relevant future time period. But their expectations are based on their previous experience. Each individual wealth-holder will not take into account the fact that his or her own attempts to run down nominal money balances will help push up prices and reduce the real value of those nominal balances. Thus, each individual will unload more money balances than they would do if they had anticipated the increase in prices likely to follow their actions. As prices rise, individuals revise upwards their anticipations of future price movements and revise downwards their evaluations of the real value of their nominal money balances. They must now try to partly rebuild their nominal money balances and their attempts to so do will reverse somewhat the increase in the level of expenditure and depress the rate at which prices are rising. This slower rate of price increase may cause individuals to revise yet again their expectations of future price movements and their consequential evaluation of their real cash balances. If they do so, their rate of expenditure may rise slightly and increase the rate at which prices are rising, though not to the level that followed the initial increase in expenditure. This cyclical pattern would continue, with the fluctuations getting smaller, until anticipated price increases coincide with actual price increases and all of the increase in the nominal stock of money is demanded.

A second reason for the cyclical nature of the adjustment process is that, at the new equilibrium, with a higher expected rate of inflation, individuals will want to hold lower real cash balances relative to their wealth and income. In the process of lowering their real cash balances as they move towards the new equilibrium position, individuals will have caused prices to rise at a faster rate than the new equilibrium rate.

We turn now to the effect of price expectations on interest rates. In his 1968 presidential address to the AEA, Friedman argued that an increase in the rate of growth of the money supply would depress interest rates initially, but raise them later. We have already seen why interest rates are forced down during stage I of the transmission process, so we now consider why they should subsequently rise. One possibility is that as expenditures, prices, and incomes rise, so will the demand for loans. Businessmen, for example, finding their stocks being run down may try to rebuild them and consequently increase their demand for bank overdrafts. Similarly they may try to borrow more on the long-term capital market in order to expand their productive capacity. Consumers, too, expecting their incomes to rise, may try to borrow more to buy consumer durable goods in anticipation of their increased ability to afford the loan repayments. According to Friedman (1968, p. 6) these effects

> will reverse the initial downward pressure on interest rates fairly promptly, say in something less than a year, [and] together they will tend after a somewhat longer interval, say a year or two, to return interest rates to the level they would otherwise have had. Indeed, given the tendency for the economy to over-react they are highly likely to raise interest rates temporarily beyond that level, setting in motion a cyclical adjustment process.

Moreover, introducing inflationary expectations into the analysis will 'definitely mean that a higher rate of monetary expansion will correspond to a higher, not lower, level of interest rates than would otherwise have prevailed' (Friedman, 1968, p. 6). If, when lenders expect prices to remain constant they are prepared to lend at a rate of interest i_r, then in order to receive the same interest in real terms when prices are expected to rise at $\dot{P}^e$ per cent, they must charge a nominal rate of interest (i_n) which is equal to $i_r + \dot{P}^e$. Similarly, the real interest cost to borrowers is unaffected by the inclusion of $\dot{P}^e$ in the nominal interest charge on loans. Expectations of inflation are therefore likely to raise nominal interest rates.

Stage II: the division of changes in nominal income between price changes and output changes

We turn now to the question of what determines how much of a change in nominal income is in the form of a change in output and how much in the form of a change in prices. It will be recalled from Chapter 5 that in the classical theory all of a change in nominal income was in the form of price changes, as output was fixed at the full employment level. In the Keynesian analysis the usual assumption was that below full employment all changes in nominal income were changes in real income, while above full employment all changes in nominal income were changes in prices.

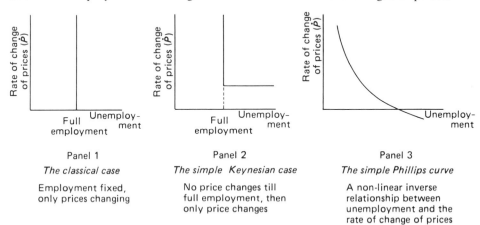

Panel 1	Panel 2	Panel 3
The classical case	*The simple Keynesian case*	*The simple Phillips curve*
Employment fixed, only prices changing	No price changes till full employment, then only price changes	A non-linear inverse relationship between unemployment and the rate of change of prices

Figure 7.1 The relationship between the level of unemployment and the rate of change of prices

These two views are illustrated in *Figure 7.1*. In all panels unemployment is measured along the horizontal axis, and rates of change of prices along the vertical. In all the panels 'full employment' is consistent with a positive level of unemployment because even though there may be equilibrium in the labour market (the usual meaning of full employment), there will always be people frictionally unemployed. Panel 1 illustrates the classical view, with unemployment fixed at the full employment level and only prices changing. Panel 2 illustrates the crude Keynesian case, where there are no changes in prices as long as employment is less than full, and changes in prices only when full employment is reached.

The expectations-augmented Phillips curve

In modern monetarism the explanation of the division of changes in nominal income between output changes and price level changes (what Friedman (1970a) called the 'missing equation') is provided by the expectations-augmented Phillips curve.

We shall be considering the Phillips curve in more detail in Chapter 9. For the present we merely need to know that it was an empirically derived curve which commanded widespread acceptance by economists during the 1960s, and which implied that there was a non-linear inverse relationship between unemployment and the rate of change of wages and prices. It is illustrated in panel 3 of *Figure 7.1*. It had the policy implication that expansions of demand could permanently reduce unemployment but at the cost of a higher rate of increase of wages and prices.

The expectations-augmented version of the Phillips curve emerged in the late 1960s and became an essential component of the monetarist framework. The expectations-augmented curve has been derived in a number of different ways and some of these will be considered fully in Chapter 9 (pp. 197–202). For the present we outline the explanation provided by Friedman. Central to this explanation is the concept of a natural rate of unemployment. This is 'the level of unemployment which has the property that it is consistent with equilibrium in the structure of *real* wage rates' (Friedman 1968, p. 8, emphasis in the original). It will be determined simultaneously with all the other relevant variables by the system of general equilibrium equations. It is the equilibrium level of unemployment in the sense that it is the level which has no tendency to change, because it is associated with equilibrium in the product and money markets and all other relevant sectors. The level of output associated with the natural rate of unemployment is, rather obviously, termed the natural level of output.

To illustrate the Friedman analysis let us assume that initially unemployment and output are at their natural levels and that prices are constant. If now the authorities expand the money supply this will set off a portfolio adjustment mechanism as in stage 1 and raise aggregate expenditure and prices. Friedman argues that employers will recognize the increase in the price of their own product before they perceive the increase in prices in general and will interpret it as an increase in its relative price. They will then try to produce more at this more favourable relative price and be prepared to pay higher money wages to attract the additional labour they will require.

Workers, too, will be slow to adjust their perception of the general level of prices, and in the meantime will see the increase in money wages as an increase in real wages, resulting in an increased supply of labour.

In the short run, therefore, the increased money supply – via portfolio adjustment and increased expenditure – will raise prices, money wages, output and employment. All of which is consistent with the Phillips curve.

But all of these results, argues Friedman, are a consequence of unanticipated inflation. They arise only because employers and employees are slow to recognize that prices in general are rising. Eventually they will alter their perceptions of prices to accord with actual experience, and when this happens the picture changes completely. Once workers realize that the increase in their money wages is matched by increases in the general level of prices they know that their real wages have not risen. The supply of labour then contracts back to its original level, and unemployment and output return to their natural rates.

Friedman's analysis, therefore, draws a clear distinction between the short-run and long-run effects of increases in the money supply. Only in the short run, i.e. that period for which there is unanticipated inflation, will there be any effects on output and employment as well as on prices. In the long run – when price perceptions have caught up with reality and unanticipated inflation has been eliminated – output and employment will be back at their natural levels and only prices and other nominal variables will have been effected. This is usually referred to as the natural rate hypothesis (NRH).

Rational expectations

Friedman's explanation of the expectations augmented Phillips curve was derived from the assumption that employers and workers were slow to adjust their perceptions of price increases to accord with what was actually happening. Expectations of price changes always lagged behind actual price changes.

This view has been criticized by economists who comprise what is known as the rational expectations school. They argue that economic agents – employers and workers etc. – would not be behaving rationally if their perceptions of price changes were always 'catching up on' actual price changes. Rational economic agents, it is argued, would try to correctly anticipate price changes rather than to always be one step behind. To do this they would base their expectations on all relevant information and not merely on their experience of actual price level changes.

Initially, of course, the information used may not be complete, and forecasting errors will arise. But the errors will not persist in a systematic manner because people will perceive the sources of their errors, remove them and incorporate new information. The way in which people form their price expectations will be continuously revised as they acquire more information about the determinants of the actual rate of change of prices. It is only when expectations are based on a forecasting model which is consistent with the way in which the rate of change of prices is actually determined, that expectations will not be systematically in error, and only then will the expectations formed be fully rational. The rational expectations approach has been described by Laidler (1978a), p. 172) as arguing

... that economic agents act 'as if' they form their expectations about the inflation rate by using the forecast that would be yielded by a correct model of the economy in which they are operating and 'as if' they expected every other agent in the economy to form his or her expectations in the same way.

If expectations are truly rational in this sense, then expectational errors could arise only as a result of random disturbances or shocks to the economy. Random shocks are, by definition, non-systematic and therefore completely incapable of being forecast. In the absence of such shocks, rational expectations implies that the expected rate of change of prices and the actual rate of change of prices, always coincide: there is never any unanticipated change in prices.

From our earlier discussion of Friedman's explanation of the expectations-augmented Phillips curve, we recall that in the absence of unanticipated price changes there can be no excess demand in the economy and output and unemployment will always be at their equilibrium or 'natural' levels. Consequently, the rational expectations hypothesis renders the portfolio adjustment mechanism redundant, by effectively short-circuiting it. Thus, an increase in money supply which would tend, via portfolio adjustment, to raise the price level, will be taken account of by rational economic agents, who will correctly forecast the increase in prices. They will then act on their correctly revised forecasts and raise their nominal wages and prices accordingly. The expectation will have been self-fulfilling and there will have been no unanticipated price changes, even in the short run. In the absence of unanticipated price changes, however, output and unemployment cannot deviate from their natural levels. The whole effect of a monetary expansion will be felt on prices. There will not even be a short-run effect on output, because at no stage are there any unanticipated price changes, and it is only unanticipated price changes which affect real variables.

Rational expectations are, of course, compatible with any view of how prices are determined. All it says is that economic agents who are forming their price expectations 'rationally' will evolve a forecasting model that will generate the same forecasts as those given by the actual price-determing mechanism, whatever it is. For example, if it is changes in the percentage of the labour force unionized that 'causes' changes in prices, then this will come to be recognized by rational economic agents. Such agents would then acquire information about the labour force and unionization and correctly forecast changes in prices. From this point of view, therefore, the rational expectations school of thought represents a branch of monetarism only because most of its members accept the basic tenet of monetarism, that changes in the money supply are the dominant cause of changes in the general level of prices.

While all monetarists accept the hypothesis of a natural rate of unemployment and the absence of a long-run trade-off between rates of change of prices and unemployment, those who also accept the rational expectations hypothesis comprise the so-called New Classical School. This statement needs modification however to recognize that two broad approaches to the natural rate hypothesis have been developed in the literature. One approach assumes continuous market-clearing (implicit in the Friedman analysis given above), while other models assuming wage and price stickiness, imply the natural rate hypothesis in the context of non-clearing markets. The new classical school is then more accurately described as combining the market-clearing natural rate hypothesis with rational expectations (for a lucid introduction to the New Classical School see Grossman 1980). We shall be considering rational expectations further in Chapter 9, where we will be looking at inflation. The policy implications of rational expectations will also be discussed in Chapter 11 (pp. 245–246). For the remainder of this chapter however we continue with other major monetarist propositions.

The inherent stability of the private sector and the unimportance of sectoral detail

Monetarist views on the demand for money and the concept of a natural rate of unemployment give rise to the proposition that the private sector is inherently stable.

The natural rate hypothesis implies that the economy has output and unemployment positions towards which it is always moving. Though the natural levels of output and unemployment may alter as a result of changes in real variables like technology and the structure of the labour force, the economy will, left to its own devices, always seek to move to those 'natural positions'.

Moreover, any deviations away from those 'natural' positions are due to authority-induced changes in the supply of money. This follows from the monetarist view considered earlier in the chapter and in Chapter 3 that the demand for money is highly stable. As Friedman (1970a, p. 195) himself has put it

> the quantity theory is ... on an empirical level ... the generalization that changes in desired real balances (in the demand for money) tend to proceed slowly and gradually or to be the result of events set in train by prior changes in supply, whereas in contrast, substantial changes in the supply of nominal balances can and frequently do occur independently of any changes in demand. The conclusion is that substantial changes in prices or nominal income are almost invariably the result of changes in the nominal supply of money.

There is also some difference of opinion between monetarists and others about the length of time it would take the economy to return to equilibrium following a disturbance. Non-monetarists tend to see this taking much longer than monetarists generally do. A policy implication of this difference of opinion concerns the desirability of discretionary economic policy and is considered in the next section.

Because monetarists believe that changes in the supply of money are the predominant cause of fluctuations in nominal income and because their transmission process, though complex, does not require a detailed understanding of the expenditure motives or behavioural peculiarities of individual sectors, they consider it sufficient to concentrate on one market – that for real money balances. Monetarists consider a detailed understanding of the different sectors – personal, business, etc. – to be unimportant. Keynesians, on the other hand, place great emphasis on understanding the expenditure motives of the different sectors. This follows from their view that shocks to the system can come from fluctuations in expenditure within any sector. For example, unemployment might result from a decision by firms to spend less on investment or from a fall in households propensity to consume. Moreover if, as Keynesians argue, the authorities should pursue a discretionary policy to minimize the magnitude and duration of cyclical fluctuations then they need to understand the expenditure motives of the different sectors in order to be able to influence the behaviour of those sectors.

It is sometimes argued that a further distinguishing characteristic of monetarism lies in its research methods. The argument is that monetarists believe that the transmission mechanism connecting money supply changes to nominal income is so complex that it cannot usefully be represented even in a large structural model. Hence, monetarists tend to prefer simple reduced form models. Keynesians, on the other hand, with their simpler transmission mechanism and concern for sectorial detail tend to prefer the structural models. This distinction is a serious over simplification, however, for both schools of thought have used a variety of research techniques. In the opinion of Laidler (1981b, p. 2) there appears '... to be no clear dividing line between the statistical methodology of monetarists and their opponents about which one can usefully generalize'.

The role of macroeconomic policy

There is now a widely held view that there no longer exists any serious disagreement between monetarists and non-monetarists about the importance of money as a determinant of money income, nor about related issues like the transmission mechanism and the interaction of output and inflation. Instead, those who hold this view argue that the major issue currently separating monetarists and non-monetarists is a policy one, namely the role that should be assigned to monetary, fiscal and incomes policies. This view has been clearly stated by the eminent Keynesian, Franco Modigliani (1977, p. 1) who, in his Presidential address to the American Economic Association, said

> There are in reality no serious analytical disagreements between leading monetarists and non-monetarists ... In reality the distinguishing feature of the monetarists school and the real issues of disagreement with non-monetarists is not monetarism, but rather the role that should probably be assigned to stabilization policies.

A similar view has been expressed by Laidler, a leading monetarist

> when it comes to propositions about the demand for money function, the relationship between money and money income and output–inflation interaction, there is a real sense in which 'we are all monetarists now'. The issues that nowadays distinguish monetarists from their opponents concern the conduct of economic policy (1981b, p. 18).

What then are the monetarist propositions about the roles of monetary, fiscal and incomes policies? Basically, there are two sets of propositions: one set states what economic policy cannot do, while the other suggests what it can be used for. Let us consider them in that order.

What economic policy cannot do

We shall distinguish two separate monetarist propositions.

(1) Monetary and fiscal policies cannot be used to fine-tune the economy. We have already seen how monetarists argue that private expenditure patterns are inherently stable. From this they go on to argue that there is no great need for the authorities to use discretionary control over monetary and fiscal policies in an attempt to stabilize the economy.

Moreover, even if there were a need for discretionary policy, it would not work. Attempts to fine-tune the economy are doomed to failure. Two different arguments are used to support this prediction. The first of these is derived from the theory considered above that employment and output can only be made to deviate from their natural levels as long as there are unanticipated changes in prices. In the long run, however, all unanticipated price changes disappear and so too, therefore, do the influences of monetary and fiscal policies on output and employment. According to the rational expectations school of monetarists, systematic policy cannot even influence output and employment in the short run.

The second argument used to support the view that economic policy should not be used to try and fine-tune the economy is very different from the first. It does not deny the ability of demand management policies to influence output and employment – at least in the short run – either to push them above their natural levels or to hasten their return to those levels if they have temporarily fallen below them. But to operate policy successfully in this way would require the authorities to have all sorts of information about the structure of the economy, and about how the economy would respond to discretionary policy changes. Monetarists argue that with our present state of knowledge the authorities do not know enough about the workings of the economic system to be able to calculate the required scale and timing of policy action.

Furthermore, policy action taken at the wrong time or on the wrong scale may not only fail to achieve its objectives, but may be positively de-stabilizing. We shall consider this argument more fully in Chapter 11 (pp. 244–250).

(2) Incomes and prices policies have no significant long-run effect on the rate of inflation. Monetarists have used a number of arguments to oppose the long-run use of controls over prices and incomes. The post-war period has seen a number of attempts to use such policies, involving a variety of schemes and forms, yet there does not appear to have been a single instance of a policy significantly influencing the rate of inflation beyond a matter of months. Monetarists argue that this was only to be expected. Trying to exert direct controls over wages and prices without controlling the rate of growth of the money supply is like trying to treat the symptoms of an illness while ignoring its cause. Moreover, for an open economy like the United Kingdom, there are added problems. With a fixed exchange rate the authorities cannot control the money supply nor the domestic price of traded goods, the latter being determined by the behaviour of world prices. Again, therefore, incomes and prices controls can at most influence the prices of non-traded goods and cannot for long have a significant effect on the general price level.

What economic policy can do

Monetarists believe that both monetary and fiscal policies have important but different roles to play. Fiscal policy should be used mainly to influence the allocation of resources and the distribution of income and wealth. Monetary policy on the other hand should be used to achieve and then maintain price stability. There is general agreement amongst monetarists that the maintenance of price stability requires the adoption of an automatic policy based on the use of rules and targets for the growth of monetary aggregates. We shall consider the arguments for and against such monetary rules more fully in Chapter 11 (pp. 250–251).

The issue of how best to achieve price stability if the initial position is one of inflation, divides the monetarist camp into two schools, which we shall call the 'gradualist school' and the 'rational expectations school'. Both agree that to restore price stability requires a reduction in the rate of growth of the money supply. They differ in their views on how best to achieve the reduction. The advocates of rational expectations believe that the reduction should be made quickly. The authorities must announce what they are going to do and insist that the policy is credible and will be strictly adhered to. Economic agents forming their expectations rationally will then feed this information about policy into their forecasting model and, provided prices are flexible, immediately bring about the desired effect on prices without any intermediate effects on output and employment.

Gradualists, on the other hand, argue that the reduction in the rate of growth of the money supply to the required target rate should be made gradually. Their advocacy of such a gradual slowing up is derived from their views that

(1) Expectations are slow to adjust and follow on behind actual experience of inflation.

(2) Prices are not perfectly flexible.

The consequence of these views is that a slowing up of the rate of growth of the money supply will only affect prices after a long and variable time lag. In the meantime the effects of the policy will be felt on output and employment and in order to minimize the magnitude of these effects a gradual reduction in the rate of growth of the money supply is advocated. The gradualist case was clearly stated by Laidler (1981a p. 158) in his evidence to the Treasury and Civil Service Committee of the House of Commons.

> the brunt of the impact of monetary policy falls not upon the price level at all, but rather upon interest rates and real income (and therefore employment). Only later do effects on the price level begin to come through. It is this belief above all which leads me to advocate a slow, rather than rapid, reduction in the monetary expansion rate as the correct response to a deeply embedded inflation.

Monetarists, fiscal policy and crowding-out

In previous sections of this chapter we have suggested that monetarists see very little scope for fiscal policy as a means of influencing the levels of output, employment and prices. In this final section we shall consider their view of fiscal policy more fully in the context of what is usually referred to as 'the crowding-out' debate.

The debate is simply over the extent to which increases in government expenditure are offset by reductions in private sector expenditure, leaving aggregate expenditure and national income unchanged. In order to set out the main issues we shall find it helpful to use *IS–LM* diagrams.

Interest-induced crowding-out

An increase in government expenditure on goods and services will, *ceteris paribus*, shift the *IS* curve to the right by an amount which is equal to the increase in government expenditure (ΔG) multiplied by the value of the goods market multiplier. Thus, in *Figure 7.2* an increase in G shifts the *IS* curve from IS_0 to IS_1.

With the *LM* curve in the position shown, the equilibrium level of income increases from Y_0 to Y_1. This increase in income is less than the full horizontal distance between the two *IS* curves. The reason for this is that the increase in income resulting from the extra government expenditure raises the demand for active money balances which, with a given money supply, pushes up interest rates. This in turn induces a contraction in any interest-sensitive expenditures, partially offsetting the increase in government expenditure, and preventing income from increasing by as much as it would otherwise have done. This is often called the interest-induced crowding-out effect, and its strength depends on the relative slopes of the *IS* and *LM* curves, i.e. the more interest-inelastic is the demand for money and the more interest-elastic are expenditures on goods and services, the more complete will crowding-out be.

We turn now to crowding-out that arises because the initial rightward shift of the *IS* curve is partially, wholly or more than offset either by the *IS* curve itself shifting back again towards the origin, or by the *LM* curve shifting back in a northwesterly direction. We will find it helpful to classify the reasons for these shifts into three kinds:

(1) Those arising out of the government's budget constraint.
(2) Those associated with wealth effects.
(3) A miscellaneous group of 'other' possibilities.

In considering the effects of these curve shifts one should also bear in mind the importance for those effects of the slopes of the curves, as outlined above.

The budget constraint

In our outline of 'interest-induced' crowding-out we paid no attention to the way in which the increase in government expenditure was financed. The concept of the budget constraint is, however, concerned with precisely that, and draws attention to the interdependence of the *IS* and *LM* curves.

The nature of the budget constraint may be stated quite briefly, thus:

$$G + TP + IP = T + M + \frac{\Delta B}{i}$$

In this statement G stands for government expenditure on goods and services, TP for government transfer payments (but not interest payments), IP for interest payments on the national debt, T for total tax revenue, M for the increase in high powered money, and $\Delta B/i$ is the change in the stock of bonds (ΔB) valued at market price ($1/i$).

The left-hand side, therefore, represents aggregate government payments, while the right-hand side shows how these payments can be financed. Subtracting T from the left-hand side gives the government deficit, which must be financed either by increasing the supply of high powered money and/or by sales of bonds. The constraint must *always* hold irrespective of the time periods concerned, and irrespective of whether the economy is in equilibrium or disequilibrium.

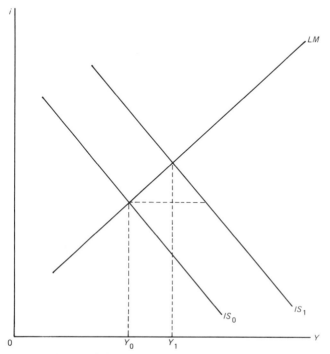

Figure 7.2 Interest-induced crowding-out

The possibility of financing increased government expenditure by new money creation or by increased bond sales makes it necessary to distinguish between stock and flow equilibriums and between temporary and permanent flow equilibriums. Stock equilibrium refers to equality between the stock of assets and the demand to hold them, while flow equilibrium refers to equilibrium in the flow of goods and services, i.e. goods market equilibrium. In the case where government expenditure is being financed by new money creation or by increased sales of bonds, then asset stocks are changing and there is stock disequilibrium. This action will alter expenditure flows and thereby the position of flow equilibrium. Thus in *Figure 7.2* if the increase in government expenditure which shifts the *IS* curve to IS_1 is deficit financed, then the level of income Y_1 is only a temporary equilibrium position. Changing stocks of money and/or bonds will have repercussions for expenditure flows which will alter the equilibrium level of income. Only when government expenditure is fully financed by tax revenue (the budget is balanced) will there be no change in asset stocks, and only then can the equilibrium level of income be regarded as permanent.

We now consider, in turn, the implications for equilibrium income of the three methods of financing an increase in government expenditure.

Tax financed

This is the familiar balanced budget multiplier case, and is illustrated in *Figure 7.3*. The increased tax rates will reduce the disposable incomes of tax-payers, therefore reducing their expenditure and shifting the *IS* curve inwards towards the origin to a

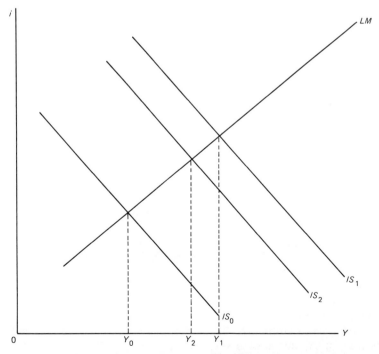

Figure 7.3 An increase in government expenditure financed by taxation

position such as IS_2. This leftward shift of the *IS* curve does not fully offset the original rightward shift, because only part of the extra tax payment would result in reduced private sector expenditure, the rest being reflected in reduced savings. The new equilibrium level of income is Y_2 and at this level the increased government expenditure is matched by an identical increase in tax revenue, the latter coming partly from the changed tax rate and partly from the higher level of income.

New money financed

The consequences of financing the increase in government expenditure by new money creation is shown in *Figure 7.4*. In this case there is no reverse shift of the *IS* curve, but instead the *LM* curve shifts to the right, reinforcing the expansionary effect of the *IS* curve shift. The *LM* curve will continue shifting to the right as long

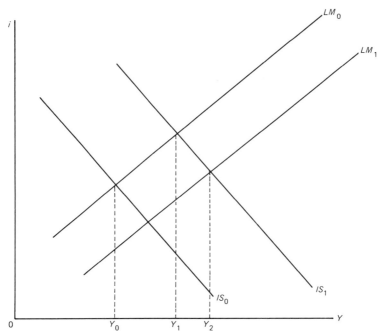

Figure 7.4 An increase in government expenditure financed by new money creation

as new money is being created to finance the budget deficit. As a result, the level of income continues to rise and with it the government tax revenue. Eventually, a new permanent equilibrium level of income will be reached at which sufficient extra tax revenue is being generated to finance the higher level of government expenditure, and there is no further need for new money creation. The permanent equilibrium level in this case must be greater than in the balanced budget case because with no increase in the tax rate a larger increase in income is necessary to generate the extra revenue needed to balance the budget. All this is illustrated in *Figure 7.4* where the level of income increases from Y_0 to Y_2.

Monetarists use this case to emphasize the importance of money, and indeed some would argue that an expansion of government expenditure financed by new money creation is really monetary policy rather than fiscal policy.

Bond financed

In this case the government initially finances the increased expenditure by borrowing from the public, i.e. by persuading the public to purchase additional government securities. This method of finance, however, further increases aggregate government outlays (i.e. the left-hand side of the budget constraint equation) because the government will now have increased interest payments to make on the greater outstanding amount of government debt. This in turn increases the disposable incomes of the debt holders, raises private sector expenditure and shifts the *IS* curve further to the right.

Of course, the sale of new bonds is not a once-and-for-all situation. It will have to be repeated every time-period as long as government expenditure is greater than tax revenue. Every new issue of bonds further increases the government interest payments and further shifts the IS curve to the right. However, as the *IS* curve shifts out, so the level of income rises and with it the government tax revenue. Eventually a new equilibrium level of income will be reached where sufficient extra tax revenue is being generated to finance the higher level of government outlays. This is shown in *Figure 7.5*, as Y_2, and exceeds the permanent equilibrium levels of income in the two other cases. This is because the level of government outlays that

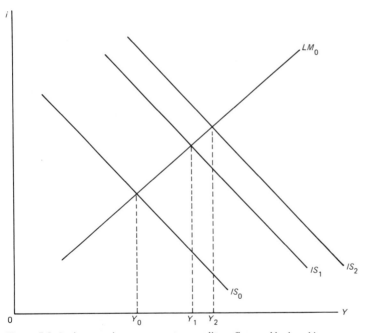

Figure 7.5 An increase in government expenditure financed by bond issues

have to be financed by taxation are greatest in the bond finance case, by virtue of the interest payments on the larger outstanding debt. Thus, Keynesians can argue that an increase in the supply of money is not necessary to make fiscal policy effective; in fact, bond finance is more expansionary.

The monetarist counter-argument to this view is that it fails to take into account the effects of the increase in wealth that has been brought about by the issue of additional bonds. Once this is done, the monetarists argue, then the expansionary effects of bond-financed public expenditure are again much less than those obtained when the public expenditure is financed by monetary expansion. Let us now consider these arguments.

Wealth effects

If the authorities finance an increase in government expenditure by additional borrowing from the public, then the private sector's holdings of bonds rises while its holdings of money and real capital assets are unaffected. Although the public initially gives up money balances in exchange for the additional bonds, the money comes back into circulation when the government uses it to finance its own expenditures. As we have seen (pp. 29–30), there is some debate over the extent to which increased holdings of government bonds do, in fact, constitute an increase in net private wealth. Moreover, the increase in the rate of interest that will be necessary to induce the public to take up the additional bonds will reduce the market value of all existing bonds, impose a negative wealth effect on the bond-holders and partially offset the increased volume of bond-holding. Additionally, the fact that government bonds have been made more financially attractive will induce a switch of funds away from public sector securities and cause a fall in their nominal value. For these reasons, Keynesians question whether bond financing of government expenditure does have any significant effect on net private wealth, and therefore whether there can be any signficant wealth effects.

But, to the extent that they do exist, we must now consider what these wealth effects are. In fact, changes in net private wealth are seen as influencing both the *IS* and the *LM* curves. The *IS* curve will be affected because the increases in wealth will lead to an increase in consumption expenditure and shift the *IS* curve further to the right. The *LM* curve will be affected because the increase in wealth will cause the demand for money to rise and therefore shift the *LM* curve to the left. These two wealth effects are therefore working in opposite directions: the rightward-shifting *IS* curve is tending to raise income, while the leftward-shifting *LM* curve is tending to reduce it. The actual outcome clearly depends on which of these two effects is the stronger. Monetarists argue that the effect on the demand for money is the stronger, so that the wealth effect works against the expansionary effect of the increase in government expenditure, and there is partial or complete crowding out.

This argument is an oversimplication, however. Long-run or permanent equilibrium requires that aggregate government outlays (on goods and services and on interest payments) are financed by equivalent tax revenues. With an increase in government expenditure on goods and services and an increase in interest payments, permanent equilibrium income must be greater than that which existed before the increase in government expenditure in order to generate the extra taxes required to balance the budget. If the perverse wealth effects reduce income below this permanent equilibrium level, then the system is unstable. The reason is that with income pushed below the budget balancing level, tax revenue will be less, there will be a budget deficit financed by further bond issues, further perverse wealth effects and a further reduction in income. And so the process would continue with income spiralling downwards.

With bond financing, therefore, either the situation will be unstable with income falling continuously, or the level of income will increase by enough to generate the extra taxes required to finance the increased government expenditure on goods and interest payments. This is illustrated in *Figure 7.6*. The curves labelled IS_0, IS_1, IS_2 and LM_0 are reproduced from *Figure 7.5*. In the absence of wealth effects, Y_2 is therefore the sustainable level of income at which the budget is balanced. If wealth effects initially shift the *IS* and *LM* curves to IS_3 and LM_1 respectively, then this would be an unstable situation because the level of income Y_3 would not generate enough taxes to balance the budget, and the whole process would be repeated. If stability is to prevail and a long-run permanent equilibrium reached, then the wealth induced shifts in the *IS* and *LM* curves must be to positions such as IS_4 and LM_2, in order for the budget to be out of deficit. With bond-financing, therefore, long-run crowding-out can only occur in an unstable situation.

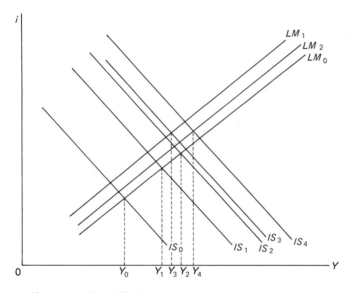

Y_0 = original equilibrium
Y_1 = equilibrium in absence of budget constraint
Y_2 = sustainable income in absence of wealth effects
Y_3 = unstable position with wealth effects
Y_4 = stable position with wealth effects

Figure 7.6 An increase in government expenditure with wealth effects

Some further reasons for crowding-out

A number of other reasons have been suggested as to why government expenditure may crowd out private expenditure, and we shall consider some of them in this final section.

Full employment price level effect

If the initial position is one of full employment, then an increase in government expenditure cannot lead to an increase in real income. Instead, prices will rise and the *LM* curve will shift to the left. This raises the rate of interest and induces a contraction in private sector investment expenditure.

Direct substitution of public for private expenditure

The argument here is that there are some areas where public and private expenditures are highly substitutable, one for the other, i.e. the expenditure by the government is on the provision of goods and services that the private sector would otherwise buy for itself. Moreover, an increase in government investment expenditure which increases the future consumption of such goods and services will result in an equivalent fall in the demand for similar consumption yielded by private investment. Thus, the increase in government investment leads to an equivalent fall in private sector investment.

Expectation effects

An increase in government expenditure which creates or enhances a budget deficit may lead to more pessimistic revisions of businessmen's expectations and thereby cause a reduction in private sector investment. In this case the tendency for the *IS* curve to shift to the right as a result of the increase in government expenditure is offset by the tendency for it to shift to the left following the fall in private investment. Thus, the level of income and the rate of interest would remain unchanged.

Alternatively, the budget deficit may reduce confidence and increase the precautionary demand for money. If it does, then the *LM* curve will shift to the left, raising the rate of interest and inducing a contraction in private sector investment.

Two major criticisms may be levelled at the above arguments for crowding out. The first is that their effects are dependent upon particular and restrictive assumptions, whose validity is highly questionable. The second is that they ignore the budget constraint, and consequently the effects they outline are only temporary and not permanent equilibrium ones. This argument is exactly the same as that considered in the previous section, i.e. permanent long-run equilibrium can only be re-established following an increase in government expenditure, if income increases sufficiently to generate the extra taxes needed to finance the higher level of government expenditure, and leave asset stocks unchanged.

Note

1. Several attempts have been made to 'list' the essential features of monetarism. See, for example, Mayer (1978), Purvis (1980) and Laidler (1982).

8

A review of the empirical evidence relating to the role of money and the effectiveness of monetary policy

In Chapter 3 we surveyed the results of empirical studies of the demand for money, and in this chapter we shall be reviewing the empirical evidence that has accumulated over the last two and a half decades on the role of money and the effectiveness of monetary policy in influencing key macroeconomic variables.

There is, of course, a number of different ways of classifying these studies, but we shall find it useful to use a fourfold classification based on the major issue with which the 'pioneering' study(s) in a particular category was concerned. We shall consider the four categories in the order in which the pioneering studies took place. First of all we shall consider the evidence from studies that have attempted to measure the length and variability of the time lag associated with the influence of monetary variables on economic activity. Secondly we shall look at those studies which have attempted to assess the relative importance of money and autonomous expenditure variables in the determination of consumption expenditure and other macrovariables. These studies were originally seen as 'races' between the simple 'Keynesian' expenditure multiplier model and the Quantity Theory. The third category embraces those studies that have attempted to assess the relative effectiveness of fiscal and monetary policies in influencing the level of economic activity. Fourthly there are studies that have attempted to consider the question of causality in the association between money and other macroeconomic variables. The categories are not mutually exclusive and several studies belong to more than one of them.

Broadly speaking, the role of money in the macroeconomy may be evaluated by using two kinds of 'model'. On the one hand there are the large structural models of the economy. These models comprise equations which set out all the main relationships between the relevant variables in the economy. Each equation will 'describe' the determination of the endogenous variables in terms of both other endogenous variables and exogenous ones. Such models will, for example, have equations explaining all the major kinds of expenditure in the economy. The complexity of such models will depend to a large extent on the degree of disaggregation that they pursue. Thus instead of having just one equation to explain the behaviour of total imports, there could be a separate equation for each of several different kinds of imports, e.g. consumers goods, raw materials, durable producers' goods, etc. Clearly these structural models can become very large and complex, embracing an extremely large number of equations and variables.

The second kind of model is the reduced form one. Such a model reduces a complex structural model to a smaller number of reduced form equations, in each of which an endogenous variable is 'explained' in terms of specified exogenous variables. For example, if we have a simple structural model comprising the following equations

$$Y = C + I + G + X - M$$
$$C = a + cY$$
$$I = \bar{I}$$
$$G = \bar{G}$$
$$X = \bar{X}$$
$$M = mY$$

where the bars denote that the variables are exogenous, then the reduced form equation for Y is

$$Y = \frac{1}{1 - c + m} \cdot (a + \bar{I} + \bar{G} + \bar{X}) \tag{8.1}$$

The argument used to support or oppose these two kinds of estimating model should be independent of the views one has of how the economy operates. A particular theory of how the economy works does not necessarily lead to a particular research methodology. Thus, as the Laidler quotation on page 160 pointed out, there is no necessity for monetarists to employ reduced form models or Keynesians to use structural ones. Each camp has in fact used both kinds of model, but it nevertheless remains true that monetarists have primarily been identified with reduced form equations, and Keynesians with more complex structural models. The majority of the evidence that we shall consider does in fact come from reduced form models.

Time lags

The first serious attempts to estimate the lag between changes in the money stock and other key macrovariables were those of Friedman (1958) and Sprinkel (1959), and were followed in the early 1960s by the major studies of Friedman and Schwartz (1963a, 1963b). Friedman's early findings which were later supported by those of Sprinkel and Friedman–Schwartz were quite startling:

> The rate of change of the money supply shows well-marked cycles that match closely those in economic activity in general and precede the latter by a long time interval. On the average, the rate of change of the money supply has reached its peak nearly 16 months before the peak in general business and has reached its trough over ... 12 months before the trough in general business. (Friedman 1969, p. 180).

Not only was the duration of the lag, on average, quite sizeable, but Friedman also pointed out its considerable variability with a range in respect of 'peaks' of 11 months and of 'troughs' of 16 months. According to Friedman the implications of these findings for the conduct of monetary policy were quite clear: monetary policy was likely to be relatively ineffective as a short-run stabilization device. Moreover, monetary policy could conceivably have a destabilizing effect upon the economy. Because of the uncertainty surrounding the timing of its operational impact on economic activity, monetary action taken some time earlier could 'disturb' the position of macrovariables that had already attained a stated equilibrium. Friedman's conclusion was that discretionary anti-cyclical monetary policy should be abandoned in favour of a monetary policy based upon a simple rule that the money supply be expanded at a pre-specified rate in accordance with the long-run growth potential of the economy.

These consistent early findings were soon subjected to severe criticism. Many of the arguments concerned the general methodological problem of using single equation tests and will be considered fully in the next section. More specifically these studies were criticized on the ground that they related the turning points of the *change* in the money stock to those of the *level* of economic activity. But 'changes in' a variable will always peak or trough before the absolute level of the variable. Thus even if the levels of the money stock and economic activity peaked and troughed at the same time, 'changes in' the money stock would peak or trough before the level of economic activity. Kareken and Solow (1963) argued that a better test for the lag would be one in which first differences of the money and economic activity series were used. They re-ran the tests along these lines and concluded that there is no uniform lag of 'monetary' changes over 'real' changes and certainly nothing like Friedman's order(s) of magnitude.

In a study using UK data, Walters (1971) found that for the data period 1955–62 the highest degree of positive association between GNP and money appears to occur when money leads income by two quarters.

Crockett (1970), also using UK data, studied the lags between movements of monetary and national income variables by using a technique known as a cross-correlogram. This is

a series of coefficients of correlation which can range between +1.0 and −1.0 and which measure the closeness of association (positive or negative) between two series with a given lead or lag. (1970, p. 461).

For example, correlation coefficients could be obtained for time-series pairing ΔY_t with ΔM_t, ΔM_{t-1}, ΔM_{t-2} ... and for pairing ΔM_t with ΔY_t, ΔY_{t-1}, ΔY_{t-2} ... These coefficients could then be plotted on a chart as in *Figure 8.1*. With the correlations

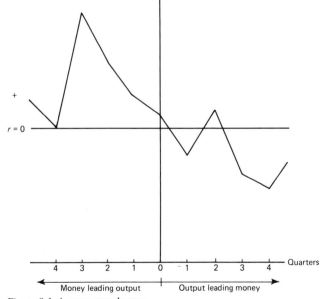

Figure 8.1 A cross-correlogram

plotted in this example money would appear to lead output rather than the other way round, with the most significant relationship occurring when money leads output by three-quarters.

Crockett in fact looked at four pairs of series:

(1) Monetary aggregates with expenditure aggregates.
(2) Monetary components with expenditure aggregates.
(3) Monetary aggregates with expenditure components.
(4) Monetary components with expenditure components.

It is the first of these which is of major interest in this context. Crockett found that movements in the money series generally preceeded that for money income and that the pattern of this lead/lag relationship was bimodal, i.e. had two distinct peaks. There appeared to be a strong relationship between ΔM and ΔY when money led income by two to three months and also when money led income by four to five quarters. This suggests that monetary action may have two effects upon economic activity: a quick-acting thrust followed by a slowly-acting influence.

Other studies, concerned primarily with different issues, have also provided some evidence on the length of time lags, and this evidence will be mentioned in later sections. The general conclusion would appear to be that in the UK, monetary policy influences income with time lags that are both long and variable.

Keynes versus the quantity theory in predicting macrovariables

We shall now consider the attempts that have been made to compare the relevant stability and predictive power of the relationship between autonomous expenditure and the money supply on the one hand and macroeconomic aggregates on the other.

The pioneering study in this field was that of Friedman and Meiselman (1963) who attempted to see whether Keynesian economics or the Quantity Theory provides the better explanation of how the economy works by comparing the relative sizes and stabilities of the money and expenditure multipliers.

The equations used by Friedman and Meiselman in their tests were based on simple and extreme interpretations of the Keynesian and Quantity Theory models. The Keynesian equilibrium condition was

$$Y = C + I + G + X - M \qquad (8.2)$$

where X stands for exports and M for imports. If taxes are deducted from both sides we have an equation in terms of disposable income.

$$Y - T = C + I + (G - T) + (X - M) \qquad (8.3)$$

Consumption is assumed a simple linear function of disposable income:

$$C = a + c(Y - T) \qquad (8.4)$$

All other variables on the right-hand side of equation (8.3) are assumed to be exogenous and collectively are referred to as autonomous expenditure, and denoted by the letter A.

$$I + (G - T) + (X - M) = A \qquad (8.5)$$

The reduced form for disposable income is then

$$Y - T = \frac{1}{1-c}(a+A) = \frac{a}{1-c} + \frac{1}{1-c} \cdot A \qquad (8.6)$$

In this $1/(1-c)$ is the 'expenditure multiplier'. However, any attempts to test for correlation between $Y - T$ and A would give biased results because A is part of Y itself. Friedman and Meiselman therefore used C as the dependent variable rather than $Y - T$.

Thus from (8.3) and (8.5) we have

$$Y - T = C + A \qquad (8.7)$$

Substituting into (8.6)

$$C + A = \frac{a}{1-c} + \frac{A}{1-c}$$

$$C = \frac{a}{1-c} + \frac{A}{1-c} - A$$

$$C = \frac{a}{1-c} + \left(\frac{1}{1-c} - 1\right)A \qquad (8.8)$$

If we denote $a/(1-c)$ by α, and $(1/(1-c)) - 1$ by β, then we have

$$C = \alpha + \beta A \qquad (8.9)$$

Turning now to the simple Quantity Theory we have

$$MV = Py = Y \qquad (8.10)$$

where M is the supply of money and V is the 'money multiplier'. It is the stability and size of this multiplier that is important in assessing the usefulness of the Quantity Theory. In order to make a direct comparison with the Keynesian equation (8.9), however, Friedman and Meiselman did not in fact use equation (8.10) as the basis of their test of the Quantity Theory, but instead employed an equation with C as the dependent variable

$$C = \lambda + \delta M \qquad (8.11)$$

The money multiplier here is δ, and is not the same as the money multiplier V in equation (8.10), and does not bear any simple arithmetical relationship to it.

From the crude Keynesian and Quantity Theory models, Friedman and Meiselman thus derived two different testable propositions. The Keynesian one was that C is primarily determined by A, while the Quantity Theory proposition is that C is primarily determined by M. This apparently simple dichotomy is shown as Causal Nexus 1 in *Figure 8.2*.

Friedman and Meiselman, using data for the period 1897–1958, obtained correlation coefficients for each of equations (8.9) and (8.11) and for variants of those equations, both for the data period as a whole and for a variety of sub-periods. Consistently the results showed a higher correlation between C and M than between C and A, the one exception being for the sub-period 1929–35. Friedman and Meiselman (1963, p. 123), interpret their results as showing that

> Except for the early years of the Great Depression, money is more closely related to consumption than autonomous expenditures ... the results are strikingly one-sided. [and] ... the stock of money is unquestionably far more critical in interpreting movements in income than is autonomous expenditure.

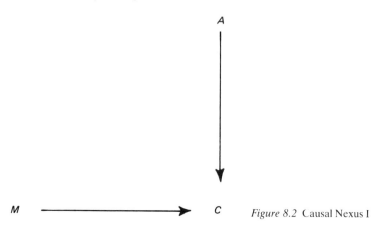

Figure 8.2 Causal Nexus I

The policy implication they argue is that

> ... control over the stock of money is a far more useful tool for affecting the level of aggregate money demand than control of autonomous expenditures.

As can well be imagined these results called forth a mass of research literature focusing criticism upon the Friedman–Meiselman methodology. Objections were raised about the fact that only two out of literally hundreds of macrorelationships had been chosen for testing, that the tests were too simple and not a valid representation of the rival theories, that the variables employed in the tests were incorrectly defined, and that the results obtained were biased.

Perhaps the major point at issue is the usefulness of simple tests of economic theories. Johnson feels that this approach can be defended on the grounds that the

> test of a good theory is its ability to predict something large from something small, by means of a simple and stable theoretical relationship. (1970, p. 86).

Other economists however, do not accept this approach and point out that a simple test of an economic theory may be a poorer predictor of economic behaviour than a more sophisticated test if the economy exhibits complex and at times incomprehensible behaviour patterns.

It may be argued that equation (8.9) does not fairly reflect the complexity of Keynesian economics. A full Keynesian model recognizes and allows for a monetary sector which equation (8.9) does not. At best equation (8.9) provides a test of the Keynesian model only in the special case of the liquidity trap with its absence of monetary repercussions. Partly in anticipation of this criticism Friedman and Meiselman also used an equation which included both the money supply and autonomous expenditure as exogenous variables. The partial correlation coefficients obtained again supported their general conclusions, but are also subject to the same criticisms. In similar vein it can be argued that equation (8.11) is not a satisfactory statement of the Quantity Theory: the presence of the constant term in particular is difficult to justify.

It is also argued that the correlation coefficient obtained on the basis of equations (8.9) and (8.11) are distorted and do not adequately distinguish between the two theories.

Consider Causal Nexus 1 again. This implies that A and M are mutually exclusive of each other. But this is not necessarily so. The behaviour of at least one of the components of A, notably investment, is not independent of the behaviour of monetary variables. A portfolio transmission mechanism links changes in $M(\Delta M)$ to changes in $A(\Delta A)$. This means that in attempting to find a significant association between ΔM and ΔC on the one hand and ΔA and ΔC on the other there will be a common cause-effect relationship linking all three, i.e. $\Delta M \rightarrow \Delta A \rightarrow \Delta C$. This suggests that for analytical convenience it might be a good idea to disaggregate the A variable into (i) a component which is influenced by the behaviour of M and which we denote by A_1, and (ii) a component which is independent of the behaviour of M (denoted A_2). The resulting causal nexus is depicted in *Figure 8.3*. Here the link MaA_1 and A_1bC, the Keynesian cost of capital channel of a portfolio transmission mechanism, is common to both the Quantity Theory and income–expenditure models.

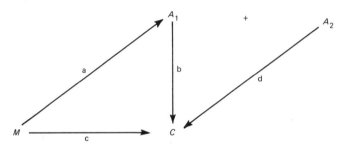

Figure 8.3 Causal Nexus II

If we make the heroic assumption that equations (8.9) and (8.11) are genuine 'reduced-form' equations, derivable directly from the underlying structural relations of the economy, and that A and M are the only exogenous variables in the economy, then one can reason that variations in C unaccounted for by ΔM must be related to ΔA and vice versa, so that if the two equations are combined one would expect the disturbance term, i.e. u in equation (8.12), to be insignificant

$$C = \emptyset + \beta A + \delta M + u \tag{8.12}$$

One way of testing the validity of this simple proposition is to subject (8.12) to a multiple regression test and see if there is a positive disturbance term. A test of this type using UK data (1878–1963) was conducted by Barrett and Walters (1966), using an equation of the following form:

$$\Delta C_t = \emptyset + \beta \Delta A_t + \delta \Delta M_t + u_t \tag{8.13}$$

They found that for the whole period approximately 44% of the observed variation in C could be accounted for by $\Delta M + \Delta A$, that in the sub-period (1878–1938) the percentage was 54%, and that in the further two periods (1878–1914) and (1921–38) it was 58% and 68% respectively. However, for the post Second World War period no positive results could be obtained. Argy's (1970) study of these relations for seventeen countries, using an equation of the form

$$\Delta C_t = \emptyset + \beta \Delta A_t + \gamma \Delta A_{t-1} + \delta \Delta M_t + \alpha \Delta M_{t-1} + u_t \tag{8.14}$$

i.e. including lagged values of A and M of one year, found that for the UK (1951–67), on average only about 33% of the variation in C_t could be accounted for jointly by ΔA and ΔM. All this suggests that there must be at least one other explanatory variable in the C function. It is theoretically possible that this other variable may account for all the residual variation, in which case it would be a better predictor of C than either A or M. Be that as it may, we have to recognize that M and A together do not have a monopoly of influence over C, so that they cannot be the only exogenous variables in the system.

It may be that the stock of money is but one of a number of 'monetary' variables of explanatory importance in the economy. For example the 'real' rate of interest and/or the availability of credit may both be capable of influencing economic activity in general, and C in particular, independently of changes in A or M. There will be occasions when variations in these non-money stock monetary variables (denoted M_v) are, in fact, directly related to ΔM. We have seen in previous chapters that there is a possible relationship between changes in the quantity of money in circulation and changes in the willingness of lenders to supply funds to the market (the credit transmission mechanism). The incorporation of these links into our 'simple' explanatory model gives us Causal Nexus III.

In this system there are now three exogenous variables which may be identified as influencing the behaviour of C: namely M, A_2 and M_{v_2}. This places a different complexion on the interpretation of the 'measured' relationship between C and M. If, in an estimating equation, a (positive) relationship exists between the independent variable (in this case M) and the error terms (such as via the credit transmission mechanism M, e, M_{v_1}, in *Figure 8.4*), this biases upwards the coefficient on the independent variable (i.e. that on M) as well as the degree of association between the dependent and independent variables (i.e. between M and C).

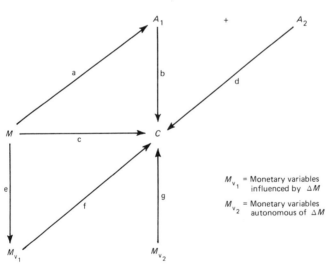

Figure 8.4 Causal Nexus III

On the 'output' side of the economy we can perceive exogenous influences upon C that take place independently of ΔM, ΔA_2 and ΔM_{v_2}. Consider, for example, the repercussions on the economy of a protracted strike, say in the motor car industry; production and wage income will fall and so too may C, with A_2, M_{v_2} and M as yet unchanged. Such factors as these will have to be included in a forecasting model because they help to explain variations in C that cannot be accounted for by ΔM, ΔA_2 or ΔM_{v_2}. This suggests that our model be extended yet again to give us Causal Nexus IV in *Figure 8.5*.

The inclusion of Z and M_v help to explain why $\Delta A + \Delta M$ appears to account for only half, on average, of the variation in C observed over an 80 year period in the UK.

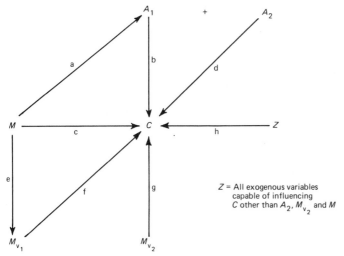

Figure 8.5 Causal Nexus IV

The ability to identify conclusively the determining influence of A and M rests upon the assumption that they are both exogenous variables. If they are not, then erroneous conclusions may be reached, as we must now endeavour to demonstrate by considering first the controversy over the definition of A. Ando–Modigliani (1965) and De Prano–Mayer (1965) both took exception to the Friedman–Meiselman definition of A as $A = I + (G - T) + (X - M)$. They argued that several components of this definition, including taxes, imports, and investment in stocks, are in fact endogenous. The inclusion of such endogenous variables in the definition of A may cause a downwards bias in the estimates of the A coefficient, as well as the coefficient of association. For example, an increase in a truly exogenous component of A will raise C and thereby raise tax revenue. This reduces the budget deficit $(G - T)$ and A, and as a result probably understates the true relationship between A and C. Similarly, an autonomous increase in, say, investment would raise disposable income and C. But if, for example, imports are a function of disposable income then M will rise and $(X - M)$ will fall. This negative correlation between C and $(X - M)$ would then cause C to have a lower correlation with A (including $X - M$) than with a genuinely exogenous definition of A. Unfortunately, it is virtually impossible to distinguish between the endogenous and exogenous components of aggregate expenditure, so that the definition of A is open to a wide variety of interpretations and the results of tests using different definitions may well be subject to large variations. For example, de Prano–Mayer recalculated the coefficients of association using the Friedman–Meiselman data on different definitions of A. They found that one particular index of A which was selected at random $(I + X)$ performed consistently better than either M, or their own index of

$A(I + G + X)$ with a coefficient of association of 0.793 (1929–63) as compared with 0.789 for M and 0.683 for $(I + G + X)$. They also found that the coefficient of association between C_t and A_t using the Friedman–Meiselman definition of $A = I + (G - T) + (X - M)$ was as low as 0.384. If we also incorporate the Barrett–Walters (1966) findings (using $A = I + G + (X - M)$) of a coefficient between M and C of 0.714 and between A and C of 0.607, it would appear that successive narrowing of the defintion of A tends to raise the explanatory power of A from 38 to 80%.

The critics of the Friedman–Meiselman study not only argued that the inclusion of negative endogenous elements in the definition of A biased downwards the results on the relationship between C and A, but they also argued that the money supply is endogenous and therefore can cause an upwards bias in the measured relationship between C and M. The question of the endogeneity of the money supply is considered elsewhere (pp. 209–211) and we shall not consider it here. What we do want to consider is the importance of a two-way chain of causation – $C{\to}M$ and/or $M{\to}C$ – for the analysis of single-equation tests of the Friedman–Meiselman variety. To see what we mean let us add to our simple macrosystem this two-way chain of causation to give us Causal Nexus V (*Figure 8.6*). If C can cause changes in M as a result of a change in the level of economic activity, so too can Z and M_{v_2}. For example, if the monetary authorities are pegging the interest rate then any increase in aggregate expenditure, whether caused by A_1, A_2, M_{v_1}, M_{v_2} or Z will raise M^d, and then M. This means that neither A_2 nor A can be regarded as totally unrelated to M and that the interdependence of A and M means that identification of their independent influence is impossible.

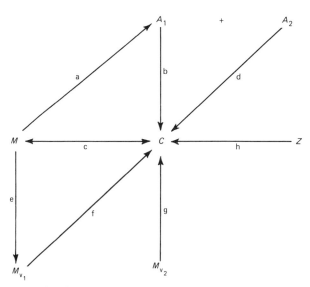

Figure 8.6 Causal Nexus V

According to our model an increase in A_2 will lead to an increase in Y, C and M etc. and an increase in M will increase A and/or M_{v_1}, and increase Y, C and M again. In this system, therefore, A, C and M are all likely to move in unison, making it impossible, as equations (8.9) and (8.1) stands, to identify and therefore estimate the independent influence of either A or M on C. If we concern ourselves with only current values of the variables, the existence of a two-way causal link between C and M yields the following conceivable sequence of events.

$Z \rightarrow C \rightarrow M \rightarrow A \rightarrow C \rightarrow M$ etc.

One possible way round this difficulty is to use lagged values of the determining variables, which offers the opportunity of isolating their effects upon C provided that C responds to A and M within a different time profile. If the hypothesis that C responds to ΔA contemporaneously, whereas it respond to ΔM with a time lag is confirmed, then the association between C_t and A_t can be distinguished from the association between C_t and M_{t-1}. We can demonstrate that this is so by integrating into our macrosystem this new relationship between M and C, giving us Causal Nexus VI (*Figure 8.9*).

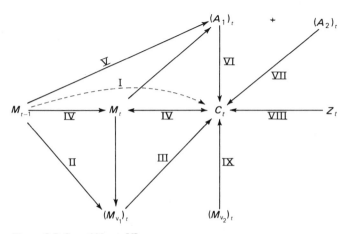

Figure 8.7 Causal Nexus VI

Let us now list the possible channels through which M_{t-1} and A_t can influence C_t.

(1) $M_{t-1} \gg C_t$ directly (I)
(2) $M_{t-1} \gg C_t$ via $(A_1)_t$ (V and VI)
(3) $M_{t-1} \gg C_t$ via $(M_{v_1})_t$ (II and III)
(4) $(A_1)_t \gg C_t$ directly (VI)
(5) $(A_2)_t \gg C_t$ directly (VII)

As links 2 and 4 are common to both as demonstrated earlier, both operating through $(A_1)_t$, there are two sources of independent influence on C_t (holding Z and $(M_{v_2})_t$ constant), $(A_2)_t$ and M_{t-1} with the latter operating directly on C_t and indirectly through $(M_{v_1})_t$. The use of lagged values in estimating equations has been standard practice in studies of the role of money since the Friedman–Meiselman one. Before looking at the results of these studies, let us consider one further complications to our causal nexus. We need to recognize that there is a possible additional link running from C to A through an accelerator mechanism. The acceleration principle of derived demand says that changes in I (a component of A) today may be in partial response to changes in C in an earlier time period. In other words, just as endogenous factors entering into the determination of M open up the possibility of a two-way chain of causation running between C and M, so an accelerator mechanism highlights the possibility of a two-way link between C and A. If we incorporate into the $(A_1)_t$ relation a lagged value of C, then we re-define our system of causal relations again *Figure 8.8*). If C_{t-1} and M_{t-1} are dimensionally equivalent (timewise) then there is a problem of a mutually interdependent system of relations. Unless the time profile of the money multiplier process $(M{\rightarrow}C)$ differs from that of the accelerator process $(C{\rightarrow}A)$ one cannot draw any firm conclusion about the relative explanatory power of M and A on C.

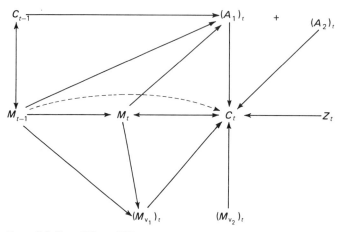

Figure 8.8 Causal Nexus VII

It may be argued that what is required in this sort of situation is (i) a greater degree of disaggregation of the variables to identify which components of C are responsive to lagged values of M and which are not, and the same for I in respect of past values of C; and (ii) a greater amount of experimentation with lag structures. For example, C and M may be dimensionally equivalent using a broad time period of, say 3 or 6 months, but dimensionally distinguishable within a narrower time structure, say, a month. Now these are the types of refinement of detail which are attempted in large-scale models of the economic system where the channels of independent influence of A and M can be more accurately specified after experimentation with more detailed disaggregation of variables and more comprehensive lag structures. In summing up the drawbacks associated with the single-equation approach, Gramlich (1969, pp. 21–26) noted that the

> appropriate degree of disaggregation to strive for in model building is at bottom a matter of taste in which the benefit of increasing the structural richness of the model is traded off against the cost of increasing the complexities of the relationships, including more mysterious feedbacks, increasing the problems of data management and being less up to date. ... but we should recognize that the one-equation approach forgoes an awful lot of structural richness.

Having sought to 'penetrate' the disarmingly simple facade of the single equation approach used in comparisons of the money and expenditure multipliers, we can now briefly review the evidence obtained from studies of this kind on UK data. The major study along the lines of the Friedman–Meiselman one was that of Barrett and Walters (1966). They estimated reduced form equations incorporating lags from data for the period 1878–1963 (excluding war years). For the period as a whole they found a marginal superiority of M over A using absolute values, but a much better fit for A than M when a 'differential' form of the estimating equations was used. Distinguishing between the three sub-periods 1878–1914, 1921–38 and 1948–63, Barrett and Walters found that in the relatively full employment period before the first World War, M appeared more important than A though the latter was not insignificant. In the inter-war period, characterized by high unemployment and falling prices for much of the time, A appeared to be the major determinant of fluctuations in C, though again a lagged M appeared significant. In the post Second World War period, neither M nor A appeared to have an significant explanatory power.

Argy (1970) made a similar study of the UK data 1951–67 as part of a broader study of 17 countries. His estimating equation included lagged values of A and M of one year, and he obtained the unusual result that the significant result for money was without a lag, while for autonomous expenditure it was with the lagged value. Crockett (1970), using his cross-correlogram technique, found low correlation between changes in money and consumption. The highest correlation coefficient obtained was 0.2 when money lagged consumption by six quarters.

Other studies of the role of money and the money multiplier have used macrovariables other than C as the dependent variable, and have not involved direct comparisons with expenditure multipliers. Walters, for example, looked at UK data for the period 1880–1962 and found that the percentage of observed variation in Y explained by changes in M was 29% for 1880–1913, 52% for 1922–38 and 7% for 1955–62.

Goodhart and Crockett (1970) tested for the influence of money on GDP (data period 1957–64) and on industrial production (data period 1953–69). They used quarterly data and a number of money supply definitions on equations of the form:

$$Y_t = a_0 + a_1 M_t + a_2 M_{t-1} + \dots a_8 M_{t-7} + u_t \tag{8.15}$$

They found

(1) The best results were obtained with the industrial output variable.
(2) M3 was the money supply best able to explain changes in both GDP and industrial output.
(3) The explanatory power of the equations was generally good, though Goodhart and Crockett suggested that the association between money and output may be 'merely a reflection of cyclical influences acting on both variables with no direct causal connection' (1970, p. 197).

An early study of the influence of money on prices was made by Walters (1971). He found for the period 1922–38 that an equation which contained first differences of M and real income (with the latter insignificant) was able to explain 61% of the change in prices. More recently Tarling and Wilkinson (1977) have looked at the influence of money on prices by using a logarithmic and 'difference' version of the simple Quantity Theory of Money ($MV = PT$):

$$\Delta \text{Log } P = \Delta \text{Log } M + \Delta \text{Log } V - \Delta \text{Log } T \tag{8.16}$$

Assuming V is constant (so $\Delta \text{Log } V = 0$) and that T changes at a uniform rate (so $\Delta \text{Log } T = \text{constant} = K$) we have

$$\Delta \text{Log } P = -k + \Delta \text{Log } M \tag{8.17}$$

Tarling and Wilkinson used a lagged version of equation (8.17) on data for the period 1960–75. For 1960–77 their results were generally poor, but the influence of

ΔM on ΔP was increased when M was lagged two years and the data period extended to 1975. However, the authors interpret their own results as rejecting the simple quantity theory explanation of inflation. Coghlan (1980) re-estimated some of the Tarling–Wilkinson equations for the period 1960–76, with ΔM lagged up to four years. His main conclusions were (i) extending the data period appeared to produce results more clearly in line with the Quantity Theory; and (ii) the importance of money appeared to be greatest when it was lagged three years.

Wren-Lewis (1981), using the retail price index and a broad definition of money, estimated an equation on quarterly data 1967–78, which had a complex lag structure but was capable of explaining a large proportion of the variation in prices over the data period. The forecasting performance of the equation in 1979 however was extremely poor. Wren-Lewis also estimated equations in which such variables as overseas prices, 'world' money, and indirect taxes were included as additional variables. In all cases the explanatory power of the equations was improved, or at least in the short run, though Wren-Lewis warns that the econometric problems are such that his results must be treated with caution.

Very little evidence on the size of the money multiplier is available from structural models of the UK. This is partly because until fairly recently the monetary sectors of most of these models were accorded relatively minor roles. Moreover, the links between the monetary and other sectors of these models is sometimes so complex that the role of money is not always clear. In a comparative simulation exercise against three of these models, Laidler (1978b) constructed a simple monetarist model which he estimated from annual data for the period 1954–70. He found that variations in the quantity of money during this fixed exchange rate period, had negligible effects on domestic output; the impact was instead overwhelmingly on the balance of payments, thus lending support to the global monetarist view.

Monetary policy versus fiscal policy

A rather different approach to the empirical assessment of Keynesian and monetarist economics was made in 1968 by Anderson and Jordan (1968) of the Federal Reserve Bank of St. Louis. They concentrated on the policy implications of the two schools of thought by trying to find out whether monetary policy or fiscal policy is more effective in influencing economic activity. Three criteria of effectiveness were used:

(1) The magnitude of effect of a policy change.
(2) The stability of the relationship between the variables of policy and the dependent variables.
(3) The speed with which the effects of a policy change are transmitted to the dependent variable.

The method used by Anderson and Jordan was again that of reduced form type equations of the kind

$$\Delta Y = a + \psi \Delta MP + \phi \Delta FP$$

where MP is monetary policy and FP fiscal policy. Two measures of monetary policy were used: the total money stock and the stock of high powered money. Three measures of fiscal policy were employed: full employment government expenditure (G), full employment government revenue (T) and the full employment government deficit or surplus $(G - T)$. The full employment measures were used in the belief that they gave a better indication of autonomous or discretionary changes in policy as opposed to income-induced changes; i.e. by measuring G, T and $G - T$ at a given level of income (conveniently full employment) the possibility that G, T and $G - T$ might change simply as a response to a change in income was removed. The equations were estimated in first differences from quarterly data for the period 1952–68, with lags on the explanatory variables estimated using the Almon technique. Their main findings may be summarized:

(1) The percentage of the variation in Y(GNP) explainable by changes in fiscal and monetary policy was over 50% in all equations tested.
(2) The coefficient on the monetary policy term was of the right sign $(+)$ with high statistical significance.
(3) The coefficient on the fiscal policy term was not always of the right sign and had low statistical significance.
(4) Y responded positively to a change in the supply of money both in the current and in the next three quarters with a total response (a money multiplier) of 5.8.
(5) Y responded positively to a change in government expenditure for the first two quarters and negatively in the next two quarters with a total response of practically zero. This would suggest that public expenditures simply crowd-out private expenditures.

Anderson and Jordan concluded that monetary policy is far more powerful, quick acting and certain in its effects upon Y that is fiscal policy. The startling results of the Anderson–Jordan study had the same sort of impact in professional and academic circles as the Friedman–Meiselman study had had half a decade earlier, and they unleashed a similar wave of intellectual indignation, particularly from those sympathizers of the Keynesian tradition who believed implicitly in the potency of fiscal policy.

Many of the criticisms of the Anderson–Jordan study were similar in principle to those that had been made of the Friedman–Meiselman study; in large measure they were connected with the problems of reduced form equations. We shall therefore discuss these criticisms rather more briefly.

De Leeuw and Kalchbrenner (1969) criticized the definitions of monetary and fiscal policy employed by Anderson–Jordan. They point out that the full employment measures of fiscal policy were useful in removing the 'drag' effect associated with an increase in real output, but of little use in eliminating the drag effect of increases in the price level. Under a progressive income tax regime, real tax revenues rise and real disposable income and expenditure falls. Some adjustment to the concept of the full employment budget surplus needs to be made to accommodate for the drag effect associated with inflation. De Leeuw and Kalchbrenner also argued that neither of the Anderson–Jordan definitions of the money stock were strictly exogenous, so that part of the association between ΔM and ΔY could be the result of a reverse influence running from ΔY to ΔM. After making an adjustment to the money base measure and to the tax variable in order to net out the influence of inflation, they re-ran the tests and found that the potency of fiscal policy was greatly enhanced.

As with the Friedman–Meisleman results there is the possibility that the Anderson–Jordan results may be biased because the reduced forms are not correctly specified. This would happen, for example, if the fiscal policy variable is endogenously determined, and this would be the case if it were varied by the authorities in an attempt to stabilize the economy. Thus if fiscal policy was operated with complete success so that all fluctuations in Y are removed, then there would be no correlation between the changes in fiscal policy and the constant level of income. Low correlation coefficients on fiscal policy could therefore be interpreted as indication that fiscal policy is a good counter-cyclical weapon.

Davis (1969) called attention to the fact that when the data period of the Anderson–Jordan study (1952–68) is sub-divided into 1952–60 and 1960–68; the explanatory power of money is very low in the former period (0.18) and quite high in the latter (0.62). Subsequent re-runs of the St. Louis model (e.g. Poole and Kornblith 1973; B. M. Friedman 1977) have provided further evidence in support of the view that the results obtained and the predictive performance of the model depend very much on the time period considered.

Artis and Nobay (1969) have run a similar type of test to Anderson and Jordan, using UK data for the period 1958–67 with two definitions of money, one broad, one narrow, a government receipts variable, and a variable denoting governmental fiscal measures which included changes in hire-purchase terms as well as tax rates. Their results are the exact reverse of those of the St. Louis experiments. Using a 'stepwise' regression programme which successively introduced additional independent variables in decreasing order of explanatory power, they found that the variable denoting government fiscal measures exhibited the highest degree of association with ΔY. Further, they were able to estimate that the impact of this variable was much quicker than that of monetary measures; 0.2 of one-quarter in the case of fiscal policy and 3.2 quarters in the case of monetary policy. Like Anderson and Jordan they found that the sign on the fiscal term alternated from $(+)$ to $(-)$, suggesting that the effect of fiscal policy, though quick-acting, was short-lived. Unlike the Anderson–Jordan study, however, Artis and Nobay found that the cumulative impact of monetary measures was only 0.2 whilst that of fiscal measures was 6.6. Artis and Nobay were very sceptical about their results and insisted that not too much importance be attached to them. This is because of the serious reservations they had about testing a 'reduced-form' equation which is not the genuine derivative of a pre-specified structural model, so that it is difficult to know what the sign and size of the coefficients ought to be and

> how they should be interpreted as representing an effect of monetary or fiscal policy variables on GDP rather than the other way round. The single-equation tests seem to us more correctly interpreted simply as measures of association. (Artis and Nobay 1969, p. 38).

Keran (1970) looked at the effectiveness of monetary and fiscal policy in the UK (data period 1953–68) as part of a multi-country study. His results presented a rather blurred picture, and only when industrial production was used as the dependent variable did either of the policies have a significant impact, and then it was monetary policy that dominated.

Some further evidence on the relative effectiveness of monetary and fiscal policies has been provided by simulations on large-scale econometric models of the economy. A number of such simulations were made in the US in the late 1960s. The Brookings quarterly model, for example, indicated that $1 bn increase in the level of unborrowed reserves through open-market operations could be expected to raise the equilibrium level of income by $8.6 bn, and that an equivalent increase in government expenditure on non-durables would permanently raise Y by 2.9 times the initial injection. Simulations on the FRB–MIT model suggested that the money multiplier may be as high as 20 (over a three-year period), whereas the fiscal policy multiplier is only about 2.4. Both studies found that fiscal policy was quicker acting than monetary policy.

A rather quicker effect for monetary policy was obtained by Anderson and Carlson (1970) in simulations on their St. Louis model. This model, though fuller than that of Anderson and Jordan, was still very small, having only three exogenous variables. It did however have separate equations for prices, interest rate, unemployment and total spending, and permitted a distinction to be drawn between changes in output and changes in prices. In this model the money multiplier was greatest after five quarters. The simulations also suggested that in the long run, monetary action had no effect on real magnitudes, only on nominal ones.

Matthews and Ormerod (1978) applied St. Louis type models to UK data for 1964–74 using the quarterly change in high powered money as their measure of monetary policy, the quarterly change in the full employment budget deficit as their measure of fiscal policy and GDP as the income variable. The results obtained were almost identical to those of Anderson and Carlson. They found that fiscal policy had the greatest initial impact, but after four quarters the money multiplier was 4.7 while that for fiscal policy was little different from zero. The authors followed Artis and Nobay in emphasizing the limitations of their results both because of the theoretical and methodological objections to St. Louis-type equations and because of the sensitivity of the results obtained to the explanatory variables used. Matthews and Ormerod also point out that their results, at least for fiscal policy, differ significantly from those generated by large-scale structural models of the UK. For example, Laury, Lewis, and Ormerod (1978) found that in simulations on the models of the London Business School, the Treasury and the NIESR, an increase in government current spending, unaccompanied by monetary expansion, generated a multiplier significantly greater than zero.

A question of causality

So far the evidence that we have considered pertaining to the role of money and monetary policy in influencing economic activity has all been concerned with the observed statistical association between money and specified macrovariables. But of course statistical association does not imply causation. The fact that money and, say, GNP move together does not necessarily mean that changes in money cause changes in income. The evidence of a statistical association is certainly compatible with that causal sequence, but it is equally compatible with a causal chain running from income to money, and also with a causal chain in which income and money are independent of one another, but both are influenced by a third variable.

The early attempts to obtain evidence that would distinguish between these different causal chains concentrated on identifying the turning points in money supply and income cycles. If it could be shown that the peaks and troughs of the money supply cycle consistently lead the peaks and troughs of the income cycle, then this could be taken as evidence that the chain of causation is more likely to run from money to income than the other way round. A second approach (Crockett 1970) is to see whether the greater correlation coefficients are obtained from money and income series when money leads income or when money lags income. If the greater association appears to exists when money leads, then this may be taken as evidence of a greater likelihood that money supply changes cause income changes rather than vice versa.

More recently studies of causality have been based on the methods of Granger (1969) and Sims (1972). Granger suggested a statistical definition of causality which may be crudely summarized thus: if better forecasts of a variable X can be obtained by using both past values of X itself and past values of another variable Y than can be obtained by using past values of X alone, then Y can be said to 'cause' X.

Sims (1972) was the first to apply this idea to the question of causality in the relationship between money and economic activity. He first tried to remove any systematic components or trend from the series he was using by pre-filtering them. This meant removing from the series for ΔM and ΔY those parts that could be predicted from knowledge of the past values of ΔM and ΔY respectively. This left the residuals in regressions of the two variables on their own past values. The filtered series could then be regressed on one another. In the regressions, not only were current and lagged values of the independent variable used, but also future values. The reason for doing this is that if ΔM 'causes' ΔY, then ΔY should not be influenced by future values of ΔM. Also, if ΔY does not 'cause' ΔM, then lagged values of ΔY should be an insignificant determinant of ΔM.

Sims applied this technique to the relationship between money and money income in the USA for the data period 1948–68. His results were in line with the view that M is exogenous and that ΔM 'causes' ΔY.

The first attempt to apply the Granger–Sims technique to UK data was made by Williams, Goodhart and Gowland (1976). Their results were rather poor, but suggested that income influenced money rather than the other way round, i.e. money appeared to be the endogenous variable. However, the period to which the study relates was one of fixed exchange rates, and as the UK is a small open economy, it may be argued that the endogeneity of the money supply was to be expected.

Mills (1980) specifically recognized the limitations of the results of Williams and his colleagues and undertook a test of Granger causality for a period characterized part of the time by fluctuating exchange rates. He used quarterly data for the period 1963(QI) to 1977(QIII). This meant that over half of the period had fixed exchange rates, but this was felt necessary in order to generate a meaningful number of observations. The money supply series used were those for M1 and M3, and the income measures used were GDP and total final expenditure (TFE). In addition to the nominal series of money and income, real values and prices were also used, giving a total of 16 pairs of series. Two kinds of test of Granger-causality were employed: a Sims-type test involving pre-filtering of the data and a 'direct' test. Mills conclusions are that:

> In general, fluctuations in real money cause fluctuations in real income, however defined, [and] It would seem that money, and especially M3, the money aggregate that monetary policy should influence, does have a causal effect on certain income and price series, particularly TFE and its components. (1980, p. 26).

Mills comments that as the major difference between TFE and GDP is imports of goods and services, these results would indicate the importance of taking into account the exchange rate and the balance of payments when considering the causal relationship between money and income.

Holly and Longbottom (1982) examined the relationship between prices and M3 using data for the period 1964–79. A number of methodological approaches were used in order to test for Granger-causality. They concluded that:

(1) Causality runs from lagged values of money to prices.
(2) There also appears to be causality running in the other direction, but the nature of this feedback suggests 'some deliberate policy response to higher inflation' rather than the passive adjustment of money to higher prices.
(3) There is some support for a proportional relationship between money and prices.
(4) There is a lag of up to four years before a change in M is fully reflected in the rate of inflation.

Though these attempts at establishing causality are clearly more sophisticated than the simpler tests of leads and lags, it is still implicit in them that causality has something to do with timing. But as several authors have argued (e.g. Kaldor 1970; Tobin 1970) sequence should not be confused with consequence, and 'statistical causality' is not the same as 'theoretical causality'. If people build up their money balances in anticipation of spending and the monetary authorities allow this to happen, then, in sequence, first the money supply rises, then expenditure and lastly, after lags of varying duration, other macrovariables, such as output and prices. But this sequence does not reflect the order of the links in a causal chain. Critics of Granger-type causality (e.g. Zellner 1979; Jacobs, Lerner and Ward 1979) suggest that the most that can be said for any pair of time series is that one is helpful/informative about predicting the behaviour of the other.

9

Inflation

Inflation is a term which has been used to mean several different things, but for the purposes of this chapter we shall define it to be a sustained rise in the general level of prices. Two points about this definition need emphasizing. First, the increase in prices must be a sustained one, and not simply a once and for all increase in prices. Second, it must be the general level of prices which is rising: increases in individual prices which are offset by falling prices are not inflationary.

To people born since the start of the Second World War it may seem hard to believe that inflation is not inevitable, but there have been notable periods of falling prices in the UK during the last three hundred years. In fact the index of prices in 1913 was lower than that of 1661. During the present century, prices rose sharply during the First World War, but fell for most of the inter-war period. The Second World War again saw prices rising rapidly and, in contrast to much of the peacetime experience of the previous three hundred years, they have continued to rise ever since. The 1970s was, for the United Kingdom, the most inflationary decade of the century. The inflation of that decade was unusual moreover, not only for its severity, but also for being accompanied by historicially high levels of unemployment.

Over the years many theories have been developed by economists to explain the nature and causes of inflation and various classifications have been used to group the theories together for purposes of comparison and contrast. In the 1950s and early 1960s, for example, it was common practice to distinguish between 'demand-pull' and 'cost-push' explanations. This classification tried to distinguish between inflations that resulted from prices being pulled up by an excess demand for goods and services, and those that resulted from prices being pushed up by rising costs. A major objection to this classification is that excess demand can arise either because of an increase in demand or a fall in supply. The latter, of course, could be a consequence of an increase in costs, so that both demand-pull and cost-push theories could be seen as excess demand explanations of inflation.

As a result the demand-pull versus cost-push distinction fell out of favour in the 1970s, being largely replaced by a classification which distinguished between economic and non-economic explanations of inflation. The non-economic explanations are regarded as sociological or socio-political, concentrating as they do on trying to explain the behaviour of trade unions and of prices in terms of sociological and political concepts. The economic theories, on the other hand, concentrate on prices as market variables, and regard inflation as the consequence of certain market conditions. The important distinction between these two broad approaches is that one regards wages and prices as being capable of rising independently of the state of demand in the goods and labour markets, while the other sees wage and price increases solely as a response to actual or expected market conditions. This distinction between economic and non-economic theories of inflation does not of course imply that all economists subscribe to the economic theories and none to the non-economic. While making the same analytical distinction we prefer not to use this discipline-based terminology but to distinguish instead between market and non-market theories of inflation.

Market theories of inflation

The inflationary gap model

The first market theory of inflation we shall consider is one which draws an important distinction between situations of unemployment and that of full employment. The theory is usually identified with Keynes and called the 'inflationary gap' model. It is illustrated in *Figure 9.1*. AD_0 is the initial aggregate demand curve, which generates an equilibrium level of income co-incidental with full employment $(Y/P)_f$. Now suppose that there is an autonomous increase in

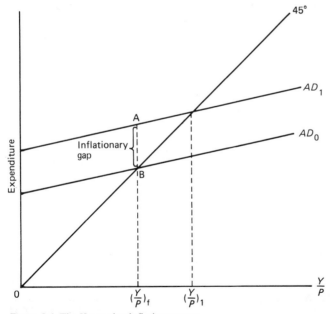

Figure 9.1 The Keynesian inflationary gap

aggregate desired expenditure which shifts the aggregate demand curve to AD_1. The equilibrium level of real income is now $(Y/P)_1$, in excess of the full employment level and consequently unattainable. At the full employment maximum, aggregate demand exceeds the real value of output by BA, and it is this that is referred to as the inflationary gap. The excess demand for goods will generate a rise in prices and probably also a rise in wages.

But we must now consider whether these would be once and for all increases, or whether they would be self-perpetuating and generate prolonged inflation. It all depends on whether the inflationary gap is removed as a result of the price increases, for as long as the gap remains prices will rise. There are in fact a number of ways in which the process of rising prices could remove the inflationary gap.

The first of these that we consider involves the money supply. As the absolute price level rises, then following the Keynesian analysis of the demand for money, the demand for transactions balances will rise. But if the total money stock does not rise, then as more and more money is used for transactions balances, less and less will be available to satisfy the demand for idle balances: the result will be an increase in the rate of interest. This in turn will induce a fall in aggregate real demand if either investment or consumption are interest elastic. In this way the inflationary gap could be removed and the inflation brought to a halt.

There are, however, other ways in which this could happen that do not directly involve the money supply. If, for example, the inflation brings about a redistribution of income, and if the redistribution is from those with high marginal propensities to consume towards those with low, then again aggregate demand will fall and the inflationary gap disappear.

One particular type of redistribution involves the government. If the tax system is progressive and if the tax structure is not altered in terms of tax-free allowances, tax bands and rates, then as people's money incomes rise during the process of inflation, they will find themselves paying a larger and larger proportion of their incomes in taxes. If the government has a lower marginal propensity to spend than tax-payers there will again be a fall in aggregate expenditure and elimination of the inflationary gap.

The foregoing discussion can be illustrated graphically using an *IS–LM* diagram. In *Figure 9.2* the original IS curve is the one labelled IS_0 and the original *LM* curve is that labelled $LM(M_0/P_0)$. The two curves intersect at a level of interest i_0 and a level of real income $(Y/P)_f$ assumed to be that corresponding to full employment. The autonomous increase in the demand for goods shifts the *IS* curve upwards to the right to the position IS_1. At the prevailing rate of interest, equilibrium in the goods market now requires a level of real income of $(Y/P)_1$, while equilibrium in the money market remains unchanged at a level of income $(Y/P)_f$. Simultaneous equilibrium in the goods and money markets requires an increase in the rate of interest to i_1 making $(Y/P)_2$ the equilibrium level of real income. But $(Y/P)_2$ represents a greater level of real income than $(Y/P)_f$, which we have defined as full employment income. Therefore there is a gap between the equilibrium level of income and the maximum that is possible – the so-called inflationary gap. The excess demand, unable to affect real output $(Y/P)_f$, will force prices up. If the nominal money supply is unchanged then the real value of the money stock will fall as prices rise and the *LM* curve will shift upwards to the left, intersecting the IS curve as it does so at higher and higher rates of interest and lower and lower levels of (Y/P). If the *IS* schedule does not shift, then eventually the leftward-moving *LM* schedule will intersect the *IS* schedule at a level of (Y/P) that represents full employment $(Y/P)_f$, but at the higher rate of interest i_2. At this new equilibrium position the inflationary gap will have disappeared and the inflation brought to an end. The higher rate of interest will have lead to a contraction in aggregate demand (a movement along the *IS* curve). If the other reasons discussed above why rising prices might reduce aggregate demand are also operative, then the *IS* curve will shift downwards to the left, towards its original position. Then the combination of the upwards-shifting *LM* curve and the dowards-shifting IS curve may lead them to intersect at the full employment level of (*Y*/*P*) and a rate of interest lower than that which would prevail if the new full employment equilibrium position were reached entirely as a result of shifts in the *LM* curve. If, however, the authorities allow the nominal money supply to increase at the same rate as the demand for money is being pushed up by rising prices, then the *LM* schedule will not change its position. In this case the inflation would only come to an end if the *IS* curve shifted back to its original position as a result of the influences mentioned earlier.

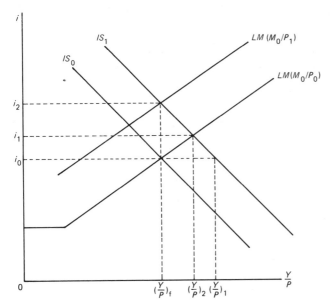

Figure 9.2 The elimination of an inflationary gap via a fall in the real value of money

If the authorities wish to stop the inflation, then this analysis suggests a prescription for policy: prevent the money supply from increasing as rapidly as the demand for it. Indeed, if the money supply was contracted, then the *LM* schedule could be shifted to the left without the need for prices to rise first. Unfortunately, however, such action will have other consequences which the authorities may consider undesirable. They then have to balance these undesirable effects against the desirability of stopping the inflation, and possibly consider alternative ways of dealing with the inflation. The authorities may be unwilling, for example, to allow interest rates to rise because of the implications for the gilt-edged market, and their management of the national debt. Moreover, the demand for real money balances will be rising fairly continuously as real output and income grow following advances in technological knowledge and other factors promoting economic growth. Unless the money supply is allowed to increase in step with this long-run growth in demand, unemployment may result. The problem for the authorities using control of the money supply to deal with an inflationary gap situation is to decide on that rate of growth of the money supply that will remove the gap without going to the other extreme and starting a recession.

The simple Phillips curve model

In the simple inflationary gap model outlined above, inflation is the consequence of an excess pressure of demand for goods and services at the full employment level of output. Increases in aggregate demand below the full employment level of output would expand real economic activity, leaving prices more or less stable. From the point of view of policy implications, this simple model suggested that if aggregate demand could be maintained at the full capacity position, full employment could be achieved with stable prices.

Actual post-war experience did not in fact justify this optimistic policy implication, and the difficulty experienced in achieving simultaneously high employment and price stability indicated there was a serious lacuna in the inflationary gap analysis of inflation and unemployment. This gap seemed to be filled by the appearance in the late 1950s of the Phillips curve relationship which implied that there was a conflict between the policy objectives of high employment and stable prices.

'Phillips curve' is the name given to the graphical relationship between the level of unemployment and the rate of change of wages that was derived from empirical data by A. W. Phillips (1958) and presented in his classic article 'The relationship between unemployment and the rate of change of money wage rates in the United Kingdom 1861–1957'. Phillips plotted a scatter diagram of time-series data for levels of unemployment and annual percentage changes in money wages for the period 1861–1913, and then fitted a curve to the plotted points. Similar data for the period 1951–57 were also observed to lie on or very close to the curve, suggesting that the relationship traced out by the curve held over the best part of a hundred years. The original Phillips curve is shown in *Figure 9.3*. Two characteristics of the curve should be noted. First, it slopes downwards from left to right implying an

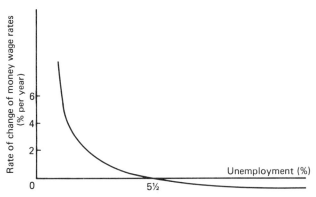

Figure 9.3 The original Phillips curve

inverse relationship between the two variables, i.e. the lower the level of unemployment the greater the rate of change of money wages. Second, the relationship is non-linear, so that equal reductions in the level of unemployment are associated with larger and larger increases in the rate of change of money wages. The position and shape of Phillips original curve were such that unemployment of 1%, 2% and 3% appeared to be associated with wage increases of about 9%, 2% and 1% respectively, while wages appeared to be stationary with unemployment of about 5½%.

The wage change–unemployment relationship of Phillips original curve was soon translated into a price change–unemployment relationship by simply assuming that wage changes are fully reflected in price changes after allowing for productivity increases. Such a derivation is shown in *Figure 9.4*. For the remainder of this chapter we shall make the simplifying assumption that productivity increases are zero, so that wage increases and price increases are the same. This does no significant harm to any of the subsequent analysis, but enables us to draw a single curve tracing both the wage change–unemployment relationship and the price change–unemployment relationship.

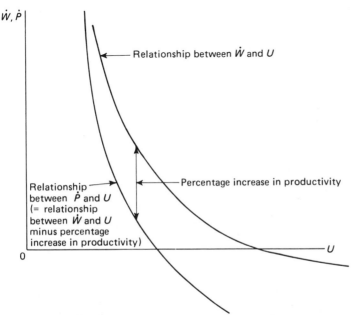

Figure 9.4 The derivation of the Phillips curve as a relationship between the rate of change of prices and the level of unemployment

What were the policy implications of the Phillips curve? To begin with it clearly demonstrated that inflation could coexist with unemployment and that unless exceptional increases in productivity could be achieved, the targets of price stability and full employment were not attainable simultaneously. The policy options offered by the curve were in fact in the form of a trade-off. In order to have less of one it would be necessary to have more of the other: to reduce the level of unemployment, for example, it would be necessary to accept a higher rate of inflation. It would be for the authorities to decide which of the various possible combinations of inflation and unemployment traced out by the curve they would seek to attain.

The Phillips curve, it must be remembered, was an empirical relationship and not a theoretical one. While Phillips himself, in his original article, attempted to provide a simple explanation of his curve it was left to subsequent writers to develop more formal theoretical underpinnings for it.

The first widely accepted theory of the Phillips curved was provided by Lipsey (1960). According to his theory the empiricially observed relationship between

wage changes and unemployment was derived from two other economic
relationships. The first of these says that rates of change of wages are functionally
related to the degree of excess demand present in the labour market, the
relationship being such that the greater the degree of excess demand, the greater
the rate of increase of wages. This may be written

$$\dot{W} = f\left[\frac{D_L - S_L}{S_L}\right], \qquad \text{where } f' > 0$$

$\dot{W}$ is the percentage change in wages and D_L and S_L are the demand for labour and
supply of labour respectively. The relationship is depicted graphically in panel 1 of
Figure 9.5.

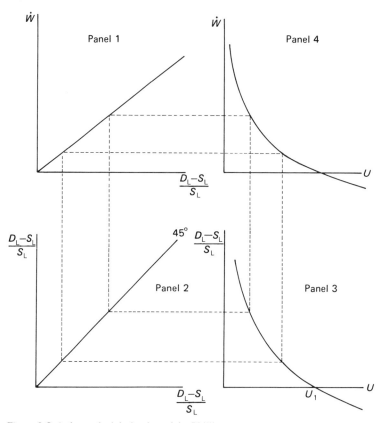

Figure 9.5 A theoretical derivation of the Phillips curve

Empirically, the excess demand for labour is not observable directly, but Lipsey
suggested that measured unemployment could be taken as a proxy variable. The
second ecnomic relationship underlying the Phillips curve in the Lipsey theory is
the functional relationship between measured unemployment and the extent of
excess demand in the labour market. This relationship may be written

$$U = g\left[\frac{D_L - S_L}{S_L}\right], \qquad \text{where } g' < 0$$

One possible graphical representation of this relationship is drawn in panel 3 of *Figure 9.5* and reflects the following assumptions and reasoning. When there is zero excess demand in the labour market, i.e. when the demand for and supply of labour are equal, there will still be some people unemployed. This will be because there are always people who are in the process of changing employment and such changes take time. There may be a variety of frictions which prevent some people who quit or lose one type of employment from becoming immediately re-employed in another, even though vacancies exist: there will always be some frictional unemployment. Thus in panel 3, zero excess demand is associated with a level of unemployment of U_1. As the extent of excess demand increases, the level of unemployment is likely to fall as the unemployed find it easier to get 'suitable' employment and spend less time 'frictionally' unemployed. But the frictions cannot disappear completely, so unemployment cannot fall to zero. Every reduction in the level of unemployment makes it more difficult for unemployment to fall further. Thus the curve tracing the relationship between $(D_L - S_L)/S_L$ and U is likely to be convex to the origin and approach the vertical axis asymtotically for all positive levels of excess demand. Where there is excess supply, however, i.e. to the right of U_1 in panel 3, this may not be the case. The simpliest assumption to make is that every addition to excess supply is an equal addition to unemployment. This will then mean that the curve tracing the relationship between $(D_L - S_L)/S_L$ and U is linear for all negative values of $(D_L - S_L)/S_L$. The Phillips curve of panel 4 in *Figure 9.5* is now readily derived from the curves depicted in panels 1 and 3.

The position and slope of the Phillips curve is clearly dependent upon the positions and slopes of the two curves from which it is derived. Thus a change in the functional relationship between W and $(D_L - S_L)/S_L$ and/or that between U and $(D_L - S_L)/S_L$ would result in a change in the Phillips curve relationship, i.e. that between W and U.

In fact the original Phillips curve relationship appeared to hold until the late 1960s. From 1958 to 1966 the wage rate changes predicted by the Phillips curve were quite close to the actual changes and were also free from bias in the sense that the errors were both positive and negative and cumulatively tended to cancel out. From the end of 1966, however, the predictive power of the Phillips curve has been very poor and consistently biased towards underprediction, culminating in underpredictions of wage increases of more than 20% in 1974 and 1975.

At about the same time that the Phillips curve was starting to significantly underpredict wage changes (i.e. the late 1960s), it was coming under attack on theoretical grounds. These theoretical developments are the subject matter of the next section. Some of the attempts to explain the empirical inconsistency of the Phillips curve with the experience of the late 1960s and 1970s were compatible with, or in the spirit of, the theoretical advances being made. Other explanations of the apparent empirical breakdown of the curve were however on a completely different track, and we postpone consideration of these until the section on non-market theories of inflation.

Expectations-augmented Phillips curve models

The initial theoretical attacks on the Phillips curve were developed independently, but at about the same time, by Friedman (1968) and Phelps (1967). Other theoretical developments of the Phillips curve have particularly been made by contributors to the new microeconomic foundations of macroeconomics.

The essential features of these developments are:

(1) The simple Phillips curve provides, at most, a short-run trade-off between steady rates of inflation and levels of unemployment.
(2) Movements along short-run Phillips curves alter the expectations of economic agents and thereby shift the position of the curve.
(3) There is no permanent trade-off between steady rates of inflation and unemployment.
(4) The long-run Phillips curve is in fact vertical at the natural rate of unemployment.
(5) The natural rate of unemployment is that which is consistent with the equilibrium level of real wages.
(6) Unemployment of less than the natural rate can be sustained only if the expectations of economic agents are continuously frustrated by an accelerating rate of inflation.

In fact one school of thought denies even the possibility of a short-run trade-off between steady rates of inflation and unemployment and thereby denies also (6) above. We shall be considering that particular view towards the end of this section, but first we need to see how (1)–(6) above are arrived at.

The theoretical developments that have generated (1)–(6) have broadly followed two different paths. One regards firms as price-fixers, while the other sees firms and workers as price-takers who instead fix quantities. We shall give examples of each approach, starting with firms as price takers.

Firms as price-takers

This approach sees firms as accepting prices fixed by the markets and adjusting their outputs to those prices. Effectively the Phillips curve is being viewed as a supply curve. The Friedman arguments outlined in Chapter 7 (pp. 157–158) were an example of this line of development, and we shall briefly repeat them here.

Friedman argued that in plotting money wages rather than real wages on the vertical axis, the Phillips curve was mis-specified. As he says, economists have always argued that the pressure of excess demand/supply in the labour markets – proxied by U in the Phillips curve – affected *real* and not money wages.

Let us develop Friedman's arguments by reference to *Figure 9.6*. We assume in the diagram that wages and prices always change by the same amount (see p. 195). $PC(\dot{P}^e = 0)$ is a simple Phillips curve, drawn on the assumption that all economic agents – firms, workers, etc. – expect a zero rate of inflation, i.e. they expect prices to remain constant. Assume that initially the economy is at point A with the goods and labour markets in equilibrium, a zero rate of inflation and unemployment of U_n. Now suppose the authorities decide that they wish to reduce unemployment below U_n, say to U_1. The simple Phillips curve suggests this could be done by accepting the higher rate of wage and price inflation of 3%, and moving to the point B. But how does the economy actually move from A to B? Obviously for unemployment to fall, i.e. employment to rise, employers must want to take on more workers, but more workers must also want to take up employment. If, however, the demand and supply of labour are respectively inverse and direct functions of the real wage, then the real wage must fall in order to stimulate an increase in the demand for labour, yet rise to increase the supply. But how can the real wage both rise and fall at the same time?

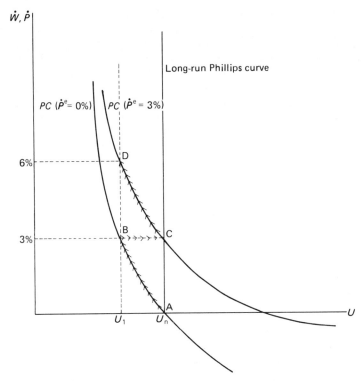

Figure 9.6 The long-run or expectations-augmented Phillips curve

Friedman's answer is that producers and workers evaluate the real wage differently. Thus, starting from point A, assume that the government engenders an increase in aggregate demand which raises market prices. Individual firms will initially believe that the increased demand is at least partly unique to them and will respond to the increased price of their particular products by trying to produce more. This will raise the market demand for labour and push up wages. To the individual producer the real wage is the ratio: money wage paid to own employee/price of own product. Thus a higher nominal wage could still mean a lower real wage as perceived by the producer.

The worker, however, spends only a very small proportion, if any, of his wage on the products he helps to produce. The real wage that matters to the worker is the ratio: own money wage/prices of products in general. If, as Friedman argues, workers are slow to adjust their perceptions of prices in general, than an increase in their money wages will be seen by them as an increase in their real wages. Thus

> a rise in nominal wages may be perceived by workers as a rise in real wages and hence call forth an increased supply, at the same time that it is perceived by employers as a fall in real wages and hence calls forth an increased offer of jobs (M. Friedman 1977, p. 13).

At point A in *Figure 9.6* workers expect prices to remain constant. If they maintain those expectations at the same time as the rate of change of money wages goes up to 3%, then the increase in money wages will be perceived as an equivalent increase in real wages. There will then be a movement along the Phillips curve to B.

But this situation is only temporary, until such time as employers and workers adjust their perceptions to accord with reality. In terms of *Figure 9.6* the fact that at point B prices are not constant but rising at 3% would eventually be recognized and alter the price expectations of economic agents. Workers would realize that the 3% increase in money wages was being matched by a 3% increase in prices, so that their real wages at point B are exactly the same as they were at point A. The supply of labour and the level of unemployment will fall back to what they were at A, but now coexisting with a rate of change of wages and prices of 3%, i.e. the movement would be to point C. Passing through point C is another simple Phillips curve, this one assuming that employers and employees expect prices to rise at 3%. It shows the trade-off between money wages and unemployment that exists as long as price expectations are held at 3%.

If the authorities, in an attempt to return unemployment to the level of U_1 further stimulate aggregate demand and thereby increase the rate of wage and price inflation to 6%, there would be a movement along the new Phillips curve to point D for so long as employers and firms held their 3% expectations. As before, however, those expectations would eventually be brought into line with the reality of 6% inflation and unemployment would once more rise to U_n.

This analysis suggests then, that there is a whole family of simple Phillips curves: a different one for every level of inflationary expectations. Each curve provides a *temporary* trade-off between unemployment on the one hand and wage and price inflation on the other.

There is no permanent trade-off, however, because as inflation expectations catch up with reality, unemployment always returns to U_n. In the long run the Phillips curve is a vertical straight line passing through U_n. Friedman termed this level of unemployment the 'natural rate of unemployment', which he defined as

> the level that would be ground out by the Walrasian system of general equilibrium equations, provided there is embedded in them the actual structural characteristics of the labour and commodity markets, including market imperfections, stocastic variability in demands and supplies, the cost of gathering information about job vacancies and labour availabilities, the costs of mobility and so on (1968, p. 8).

The actual number of unemployed to which the natural level of unemployment relates is not fixed over time, but will depend on a variety of factors, some technological, some man-made, but all of them 'real' as distinct from 'monetary'. Such factors would include

> the effectiveness of the labour market, the extent of competition or monopoly, the barriers or encouragments to working in various occupations, and so on (Friedman 1977, p. 15).

Given the natural level of unemployment, the only way the authorities can maintain a lower level is by continuously frustrating the inflationary expectations of employers and workers. This follows from the argument that wherever actual and expected rates of inflation coincide, unemployment will be at its natural level. If inflation expectations are to be frustrated, then actual rates of inflation cannot be held steady, but must accelerate. In *Figure 9.6* for example, unemployment of U_1, could only be maintained by having actual rates of inflation of 3%, 6%, 9%, etc.

Similar conclusions to all of these can be reached by using rather different reasoning. Consistent with the above approach of treating producers and workers as price-takers are several contributions associated with the microfoundations of inflation and unemployment. Considerations of space preclude us from giving anything more than a brief outline of the nature of these views, and the interested reader is referred for further elaboration to Phelps (1971).

The natural rate of unemployment is regarded as largely comprising workers who are engaged in a search activity for information about job opportunities. The activity of search generates both costs and benefits for the unemployed person. The costs are in the form of wages forgone by not accepting wage offers already received, minus unemployment benefit. Benefits are the discounted present value of the increased wage offer that the worker expects to turn up during the period of search.

Additional periods of search should be undertaken as long as the benefits of searching for that period exceed the costs, i.e. as long as the marginal benefits of search exceed the marginal costs. The wage offer that a worker may expect to discover during a period of search will reflect his views on the 'state of the market', a view which in turn is likely to reflect the worker's previous experience of 'the market'. Thus a newly unemployed worker may expect to discover a wage close to the one he had previously been receiving in employment. At the start of each period of search the unemployed worker will have, based on the costs and benefits of search, an acceptance or reservation wage. If during the search period this acceptance wage turns up, the worker will accept it and enter employment; if it does not, then the worker continues to search.

If the authorities stimulate demand and raise the rate of wage and price inflation, and if unemployed workers do not accordingly quickly revise upwards their perceptions of inflation, then they are likely to receive unexpectedly high wage offers which meet acceptance levels and lead to the cutting of search activity and a fall in unemployment.

Eventually, however, perceived rates of inflation catch up with actual rates, and workers revise upwards their acceptance or reservation levels of wages. Levels of search are again extended and unemployment returns to its 'natural' level. There is a short-run trade-off between money wage inflation and unemployment, but no long-run one.

Firms as price-fixers

In contrast to the two approaches outlined above, Phelps's analysis takes firms to be price-fixers. According to this view, firms attempt to set relative prices and wages; i.e. they fix their prices and wages so that they bear a particular relationship to the prices and wages being set by other producer–employers. Thus a firm that wishes to maintain its share of the market and its level of employment will *ceteris paribus* attempt to set prices and wages which are unchanged relative to those being fixed by other producers. If, however, the firm wishes to expand its market share and its level of employment, then it will attempt to set a lower relative price. If it wishes to contract its market share and level of employment it will attempt the converse.

If, having set its prices and wages, the firm finds itself faced with an excess demand for its product, i.e. an ability to sell more than it had planned, then it will raise its price; likewise it will lower its price if it is unable to sell all it had planned. The price fixed by a firm will therefore reflect two considerations: a relative price to determine the firm's share of the market and an adjustment to reflect any excess demand or supply.

In order to fix a relative price, the firm must formulate a view of the prices its competitiors are going to charge. If the firm wishes to maintain its relative price and it expects all other firms to maintain their current prices, then the firm will maintain its own current price; if, however, it expects all other firms to raise their prices by 10%, then it will raise its own price by 10%. If all firms wish to maintain their relative prices, then all will raise their actual prices at the rate they expect the other firms to raise theirs. For every firm, expected price increases are equal to actual price increases, and an index of actual prices for all firms together will increase at the same rate as an identically weighted index of expected prices. A general excess demand in the economy would result in many firms raising their prices more than they had originally intended. Thus the actual rate of inflation will exceed the expected rate. In the case of a generalized excess supply, the actual rate of inflation would be less than the expected rate.

According to this approach therefore, the actual rate of inflation is dependent upon the expected rate of inflation and the extent of excess demand/supply in the economy. There is no longer a simple Phillips curve relationship between inflation and excess demand alone. The relationship has been augmented by the introduction of the expected rate of inflation.

The inflation–expectations coefficient

All of the three approaches to the expectations-augmented Phillips curve that we have outlined above come to essentially the same conclusions. Let us now set out the simple Phillips curve and the expectations-augmented version in notational form. We shall concentrate on the determination of the rate of inflation rather than the rate of change of money wages. The simple Phillips curve may be written as

$$\dot{P}_t = a(E)_t \tag{9.1}$$

where $\dot{P}$ is the rate of inflation and (E) a measure of the deviation of output from its full employment or 'natural' level (i.e. the level associated with the natural rate of unemployment).

The expectations-augmented version adds the expected rate of inflation as a determinant of the actual rate of inflation and may be written as

$$\dot{P}_t = a(E)_t + b\dot{P}_t^e \tag{9.2}$$

where $\dot{P}^e$ is the expected rate of inflation.

The value of the coefficient b is of vital importance. A value of unity means that all of the expected rate of inflation is passed on to the actual rate of inflation, while a value of less than unity means that only part of the expected rate of inflation is reflected in the actual inflation rate.

Equation (9.2) can be rearranged to give

$$\dot{P}_t - b\dot{P}_t^e = a(E)_t \tag{9.3}$$

If $b = 1$ then the equation says that it is unexpected inflation (the difference between actual and expected inflation) which is related to excess demand (i.e. the deviation of output from its natural level). When inflation is fully anticipated (where $\dot{P}_t - \dot{P}_t^e = 0$) there is no excess demand and output will be at its natural level. Moreover the natural level of output is consistent with any actual rate of inflation, provided that it is fully anticipated (i.e. $\dot{P}_t = \dot{P}_t^e$). To maintain output above its natural level requires that $\dot{P}_t > \dot{P}_t^e$ also be maintained. The views outlined earlier in the section which suggested that inflation expectations will eventually catch up with a steady rate of actual inflation leads to the conclusion that actual inflation can exceed expected inflation only if the former is accelerating.

If b has a value of less than unity, however, then a trade-off between E and $\dot{P}$ is possible even in the long run. In the extreme case, if $b = 0$ then equation (9.2) reverts back to the simple Phillips curve relationship. If $0 < b < 1$ then the long-run Phillips curve will be non-vertical but steeper than the simple short-run curve. The various possible trade-offs are shown in *Figure 9.7*.

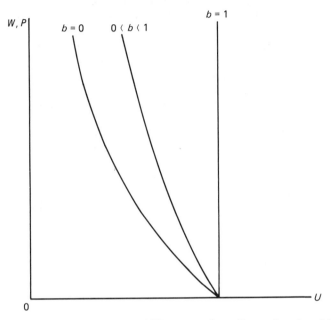

Figure 9.7 Possible long-run Phillips curves, depending on the value of the inflation-expectations coefficient

There is now fairly general agreement amongst economists that $b > 0$. Whether $b = 1$ or $b < 1$ is still however uncertain. The matter cannot be resolved on the basis of *a priori* reasoning. There is not, for example, complete agreement on exactly what it is that b 'measures'. Some writers have argued that it is a measure of money illusion. If this is the case then b will have a value of less than unity to the extent that increases in money incomes are desired for themselves even though they do not result in equivalent increases in real incomes. Monetarists argue that such money illusion does not exist, particularly when inflation reaches relatively high rates, and as economic agents become more sophisticated in their general economic awareness.

The coefficient b has also been interpreted as a measure of the ability of trade unions to pass on fully into wage increases their expectations of price increases. Thus although unions may not suffer from money illusion as such, they may be unable to achieve the increases in money wages that would be necessary to offset their correct perceptions of the rate of inflation.

The precise value of b is a matter of empirical research and a number of studies have been made to try and ascertain its value. The early studies (Solow 1969; Turnovsky and Wachter 1972; Cukierman 1974) generally found values of b that were significantly less than unity, supporting the view that there was a trade-off between the rate of inflation and the level of unemployment, even in the long run. Later studies of the UK, the USA and an aggregate of the Group of Ten countries tended, however, to obtain results for *b* which were closer to, or even equal to 1 (Mackay and Hart 1974; Duck *et al* 1976). (These later studies incorporated data for a period in which both the rate of inflation and the level of unemployment were rising.)

Wages, however, were able to keep fairly closely in line with the rate of inflation. One possible explanation for this is that the higher the rate of inflation, the more important it is for labour to anticipate it and allow for it in wage claims. If inflation is proceeding at 2% per annum unions may not worry too much if wages are one step behind, but if inflation is, say, in double figures and accelerating, unions may become very concerned to try and anticipate the rate of inflation, and incorporate these expectations into their wage claims.

The period also probably witnessed a change in the relationship between unemployment and the pressure of demand in the labour market, with higher levels of unemployment than hitherto being associated with given levels of demand. The natural rate of unemployment almost certainly increased, though there is no general agreement on what it is (Saunders 1978).

The period also saw the breakdown of the Bretton Woods system and the movement away from fixed exchange rates. As we shall see in the final section of the chapter, for small open economies operating fixed exchange rates international factors are a major determinant of their rates of inflation. One would expect inflationary expectations in such countries to be influenced not only by domestic factors but also by international ones. However, virtually all the studies of the *b* coefficient make no allowance for the openness of the economies, though for the USA this is not a great problem given the size of its domestic market *vis-à-vis* its foreign trade. Cross and Laidler (1976) however did allow for international influences on the formation of expectations in their multi-country study and they found that this did improve their results.

This leads us on to the very important problem of how best to incorporate inflation expectations into the tests. This is a methodological problem which all econometric studies that involve expectations have to face up to. Indeed we have already encountered it in the context of demand for money studies. The problem arises because expectations are not a directly observable variable, and consequently an 'indirect' way of measuring them has to be found. In the current context, studies that attempt to obtain a value for *b* must include a series of values for $\dot{P}^e$. But there are no statistics of $\dot{P}^e$ because it cannot be observed directly. Consequently some alternative way of measuring it has to be found. This means that every empirical test of the value of *b* is also a test of the adequacy of the indirect measures of expectations which are embodied in the study.

Two approaches have been adopted to the measurement of $\dot{P}^e$. The first is to take some directly observable variable as a proxy for inflation expectations. This has been the most widely used approach, and it has generally been assumed that economic agents form their expectations about inflation in the light of their experience of actual inflation. This is of course the adaptive expectations approach which was considered on pp. 73–74. In this context it means that inflation expectations are adapted (i.e. revised) whenever actual inflation rates differ from those that had been expected. Thus if inflation is expected to be at a rate of 15%, but actually turns out to be 20%, then people will revise upwards their expectations of inflation for the next period. It is possible that expectations are always adjusted by the whole of the difference between expected inflation and actual inflation, which is only another way of saying that the inflationary expectations of the current period are always equal to the actual inflation of the last period. More generally, expectations are seen as being adjusted by some fraction of the gap (i.e. expectation error) that arises whenever the actual rate of inflation turns out to be different from the rate expected. This may be written

$$\dot{P}^e_t - \dot{P}^e_{t-1} = b(\dot{P}_{t-1} - \dot{P}^e_{t-1})\,0 < b < 1 \qquad (9.4)$$

This is equivalent to (see p. 73)

$$\dot{P}^e_t = b\dot{P}_{t-1} + b(1-b)\dot{P}_{t-2} + b(1-b)^2\dot{P}_{t-3} + \dots \qquad (9.5)$$

This is a geometrical progression so that current inflation expectations are equal to a geometrically weighted average of past rates of inflation. The weights decline geometrically over earlier and earlier time periods: this simply means that people are seen as giving greater emphasis to the more recent past when forming their inflationary expectations. How rapidly the weights decline depends on the relative importance attached by economic agents to the recent rather than the earlier history of actual inflation rates. The weights in equation (9.5) sum to unity so that a constant rate of inflation will eventually result in equality between the actual and expected inflation rates. If however, inflation is accelerating or highly volatile then equation (9.5) would generate forecasts which were very inaccurate.

The other approach to 'measuring' $\dot{P}^e$ is to attempt a direct estimate by using the data generated by questionnaire-type surveys. Carlson and Parkin (1975), for example, used information obtained from a monthly survey which asked people the direction they expected prices to go in order to generate a series for expected inflation which was couched in quantitative terms, i.e. % change p.a. They found that the $\dot{P}^e$ series thus generated was best fitted by a second-order error learning process, i.e. inflation expectations adjust to the difference between the actual and expected rates of inflation for the last two periods.

Rational expectations

The adaptive expectations view of how expectations are formed has been criticized on the grounds that it implies exceptionally naive behaviour on the part of economic agents. Surely, it is argued, people would not form their inflation expectations simply on the basis of past rates of inflation without taking into account information about other variables which may have an effect on the inflation rate. Such events as a change of government, a wage freeze, or a world recession might all be expected to affect the rate of inflation, and failure to take account of them in forming inflation expectations may be regarded as irrational. People must be forming their expectations in a way which is inconsistent with the mechanism actually determining the rate of inflation.

By tying their inflation expectations to a mechanical rule which is inconsistent with the way inflation is actually generated, economic agents will generate forecasts which are systematically in error. To continue to use adaptive expectations in such a situation would be irrational; rational behaviour would require the abandonment of the model and its replacement by one which gives more accurate forecasts.

An alternative hypothesis of the way people form their expectations, explicitly assumes that people behave rationally and is known as the rational expectations model. It was considered on pp. 158–159. The main points of the rational expectations hypothesis which are relevant to our discussion of inflation are:

(1) Economic agents use information efficiently in the sense that they try to eliminate all systematic errors in their forecasting.
(2) If forecasting models do not make systematic errors, then they will generate inflation expectations which resemble those given by the actual inflation-generating mechanism.
(3) Systematic policies to influence the rate of inflation will be recognized and fed into the forecasting model and reflected in inflation expectations.
(4) Consequently systematic policies cannot generate unanticipated inflation. Only random fluctuations in the actual rate of inflation can do that.
(5) If systematic policies cannot induce unanticipated inflation, there can be no systematic policy-induced deviation from the natural rates of unemployment and output, even in the short run.

These ideas may be presented notationally in a simple model. The first element of the model is the relationship between excess demand and unanticipated inflation incorporated in the vertical expectations-augmented Phillips curve.

$$\dot{P}_t - \dot{P}_t^e = f(E) \tag{9.6}$$

where the symbols have the same meaning as for equations (9.1) and (9.2).

The second element is the actual inflation generating mechanism. Let us adopt the monetarist hypothesis that the rate of inflation is determined by the rate of growth of the money supply and a random influence. This gives us

$$\dot{P}_t = \dot{M}_t + R \tag{9.7}$$

where $\dot{M}$ is the rate of growth of the money supply and R is a random shock variable.

Rational expectations implies that the expected rate of inflation is that generated by a forecasting model which yields the same results as the actual inflation generating mechanism. We therefore have

$$\dot{P}_t^e = \dot{M}_t^e + R^e \tag{9.8}$$

where the superscript e again denotes the expected values of the variables. If we assume that the random shock variable has a mean expected value of zero, then it drops out and we are left with

$$\dot{P}_t^e = \dot{M}_t^e \tag{9.9}$$

The next element of the model is the policy function of the monetary authorities. We assume that the authorities adjust the current rate of growth of the money supply according to the excess demand in the previous period, but subject also to a random disturbance. This may be written

$$\dot{M}_t = m(E_{t-1}) + \alpha \tag{9.10}$$

The expected value of the money supply generated by rational expectations is the same as that given by the authorities policy function. Assuming that the random disturbance term has a mean expected value of zero and therefore drops out, we are left with

$$\dot{M}_t^e = m(E_{t-1}) \tag{9.11}$$

By substitution of equations (9.7)–(9.11) into (9.6) we derive the model's reduced form equation:

$$\alpha + R = f(E) \tag{9.12}$$

This states that excess demand can exist (i.e. ouput and unemployment can differ from their equilibrium or 'natural' levels) only as a result of random shocks, either to the rate of inflation or to the money supply. Systematic policy can have no effect on demand, output or employment, even in the short run.

Rational expectations clearly represents an attempt to bring the analysis of price expectations into line with the rest of economics, where the dominating view is that economic agents behave rationally. An approach which says that people do not go on continually making the same mistakes would appear to be more plausible and appealing than alternative approaches which suggest that people do in fact behave in such a way. There are however a number of criticisms of rational expectations, but consideration of them is postponed until Chapter 11.

The role of money

To conclude our discussion of the expectations-augmented Phillips curve analysis of inflation, we shall now consider the role that is played in that analysis by the rate of growth of the money supply. We shall concentrate on the version of the model that incorporates adaptive expectations and a vertical long-run Phillips curve at the natural rate of unemployment.

According to this theory, the rate of inflation is determined by excess demand and inflationary expectations. Recall equation (9.2).

$$\dot{P}_t = a(E)_t + b\dot{P}_t^e, \quad \text{where } a > 0, b = 1$$

Inflationary expectations are influenced by previous rates of inflation and hence by previous levels of excess demand. Recall equation (9.5).

$$\dot{P}_t^e = b\dot{P}_{t-1} + b(1-b)\dot{P}_{t-2} + b(1-b)^2\dot{P}_{t-3} \dots$$

Excess demand means, in this model, the excess of actual demand over that which is necessary to maintain output and employment at their natural levels.

But what generates such excess demand? Monetarists of course argue that it is the consequence of an over-rapid expansion of the money supply. Some expansion of the real money supply is necessary to meet the expanding demand for real money balances which results from an increase in the natural level of output, itself brought about by technological advances etc. The rate of growth of the real money stock is the rate of growth of the nominal money stock minus the prevailing rate of inflation. If the rate of growth of the real money stock is in excess of that required to satisfy the demand generated by the growth of the natural level of output, then the surplus gap will be reflected in an excess demand for goods and services. If we assume a constant income elasticity of demand for real money balances of unity then we have

$$E = (\dot{M} - \dot{P}) - \dot{y}n \tag{9.13}$$

where $\dot{y}n$ = growth of natural level of output

In the short run the excess demand will, according to monetarist doctrine, influence the real variables of output and employment, and only after a long and variable time lag will prices be affected. In the long run, when inflationary expectations have caught up with actual inflation and unanticipated inflation has been eliminated, then output and employment will return to their natural levels and excess demand will disappear.

Setting $E = 0$ in equation (9.13) and rearranging gives

$$\dot{P} = \dot{M} - \dot{y}n \tag{9.14}$$

This says that the long-run equilibrium rate of inflation is given by the difference between the growth rates of the money stock and of the natural level of output. Equations (9.2), (9.5), (9.13), (9.14) therefore provide a highly simplified summary of the monetarist model of inflation. An implication of the model is that expansion of the money supply is a sufficient condition for the initiation and continuance of inflation.

This conclusion however is dependent on the validity of equation (9.13), i.e. that an expansion of the nominal money supply in excess of the growth of the natural level of output will generate excess demand. If however the velocity of circulation is unstable such that 'excessive' expansions of the money supply simply disappear into idle hoards and have no effect on expenditure, then an expansion of the money supply is not a sufficient condition for setting off an expectations-augmented Phillips curve type inflation.

We must now consider whether the expansion of the money supply is a necessary condition for inflation. To answer this we shall consider a situation where the money supply is held constant and excess demand emerges as a result of businessmen becoming more optimistic about future business prospects and raising the level of investment.

We assume that initially the economy is in long-run equilibrium with output and employment at their natural levels. The expected rate of inflation is equal to the actual rate of inflation, which for simplicity's sake we will assume is zero. In *Figure 9.8* the economy is at point U_n. The emergence of the excess demand will result in a north westerly movement along the short-run Phillips curve labelled $PC(\dot{P}^e = 0)$. Let us assume that the excess demand is sufficient to move the economy to point A where unemployment has fall to U_1, but the rate of inflation has risen to 3%. With adaptive expectations the divergence between actual and anticipated inflation rates will disappear and there will then be a movement back to the natural rates of unemployment and output, i.e. a movement to point B. At this point inflation is proceeding at a steady 3%. In the absence of any expansion of the nominal money supply the inflation will depress the real value of the money balances held by economic agents below their desired levels, given the pattern of relative real yields. Interest rates will rise and via a process of portfolio adjustment expenditure will fall. The fall in expenditure will lower output and employment below their natural levels and reduce the rate of inflation. In *Figure 9.8* there will be a movement in a southeasterly direction along the short-run Phillips curve labelled $PC(\dot{P}^e = 3\%)$. Inflationary expectations will adapt to the experience of lower actual rates of inflation and the economy will move on to a lower short-run Phillips curve. In *Figure 9.8*, this is assumed not to happen until the actual inflation rate has fallen to 0 per cent (i.e. at point C). When both the actual and the expected rates of inflation are equal to zero the economy will be back at the point U_n.

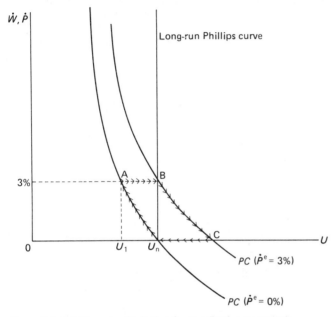

Figure 9.8 A falling rate of inflation due to a fixed money supply

In the foregoing illustration we assumed that inflation did not start to reduce aggregate demand until the long-run equilibrium rate of inflation had been reached. It is of course probable that this effect on expenditure will happen much sooner, in which case the adjustment path is rather different to that shown in *Figure 9.8*. The illustration also ignored any effect inflation expectations may have on the demand for real money balances. Nevertheless, the illustration suffices to show that in the absence of an expansion of the money supply, inflation of this kind can only be a temporary phenomenon. Most economists would now agree with the view of Kahn that

> it can be readily conceded to the monetarists that an increase in the quantity of money, though not the *cause* of inflation is a necessary condition (1976, p. 6).

Perhaps the major controversy about the role of money in the inflationary process is not whether an expansion of the money supply is or is not a necessary and/or sufficient condition for inflation but whether the expansion itself is actively or passively generated. This is usually referred to as the endogeneity/exogeneity debate (see note 1, p. 104). More precisely the debate is about whether changes in the money supply are the result of deliberate action taken by the monetary authorities (exogenous) or simply passive responses to changes in the private sectors demand for money (endogenous).

There are two main issues in this debate. The first concerns the *ability* of the monetary authority to control the money supply, while the second concerns their *willingness* to do so. On the first of these issues, monetarists argue that (i) the authorities are able to control the monetary base (supply of high powered money); and (ii) that the monetary base is the main determinant of the total money supply. Both of these links in the monetarist argument have been subjected to extensive criticism and the major aspects of the debate were considered in Chapter 4. In considering the arguments and counter-arguments it is important to remember, however, that the monetarist view of inflation does not require the authorities to have perfect control over the money supply, but only that they are able to exert the dominant influence.

The debate about the *willingness* of the authorities to control the money supply is really about the direction of causation between changes in the supply of money and changes in expenditure. The monetarist view is that changes in the money supply are primarily the result of policies *actively* initiated by the authorities for purposes which are independent of the current values of endogenous variables. In this view the causal links between money and expenditure are:

Authority initiated changes in high powered money	$\Rightarrow$	Change in total money supply	$\Rightarrow$	Change in expenditure and income

Keynesians on the other hand, argue that the direction of causation is reversed, i.e.

Exogenous change in planned expenditure	$\Rightarrow$	Change in total money supply	$\Rightarrow$	Accommodating changes in high powered money

In this latter sequence the money supply is seen as passively adjusting to changes in the demand for it. Several arguments have been put forward to support this view. The credit nature of money is often emphasized, and the point made that spenders seek credit (e.g. a bank loan) only if they have already taken a decision to spend. The corollary is that loans cannot be forced on unwilling borrowers, the supply of credit money is essentially demand determined. This view has clearly been stated by Kaldor and Trevithick (1981, p. 7):

> Unlike commodity money, credit money comes into existence as a result of borrowing from the banks (by businesses, individuals or public agencies) and it is extinguished as a result of the repayment of bank debt (which happens automatically under a system where an excess of receipts over outlays is directly applied to a reduction of outstanding overdrafts). Hence in a credit money economy, unlike with commodity money, the outstanding 'money stock' can never be in excess of the amount which individuals wish to hold: and this alone rules out the possibility of there being an 'excess' supply of money which should be the cause (as distinct from the consequence) of a rise in spending.

A second argument concerns the role of the monetary authorities. Essentially the authorities are seen as playing a passive role, and providing any additional reserves which may be required to support the demand-induced expansion of the total money supply. This passivity of the authorities is usually seen as a consequence of their concern for the gilt-edged market and the level and structure of interest rates. The point being made is quite simply that the authorities can control either interest rates or the supply of money but not both. In the face of an increased demand for money any attempts to keep the supply of it constant will drive up interest rates. If the authorities are committed to pegging interest rates, then they must allow the supply of money to adjust to the demand for it. The supply of money becomes demand-determined.

Suppose, for example, that there is an increase in the level of planned consumption expenditure which leads to a rise in the demand for bank loans. If the banks are fully loaned up with no excess reserves then they can only satisfy the increased demand either by switching from investment to loans, or by attracting additional reserves from the non-bank public or by 'over-lending'.

Switching will be encouraged if the increased demand for loans makes them relatively more profitable *vis-à-vis* investments. An attempt by the banks to sell securities will depress security prices and push up interest rates. If the authorities are concerned to maintain stable interest rates, then they will step into the market and buy up securities. In so doing they inject additional cash reserves into the system and facilitate an expansion of the money supply. A similar consequence would result from a decision by households to finanace the increase in their planned expenditure by selling securities themselves. As long as the authorities are trying to peg interest rates, then any increases in the supply of securities on the market will result in an increase in the supply of money.

If the banks respond to an increased demand for loans by 'over-lending', then they will experience an excessive cash drain and find their reserves depressed below the required minimum level. The banks will then be forced to borrow, directly or indirectly from the central bank. If the central bank is concerned to see interest rates not rise then it will 'support' the lending banks by providing them with the required reserves at non-penal rates. Similarly, if the banks try to acquire additional reserves from the non-bank public by offering higher interest rates then the authorities concern to stabilize interest rates will lead them to supply the additional reserves themselves.

Non-market theories of inflation

We turn now to theories of inflation that are based on the hypothesis that wages and prices are capable of rising independently of the state of demand in the labour and goods markets. They are seen as reflecting instead sociological and political variables. We shall not consider these theories in any detail but simply set out some of their common features and pay particular attention to the role that is played by money.

The view that prices are pushed up by non-market forces has been used to provide an explanation of inflation in Britain since the end of the war, and has gained particular momentum since the 1960s.

These non-market theories of inflation are generally based on a particular view of modern capitalist societies. They emphasize the monopoly power which is possessed by trade unions, and the dominance of oligopolistic market structures. The unions are seen as using their monopoly power to try and raise the share of wages in the national income and to protect material standards of living. Individiual unions seek to maintain the relative status of their members *vis-à-vis* members of other unions. The oligopolistic structure of industry is reflected in greater concern for non-price competition and a more ready willingness to pass increased costs on into higher prices.

Within the inflationary process certain wage settlements are seen as being 'key settlements' in influencing the movements of wages in other sectors. Thus a 'key' group of workers may achieve a significant increase in wages because they find themselves in a particularly strong bargaining position. They may, for example, have achieved substantial increases in productivity, or there may have been an increase in the foreign demand for the goods they make, or the employers' profits may have risen considerably. But the unusually large increase in wages achieved by this group will disturb differentials between them and other groups. This in turn will lead to pressures to restore differentials which are regarded as traditional or normal. The key group in its turn may try to maintain what it regards as a justified improvement in its relative position. As a result there is general upward pressure being exerted on wages.

The oligopolistic structure of industry will result in a greater willingness, than would exist under more competitive conditions, to concede wage increases rather than face strikes and the loss of output and contracts.

Within this very broad scenario of non-market induced inflation there is scope for considerable differences of emphasis. Some writers concentrate on the class struggle between labour and capital, some pay particular attention to inter-union rivalry and the importance of 'accepted differentials', while yet others emphasize the resistance of trade unions to any cuts in real wages. There would however be general agreement with the view expressed by Kaldor and Trevithick (1981, p. 16) that

> the inexorable rise in industrial prices in the post-war period was in the main, cost-induced: it had virtually nothing to do with excess demand. It was a consequence of the increased concentration of economic power both on the side of capital and on the side of labour – of militant trade unionism combined with monopolistic price policies in industry.

Non-market explanations have also been put forward for the apparent breakdown from the late 1960s of the simple Phillips curve relationship. Such explanations have included

(1) Greater aggressiveness on the part of trade unions because of the advent of more militant leaders and a belated recognition of the power they possessed.
(2) Less concern by trade unions about the effects of wage claims on unemployment because of improved financial provision for the unemployed.
(3) Increased socio-political tensions as witnessed by the student riots of the late 1960s.
(4) Resistance to cuts in real standards of living caused by higher import prices and deflationary government policies.
(5) The extension of wage comparability to inter-country comparisons of relative wages.

As we did with the market theories of inflation so we must now consider the role of the money supply in the non-market theories. If prices rise because of upward pressure being exerted on costs, then in order to 'finance' the same volume of real transactions there must either be an increase in the velocity of circulation of money or the money stock must rise. Let us assume for the moment that neither of these possibilities occurs. What will be the result? Clearly there must be a fall in the volume of transactions. Interest rates will rise because the demand for real money balances exceeds the supply, and there will be a fall in interest-sensitive expenditures. If initially there was equilibrium in the goods and labour markets then the fall in demand will result in an excess supply of goods and of labour. If wages are pushed up independently of the state of the goods and labour markets, then the rise in unemployment should not make any difference to the inflationary pressures. It would, however, seem more likely that if unemployment rises far enough, then the upward pressure on wages must be affected, and eventually the inflation brought to a halt.

As with all other theories of inflation it would appear that non-market theories require an expansion of the money supply. The only other possibility is that the velocity of circulation of money rises. The extreme view on this possibility was stated by the Radcliffe Committee (1959) when they said 'we cannot find any reason for supposing, or any monetary experience in history indicating, that there is any limit to the velocity of circulation' (para 391). Very few economists would now go along with that view. Nevertheless many would argue that the ingenuity of the financial system for developing money substitutes does mean that inflation may continue for sometime before the brake of falling real money balances brings it to a halt.

Most supporters of non-market theories of inflation however argue that it is an expansion of the money stock which in fact 'finances' the inflation.

They argue that the money supply is an endogenous variable, passively adjusting to the demand for it. The authorities are seen as being prepared to let the money supply adjust in this way because of their concern for the level of unemployment. If the authorities do provide an accommodating expansion of the money stock then the resulting inflation may be seen by some as a monetary phenomenon resulting from the failure of the authorities to control the rate of growth of the money supply. On the other hand non-monetarists will agree with the view expressed by Goodhart (1975a, p. 217) that

> If the control of inflation by demand management, by monetary restriction sufficient to cause considerable unemployment and distress – even if for some finite but indefinite period – is so unpopular, it does not really help to blame the authorities for responding to the general will of the public in being reluctant to take sufficiently strong measures to halt inflation.

Goodhart in fact argues that the importance of non-market forces is in influencing the natural rate of unemployment. He suggests that the natural rate depends on all manner of forces including social and structural ones, so that 'cost-push pressures can perhaps be defined as those forces pushing the equilibrium or natural rate of unemployment upwards' (Goodhart 1975a, p. 219).

Inflation in an international context

Our discussion of inflation has so far implicitly been confined to closed economies. The 1970s, however, saw inflation being increasingly considered as an international phenomenon. In this final section we shall therefore extend our analysis to consider the generation and international transmission of inflation in a context of open economies.

The various approaches to the analysis of inflation in countries that engage in international transactions can again be classified into market and non-market ones. We shall devote most space to a consideration of the market approaches.

Market theories

We shall subdivide the market theories into two groups. First of all we shall consider the approach commonly known as global monetarism. We shall then put all other market theories into one group and conveniently label them 'Keynesian'. Both groups will be considered under fixed and fluctuating exchange rates.

Global monetarism with fixed exchange rates

The major features of this approach may be summarized thus:

(1) Inflation rates within individual open economies cannot remain above or below rates in other countries.
(2) National rates of inflation therefore converge on a common rate.
(3) As a 'world' problem, inflation can be explained only by events at a world level.
(4) World inflation is in fact caused by an excessive rate of growth of the world money supply.

Global monetarism incorporates, but is not synonomous with, the monetary approach to the balance of payments. The latter is explained fully on pp. 223–228, but we must briefly summarize it here. Assume a small country in which the demand and supply of money are equal and increasing at the same rate. If the monetary authorities of that country then increase the rate of growth of the supply of money there will be an excess supply. According to the monetary approach to the balance of payments, the excess supply of money will be used by the domestic residents to acquire goods, services and assets from foreign residents. This action will generate a balance of payments deficit, a loss of foreign exchange reserves and a reduction of the domestic money supply. Similarly, if a country's rate of growth of its money supply falls behind the rate of growth of the demand for money, then domestic residents will try to exchange goods, services and assets for money balances from abroad. This will generate a balance of payments surplus and an inflow of money. The conclusion of this approach is that with a system of fixed exchange rates, national authorities cannot control their own domestic nominal money supplies.

The second tenet of global monetarism is the 'law of one price'. This simply states that there is a single price which prevails for each good throughout the world. This is derived from the argument that if there is free international trade in goods, then commodity arbitrage will eliminate all differences in commodity prices between countries. This means that if the prices of goods are lower in one country than in another, traders will buy in the cheaper market and sell in the dearer. Exactly how this equalizes prices in the two countries depends on the exchange rate regime in operation. To illustrate, let us assume that prices in Britain rise above those prevailing in America. Traders will switch their demand from British goods to American. This increases the demand for dollars but reduces the demand for pounds. With fixed exchange rates the central banks of both countries are obliged to enter the foreign exchange market and undertake appropriate purchases or sales in order to maintain the exchange rate. The US central bank will sell dollars and in so doing expand the US money supply (or more likely its rate of monetary expansion). This finances the increased demand for American goods and raises their prices. The reverse process takes place in Britain until prices in the two countries converge. The law of one price is also seen as applying to financial assets, so that interest rates as well as commodity prices will be equalized.

The law of one price is the basis of the purchasing power parity theory, which states that the ratio of the domestic price levels in two countries is the reciprocal of the rate of exchange between their currencies. If the rate of exchange between the pound and the dollar is £1 = $2 then PPP says that the dollar price level in the US will be twice as high as the pound price level in the UK. Thus £1 in Britain will buy the same quantity of goods as $2 in the US.

The implication of all this for inflation is that no one country's rate of inflation can differ from that in the rest of the world. Suppose a country unilaterally tries to reduce its own rate of inflation below the world rate by pursuing a contractionary monetary policy. According to the foregoing argument there will be a switch of demand towards that country's goods and services and an inflow of money across the foreign exchanges. The result will be that the country's rate of inflation will be pushed back up to the world rate. Similarly, if the country's inflation rate initially exceeded the world rate, its domestic money supply would contract as there was a net outflow across the foreign exchanges. This would slow up the rate of inflation until it fell into line with that in the rest of the world.

The analysis so far has led to the conclusion that there is a 'world' rate of inflation to which national rates of inflation must conform. But what determines this 'world rate'? According to the global monetarists' approach the answer is simple: it is the rate of growth of the world money supply which determines the rate of 'world inflation'. Essentially the argument is that a world economy based on fixed exchange rates is the same as a closed national economy. The countries within the world economy are like the regions within a country. The essential assumptions and arguments of the monetarist view of inflation within a closed economy are then applied to the world economy. The world demand for money (and its reciprocal, the velocity of money) are assumed to be stable functions of a small number of variables, while output and employment are seen as being at their natural levels. Under these conditions a rate of growth of the world money supply in excess of the rate of growth of the world demand for money will, through portfolio adjustments, result in inflation.

As to what determines the rate of growth of the world money supply, there is some disagreement. One view is that it depends, in one way or another, on the rate of growth of international liquidity (Jackman, Mulvey and Trevithick 1981). Parkin, Sumner and Ward (1976, p. 45), however, having developed a model of the world money supply 1961–71, suggest

> that there was no well defined relationship between the aggregate of domestic credit policies and the growth of foreign exhange reserves.

Instead they conclude

> that the growth of the world money supply was in an important and predictable way influenced by the growth of world high powered money (p. 43).

The policy implication of this latter view is that control of the rate of growth of the world money supply cannot be achieved through control of the rate of growth of international liquidity; instead it

> could be achieved by detailed control over the domestic credit policies of each member of the fixed exchange rate system (p. 43).

The main criticisms of this 'global monetarist' approach to world inflation include the familiar criticisms of monetarism that we have already considered. Thus, doubts are cast on the stability of the world demand for money, and on the tendency for output and employment to stay at or close to their natural levels. Criticisms are also made of PPP and of the argument that individual country price levels and interest rates must conform to the world level.

There is some empirical evidence to support the global monetarist theory, but it is far from conclusive. Gray, Ward and Zis (1976) found for the fixed exchange rate period 1957–71, and for the world defined as the Group of Ten, that there was a stable world demand for money function. As we have seen Parkin *et al* (1976) found evidence that the rate of growth of the world money supply is determined by the rate of growth of the world monetary base. Duck *et al* (1976) have provided evidence that for the Group of Ten as a 'world economy' there was an expectations-augmented Phillips curve during the period 1956–71 with no long-run trade-off between inflation and unemployment. This study however, while arguing that world inflation is caused by excess demand, does not attempt to show that the excess demand itself is a result of the rate of growth of the world money supply. Other studies have provided evidence linking the world price level to the world money supply (e.g. Heller 1976; Genberg and Swoboda 1975).

Global monetarism under floating exchange rates

Under a regime of floating exchange rates there is no convergence on a common world rate of inflation. Instead each country's rate of inflation depends on its own rate of growth of its money supply. The basic reason for this is that with flexible exchange rates there are no significant changes in a country's reserves as the exchange rate itself moves so as to equate the demand for and supply of a country's currency on the foreign exchange market. This insulates a country's money supply, and with it its rate of inflation, from external influences.

Suppose a country accelerates the rate of growth of its money supply so that supply exceeds demand. People will try to eliminate their surplus money holding, by at least partly exchanging their domestic money for foreign goods, services and assets. This will increase the supply of the domestic currency on the foreign exchange market and increase the demand for foreign currencies. The results will be a depreciation of the domestic currency on the foreign exchange market and rising domestic currency prices of imports. Thus for global monetarists excess money supply growth results in a depreciating exchange rate and an acceleration in the rate of inflation.

A flexible exchange rate is also seen as insulating a country's economy from inflation originating in the rest of the world. Thus the monetarist view is that the long-run rate of inflation in a country with a flexible exchange rate is determined by its own domestic monetary policy, just as it is in a closed economy.[1]

'Keynesian' inflation under fixed exchange rates

The term 'Keynesian' is in fact applied to a range of open-economy models of inflation which differ in the assumptions they make and the conclusions they come to. Some models emphasize that considerable differences in national inflation rates can exist because

(1) Domestic monetary authorities can control their own domestic money supplies through their ability to sterilize the country's external balance.
(2) Countries produce goods and services which are imperfect substitutes for those produced by other countries.
(3) Many goods and services are non-traded.

Other 'Keynesian' models have been developed however, to show that national price levels will in fact converge (e.g. Branson 1975). These models focus on the pressure of demand in domestic markets and recognize that this pressure can be affected by external factors.

Suppose for example that there is an increase in prices in the rest of the world *vis-à-vis* one country. This will affect that country's own price level in two ways. Firstly the higher import prices will feed into the country's own price level both directly through finished goods prices and indirectly through costs of production. Secondly, the higher prices in the rest of the world will affect the level of domestic demand in the country because the rise in world prices will make the country's exports more attractive in world markets and its imports less attractive to its own domestic residents. There will therefore be an increase in both the foreign and the domestic demand for the country's goods and services, the magnitude depending upon the appropriate elasticities. This in turn will stimulate the demand for labour, reduce unemployment, and, in line with the Phillips curve, push up the domestic wages and prices. The money supply is assumed to adjust passively. The process will continue until domestic prices have been brought into line with those in the rest of the world, and the pressure of demand reduced to its former level.

An extension of this approach has been to try and relate it to the expectations-augmented Phillips curve rather than the simple Phillips curve, by recognizing that the expected rate of inflation may affect the actual rate of inflation, and then arguing that the expected rate of inflation depends on world-wide rather than purely domestic influences. Some tentative evidence in support of this argument is provided by Cross and Laidler (1976).

'Keynesian' inflation under floating exchange rates

We have earlier argued that with floating exchange rates, an open economy effectively operates as a closed one as far as its long-run rate of inflation is concerned. The Keynesian explanation of inflation under such conditions would then be in terms of an expectations-augmented Phillips curve where

(1) The excess demand is due to an autonomous increase in expenditure.
(2) The money supply passively adjusts to the demand for it.
(3) Expectations of domestic inflation are not influenced by expectations of world inflation.
(4) The long-run Phillips curve is non-vertical.

Non-market theories

The non-market theories of world inflation see it as being simply the aggregate of separate and independent national rates, each determined by non-market forces within the individual countries. The arguments are essentially as we have already outlined them. For an open economy, attention is often drawn to the effect of rising import prices, both in raising domestic costs of production and thereby prices, and in stimulating trade unions to seek offsetting inflationary increases in money wages. The money supply is usually assumed to adjust passively.

Any tendency for rates of inflation in different countries to move together is usually explained by reference to 'demonstration effects'. Militant aggressive unions in one country who successfully achieve inflationary wage increases 'demonstrate' to unions in other countries what can be achieved by militant action. This prompts similar trade union action in these other countries, and in this way inflation is transmitted from one country to another. Again the monetary authorities in each country are regarded as passively allowing their domestic money supplies to expand in order to finance the inflation.

Note

1. A flexible exchange rate does not insulate a domestic economy from all external shocks. Thus a change in the real terms of trade, such as occurred with the dramatic increase in oil prices in the 1970s, will have consequences for a country's level of real income and pattern of *relative* prices.

10

The balance of payments and the foreign exchange rate

In the previous chapters we have examined where appropriate the role of money in the context of an open economy such as the UK's, (for example, the impact of balance of payments flows on money supply determination in Chapter 4). In this chapter we concentrate specifically on the role of money in the balance of payments adjustment process and in the determination of the foreign exchange rate. Because of the growing importance of external influences on economies in an increasingly integrated world economy this extension of monetary analysis to open economy situations is considered essential.

In a fixed exchange rate system, where the authorities intervene in the foreign exchange market to maintain a given parity rate, any disturbance to a country's external position would be reflected in fluctuations in the balance of payments. Thus with such a system the focus of attention would be on the behaviour of the balance of payments, and in the first part of this chapter we consider the main theoretical approaches to balance of payments adjustment. With a floating exchange rate system, where there is no (or very little) intervention by the authorities in the foreign exchange market, the exchange rate adjusts in response to market forces to equate the demands for and supplies of currencies arising from international transactions. Thus, with such an exchange rate regime external disequilibrium would be reflected not in balance of payments fluctuations but in movements in the exchange rate and the focus of attention therefore would be on the behaviour of the exchange rate. Since the breakdown of the Bretton Woods system of fixed exchange rates in the early 1970s, increasing attention has been paid to the question of exchange rate determination, and in the second part of this chapter we concentrate on the main theories which seek to explain exchange rate fluctuations in a world of flexible exchange rates.

Monetary and other approaches to the balance of payments

One can distinguish broadly three analytical approaches to the balance of payments: (i) the elasticities approach; (ii) the absorption approach and (iii) the monetary approach.

The elasticities approach

The traditional elasticities approach, developed originally in the 1930s by Robinson (1937), concentrates on the elasticity conditions necessary for a devaluation to improve the current account component of the balance of payments. It is a partial equilibrium model, which focuses on the response of exports and imports to changes in relative prices and ignores income effects, capital flows and the money market.

In order to derive the elasticity conditions we first set out the current account equation:

$$B = X(P_d/P_f, E) - E\,F(P_d/P_f, E) \tag{10.1}$$

where B is the balance of payments on current account measured in domestic currency. Exports, X, measured in domestic currency and imports, F, measured in foreign currency, are both seen as functions of their relative prices (P_d is the domestic price of exports; P_f, the foreign price of imports) and the exchange rate, E, defined as units of domestic currency required to purchase one unit of foreign currency (a depreciation would increase E). X is a direct function of E, and F an inverse function of E.

In its basic form, the approach assumes, given spare capacity, that the supply elasticities of exports and imports are infinite so that their prices can be treated as constant. The current account expression therefore reduces to

$$B = X(E) - E\,F(E) \tag{10.2}$$

The effect of a change in the exchange rate is found by differentiating B with respect to E:

$$\frac{dB}{dE} = \frac{dB}{dE} - E\frac{dF}{dE} - F$$

$$= F\left(\frac{dX}{dE}\frac{E}{X}\frac{X}{EF} - \frac{dF}{dE}\frac{E}{F} - 1\right) \tag{10.3}$$

Now equation (10.3) contains the expressions for the elasticity of demand for exports, e_x, and the elasticity of demand for imports, e_F, where

$$e_x = \frac{dX}{dE}\frac{E}{X} \quad \text{and} \quad e_F = -\frac{dF}{dE}\frac{E}{F}$$

Substituting the demand elasticities in (10.3) we obtain

$$\frac{dB}{dE} = F\left(\frac{X}{EF}e_x + e_F - 1\right) \tag{10.4}$$

The approach assumes that initially the value of exports equals the value of imports ($X = EF$). Thus (10.4) will reduce to:

$$\frac{dB}{dE} = F(e_x + e_F - 1) \tag{10.5}$$

This is the well known Marshall–Lerner condition, which states that devaluation will improve the balance of payments on current account if the sum of the price elasticities of demand for exports and imports exceeds unity.

The approach can be extended to incorporate income effects that may arise from changes in relative prices. Such changes will have repercussions on flows of expenditure and these in turn will feed back on to domestic output and employment. The consequences of such effects, however, do not essentially alter the basic Marshall–Lerner condition.

Thus the elasticities approach suggests that payments imbalances are likely to be the result of movements in relative prices, and that the restoration of equilibrium requires relative price adjustment, either through an exchange rate change, or via an absolute reduction in domestic prices if the foreign price level is constant, or a relatively smaller increase in domestic prices if the foreign price level is rising. Exchange rate devaluation improves the current account by switching both domestic and foreign expenditure towards domestic output. In its basic form, however, the approach ignores the possibility of a cost-price transmission running from import to export prices. More recent models of devaluation (for example Wilson 1976) focus attention on the inflationary effects of exchange rate depreciation. These models predict that, if workers succeed in maintaining the purchasing power of their incomes, the rise in domestic prices and wages following depreciation would eventually wipe out any initial competitive gains from depreciation.

The absorption approach

The first specific statement of this approach was contained in Meade's *The Balance of Payments* (1951). It represents the extension to an open economy of the Keynesian income-expenditure analysis. It focuses specific attention upon the product market, rather less on the foreign exchange market, and appears to ignore completely the money market. By concentrating its attention upon income and expenditure flows it omits, as important explanatory variables, cash balances, other monetary variables and relative prices. From a country's national income accounts:

$$Py = G + I + C + X - F \tag{10.6}$$

the following expression for a country's trade balance can be obtained

$$B = X - F = Py - (G + I + C) \tag{10.7}$$

where the bracketed term on the right-hand side is aggregate domestic expenditure, referred to as 'absorption', to use Alexander's (1952) terminology. The absorption approach assumes that the level of income is the prime determinant of the level of absorption and that the trade balance is primarily determined by the level of absorption; hence we have

$$B = \overline{X} - F(A) = Py - A(Py) \tag{10.8}$$

where $A = G + I + C$ and $\overline{X}$ denotes that exports are exogenous (imports (F) are measured here in domestic currency).

The absorption approach emphasizes the fact that payments imbalances are 'characterized' by (but not necessarily 'caused' by) *ex ante* divergences between aggregate income receipts and aggregate domestic expenditure (absorption). In some situations a strong causal connection between Py and A on the one hand, and X and F on the other, can exist. For example, an increase in A holding Py constant, creates an excess of aggregate payments over aggregate receipts, causing the increase in A to spill over on to imports and deteriorate the balance of trade. This suggests that whenever $Py > A$, $X > F$, and that whenever $Py < A$, $X < F$. The reader will probably have noticed our reluctance to assert that trade imbalances are always the 'result' of an ex ante divergence of Py from A. This is because the whole 'structural form' of the absorption equation does not lend itself easily to conclusive specification of directions of causation between trade variables, absorption variables and the level of domestic income. For example, imagine that there is an 'autonomous' decline in the domestic country's export sales because of a change in foreign tastes away from domestic goods. Mathematically this means that the value of X on the left-hand side of equation (10.8) falls, as there is a direct deterioration in the trade balance. Now the reduction in export sales will cause exporters to cut back planned production and/or increase their sales effort to the home market. If it is the former Py will decline; if it is the latter A will rise. Whichever it is, the value of the right-hand side of equation (10.8) will fall by exactly the amount of the initial drop in X. *A posteriori* analysis will reveal that there has been a deterioration in the trade balance accompanied by an increase in A relative to Py. To infer from this that the trade deterioration was the 'result' instead of the 'cause' of the divergence of Y and A would clearly be wrong. Even where it is possible to specify that the chain of causation runs from Py and A to B, as the absorption model suggests, one wonders how useful such information is, especially in view of the fact that the formulation can throw no light on the 'causes' of the divergence of Y from A. Is the divergence the result of endogenous factors, e.g. a sudden change in the community's willingness to save, or the exogenous factors such as a change in the level of public expenditure?

The policy implications of the absorption approach has been clearly stated by Johnson (1958). There are two kinds of policy control that the authorities can exercise in bringing Py and A into line with each other. First, there are expenditure-variation controls which seek to operate directly on the schedule of absorption in the economy and include variations in the level and composition of the budget, as well as manipulation of the cost and availability of credit. Secondly, there are expenditure-switching controls which are designed to divert domestic expenditure away from foreign output on to domestic output and also foreign expenditure on to domestic output, with the intention of influencing Py through the familiar expenditure multiplier process. Devaluation and import restrictions, such as tariffs and quotas, are examples of expenditure-switching policies. The general message which emerges from the absorption model is that the elimination of a trade deficit requires that Py rise relative to A, or that A fall relative to Py, for only then will aggregate foreign receipts increase in relation to foreign payments.

The absorption approach has been criticized on the grounds that it is incomplete if it is to be interpreted as ignoring 'monetary conditions' completely, and unsatisfactory, if it is interpreted as postulating highly questionable assumptions about the behaviour of certain strategic monetary variables. However by pointing out that a balance of payments deficit implies an excess of payments over receipts and must therefore have implications for the money supply or its velocity, the absorption approach drew attention to the monetary nature of balance of payments deficits and surpluses. It was these monetary implications which were taken up by some economists and developed by them into the monetary approach to the balance of payments. It is to that approach that we now turn.

The monetary approach

According to Johnson (1977, p. 260):

> the essential difference between the monetary approach and the other post-Keynesian approaches ... is that the monetary approch formulates the problem of the balance of payments as a monetary phenomenon to be analysed with the tools of monetary theory, whereas the other approaches formulate it as a residual difference between real flows determined by other flows and relative prices.

It is the balance of payments as a whole which is the focus of attention of the monetary approach, with a balance of payments disequilibrium defined as a change in the level of foreign exchange reserves. These changes in reserves are seen as both reflecting a disparity between actual and desired money balances and, at the same time, providing an automatic mechanism by which equilibrium in the money market is restored.

There are two key elements to the automatic adjustment mechanism between the balance of payments and the money market. The first of these is the direct relationship which exists for an open economy with a fixed exchange rate, between its domestic money supply and its balance of payments. As we explained in Chapter 4, for such an economy, total domestic money supply effectively becomes an endogenous variable, with the national monetary authorities able to exert, at most, control over the domestic sources of change in the monetary base. A balance of payments surplus will result in an expansion of the monetary base and hence of the total domestic money supply, while a balance of payments deficit will contract the monetary base and money supply. This direct relationship between balance of payments flows and the domestic money supply does however depend on the key assumption that the national authorities do not or cannot engage in sterilization operations in order to offset the domestic monetary consequences of balance of payments deficits and surpluses. The monetary approach does not consider such sterilization operations feasible in a world of integrated financial markets and a high volume of interest-sensitive international capital flows.

The second element of the automatic adjustment mechanism is the demand for money. The monetary approach emphasizes that the demand for money is a stock demand and not a flow demand, and argues that it is a stable function of a small number of variables.

We can now combine these two elements and see how the automatic adjustment mechanism would work. Assume that initially we have equilibrium in the money market with the stock demand for money equal to the supply of money and the balance of payments in equilibrium with zero change in reserves. Now suppose the monetary authorities increase the domestic component of the money supply so that the total money stock now exceeds the demand to hold it. The excess supply of money will induce domestic residents to adjust the composition of their portfolios as they try to reduce their actual money holdings to their desired levels. The portfolio adjustment emphasized by the monetary approach to the balance of payments is the exchange of money for foreign goods and assets. This increases the flow of expenditure on the current and capital accounts and generates a balance of payments deficit which will be accommodated by a loss of foreign reserves, as the authorities sell foreign exchange and purchase sterling in order to maintain a fixed exchange rate. The loss of reserves means a fall in the total domestic money supply, and the process will continue until all the excess supply of money has been eliminated. With stock equilibrium restored to the money market, the balance of payments will again be in equilibrium.

In similar fashion, a contraction in the rate of growth of the domestic component of the money supply such that the total stock of money is less than the demand for it will guarantee portfolio adjustments that give rise to a balance of payments surplus. The surplus expands the foreign reserves and the total domestic money supply until both the money market and the balance of payments are in equilibrium.

A balance of payments surplus or deficit is thus seen as a transitory disequilibrium situation reflecting the process of adjustment of actual money balances towards the desired stock of money. In other words, a balance of payments disequilibrium is self-correcting through adjustments in the money market, the balance of payments itself providing the main adjustment mechanism. In Johnson's words, balance of payments 'deficits and surpluses represent phases of stock adjustment in the money market and not equilibrium flows' (Johnson 1976, p. 153).

In the example considered above, the initial disequilibrium originated in the activities of the domestic monetary authorities. It is possible, however, that the initial disturbance originates abroad. Thus if there is money market equilibrium in the economy, while the money supply in the rest of the world increases in excess of the demand for it, then there will be portfolio adjustments in the rest of the world which will result in a balance of payments surplus. But the surplus will increase the reserves of the country and thereby its domestic money supply. The country thus has money market disequilibrium with an excess supply of money, and as explained above this will result in a portfolio adjustment which will lead to an outflow of money and restoration of balance of payments equilibrium. Likewise a change in the rate of growth of the money supply in the rest of the world which causes a deficit will give rise to portfolio adjustments which restore equilibrium both in the balance of payments and the money market.

Accordng to the monetary approach then, it would appear that what is happening to a country's balance of payments will depend, given the demand for money in that country and in the rest of the world, upon the rate of growth of the money supply in the country *vis-à-vis* the rate of growth of the money supply in the rest of the world.

It is also possible within the monetary approach for non-monetary variables to instigate a balance of payments deficit/surplus, but their impact is seen as operating through their effect on the demand for, or supply of, money. Thus if demand and supply of money are equal and growing at the same rate both in the economy and in the rest of the world, then a fall in the rate of growth of the economy's output will induce a fall in the rate of growth of its demand for money, causing it to fall behind the growth of the money supply. The resulting excess supply of money will, via portfolio adjustment, generate a balance of payments deficit. The automatic adjustment process will eventually restore equilibrium in both the money market and in the balance of payments.

This adjustment process may however be counteracted if the authorities allow an excessive expansion of the domestic sources of change in the money supply. In this case the temporary balance of payments deficit would be turned into a chronic balance of payments deficit, caused not by the initial change in the real variable but by 'monetary accommodation' by the authorities.

The distinctive feature of the monetary approach then is its emphasis on the importance of monetary factors in the determination of the balance of payments. There can only be long-run equilibrium in the balance of payments, i.e. no changes in reserves, if there is full stock equilibrium in the money market. As to the exact nature of the adjustment process by which long-run equilibrium is achieved, Helliwell (1978) has pointed out that the monetary approach literature contains a variety of versions. Johnson (1976), for example, assumed fast-clearing world goods and capital markets and had instantaneous adjustment of money supply to money demand, while other writers (Dornbusch 1976b) has assumed a delay in the adjustment process. The assumptions required to achieve instantaneous adjustment in the money market are not crucial to the monetary approach, for as Mussa (1976) has emphasized, the monetary approach can incorporate different views on the nature and speed of the adjustment process, for it is concerned primarily with the longer-term balance of payments position.

> The monetary approach seeks to outline a relatively general theory of long-run behaviour with a number of different models of the process of adjustment. (p. 193).

The price level and the interest rate reflect the longer-run perspective of the approach, and are usually taken to be fixed at world levels under conditions of internationally integrated goods and capital markets, while income is assumed supply-constrained at full capacity utilization. With these assumptions the monetary approach is synonomous with the international or global monetarist model (see pp. 214–216). However, as Johnson (1977) has pointed out, these assumptions are not essential to the monetary approach, and more complex models can be constructed incorporating shorter-term adjustment mechanisms (see, for example, Jonson 1976).

What is crucial to the monetary approach is the assumption of a stable demand for money. If it were unstable, as for example in the Keynesian liquidity trap situation, excess money balances arising from a balance of payments surplus would be absorbed into idle money balances and the automatic balance of payments adjustment mechanism would not operate. We can now summarize the main features of the monetary approach to the balance of payments by setting out a very simple monetary approach model.

The first element of the model is the demand for money. This is taken to be a stable function of real income (y), the rate of interest (i) and the price level (P).

$$M^d = L(y, i, P) \text{ where } L(y), L(P), > 0; L(i) < 0 \tag{10.9}$$

The second element is the supply of money, which is defined as the sum of the domestic assets of the banking system (domestic credit, D) and the country's foreign exchange reserves (R).

$$M^s = D + R \tag{10.10}$$

Abstracting from the short-run adjustment process, in the long run there is equilibrium in the money market.

$$L(y, i, P) = D + R \tag{10.11}$$

Taking first differences and re-arranging gives

$$\Delta R = \Delta L(y, i, P) - \Delta D \tag{10.12}$$

But ΔD = DCE (Domestic Credit Expansion) $\tag{10.13}$

So

$$\Delta R = \Delta L(y, i, P) - \text{DCE} \tag{10.14}$$

Equation (10.14) summarizes the basic contention of the monetary approach to the balance of payments: that a deficit or surplus – as represented by changes in the country's foreign exchange reserves – is equal to the difference between the change in the demand for money and the change in domestic credit (i.e. domestic credit expansion). It follows that a continuous balance of payments deficit can occur only if the authorities allow domestic credit to expand faster than the demand for money.

Equation (10.14) also contains a number of other important propositions of the monetary approach. The first of these is that the growth of international reserves is positively associated with increases in real income. The reason for this direct relationship is that real income expansion increases the demand for money which can only be met, in the absence of domestic credit expansion, through a balance of payments surplus. This is in contrast to the traditional Keynesian approach, where real income expansion leads to a deterioration in the balance of payments. Other monetary approach propositions implied by equation (10.14) are (i) an increase in P improves the balance of payments and (ii) an increase in i worsens the balance of payments. Both (i) and (ii) are in contradiction to the conventional Keynesian argument.

The key feature of the monetary approach is the automatic balance of payments adjustment mechanism, i.e. a balance of payments surplus or deficit is removed by the adjustment of money supply to money demand. Long-run stock equilibrium in the money market ensures long-run balance of payments equilibrium. Balance of payments disequilibria are thus seen as essentially short-run monetary disequilibria. It therefore follows that persistent balance of payments deficits can only occur if the adjustment mechanism is frustrated by the continuous creation of excess domestic credit by the monetary authorities. The appropriate policy measure in this situation is for the authorities to reduce domestic credit creation in order to restore equilibrium in the money market.

The monetary approach considers that conventional balance of payments policy measures such as devaluation can only affect the balance of payments position through their effects on the demand and supply of money. They will only, however, have a short-term impact on the balance of payments and are seen by the monetary approach as essentially a temporary substitute for monetary contraction. Exchange rate devaluation, for example, by reducing the real value of nominal money balances through an increase in the domestic price level, may result in a transitory impact on the balance of payments, but cannot, in the case of a chronic balance of payments deficit, achieve a permanent effect.

> the only possible long-run remedy within the control of the national policy making authorities is a reduction of the rate of domestic credit expansion (Johnson 1976, p. 283).

We conclude this section by briefly considering some of the criticisms that have been made of the monetary approach. First of all it is necessary to recognize that some of these criticisms are really criticisms of global monetarism. As we have already pointed out, while the monetary approach to the balance of payments is an integral part of global monetarism, it is not synonomous with it. Certainly the more restrictive assumptions of global monetarism have sometimes been used in a number of expositions of the monetary approach, but this has usually been for pedagogic reasons.

It will be recalled that the two essential elements of the monetary approach are the stability of the demand for money and the direct link between the balance of payments of a country and its total money supply. The validity of both of these elements has been questioned. This issue of the stability of the demand for money has been considered elsewhere (pp. 76–79) so we shall say no more about it here.

The question of the link between the balance of payments and the money supply centres around the ability of the monetary authorities to neutralize the inflows and outflows of money associated with balance of payments deficits and surpluses. Apart from the USA which because of its size and reserve currency status is in a unique position, empirical studies have, according to Whitman (1975, p. 523), indicated 'that at least some degree of sterilisation has been or could be undertaken in the short run by the country's surveyed'. Although it may be possible in the very short term for the authorities to use open-market operations to achieve some degree of sterilization of external flows, it seems doubtful, as explained in Chapter 4 (p. 94) that sterilization would be possible in the longer run, given the growth of international financial markets and the increasingly integrated nature of national financial markets.

A related criticism is that a disequilibrium in the money market does not necessarily have to be reflected in a balance of payments deficit or suplus, because it could be offset instead by a deficit or surplus on the government's budget. It is an essential feature of the monetary approach that balance of payments deficits and surpluses are consequences of stock adjustments in the money market. Full long-run equilibrium in the balance of payments can only be achieved when there is stock equilibrium in the money market. It has been pointed out that this approach has much in common with the analysis of the government's budget constraint and the stock/flow implications of government budget deficits (see pp. 164–169). In that analysis national income can only be in full equilibrium when the government's budget is balanced, for otherwise the stock implication of financing the budget will result in a changing level of aggregate demand and national income.

However, in the context of an open economy with fixed exchange rates, neither a government budget imbalance nor a balance of payments imbalance will necessarily have any effect on private sector stock equilibrium. The reason is simply that they could neutralize one another. Thus the inflow of money from a balance of payments surplus need not disturb the equilibrium of the money market if accompanied by a government budget surplus. Thus Currie (1976, p. 510) has argued that

> the monetary analysis of the balance of payments has overlooked the fact that sterilization can be effected by running a government budget surplus/deficit, and that this involves no continuing disturbance to private sector stock equilibrium.

Of course, in the case of a balance of payments deficit it cannot be 'neutralized' indefinitely by a deficit on the government's budget, because sooner or later the government will run out of reserves. In the case of a surplus the neutralization argument has been countered on the grounds that

> even the most casual observation of governmental behaviour suggests that it is rare indeed (if not altogether unknown) both for a government to pursue a policy of continual surplus budgeting for the explicit purpose of accumulating reserves without limit ... and for a government with a strong reserve and balance of payments position not to take monetary and budgetary steps to correct its balance of payments surplus (Nobay and Johnson 1977, p. 769).

Currie has also criticized the monetary approach on the grounds that once explicit account is taken of the government's budget constraint, then in the context of an underemployed Keynesian fixed-price model the longer-run effects of expenditure-switching policies (devaluation, tariffs, quotas) are not automatically nullified by the ensuing changes in money flows and the consequential stock-flow adjustments made by the private sector. The essence of the argument may be illustrated by assuming that initially the balance of payments, the money market and the governments budget are all in equilibrium and that the government then devalues the currency. If the elasticity conditions are satisfied then the devaluation will shift the balance of payments into surplus and raise national income. The increase in income will raise the government's tax revenue and move the government's budget into surplus. In this way the surplus on the balance of payments is neutralized by the surplus on the government's budget, and there is no effect on private sector stock equilibrium.

Thus while agreeing that the monetary approach is correct in pointing out that control of the balance of payments must involve restraint of domestic credit, Currie argues that this restraint can be achieved by expenditure switching policies working through real flows and the governments budget.

The monetary approach has also been criticized for suggesting that all balance of payments deficits are caused by lax monetary control and for ignoring all real and structural causes of payments imbalances. This is an unjustified criticism, however, for the monetary approach does not in fact claim that all deficits are caused by monetary factors; it simply argues that all deficits have monetary symptoms and implications and that because of them there is an automatic tendency to balance of payments correction.

A somewhat different version of this criticism is that because the monetary approach emphasizes the link between changes in reserves and all other transactions together, and because it pays virtually no attention to changes in the composition of the current and capital accounts, it ignores much of what is important in the balance of payments for economic welfare and for the conduct of economic policy.

Finally we refer to the criticism that is directed at the emphasis that the monetary approach places on long-run equilibrium analysis. The critics argue that the duration of the short run is important because (a) the longer it is the greater the likelihood that disturbances will occur that will divert the economy from its initial adjustment path, and (b) it will influence the social costs associated with adjustment. Moreover, policy-makers work with fairly short time horizons and must concern themselves with the nature of adjustment paths. It has therefore been argued that the monetary approach's 'concentration on the long run assumes away all of the problems that make the balance of payments a problem' (Krause 1975, p. 547).

Foreign exchange rate determination

In this section we shall distinguish four main approaches:

(1) The Mundell–Fleming model.
(2) The monetary model.
(3) The broader portfolio approach.
(4) The overshooting model of Dornbusch.

The Mundell–Fleming model

We have already encountered this approach as the standard open-economy version of the Keynesian model (see pp. 137–141), so it will suffice here simply to state its main points. The exchange rate is determined within a standard macroeconomic framework in which net exports are an inverse function of income, and the net capital inflow a direct function of domestic interest rates, given constant foreign rates of interest. The exchange rate is a factor in this model because it influences the price competitiveness of exports and import substitutes and thereby net exports. Thus from a position of equilibrium in the goods market, the money market and the foreign exchange market, an expansion of the money supply would depress interest rates, stimulate interest-sensitive expenditures, and raise the level of income. Because of this, net imports would tend to rise and net capital inflow fall. As a result the currency would depreciate, stimulating exports until equilibrium is restored to all three markets again. The extent of the necessary depreciation will depend upon the marginal propensity to consume as well as a number of elasticities, such as the interest elasticities of the demand for money and domestic expenditure, and the income elasticity of the demand for money.

Several criticisms have been made of this approach to exchange rate determination. Firstly, no importance is attached to exchange rate expectations, so that international differences in interest rates cannot be due to expectations of exchange rate changes. The second criticism is that no allowance is made for the effect of the depreciation on domestic prices and thereby on the real value of the money supply. Thirdly there is an absence of any dynamics, such as lags in response of output and trade flows. Lastly, the treatment of capital flows in the model would appear to be appropriate only for very short-run analysis. The approach implies that for a given interest differential between domestic and foreign interest rates, there would be an indefinite capital flow resulting in a potentially infinite accumulation of assets either by domestic residents or by foreigners. Capital flows, however, cannot continue indefinitely in a stationary world: they represent adjustments to inequalities between actual and desired stocks, and once stocks are optimally allocated, capital flows would cease. Thus a change in the interest differential will initially result in capital flows but will eventually cease when asset equilibrium is restored. The problem of how asset portfolios are optimally allocated is ignored in the Mundell–Fleming model.

In contrast to the Mundell–Fleming model, which focuses on the *flow* demands and supplies in the foreign exchange market, the more recent approaches to exchange rate determination view the foreign exchange market as an asset market with exchange rates being determined in the short run by equilibrium conditions in domestic and foreign asset portfolios. We consider below three main asset market equilibrium models, starting with the monetary model which focuses on the role played by the money market in exchange rate determination.

The monetary approach

Under fixed exchange rates, the monetary approach provides a theory of balance of payments determination. Under floating exchange rates the monetary approach converts into a theory of exchange rate determination, with the exchange rate seen as essentially a monetary phenomenon determined by stock equilibrium conditions in the money market. Without official intervention in the foreign exchange market, the link between the domestic money supply and the balance of payment flows is effectively severed, the monetary base being determined solely by domestic influences.

In the fixed exchange rate case, if an expansion of domestic credit results in an excess supply of money, equilibrium in the money market is re-established through the balance of payments adjustment mechanism. The excess money balances increase spending on foreign goods and assets, putting downward pressure on the exchange rate, and forcing the authorities to sell foreign exchange. This contracts the international reserves component of the monetary base, until eventually equilibrium in the money market is restored. With a freely floating exchange rate excess money balances again put downward pressure on the exchange rate, which, in the absence of official intervention, will then depreciate. The domestic price level thereby rises, reducing the real value of the money supply, until eventually the supply and demand for real money balances are once more in equilibrium. Thus it is the depreciating exchange rate which provides the mechanism whereby stock equilibrium is restored in the money market. In the monetary approach then, the long-run equilibrium exchange rate is determined by the relationship between the supply of and demand for real money balances.

There is clearly a long-run symmetry between the monetary approach operating under conditions of fixed exchange rates and operating under conditions of flexible exchange rates. There is a significant difference however between the two regimes in the way in which the adjustment process works. As Whitman (1975, pp. 516–17) has pointed out:

> Under fixed exchange rates, quantities adjust gradually, in the form of reserve flows, to bring about equality between the actual stock of money and the desired level of real balances. Under flexible rates, with the nominal quantity of money fixed in each country, changes in the valuation of the stock through changes in the exchange rate bring about instantaneous full stock adjustment in the money market.

An essential difference between the monetary approach to the balance of payments under fixed exchange rates and the monetary approach to the determination of the exchange rate under a floating system is that under the former the price level is fixed at a 'world' level, with the domestic nominal money supply adjusting in response to changes in foreign exchange reserves. With floating rates it is the foreign exchange reserves which are tied down, leaving the money supply under the potential control of the monetary authorities.

The basic monetary model of exchange rate determination may be usefully set out in the form of four simple equations. Equation (10.15) is the condition for equilibrium in the domestic money market and assumes that the demand for money is a (stable) function of the price level, real income, and the rate of interest.

$$M = L(P, i, y) \tag{10.15}$$

In real terms

$$\frac{M}{P} = L(i, y) \tag{10.15a}$$

Making corresponding behavioural assumptions for the rest of the world generates a similar equation for foreign money demand and supply, i.e. equation (10.16) where the subscript f denotes 'foreign'.

$$M_f = L_f(P_f, i_f, y_f) \tag{10.16}$$

or in real terms

$$\frac{M_f}{P_f} = L_f(i_f, y_f) \tag{10.16a}$$

International commodity arbitrage is assumed to ensure purchasing power parity (PPP). Thus if a product sells for $10 in USA, and the rate of exchange between the pound and the dollar is £0.5 = $1, then that good will sell for £5 in the UK. PPP may thus be written:

$$P = E P_f \qquad (10.17)$$

where E is the rate of exchange
Re-arranging (10.17) gives

$$E = \frac{P}{P_f} \qquad (10.17a)$$

Substituting the 'real' versions of the monetary equilibrium equations into (10.17a) gives:

$$E = \frac{M \cdot L_f (i_f, y_f)}{M_f \cdot L (i, y)}$$

In the monetary approach the exchange rate is the relative price of national monies, and is determined by the demands for and supplies of those monies.

In its simplest or most extreme form, the monetary approach also assumes that real income and real interest rates are given. Income is taken to be at its full or 'natural' level, while the real interest rate is assumed fixed by foreign rates and exchange rate expectations. This latter point is the so-called interest parity condition, which states that the difference between domestic and foreign interest rates is equal to the expected change in the exchange rate, i.e. if interest rates in the domestic economy are, say, 4% higher than 'world' rates, then the domestic currency will be expected to depreciate by 4%. In other words there will be no expected net financial advantage from depositing money in either the domestic economy or the rest of the world. If there were such an anticipated net gain, then interest arbitrage would remove it. The interest parity condition may be stated thus:

$$i - i_f = \frac{E^e - E^s}{E^s}$$

where $(i - i_f)$ is the interest differential and $(E^e - E^s)/E^s$ is the percentage excess of the expected future spot rate (E^e) over the current spot rate (E^s), i.e. the expected depreciation of the domestic currency.

An increase in the domestic money supply will cause an increased demand for goods, services and assets. With domestic real income and interest rates fixed, and domestic prices tied through PPP to foreign prices, the excess demand is directed towards foreign goods, services and assets. This results in a depreciation of the exchange rate, and thereby a rise in domestic prices in line with PPP. With a price elasticity of unity in the demand for money, the increase in domestic prices (and also therefore the depreciation of the currency) must be in the same proportion as the increase in the money supply, leaving the real money supply unchanged.

The portfolio balance approach

Whitman (1975) has described the monetary approach as a 'stripped-down' version of the asset or portfolio balance approach to exchange rate determination. In this latter approach, the exchange rate is viewed as one of a range of prices that equilibrate the demands for and the supplies of the complete spectrum of assets which comprise wealth portfolios. Kouri (1980, p. 79) has summarized the portfolio equilibrium model thus:

> In line with the modern asset market view, the foreign exchange market is viewed as an efficient speculative market dominated in the short run by speculation and capital account transactions rather than by payment flows associated with merchandise trade. In particular, the short-run equilibrium value of the exchange is determined together with other asset prices by conditions of equilibrium between the demands for and the supplies of different assets.

The portfolio approach clearly differs from the monetary one in that it does not confine its attention to just one asset (money), assuming all others to be perfect substitutes. Instead it recognizes that the demands for and supplies of all assets have to be taken into account in analysing the equilibrium of wealth portfolios. It therefore extends the monetary approach by acknowledging that exchange rate movements are not the consequences solely of changes in the conditions of money supply and demand.

If we assume that there is just one non-money domestic asset, and one foreign asset, then we can illustrate some of the main features of the portfolio balance approach by using a simple diagram. In this 'model' the role of the exchange rate is to influence the domestic currency price of foreign assets and thereby the value of the total wealth portfolio.

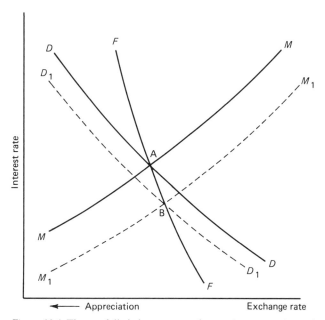

Figure 10.1 The portfolio balance approach to exchange rate determination

In *Figure 10.1* the curve labelled *MM* is the money market equilibrium curve, tracing out the various combinations of interest and the exchange rate that equate the demand for with the supply of money. The higher the rate of interest the lower is the demand for money, so if monetary equilibrium is to be maintained then the domestic currency must depreciate in order to raise the domestic currency price of foreign assets and hence wealth. The increase in wealth raises the demand for money and keeps the money market in equilibrium i.e. high interest rates must be accompanied by a depreciation of the exchange rate if the money market is to be kept in equilibrium.

The curve labelled *DD* in the diagram traces out the different combinations of interest and exchange rate that keep the domestic asset market in equilibrium. Higher interest rates increase the demand for the asset, so an appreciation of the currency is required to restore equilibrium via a fall in the value of wealth and hence the demand for the asset.

In similar fashion the curve labelled *FF* is the locus of interest rate and exchange rate combinations that maintain equilibrium in the foreign asset market.

We can now trace the consequence of a monetary expansion. Starting from point A in the diagram, with equilibrium in all three markets, an expansion of the money supply would create an excess supply of it. This would shift the *MM* curve downwards to the right (say to $M_1 M_1$) as the money market equilibrium now requires a depreciation of the currency and/or a lower rate of interest. The excess supply of money would generate an excess demand for the domestic asset and would shift the *DD* curve downwards to the left (say $D_1 D_1$) as the maintenance of asset market equilibrium would now require a depreciation of the currency or a fall in the interest rate. The fall in interest rates will increase the demand for the foreign asset. Given the fixed stock of foreign assets held by domestic residents, the foreign exchange rate depreciates. Thus the two domestic market curves *MM* and *DD* slide along the foreign asset market curve, to reach a new position of portfolio balance at point B. The expansion of the money supply has unambiguously depreciated the currency, which has played 'a balancing role by affecting the valuation of assets' (Dornbusch 1980, p. 14). However, the portfolio approach recognizes that such exchange rate changes may follow from changed supply or demand conditions for foreign assets and non-money domestic assets, as well as changes in money market conditions.

So far, none of the models of exchange rate determination that we have considered has given any attention to the role of expectations and dynamics. We shall therefore conclude our discussion of theories of the exchange rate by looking at one approach which does so in an attempt to explain the phenomenon of 'overshooting'.

Exchange rate dynamics and overshooting

The model that we shall briefly describe in this section was originally developed by Dornbusch (1976a). The model incorporates certain aspects of the monetary approach, particularly the demand for money function and the assumption of perfect capital mobility (and hence interest parity).The foreign exchange market is taken to be dominated by agents who form their expectations rationally and it is assumed that interest rates and exchange rates adjust to shocks more rapidly than do goods prices and wages. Output is fixed at its natural level and money is neutral in the long run in the sense that an X% rise in the money stock eventually results in domestic prices rising by X% and the currency depreciating by X%.

Suppose now there is an increase in the money supply. With the demand for nominal money a function of prices, current real income, and interest rates, money market equilibrium can be restored only through an increase in price and/or real income, or through a fall in interest rates. But real income is fixed at its natural level, while prices are assumed slow to adjust. Consequently the money market initially clears through interest rates falling. But this opens up an international interest differential so that interest parity no longer holds. To restore it, the exchange rate must be expected to appreciate, and with expectations formed rationally it must appreciate.

In the long run, however, the consequence for the exchange rate of an expansion of the money supply is a depreciation of the currency. Economic agents forming their expectations rationally will expect such a long-run depreciation.

But how can the exchange rate be expected to both appreciate and depreciate? The answer is that it initially depreciates by more than is required for long-run equilibrium, and then appreciates back up to that new long-run level, i.e. it initially 'overshoots'. This is illustrated in *Figure 10.2*. The original equilibrium exchange

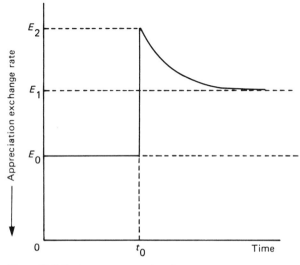

Figure 10.2 Exchange rate overshooting

rate is E_0. An expansion of the money supply at t_0 generates a new long-run equilibrium exchange rate of E_1. Initially, however, the exchange rate depreciates very sharply (to E_2) taking the spot rate above its new long-run equilibrium value. Thereafter the rate appreciates till the new equilibrium level is reached. According to Dornbusch (1980, p. 19) 'This "overshooting" of exchange rates is an essential counterpart of permanent monetary changes under conditions of short-run price stickiness and perfect capital mobility.'

11

Monetary policy: targets, indicators, rules and discretion

This is the first of three chapters in which we shall consider a number of issues relating to monetary policy. In this chapter we will be discussing two of them:

(1) What is the best target of monetary policy and what variable(s) provides the best indication of whether the policy is on course?
(2) Should policy be conducted at the discretion of the authorities or should it be based on a pre-determined rule?

In Chapter 12 we describe and briefly assess the major techniques of policy available to the authorities, while in the final chapter we survey the targets and methods of monetary policy as it has been applied in the UK since the end of the Second World War.

Before considering the question of targets and indicators we will first outline the broad nature of monetary policy.

Monetary policy may be used by the authorities as one of several different ways of trying to achieve certain macroeconomic goals:

(1) A high level of employment.
(2) A low rate of inflation.
(3) Balance of payments equilibrium.
(4) A satisfactory rate of economic growth.

These goals are sometimes called the ultimate targets of policy, but as we shall be using the term target to mean something else, we shall refer to them simply as the goals of policy.

The monetary authorities do not have direct control over these goals, but instead can act only on certain instruments of policy, or instrumental variables as they are usually called, which are under their direct influence. These instruments include open-market operations, special deposits and possibly the discount rate of the central bank. The instrumental variables do not however exert any direct influence on the goals of policy. Instead they work through intermediate variables, a category which embraces such things as bank reserves, the level of short and long-term interest rates and the total money supply. Many of the intermediate variables are linked together. For example, a change in the level of bank reserves may bring about a change in bank deposits and the total money stock. Thus some intermediate variables lie closer to the instruments of policy and are influenced by policy action in the shorter run, while others are further away from policy, lying closer to the goals, and are influenced by policy action only in the longer run.

The category of intermediate variables embraces what are known as the indicators and targets of monetary policy. The indicators are those intermediate variables which usually lie close to the instruments of policy and 'indicate' the direction and strength of monetary policy. The targets, on the other hand, are usually included in those intermediate variables which lie closer to the goals of policy and which are seen as having a fairly predictable effect on those goals. Thus, for example, if the money supply is considered to bear a stable causal relationship to the rate of inflation, then policy which is directed at influencing the rate of inflation may well aim to control the money supply; the money supply would be a target of policy. It must be remembered of course that the targets are not ends in themselves but only means towards the end of achieving the goals of policy.

In trying to decide what action to take on the instrumental variables, the authorities are faced with a number of difficulties. To begin with the structural relationships of the macroeconomy may not be known to the authorities; that is, they may not know how the instrumental variables are related to the intermediate variables, and how the intermediate variables are related to the goals of policy. The authorities are confronted with a number of different models incorporating a variety of relationships between the instruments, the intermediate variables and the goals of policy. Secondly, both the intermediate variables and the goals are subject to exogenous influences i.e. influences which are independent of policy. For example, if the money supply is determined by the supply of high-powered money together with the reserve ratio of the banks and the public's desired cash to deposits ratio, then if either of the latter two change, the money supply will change also, even though there has been no policy-induced change in the stock of high-powered money. If the authorities know what changes are taking place in these exogenous influences, then appropriate action can be taken on the instrumental variables. Unfortunately, knowledge of changes in the exogenous influences can at best be obtained only after a time lag. Thus the policy-makers are impeded in the formulation of their policy because they do not have complete knowledge either of the relevant structural relationships or of the values of the non-policy determined variables entering into those relationships. These arguments are summarized in *Figure 11.1*.

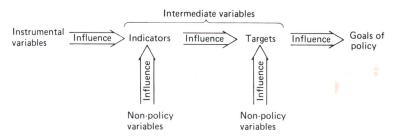

Figure 11.1 The variables of macroeconomic policy

It is under these conditions of uncertainty that the monetary authorities may want to use targets and indicators as a means of helping them make sure that policy is influencing the goals in the desired way.

The choice of targets and indicators

Targets

A target is an intermediate variable which the authorities are trying to influence in the belief that it bears a predictable and stable relationship to one or more of the goals of policy. Clearly there can only be an advantage in using an intermediate variables as a target of policy so long as it avoids some or all of the problems involved in the direct use of the goals themselves as targets. The criteria for a good target are:

(1) It must be affected by the policy instruments with a shorter time-lag than is involved with ultimate goals.
(2) The target must be readily observable with little or no delay.
(3) It must be stably related to one or more of the goals of policy.
(4) The non-policy influences on it should be separable from the policy influences, and be identifiable.

In deciding on a target the authorities have basically to choose between a quantity and a price. Examples of a quantity would be the various measures of the money supply, the monetary base and domestic credit expansion, while examples of a price target would be short or long-term interest rates, and equity yields.

Poole (1970) argued that if the goal of policy is to minimize the fluctuations in national income, then the choice between an interest rate and a money supply target depends on whether the money market or the goods market is the more subject to non-policy influences. This is illustrated in *Figures 11.2* and *11.3*.

Figure 11.2 illustrates the different effects of using money supply and interest rate targets in the face of goods market fluctuations. Thus if the *IS* curve is initially in the position labelled IS_0 then the rate of interest is i_0 and national income Y_0. An

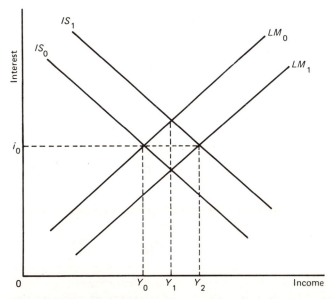

Figure 11.2 The different effects on income of targeting on the money supply and interest rates in the face of goods market disturbances

increase in aggregate demand would shift the *IS* curve to the right, say to the position IS_1. If the authorities are targeting on the money supply and allowing interest rates to fluctuate, then national income will rise to Y_1. If, however, the authorities are targeting on the level of interest rates and allowing the money supply to fluctuate, then the *LM* curve will shift to LM_1 and the level of income will rise to Y_2. In the face of goods market fluctuations it would appear that stabilizing the money supply will generate smaller income fluctuations than will stabilizing interest rates.

Figure 11.3 is concerned with money market fluctuations. If the *LM* curve is initially in the position labelled LM_0, then the rate of interest is i_0 and the level of income Y_0. Suppose now there is a fall in the demand for money which shifts the *LM* curve to LM_1. If the authorities are aiming to stabilize the money supply then the rate of interest will fall to i_1 and the level of income increase to Y_1. On the other hand, if the authorities stabilize interest rates, passively allowing the money supply to adjust, then the *LM* curve will shift back to LM_0, and there will be no change in the rate of interest or the level of income.

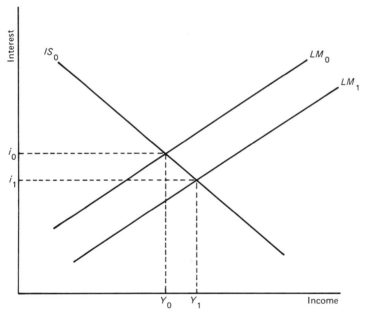

Figure 11.3 The different effects on income of targeting on the money supply and interest rates in the face of money market disturbances

In the case of both goods market and money market fluctuations, the extent of the differences outlined above concerning the fluctuations in income which result from using money supply or interest rate targets will depend on the slopes of the *IS* and *LM* curves. For example, in *Figure 11.4* the steeper the slope of the *IS* curve, the smaller will be the difference in the magnitude of income fluctuations resulting from the two different targets in the case of goods market disturbances.

Let us now consider some of the other advantages and disadvantages of the money supply and interest rates as targets.

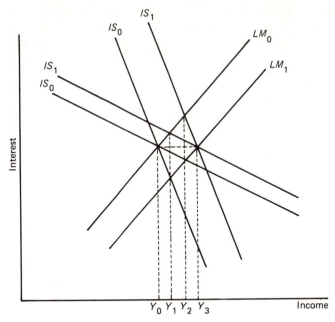

Y_0 = Original level of income

Y_3 = Level of income with interest rate as target

Y_1 = Level of income with money supply as target and elastic *IS* curve

Y_2 = Level of income with money supply as target and inelastic *IS* curve

Figure 11.4 The importance of the slopes of the *IS* and *LM* curves for the income consequences of money supply and interest rate targeting

Money supply

The target advocated by monetarists is the money supply or, more precisely, the rate of change of the money supply. Several arguments have been used to support this view. To begin with it is argued that monetary policy cannot be used to influence real magnitudes but only nominal ones such as the price level and nominal national income. Reference is then made to a considerable body of empirical evidence suggesting well-determined links between the money supply and the nominal goals of policy. The stability of the demand for money is particularly emphasized, for as Friedman put it in his classic article on monetary policy:

> In principle, 'tightness' or 'ease' depends on the rate of change of the quantity of money supplied compared to the rate of change of the quantity demanded, excluding affects on demand from monetary policy itself. However, empirically demand is highly stable, if we exclude the effect of monetary policy, so it is generally sufficient to look at supply alone. (1968. p. 7).

Moreover, because of the stability of the demand for money, it is argued that goods market fluctuations are greater than those in the money market. From Poole's arguments outlined above it then follows that it is preferable to stabilize the money supply rather than the rate of interest.

Minford, however, has argued that the rationale for monetary targets is quite independent of the stability of the demand for money. His rationale 'is that if the exchange rate is floating then the money supply must be controlled, and interest rates must not because of problems of determinacy and stability', (1981, p. 47). Minford's argument is that as long as a demand for money exists, even though it is not a highly stable one, then with inflationary expectations, a determinate (and probably stable) rate of inflation will emerge only if there is control over the money supply. With adaptive expectations a given supply of money will generate a determinate inflation rate in the long run, though not in the short run. With rational expectations the rate of inflation is determined by the supply of money (subject to random shocks) both in the short and long runs. In contrast, control of interest rates will make the price level and rate of inflation indeterminate in the long run if expectations are formed adaptively, and indeterminate in both the short and long runs if expectations are formed rationally.

> Interest rate stabilisation implies failure to control the price level, either totally (rational expectations) or asymptotically (adaptive expectations). (Minford 1981, p. 48).

If the money supply is to be used as the target of policy, then the authorities must decide to which, if any, of the number of monetary aggregates they will accord primary importance. Three main criteria have been used in evaluating the suitability of the various aggregates:

(1) The closeness and stability of the relationship between changes in the monetary aggregate and changes in the goal variables.
(2) The controllability of the aggregate.
(3) Its measurability.

The usefulness of the first criteria however is questioned by Goodhart's law', which states 'that any observed statistical regularity will tend to collapse once pressure is placed upon it for control purposes' (1975b, p. 5). Thus while the case for using M1 as the target variable rests primarily upon it appearing to have a more stable demand function than the broader monetary aggregates, because of its narrowness it is probably most at risk from the operation of Goodhart's law. Similarly while M2 is probably closer than M1 to being the aggregate that measures the stock of transactions balances, it is based on a somewhat arbitrary classification and is regarded by many commentors as being still too narrow an aggregate upon which to target. In any case, as a new measure there is little evidence on its relationship to the goal variables.

The case against using the broader aggregates is the apparently greater instability of their demand functions. As the Governor of the Bank of England put it:

> On occasion the path of M3 can be significantly influenced by changing competitive conditions within the banking industry – conditions which can change for reasons quite separate from the course of nominal incomes in the economy, or the actions of the monetary authorities. (Bank of England 1978a, p. 36).

On the other hand £M3 has an advantage from the point of view of contrallability and measurability because:

> it can be linked to changes in certain key credit counterparts, such as the PSBR, bank lending, government debt sales, DCE and external financial flows, in a way that helps our understanding of the course of monetary developments. It has also some comparative statistical advantages; for example it is proportionately less disturbed by transit items – somewhat arbitrarily treated as they are – than M1. (Bank of England 1978a, p. 36).

Interest Rates

Until money supply targets became fashionable in the late 1970s, interest rates were the most popular choice of intermediate variable to act as a target of monetary policy, and they still command significant support amongst particular groups of economists.

Those economists, for example, who believe that the demand for money is unstable and that as a result the money market is more subject to stochastic shocks than is the goods market, following the Poole analysis outlined above, argue for an interest rate target on the grounds that it will result in smaller fluctuations in nominal income. As a target, interest rates have the attributes that they are observable, and that the observations are available with a minimum delay.

There are however a number of disadvantages attached to the use of interest rates as intermediate targets. As with money supply measures, so there is more than one rate of interest, and no clear criteria for deciding which is the 'right' one or the 'right' range.

Second, the observed nominal interest rates that act as the targets of policy are not the relevant ones, from the point of view of influencing decisions to lend and to borrow. Some writers draw attention to the role of expectations and speculation. Lenders and borrowers may be influenced not only by the nominal rate of interest but also by any capital gain or loss. So if there is a general belief that interest rates are going to fall, causing a capital loss, then the unobserved total yield is less than the observed nominal rate, perhaps by a significant amount. Similarly it is the real rate of interest, not the nominal one, which matters, and while the authorities can control and observe the nominal rate they cannot observe the real rate because the latter depends upon expectations of price changes which vary from one person to another and from one period of time to another.

Another problem is that interest rates are particularly susceptible to non-policy influences, and because these influences are difficult to separate from those of policy, it is very difficult (some would say impossible) to assess the impact of policy on the economy. Suppose, for example, that the authorities believe that there is an inverse relationship between rates of interest and the level of aggregate demand. The use of interest rates as a weapon of stabilization policy will then mean raising them when aggregate demand is high and lowering them when aggregate demand is low. In the absence of positive policy action, interest rates will tend to move in a pro-cyclical manner; in periods of rising aggregate demand interest rates will tend to rise, while in periods of falling aggregate demand they will tend to fall. If the authorities merely rely on observed interest rates as the target of their policy, then they may get the 'wrong' signal, because the change in the observed rate is compounded of the policy effect and the exogenous effect. Thus in the boom phase of the cycle, interest rates will have a tendency to rise independently of policy action. The desired policy action, on the assumption of an inverse relationship between aggregate demand and interest rates, is to raise the latter. But the policy actually implemented may have the effect of lowering rates. If, however, the exogenous effect on interest rates is strong enough, it will outweigh the policy effect and interest rates will actually rise. It is the actual rise that the authorities observe and they consequently get the impression that their policy is having the right effect on the target – which in fact it is not.

A final disadvantage of using interest rates as targets is that for any given kind of monetary policy they will move first in one direction and then in another. As we saw in Chapter 7 (pp. 155–156), Friedman argues that an expansionary monetary policy will at first lower interest rates, but will eventually raise them.

Equity yields

The case for using equity yields as a target starts from the view that the 'principal channel through which financial policies and events affect business activity (the real economy) is the demand for storable and durable good⁻' (Tobin 1969a, p. 173). The incentive to undertake real investment depends upon the value of existing capital equipment relative to the cost of constructing new. An increase in the market value of existing capital, relative to the cost of producing new capital, would provide an incentive to undertake additional capital construction, while a fall in the value of existing capital relative to the costs of producing new would reduce the incentive to undertake additional construction. Thus monetary policy will be 'easier' if it leads to a fall in the cost of producing new storable and durable goods relative to their current market value, and 'tighter' if it does the opposite. According to this view, 'the valuation of investment goods relative to their cost is the prime indicator and proper target of monetary policy'. (Brainard and Tobin 1968, p. 104).

The valuation of existing investment goods is reflected in stock market prices of equity capital and in equity yields. When the real rate of return on equity capital rises this is likely to be because the market has lowered its valuation of existing capital equipment, and the converse is true when the real rate of return on equity capital falls. Thus an advantage of this type of target is that it is fairly readily observable, and easily compared with a price index of new investment to give an indication of the thrust of policy.

However, suitable indicators are not so readily available for all types of stockable and durable goods. This is particularly the case, for example, with consumer durables.

Even in the equity market it is not always the case that equity yields, which reflect the view of financial investors, equally reflect the views of those responsible for undertaking real investment. Under some circumstances, such as the peaks and troughs of the trade cycle, stock market prices may be influenced more by speculative attitudes and less by a rational evaluation of the future profitability of companies. On the other hand the efficient markets hypothesis does imply that stock prices are determined rationally and will reflect economic considerations and not simply speculative attitudes. Tobin himself does 'not share the common view that the stock market is a speculative sideshow without relevance to the main economic circus'. (1969a, p. 174).

Domestic credit expansion

In so far as the money supply is a good target of policy, it is sometimes argued that it needs modifying in an open economy which is operating a fixed exchange rate system, in order to take account of net inflows/outflows of money across the foreign exchanges.

Domestic Credit Expansion is, briefly, the change in the money supply adjusted to take account of the effect on it of any external surplus or deficit.

> DCE is thus approximately equal to the increase in the money supply plus those sterling funds accruing to the authorities by their provision of foreign exchange, from one source or another, for the accommodation of an external deficit (or conversely, minus the sterling finance required to accommodate an external surplus). (Bank of England 1969, pp. 363–364).

When DCE has been advocated as a target of policy it has usually been as a supplementary one for use with a money supply target. Thus a tight money supply target could be met either by a restrictive domestic monetary policy (low DCE) or a high DCE coupled with a large payments deficit. The additional use of DCE as a target would enable the authorities to make sure that the money supply targets were being met by the appropriate domestic policies.

Indicators

An ideal indicator is an intermediate variable that gives the authorities an early and unambiguous signal of the direction and strength of policy.

Saving (1967) has emphasized the need for indicators to show the extent to which changes in intermediate targets are due to policy and to what extent due to non-policy influences. Intermediate target variables may reach desired levels partly as a result of changes in the non-policy variables acting upon them, and not only as the result of policy action. Where this is the case attainment of the targets of policy may not mean attainment of the goals. For example, if interest rates are taken as the target of policy, they may be influenced not only by policy action but also by changes in such factors as the productivity of capital, and businessmen's expectations. Suppose the current economic structure is characterized by inflation and that price stability is a goal of policy. If the authorities believe that interest rates and the rate of inflation are inversly related, then with interest rates as the target, they will take action to raise them. But while their policy is taking effect, businessmen may become more pessimistic, lowering the investment schedule and consequently also lowering the equilibrium rate of interest, possibly well below the pre-policy market level. In this case investment and aggregate demand would have fallen, possibly by enough to secure price stability. But the policy has raised market interest rates above their pre-policy level, with the result that investment falls even further, possibly causing unemployment. The actual movement of interest rates is thus affected by both policy and non-policy influences, which in this example are pulling in opposite directions: policy is raising rates while the change in businessmen's expectations is tending to pull them down. According to Saving (1967, p. 450) what the policy maker wants under these sorts of circumstances is

> a separation of the change in this target variable into a policy effect and an exogenous effect. Since observation of the changes in the target variable yields only the total effect, some other variable or combination of variables is required to reflect the policy effect.

Brunner and Meltzer (1969) have drawn attention to the need for monetary indicators wherever monetary policies are being compared from the point of view of their effect on the economy. If comparisons of this sort are to be made, then there must be a kind of scale to which reference can be made. The problem is similar to that involved in making all kinds of comparisons. For example, if we wish to know whether today or yesterday was the warmer then we must have some observable indicator of warmth, such as the extent to which mercury moves along a glass tube.

If an indicator is satisfactorily to fulfil these functions of measuring the direction and strength of policy, then there are several desirable characteristics that it should possess. Firstly it should be observable. Secondly, the indicator must be close to the instruments of policy, and have a stable relationship to them so that the thrust of action can be quickly reflected in the indicator. Thirdly the indicator should primarily be influenced by policy action and only to a much lesser extent influenced in the same period by non-policy variables, or it must be possible to separate and identify the policy and non-policy influences on the indicator. Finally the indicator should bear a stable and close relationship to the target of policy.

Clearly the possible indicators of policy are likely to exhibit these desirable characteristics in varying degrees. Many intermediate variables have been suggested as indicators, including all those that we have already discussed as possible targets. The choice of target will influence the choice of indicator. Thus if the money supply (in one or other of its versions) is chosen as the target of policy then something like the supply of high-powered money (i.e. the monetary base) may well be chosen as the indicator. Other widely suggested indicators include the assets and liabilities of the banks and short-term interest rates.

Rules versus discretion

In this final section we consider the question of whether monetary policy should be conducted at the discretion of the authorities or on the basis of a predetermined rule or automatic pilot. Discretionary monetary policy means operating the weapons of monetary control in the direction, manner and extent considered appropriate by the monetary authorities in the light of the relevant economic circumstances and the desired economic goals. Monetary rules means operating monetary policy according to a predetermined rule, largely irrespective of prevailing economic circumstances. Several rules have been suggested, but perhaps the most widely discussed is that by which the money supply would be expanded at a fairly uniform rate over time.

The monetarist case for the abandonment of discretionary or activist monetary policies and the adoption of a monetary rule has several strands to it. We shall find it useful to consider them under three headings:

(1) Activist policies are unnecessary.
(2) They can not be successful and may be positively harmful.
(3) There are definite benefits of using a monetary rule.

Activist policies are unnecessary

Monetarists argue that an activist monetary policy is unnecessary because the economy is inherently stable and any fluctuations that do occur will be short-lived. This view was originally presented in terms of the slopes and stability of the *IS* and *LM* curves. In the absence of authority initiated changes in the supply of money, the monetarist view on the stability of the demand for money and on its interest elasticity suggested a stable and steeply sloped *LM* curve. The *IS* curve too was regarded as being fairly stable because the private sector expenditures from which it is largely derived were also considered to be stable. Friedman's work on the consumption function for example, where consumption is seen as a function of permanent income, implies that fluctuations in current income will induce relatively small changes in consumption. The *IS* curve was also considered by monetarists to have a fairly flat slope because they believed that a change in interest rates would affect a wide range of expenditures. These views are illustrated in *Figure 11.5*.

Shifts in the *IS* curve are seen as being infrequent and small, e.g. from IS_0 to IS_1, while in the absence of money supply changes the *LM* curve is virtually stationary and fairly steeply sloped. The consequence is that *IS* curve shifts, when they do occur, have little effect on output, being largely offset by consequential changes in the rate of interest. Thus in *Figure 11.5* the shift of the *IS* curve raises the rate of interest from i_0 to i_1 but increases income only from Y_0 to Y_1.

The non-monetarist counter-argument is that while normal consumption expenditure may indeed be relatively stable, other components of aggregate demand are not. Investment, for example, will depend very much on the state of businessmen's expectations, which themselves are peculiarly prone to waves of optimism and pessimism. Export demand too may fluctuate significantly, as may the demand for consumer durables.

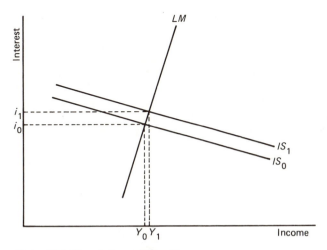

Figure 11.5 The relative stability of income

The second attack on the necessity for discretionary policy came when Friedman and Phelps developed the vertical Phillips curve and the concept of the natural rate of unemployment. According to this analysis, flexible wages and prices will ensure that output and employment will always converge onto their natural or full employment levels and the destabilizing influence on output of changes in demand are only temporary and disappear before an activist policy could become effective.

Discretionary policy has been defended against this argument on two main grounds. First, it is argued that the long-run Phillips curve is not vertical, so that an activist policy is required to prevent output and employment settling at less than their natural levels. Secondly, even if the long-run Phillips curve is vertical, the long run may be a long time in coming, in which case activist policy is necessary to hasten the movement of output and employment towards their natural levels.

With the emergence of the Rational Expectations school, the case against the necessity of discretionary policy appeared complete. The integration of rational expectations into the vertical Phillips curve analysis implied that there would not even be short-run fluctuations away from the natural rates of output and unemployment (see Chapter 9, pp. 205–207). Any anticipated shock would be fed into their expectations by rational economic agents and thereby would ensure the coincidence of expected and actual rates of inflation and the maintenance of output and employment at their natural levels. There would not appear to be any need for discretionary policy, even in the short run.

This conclusion however has been criticized from several different viewpoints. Some writers do not accept that expectations are formed rationally, while others argue that even accepting that rational expectations exist there may still be scope for discretionary policy. Let us consider some of the major criticisms.

To begin with there is the argument that economic agents do in fact often behave in a non-rational manner. Price expectations may well be formed without reference to all available information and forecasting errors continue to be made, especially in the short run, which may be of considerable duration.

A second criticism says that information may not be freely available. In this case the accumulation of information generates costs which must be set against the benefits of being able to make improved forecasts. The economically rational agent would then continue to collect information until the marginal cost of doing so was equal to the marginal benefit. Under such circumstances, economic agents may not anticipate and offset shocks to the level of output and employment even though they are behaving rationally in the sense of comparing the costs and benefits of acquiring information.

Thirdly it is argued that markets do not clear because prices and wages are inflexible and may not respond fully and immediately to new relevant information. Thus it is argued that because of such things as long-term contracts, it may be impossible or costly to adjust prices quickly, and consequently they remain somewhat sticky. Of course the flexibility of prices may increase over time, making the natural levels of output and employment eventually attainable, but the time-lag involved may be intolerably long, particularly from the point of view of politicians. In this case, even if information were freely available there may still be a need for discretionary policy, at least in the short run.

Another assumption of the rational expectations hypothesis that has come under criticism is that the authorities do not have any information advantage in the sense of having access to information which is not similarly available to all other economic agents. If they do have an advantage there may be a need for policy action, at least until the authorities loose their advantage.

Finally, some critics have drawn attention to the incompatability of the predictions of the rational expectations hypothesis with the experience of the real world. As Modigliani (1977, p. 6) has put it,

> the most glaring flaw of ... [rational expectations] ... is its inconsistency with the evidence: if it were valid, deviations of unemployment from the natural rate would be small and transitory – in which case the General Theory would not have been written

Many supporters of rational expectations concede that if prices are inflexible, information costly to obtain, and the authorities possess information advantage, then there is indeed scope for policy action to influence real variables. But it is not a desirable policy they argue, because it rests on the ability of the authorities to deceive economic agents into making forecasting errors. It is policy based on deception. Instead of such a policy, it is argued that the authorities should aim to improve the flow of information, reduce the costs of acquiring it and try to improve the flexibility of prices.

Activist policies won't work

Monetarists argue that the vertical Phillips curve not only makes activist monetary policies superfluous but also makes them impotent as far as influencing real variables are concerned, at least in the long run. Similarly, rational expectations are considered to render activist policies impotent even in the short run. The counter-arguments presented by the activists are those considered above in the context of the need for discretionary policy. Additionally it is suggested that discretionary policies may be capable of exerting an influence on real variables during the time lag before economic agents discover what the policy is. A change of policy may initially be interpreted by economic agents as random deviations from the original policy. Gradually of course people will come to recognize that there has been a change of policy and adjust their behaviour accordingly. During this intervening period systematic forecasting errors may be made. The rational expectations school however argue that changes in policy are usually widely publicized and therefore immediately, or at least very quickly, recognized as such by economic agents.

Some critics of rational expectations have pointed out that even if policy is not changed, economic agents may expect it to be. If, for example, a government has pursued a restrictive monetary policy during its period of office, people may expect it to relax the policy in the pre-election period. If the policy is in fact adhered to, then forecasting errors may be made by economic agents.

A different and older argument for believing discretionary policies cannot work, does not depend on the presence of flexible prices, a vertical Phillips curve, or rational expectations. The argument is simply that the authorities do not have, in the present state of knowledge, sufficient information to be able to operate their policies successfully. Indeed, the pursuit of activist policies under such circumstances may actually prove destabilizing.

One of the major problems faced by any monetary authority conducting an activist policy is the existence of time lags, which may be either discrete or distributed. A discrete time lag is one where the time interval between the two relevant events is definite and clear-cut. For example, when a person makes out a cheque there will be a definite time lapse before his account is debited. To say that the time lag is definite is not to say that it is fixed in the sense of being the same duration for all similar pairs of events. Thus when a person makes a cheque out to cash in order to obtain coins and notes, the time lag before his account is debited is likely to be shorter than when he makes a cheque out payable to a customer of another bank. In both cases, however, the time lag is clearly defined: there is a clear beginning to the time lag and a clear-cut end to it. With distributed time lags, however, this is not the case. Either the beginning of the time lag is not definite, or the end is not, or perhaps both. This will happen if the 'event' at the start of the

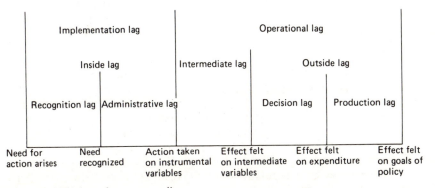

Figure 11.6 The lags of monetary policy

time lag is spread out over a significant period of time, or if the consequences of that event which brings the time lag to an end is distributed over time. Examples of distributed time lags will presently emerge in our discussion of the various lags associated with monetary policy.

There are of course many ways of classifying all the different lags and *Figure 11.6* sets out one such classification. Basically the lags can be divided into those associated with the implementation of policy and those associated with its operation. The implementation lags are those of recognition and administration while the operational lags are intermediate, decision and production.

The recognition lag

This is the time interval between the need for monetary action arising and the time when that need is recognized by those who take the decision to act. It arises partly because the need for action is not likely to be acknowledged until it is reflected in the statistical data and other indicators upon which forecasts are based and decisions subsequently made. Its length will also depend upon the time it takes for the 'evidence' to work its way through the organizational structure of policy-making from those who prepare the evidence to those who take the decisions.

The administrative lag

This refers to the interval between the time when the decision-taking authorities recognize the need for some sort of action and the time when they actually take that action. Its length depends principally upon the administrative procedures involved and partly upon the attitude of the authorities towards taking action quickly, frequently, and in small doses, rather than more slowly, infrequently and in larger doses. It is usually argued that the administrative procedures involved in monetary policy are fairly straightforward and the length of this lag fairly short.

The intermediate lag

This is the time lapse between the authorities taking action and the effect of that action being felt on the intermediate variables such as the money supply, the level of interest rates or the availability of credit. This is a distributed lag, for the effect on the intermediate target variables of the authorities' actions may build up over a period of time.

The decision lag

The decision lag pertains to the interval between changes in intermediate target variables and changes in the level and composition of expenditures. The expenditure decisions will be influenced by the intermediate target variables through a variety of routes. Consequently some decisions will be affected before others, so that the effects of changes in the intermediate target variables will be distributed over time. Moreover, changes in some types of expenditure decision will affect other types of expenditure decision. For example, changes in the decision to consume may have repercussions on investment expenditure decisions. The decision lag then is very much a distributed one.

The production lag

This is the lag between changes in expenditure and the effects of those changes being felt on employment, output and prices.

The existence of these lags means that the total time lapse between the need for action arising and the effect of the action being felt on the goals of policy may be considerable. During this time lapse it is quite possible that the underlying situation may have changed, so that by the end of the complete lag, when the monetary action taken at the beginning of the lag is pushing the goal variables in a particular direction, the real need at that point in time may be for a monetary policy working in the opposite direction. In this case monetary policy would be aggrevating the situation; it would be destabilizing rather than stabilizing.

Of course, the more effective monetary policy is in influencing its goal variables the more important the time lags become. If monetary policy were a completely impotent weapon of control, then the existence of time lags would be of little consequence. If monetary action had no effect on the goals of policy and were incapable of influencing them in any direction, then it would be nonsense to talk about monetary policy working in the wrong direction. If, on the other hand, monetary policy is a very effective weapon, in the sense of being able to achieve quantitatively large changes in the goals of policy, then inappropriate timing of its use could prove very harmful.

The existence of lags would not be such an obstacle to the effective operation of monetary policy if they were always of the same duration, and if their duration were known with certainty. Then provided the need for action could be forecast sufficiently far in advance, policy could be implemented at that point in time, which with due regard to the length of the time lags, would mean it was operating in the right direction at the right time. When the lags are variable however, and there is much evidence to suggest that they are, then it becomes much more difficult to decide on the right timing of monetary policy.

Whether the existence of lags provides support for the abandonment of discretionary monetary policy and the adoption of a monetary rule clearly depends, in the first instance, on the length of the time lags, their variability and the potency of monetary variables.

Even if the timing of monetary policy were perfect, however, there would still remain the problem of the scale on which the policy should be implemented. If, starting from a position of equilibrium, a need for action arises as a result of a non-policy disturbance there are the questions of how much and what sort of a response is required to just offset the 'shock' to the system. Unfortunately our knowledge of the quantitative effectiveness of changes in monetary variables is sadly deficient.

This quantitative uncertainty of effect means that it is extremely unlikely that monetary policy could be used to keep the economy on the desired path and indeed opens up the possibility of an 'over-reaction' which creates a situation which may be worse than the one with which it was designed to deal.

Against these criticisms, those who favour discretionary monetary policy may counter-argue that past experience is a poor guide to assessing future performance. Experience of mistakes in the past is bound to improve performance in the future. Techniques of control are becoming more refined and sophisticated, while the vast amount of empirical evidence being accumulated is helping to improve our understanding of the working and effectiveness of monetary policy. Improvements in forecasting techniques and performance are likely to lead to better timing of monetary action.

In any case, even if we do not yet have all the knowledge necessary for the effective operation of monetary policy, and even if the techniques of monetary control are still rather clumsy, it would be foolish to abandon discretionary monetary policy altogether, for to do so would simply make it impossible for us to improve our knowledge and techniques and to move closer to that state of affairs where monetary policy can be used to 'fine-tune' the economy.

The weight that one attaches to these counter-arguments depends in large measure on the extent to which it is believed that performance in the operation of monetary policy has in fact improved in the past and is likely to improve in the future. Monetary rule advocates clearly believe that the past and the expected improvements are not sufficient to justify the continued operation of discretionary policy. Certainly we can hope that the continued operation of such a policy would dramatically improve performance, but we cannot be certain that it would. The question is whether it is worthwhile to bear the current cost of operating a discretionary policy in the hope of an uncertain benefit in the future.

Another line of argument against the effectiveness of activist policies concerns the subjugation of economic policy to the political goals of government. The argument is quite simply that governments are likely to follow restrictive policies early in their life and then to generate booms just before an election in order to increase their chances of being re-elected. Evidence for such a political business cycle in the UK, however, is far from conclusive.

In similar vein, it has been argued that the way in which discretionary monetary policy is used will reflect the ideological views of the government of the day. Different governments will have different priorities; one may be more willing to use exchange rate changes as the means of achieving external balance using monetary policy for internal balance, while another may prefer to use monetary policy to attain external balance and fiscal policy for internal. Changes of government may well mean an abrupt change in the way in which monetary policy is used.

The benefits of a monetary rule

There are a number of different rules that have been suggested, but probably the best known is the demand standard rule which advocates expanding the money supply at a uniform rate per annum, roughly the rate at which real full employment output is growing. The rationale for this rule is derived simply from the formula $MV = Py$. The formula is true for any time period, so we have

$$M_t \, V_t = P_t \, y_t$$
$$M_{t-1} \, V_{t-1} = P_{t-1} \, y_{t-1}$$

If we substract the second of these expressions from the first and divide the difference by the first we get

$$\frac{M_t V_t - M_{t-1} \, V_{t-1}}{M_t \, V_t} = \frac{P_t \, y_t - P_{t-1} \, y_{t-1}}{P_t \, y_t}$$

If we now assert that V is constant, then $V_t = V_{t-1}$ and the Vs cancel out in the left-hand side of the expression. Similarly, if we want a constant price level, then we want $P_t = P_{t-1}$. Again the Ps cancel on the right-hand side of the expression.

The whole expression has reduced to

$$\frac{M_t - M_{t-1}}{M_t} = \frac{y_t - y_{t-1}}{y_t}$$

The left-hand side is the proportionate increase in the money supply and the right-hand side the proportionate increase in real output. Thus, if it is desired to stabilize the price level, as we have assumed above, then the implication for the money supply is clear. It must grow at the same rate as that for real output. If it is believed that in the long run V falls somewhat, then the rule would need to be adjusted so as to allow for larger increases in nominal M. Similarly, if a slightly rising rather than constant price level is required, then again the rule would have to be adjusted to permit a more generous growth of nominal M.

The rule is concerned primarily with the long run rather than the short run. It recognizes that V is not in fact a constant, having short-run seasonal and cyclical fluctuations, but in the long run is a highly stable phenomenon. Again, the rate of growth of y may vary in the short run, so that it is with the much more stable long-run rate of growth that the rule should be concerned.

The first positive argument in favour of a monetary rule of this sort is that it provides a built-in stabilizer for dealing with short-run cyclical fluctuations. In recessions the supply of money will be increasing at its nominal 'rule' rate, but the demand for money will fall below its long-run trend rate. This will create an excess supply of money, without the need to increase the nominal money stock above its rule rate, as discretionary monetary policy would probably do. Similarly, in booms the rule would require the money supply to increase at its nominal rate while the demand for money would rise above its trend rate, creating an excess demand for money – a situation similar to that which discretionary monetary policy would try to create. Thus under this type of monetary rule:

> Both recessions and boom would call forth automatically the kind of imbalance between supply of, and demand for, money that is cyclically corrective. No one has a principle for doing any better by discretionary means. (Shaw 1969, p. 111).

If however the demand for money does not grow at a uniform rate, then uniform growth in the money supply might well be destabilizing rather than stabilizing.

A second argument in favour of a rule is that it would create a more stable environment conducive to the long-term planning and investment necessary for rapid economic growth. Money, it is argued, is at its best when it is unobtrusive, and this is when it is increasing according to a rule that is known to everyone.

Another argument is that a well publicized rule for monetary growth will influence the behaviour of those involved in collective bargaining by making it clear that the authorities will not expand the money supply so as to accommodate inflationary wage increases. The implication implicit in this argument is that in the absence of such finance inflationary wage increases will result in unemployment. How successful a monetary growth rule would be in restraining wage increases then depends on:

(1) Whether wage bargainers believe the authorities will keep to their rule.
(2) The extent to which they think that inflationary wage increases which are not accommodated by monetary expansion will result in unemployment.
(3) How much importance they attach to such prospective unemployment.

The final argument is that a monetary rule will impose a discipline on governments, preventing them from using economic policy primarily for electoral purposes.

12

Techniques of monetary control

In this chapter we will consider the main techniques available to the authorities for controlling the stock of money. We shall take as our definition of the money stock, sterling M3.

$$\text{Money stock} = \begin{array}{l} \text{Sterling deposits of} \\ \text{UK residents} \end{array} + \begin{array}{l} \text{Notes and coin in circulation} \\ \text{with the public} \end{array} \quad (12.1)$$

The currency component of the money stock is relatively unimportant, and no attempt is made by the authorities to control it for the purpose of altering the total stock of money. We shall therefore ignore it and concentrate our attention on the techniques for the control of deposits. Broadly there are two approaches to the control of deposits. The first is to use instruments of policy that act directly upon the demand for or supply of deposits themselves. The other is to use instruments that are aimed at one or more of the so-called supply side counterparts of the volume of deposits. We will first explain the difference between the two broad approaches and then move on to consider the actual techniques.

Deposits appear on the liabilities side of the balance sheets of monetary institutions. But they must be matched in total by credit counterparts featuring on the assets side of those same balance sheets.

The consolidated balance sheet of the monetary sector may be shown as:

Monetary Sector Balance Sheet (12.2)

Liabilities	*Assets*
Sterling deposits of:	Sterling lending to:
UK residents	UK public sector
Overseas sector	UK private sector
Net foreign currency deposits	Overseas sector
Non-deposit liabilities	

In this presentation of the monetary sector's balance sheet the assets are shown by borrowing sector and not, as is more usual, by the type of asset held. Since total liabilities equal total assets, we can, by substituting the money stock definition (12.1) into the balance sheet (12.2), express changes in the money stock in terms of changes in the other items in the balance sheet.

Increase in money stock   =   Increase in: (12.3)

                                              Currency in circulation

                               + Change in sterling lending to:
                                                UK public sector
                                                UK private sector
                                                Overseas sector

                               − Increase in:
                                                Overseas sterling deposits
                                                Net foreign currency deposits
                                                Non-deposit liabilities

We can now set out the public sector borrowing requirement (PSBR), showing the sources of finance by lending sector.

    PSBR = Increase in currency in circulation   (12.4)
                + Sales of public sector debt to non-bank private sector
                + External (overseas) finance
                + Sterling borrowing from the banking sector

By re-arranging (12.4) to express the item 'sterling borrowing from the banking sector' in terms of the other items in the public sector financing expression (12.4), we can, by substituting into (12.3) (replacing 'sterling lending to U.K. public sector'), obtain the accounting relationship which links the money stock to the PSBR.

Increase in   = PSBR   (12.5)
money stock − Sales of public sector debt to non-bank private sector
                + Increase in sterling (bank) lending to private sector
                − External (overseas) finance
                − Increase in
                         Overseas sterling deposits
                         Net foreign currency deposits
                         Non-deposit liabilities
                + Increase in sterling lending to overseas sector

By combining all external influences and ignoring non-deposit liabilities, this relationship may be simplified to:

Increase   = PSBR − Sales of public   + Increase in   + Net   (12.6)
in money   sector debt to   bank lending   external
stock   the non-bank   to the   flows
                              private sector   private
                                               sector

This expression (12.6) highlights the 'supply side' counterparts of the money stock. A change in that stock must be associated with a change in one or more of these counterparts. It should be emphasized, however, that the expression is an identity and not a behavioural relationship. There is not, for example, a simple one-for-one relationship between changes in the PSBR and the stock of money. Changes in the PSBR may, for instance, be associated with changes in private sector financial wealth which could, in turn, affect bank lending and private sector purchases of public sector debt. Thus a change in one of the components of the identity is likely to have repercussions on the other components. (These complex interrelationships among the components are explored by using a large-scale structure model of the financial system (see Middleton *et al.* 1981). Despite this qualification to the use of the accounting identity, expression (12.6) does focus attention on those variables that the authorities could seek to influence as a way of controlling the money supply.

Summarizing so far, we have shown that in order to control the money stock the authorities could aim directly at bank deposits, using techniques which would have a fairly direct effect on that particular aggregate. Alternatively the authorities could aim to control the money stock more indirectly by influencing the supply side counterparts set out on the right-hand side of expression (12.6).

We can now consider the variety of techniques available to the authorities to influence the money stock via either of the two approaches we have identified. The actual number of techniques that may be specified is largely a question of classification, i.e. the degree of aggregation or disaggregation that is being entered into. Classifications, like definitions, are not right or wrong, but only more or less useful for the purpose in hand. Thus for some purposes it may be most appropriate to distinguish between market instruments and direct controls. The latter would embrace 'directives' or 'orders' issued to those who supply deposits and/or supply-side counterparts, or to those who demand them. In practice, such controls are invariably imposed on the suppliers. They usually relate directly to the price or quantity of the variable, but not necessarily so. Thus an order to banks that they must keep an X% backing of 'cash' to deposits would be a direct control aimed at influencing bank deposits. Market controls would embrace all those techniques which work through market forces to influence the price and quantity of the variable being aimed at. They usually involve the purchase or sale of financial assets by the monetary authorities. Such a classification may not be all-embracing however, and another category may have to be included. Thus some of the techniques that may be used to influence the PSBR do not readily fit into the market or direct control categories, and may be more usefully categorized separately. A variation on the market/direct controls classification separates the market controls into those that act on prices (interest rates) and those that act on the supply of reserve assets to the banks (sometimes called reserve base control, sometimes called – more narrowly – monetary base control).

Another classification simply distinguishes between techniques that aim to influence prices with quantities adjusting accordingly, and those that aim at quantities with prices adjusting accordingly.

It is of course quite possible to devise other classifications, but those we have mentioned are sufficient to illustrate the point that there is no 'right' classification and no fixed number of control techniques.

In what follows we shall find it useful to draw a broad distinction between direct controls and market controls, while treating control of the PSBR as a distinct category. In discussing market techniques we shall pay particular attention to reserve base control. A schematic summary of the techniques we shall consider is set out in *Figure 12.1*.

Any assessment of monetary control techniques, like the assessment of any instrument of policy, requires the answer to two basic questions: (i) does the instrument achieve its aims? (ii) what side-effects does it have? The latter question is usually considered from the point of view of the twin criteria of equity and efficiency. Consideration of space will necessitate us giving only the briefest

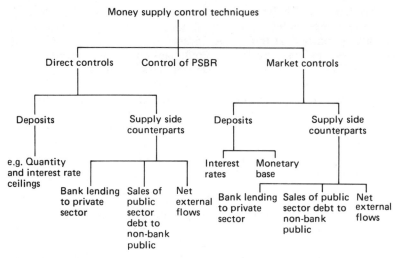

Figure 12.1 A classification of techniques for controlling the money supply

consideration to the equity and efficiency arguments, but a good account is provided by Gowland (1982).

We shall consider first the direct controls, which can be applied either to deposits or to the supply side counterparts.

Direct controls over deposits

We can illustrate the nature and variety of such controls by considering three kinds:

(1) Imposing a ceiling on the rate of interest that can be paid on deposits. An example of such a scheme is Regulation Q in the United States. This kind of control was also used in the UK in 1973. The aim is to reduce the relative attractiveness of holding bank deposits and thereby encourage depositors to hold other kinds of financial assets instead, particularly deposits with building societies. Often the regulation is applied in a way which discriminates between large and small deposits, with the latter bearing the restriction or greater restriction. In this form it is often evaded by such means as aggregating small deposits. It is widely condemned by economists. Gowland, for example, has said (1982, p. 77): 'Of all controls, this one is the most unfair, least effective and most disastrous in its effects.'
(2) The authorities may impose reserve ratios on the banks over and above those that might be imposed for prudential reasons. This is one way of operating a reserve asset system of control, the pros and cons of which we shall be considering later. This particular control can be applied selectively, so as to distinguish between different kinds of deposits, e.g. encourage/discourage the rate of growth of time deposits *vis-à-vis* demand deposits.
(3) Imposing a quantitative restriction on banks which is directly related to a particular level or rate of growth of deposits. This could take various forms including absolute ceilings on deposits with penalties imposed for exceeding the ceiling. One possible penalty would be to require banks to place a percentage

of their excess deposits with the central bank. To the extent that these 'official' deposits earn less interest than could be obtained elsewhere, they affect the profit maximizing 'output' of the banks. In essence such official deposits are tantamount to a tax on banks. If, for example, banks are required to place in a non-interest-bearing account with the central bank one-half of any extra deposits they receive, then only one-half of the extra deposits can earn interest. This has the same effect on the banks as leaving them with all their extra deposits, but taxing away one-half of the revenue that the deposits earn for them. How effective the 'tax' is depends on the percentage of deposits called for, and the difference between any interest paid on the official deposits and that which could be earned on them in their most profitable employment. The larger the percentage call, and the bigger the interest difference, the greater the 'tax'.

Direct controls on deposits suffer from much the same disadvantage as any other kind of direct control, namely evasion, inefficiency and inequity. Let us illustrate. Many of those affected by the direct controls will try to find ways of circumventing them. For example, ultimate borrowers and lenders may deal directly with one another instead of going through a bank, a process known as disintermediation. Sometimes the bank may still be involved in such transactions, but acting more as a broker than a dealer. Similarly a bank may provide an acceptance credit, whereby it guarantees a bill made out by, say, company A and then sold to B. In this way B's holding of the bank guaranteed bill is a substitute for holding a bank deposit, while A has obtained credit via the bank-guaranteed bill instead of directly from the bank. Thus to all intents and purpose the bank's normal deposit/loan business has been maintained.

Another likely outcome of using direct controls is that non-controlled intermediaries may start dealing in similar kinds of deposits, i.e. so-called parallel markets may arise.

A third possibility is that the controlled intermediaries will if possible develop substitutes for the controlled liabilities and engage in liability management. To illustrate, if the direct control applies only to the bank's interest-bearing deposits then they could encourage depositors to switch from interest-bearing to non-interest-bearing deposits.

Clearly there are numerous opportunities for evading the direct control. Such evasion, moreover, generates inefficiency and inequity. The controlled intermediaries are being 'unfairly' discriminated against and prevented from competing for business. The parallel markets and disintermediation are likely to be less efficient than the original markets and business that they replace, for otherwise they would not need the protection of the direct control to stimulate their growth.

Further, as a result of these evasive practices, the reliability of the money supply statistics will be thrown into question. The introduction and subsequent removal of such controls is likely to mean that the observed change in the money supply figures overstates the real change in the underlying situation.

The extent to which evasive techniques are employed depends to a large extent on how long the direct controls over deposits are kept in force. If they are used only for short periods then it may not be worthwhile incurring the costs involved in developing the evasive techniques. Such direct controls therefore are most likely to be effective if employed as a short-duration weapon.

However even if the control is used for a prolonged period and as a result is largely evaded, it could still have some effect. The evasion is likely to be less than complete, and in any case the economic behaviour of those involved in the evasion procedures may be affected. If people, who in the absence of the control would have preferred to hold bank deposits, now hold instead some alternative asset, then that asset, be it a bank guaranteed bill or whatever, is a less than perfect substitute for the bank deposits. As a result the holders may alter their economic behaviour in ways which the authorities were looking for when they imposed the direct control. The importance attached to this argument depends to a large extent on the view one has of the uniqueness of money and of the monetary transmission mechanism.

Direct controls over supply-side counterparts

Bank lending to the private sector

These controls usually take the form of ceilings on bank credit and may be applied so as to discriminate between particular kinds of borrower or between loans for particular purposes. For example, the ceiling may be imposed on loans to persons but not on loans to businesses, or it may apply to loans for speculative use but not to loans that promote exports.

These controls, like those on deposits, are likely to stimulate the development and use of evasion techniques. If, for example, the controls are applied to some kinds of bank lending but not to others, then borrowers may claim to be borrowing for an unregulated purpose but in fact use the credit obtained for a regulated one. This does not mean the borrower is making false statements to the banks, but simply re-deploying the total funds available to him. As an example take a borrower who has two kinds of expenditure in mind, say an improvement to his house and the purchase of a new car. He has funds available for the finance of one expenditure, but has to borrow to finance the other. If credit is not available at all then the borrower would only undertake the house improvement. If there are restrictions on the availability of bank credit for the car purchase, but not for house improvements, then the borrower would simply claim to be borrowing for the latter unregulated use, and employ his own funds to finance the purchase of the car.

Because of the virtual impossibility of controlling all credit channels, imposing a control on only some of them is likely to divert borrowers to the uncontrolled channels. However, as with direct controls over bank deposits, the evasion of these controls may not be complete even in the long run. In any case there may be some relevant effects on the behaviour of those involved in the evasion process.

Whether or not the controls are effective, they are criticized for being unfair and inefficient. They are unfair in discriminating against particular providers of credit and particular kinds of borrower. The controls generate inefficiency for two main reasons. Firstly they prevent the more efficient banks from growing at the expense of the less efficient ones and thereby create a mal-allocation of resources within the banking sector. Similarly a larger proportion of total credit flows are being provided by methods and institutions which are less efficient than those they have replaced. Secondly, because the banks cannot lend as much as they would wish, they are likely to favour the larger, well established, 'safe' customers. For this reason, small, new, but efficient and growing firms are discriminated against with adverse effects on industrial efficiency and economic growth. It has been argued that

the main purpose for introducing such controls in this country has been to reduce the need to raise interest rates at least in the short term, by causing banks to ration their lending (Green Paper, 1980).

While it may be true that the 'price' of the controlled credit may be kept down in this way, the increase in the demand for uncontrolled credit may well push up its price, possibly to such an extent that the average price of credit actually increases.

In summary, direct controls on credit suffer from all the same limitations and disadvantages as direct controls on deposits, and enjoy the same qualified merits.

Sales of public sector debt to the non-bank private sector

This technique implies 'forcing' the non-bank private sector to lend to the public sector. It is generally unpopular in the UK because of the political implications and consequently is most likely to be resorted to on any significant scale either in times of war or as a by-product of some other objective. Thus the two best-known examples of this technique in the UK are post-war credits and import deposits. Under the former, the government during the Second World War reduced certain personal income tax allowances, but credited to the tax-payers the extra tax that they paid, the actual refund of the tax to be made when the war was over. Import deposits were introduced in the UK in November 1968. Importers had to deposit with the authorities, interest-free for a period of six months, 50% of the value of their imports (with the exception of food and raw materials). Effectively therefore these deposits were interest-free loans to the authorities for a period of six months.

Net external flows

Attempting to influence the money supply by acting upon net external flows necessarily means trying to 'worsen' the balance of payments, i.e. reducing a surplus or going from surplus to deficit, etc. But the balance of payments is itself a goal of policy, so to use it as an instrument of monetary control in the way required could be seen as counterproductive. However, there may be a case for a short-run worsening of the balance of payments to reduce the rate of growth of the money supply if by so doing the longer-run prospects are improved.

The most obvious direct controls over net external flows are exchange controls. In the UK these controls have usually been employed to protect the balance of payments and restrict the net outflow of money. In so doing they have kept the money supply higher than it would otherwise have been. The relaxation or removal of such controls, as for example in November 1979, may be regarded as a way of encouraging an outflow of money. Other countries (e.g. W. Germany) have designed and employed inward exchange controls, restricting the inflow of money.

Market controls over deposits

The term market controls, as it is being used in this context, implies two conditions. Firstly, the authorities are trying to influence the stock of money by influencing the conditions of money supply and/or money demand. Secondly, they are doing this by means other than 'directing' what those conditions will be. Thus, imposing a ceiling on the rate of interest payable on deposits is a direct control. Carrying out open-market operations to influence that rate is a market control.

We will find it helpful to sub-divide the market controls over deposits into two categories. The first of these embraces those techniques which are intended to influence the price of deposits, with quantity adjusting passively. The second category covers those market controls which are aimed at influencing quantity, with price being the passive adjuster. Given the interdependence between price and quantity this division of technique is clearly arbitrary. Nevertheless it will help us to distinguish between the main kinds of market control.

Interest rate controls

This particular technique aims to control the level of deposits by means of interest-induced changes in the demand for them. The rationale for the technique is that the demand for deposits is a stable function of a small number of variables, notably the price level, the level of real output and the opportunity cost of holding deposits. The opportunity cost is assumed to be the interest on near-money assets.

If then the authorities can push up interest rates, there will be some switching out of bank deposits and into interest-bearing assets. The loss of deposits (liabilities of the banks) will have to be matched by an equivalent fall in bank assets, i.e. there will have to be a fall in bank lending to the public and/or private sectors. If one envisages a demand curve for bank deposits which is inversely related to the rate of interest (on other assets), then this technique sees monetary control being achieved by sliding along that curve.

There are several problems associated with this technique. First of all, in order for the authorities to be able to operate the technique effectively the demand for deposits function must be stable and its interest elasticity known. If these conditions are not met, then the authorities cannot know what change in interest rates is necessary in order to induce the required change in demand.

A second problem is that some bank deposits bear interest. In their case the effective opportunity cost of holding them is the differential between the rate of interest available on other assets and the rate being paid on these deposits. Consequently a general increase in interest rates may simply encourage depositors to switch fron non-interest-bearing deposits to interest-bearing ones. In this case the total demand for deposits may remain unchanged. The real opportunity cost of holding deposits is the difference between the own rate of interest on deposits and those available elsewhere, and it is this differential that the authorities must act upon if they are to secure movements along the demand for deposits curve. In fact, because deposit rates tend to be very flexible, it is possible (and indeed has happened) that at times of monetary restriction they are bid up more than other interest rates, so that the differential behaves 'perversely' and the demand for deposits actually rises.

Monetary base control

Monetary base control is one particular version of a broader category of controls which sees the volume of bank deposits being regulated through the quantity of reserve assets held by the banks. The monetary base proposal picks out the cash reserves of the banks as being the appropriate reserve assets to act upon.

The proposal for monetary base control is closely related to the monetary base model of money supply determination which we considered in Chapter 4. The view likely to be taken of this particular control technique will depend very much on how adequately one considers the monetary base approach explains the determination of the money supply.

At the intuitive level the case for monetary base control has been stated clearly by Friedman:

Trying to control the money supply through 'fiscal policy ... and interest rates' [Quoting the Green Paper on Monetary Control] is trying to control the output of one item (money) through altering the demand for it by manipulating the incomes of its users (that is the role of fiscal policy) or the prices of substitutes for it (that is the role of interest rates). A precise analogy is like trying to control the output of motor cars by altering the incomes of potential purchasers and manipulating rail and air fares. In principle, possible in both cases, but in practice highly inefficient. Far easier to control the output of motor cars by controlling the availability of a basic raw material, say steel, to the manufacturers – a precise analogy to controlling the money supply by controlling the availability of base money to banks and others. (1980, p. 58).

Rather more formally, the proposal for monetary base control may be derived, as we have indicated, from the monetary base approach to the determination of the money supply. Recalling equation (4.14) this may be written

$$M = mB$$

where M is the money stock, B the monetary base, and m the money supply multiplier. If m is reasonably stable, then a change in B will cause a multiple change in M.

In fact there are two broad approaches to monetary base control which can be derived from equation (4.14). The first of these is the non-mandatory approach and is in fact the one we have been concerned with so far. In this approach the money supply multiplier reflects the cash reserve ratio which the banks have voluntarily imposed upon themselves for prudential reasons. The second approach is that based on a mandatory requirement placed on the banks to observe a minimum specified cash reserve ratio. It is the non-mandatory scheme which has probably been most strongly advocated for the UK, and at the same time has been the most strongly condemned. Thus for example, Griffiths, one of the major advocates of monetary base control in the UK, has argued

The banks' demand for base money, their cash ratio, depends on the maturity structure of deposits, the frequency of cash withdrawal, the opportunity cost of holding cash as measured by day to day interest rates, and the banks' aversion to risk. As these will differ from bank to bank, so will each bank's desired cash ratio. However, a uniform cash ratio is not necessary for monetary control; all that is required is that banks' demands for cash are reasonably stable ... (Griffiths 1979, p. 39).

On the other hand, Gowland concludes his survey of monetary base techniques by saying:

It seems clear that sole reliance on a non-mandatory reserve or monetary base system would lead to disaster. (Gowland 1982, p. 74).

Some of the reasons for these differences of opinion will emerge if we now go on to consider problems of implementing the schemes, and some of their major advantages and disadvantages.

Some problems of implementation

The critics of monetary base control argue that the problems of implementation are such as to make it ineffective as a mechanism for achieving short-run control over the money supply. This is thought to be particularly true of the non-mandatory version.

To begin with it is argued both that the money supply multiplier is unstable and that the authorities cannot control the base itself. These arguments were considered fully in Chapter 4. Summarizing those arguments, advocates of monetary base control claim that the money supply multiplier is stable, and that changes in its numerical value can be predicted either from a detailed structural model of the financial sector or, following the St. Louis approach, from single equation estimates. On the other hand critics of the approach would support the view of Savage that:

> Forecasting the money supply multiplier would ... pose formidable problems under existing institutional arrangements since it would depend on the entire vector of variables (income, wealth, relevant interest rates, and so on) which influence banks' portfolio behaviour and the publics asset preferences. (1980, p. 82).

In the context of a non-mandatory scheme the variability of the banks' cash reserve ratio is particularly emphasized by critics. It has been suggested that the minimum ratio to which the banks could operate may well be 1% or less.

As far as the base itself is concerned advocates of the technique argue that as it comprises the liabilities of the monetary authorities and is produced solely by them, then they have sufficient if not complete control to make the technique effective. The opposite view has again been expressed by Savage.

> ... in the present institutional setting it would seem difficult to regulate the base at all precisely since it would be affected by fluctuations in gilt sales, errors in forecasting the public sector borrowing requirement and changes in foreign exchange reserves – the very problems which bedevil attempts to control the money supply under the present system. (1980, p. 82).

Let us now consider some of the other arguments surrounding monetary base control. It has been suggested for example that the effects of the control may be evaded via the growth of certain banks and other institutions not signficantly affected by the monetary base regulations. Institutions other than the clearing banks need far less cash to meet the demands for it of their depositors, and settle debts between themselves by using their accounts with the clearing banks. For these reasons the non-clearing banks' holdings of base money are extremely small, and they will be affected by monetary base control only to the extent that it will increase the cost to them of competing for and attracting the deposits needed to support their lending.

Opponents of monetary base control argue that in fact it is the same as interest rate control, but that the interest rate fluctuations would be greater. We consider first whether monetary base control is only another guise for interest rate control. That it is was clearly stated in the Green Paper on Monetary Control (p. 8).

> This approach therefore is intended to provide a means for the markets to generate the interest rates necessary to bring the rate of growth of the money supply back towards the desired path.

The opposite view has been put forward by Friedman (1980, p. 57):

> Direct control of the monetary base is an alternative to fiscal policy and interest rates as a means of controlling monetary growth. Of course, direct control of monetary base will affect interest rates ... but that is a very different thing from controlling monetary growth through interest rates.

The former of these two views can be illustrated by using a simple supply-demand diagram. *Figure 12.2* refers to the asset side of banks' activities but the implications for deposits and the money supply are very much the same. The supply curve of credit is shown to be a direct function of the rate of interest on loans and investments, reflecting the portfolio approach to bank behaviour (see Chapter 10). The position of the curve will depend upon the cash reserves of the banks; a reduction in these reserves will shift the curve to the left. The demand for credit is shown as an inverse function of the 'same interest rates. If we assume that the market clears by price, i.e. by the rate of interest, then the quantity of credit will be *OA*. *Figure 12.2* demonstrates that if the authorities wish to reduce the quantity of credit to OB they can do so either by acting on interest rates and pushing them up to i_2 or by reducing the cash reserves of the banks such that the supply curve of credit shifts to S_2S_2. The end result is the same in both cases – an interest rate of i_2 and quantity of OB.

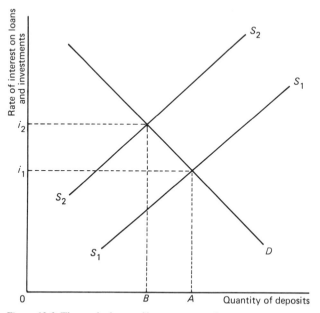

Figure 12.2 The equivalence of interest rate and monetary base control

This result, however, is a consequence of the assumption that the position and elasticity of the demand curve and the elasticity of the supply curve are known. In practice of course there will be some uncertainty about all of these. Let us illustrate the consequences by assuming that the authorities are unsure of the elasticity of the demand curve. In *Figure 12.3* there are two possible demand curves and we assume that the authorities believe that there is an equal likelihood of either of them being the 'true' one. Initially the quantity of credit is OA and the rate of interest i_1. If now the authorities want to reduce the quantity of credit to OB then they cannot be certain about what is required either using interest rate controls or monetary base control. If they use interest rates then they would need to raise them to i_2 in the case of the D_1D_1 curve and to i_3, in the case of the D_2D_2 curve. If the authorities believe there is an equal likelihood of either of them being the 'true' curve then they may opt for an interest rate mid-way between i_2 and i_3, i.e. i_4. At that rate of interest the quantity of credit would be OC in the case of the D_1D_1 curve and OD the case of the D_2D_2 curve. If the authorities use monetary base control instead, they would aim to shift the supply curve to S_2S_2. If the demand curve then turned out to be D_1D_1 the quantity of credit would be OE while if the demand curve were D_2D_2 the quantity would be OF. Clearly monetary base control enables the authorities to get closer to their target than does interest rate control.

Other differences between interest rate and monetary base control have been identified. Artis and Lewis (1981) for example argue that monetary base control gives the banks a more active role to play in the process of monetary control and

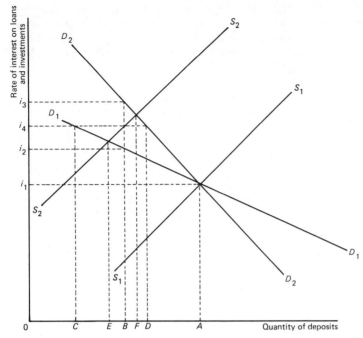

Figure 12.3 The non-equivalence of interest rate and monetary base control

allows them to choose the mechanism by which adjustment to a more expansionary or contractionary policy will be made. They particularly emphasize the point that because of the cost to the banks of adjusting to a shortage of reserves they would be

> likely to exercise much greater care in future when granting facilities and open credit lines ... There would also be an incentive for banks to refrain from lending and build up reserves when reserve shortages are anticipated. Accordingly, surges in monetary growth may be less likely to occur. (Artis and Lewis, 1981, p. 124).

But would interest rate fluctuations be greater with monetary base control? Certainly this was the view of the three Bank of England economists who argued that monetary base control 'would continually threaten frequent and potentially massive movements in interest rates, if not complete instability' (Foot, Goodhart and Hotson 1979, p. 153).

There are clearly problems of deciding which interest rates are being referred to, but the analysis based on *Figure 12.3* certainly supports the view that there would be greater variability in interest rates on bank credit. Gowland, however, has argued that this is a consequence of assuming that markets always clear by price. In his view it is quite likely that they do not, in which case a reserve base system may reduce variability in rates.

Griffiths (1979) argues that monetary base control would generate more frequent, but relatively small adjustments to interest rates. But this he suggests, would avoid the need for the less frequent, but much larger changes in interest rates which characterize alternative methods of monetary control.

The final criticism of monetary base control which we shall consider is the one that argues that in order to make this method of control effective there will need to be institutional changes which in themselves are undesirable. It is true that those who advocate monetary base control have made various suggestions for changes in financial structure and practice. One suggestion is that there should be only a single reserve asset, say deposits held with the central bank. Another proposal is that if the central bank's 'lender of last resort' facility is not to frustrate monetary base control, then the central bank must refrain from acting as a lender of *first* resort and instead fulfil its proper role of lender of *last* resort. If it does, then since such last resort loans are for a limited period and at a price that the central bank can decide, then over a period of, say, three months the pursuit of monetary base control need not be made impossible by this central bank facility. It has also been suggested that the method of selling government stock should be by market clearing tender. Such changes would indeed have implications for institutions such as the discount houses and the stock jobbers, but Griffiths (1979, p. 41) argues that such structural changes as may follow need not be undesirable because 'it is difficult to justify the present structure if it involves imposing artificial requirements which are effectively a form of subsidy'.

Market controls over supply-side counterparts

Most of the market controls that we shall consider in this section are designed to work through interest rates.

Bank lending to the private sector

The assumption underlying this technique is that the demand for credit is inversely related to the price that has to be paid for it, i.e. the rate of interest charged on bank credit. Then if policy can induce the banks to put up those interest charges there will be a contraction in the demand for credit and a fall in the quantity of it supplied.

If the authorities are to have any hope of success in using this technique then the demand for credit must be stable and its interest-elasticity known. If these conditions are not met the authorities will have no idea what increase in interest is required to bring about the desired reduction in the volume of bank lending.

A limitation of this technique is that an increase in the interest charge on bank loans may well, either through competitive pressures and/or conventional practice, result in an increase in interest rates being paid on bank deposits. To the extent that this happens bank deposits become more attractive to hold, which is in conflict with the authority's attempt to reduce bank deposits.

A further difficulty with this technique is that it may be frustrated by the inflation expectations of borrowers. An increase in the nominal interest charge on bank loans may not lead to a contraction in the demand for them if potential borrowers believe that prices will rise by a bigger percentage than the increase in nominal interest rates. In other words the demand for credit may well be a function of real, rather than nominal, interest rates. If it is, then in an inflationary context the authorities must raise nominal interest rates quickly and sharply if they are to avoid the situation where nominal interest rates lag behind inflation expectations and real rates thereby fall.

Another possible source of frustration for the technique arises if it is used as part of a package to deflate the economy. This may depress profits and squeeze firms of their liquidity. As a result their demand for credit may increase. In this case the contraction up the demand curve in response to higher interest rates is offset by a rightward shift of the entire curve.

A final disadvantage of this technique is common to all those controls that work through changing interest rates. Frequent variations in, and high levels of interest rates, have a number of drawbacks. To begin with they are politically unpopular. One of the major reasons for this is because of their effect on the cost of mortgages and through this the likely voting behaviour of mortgagees.

Business confidence is also likely to be adversely affected by frequent changes of interest rates. As a result, levels of investment and economic growth are likely to be lower then they would be with more stable interest rates. There are also likely to be some directional effects. One reason for this is that interest rate changes have their greatest impact upon investments which are long-lived and relatively risk-free. It is partly for these reasons that industries such as construction are particularly badly affected by fluctuating interest rates.

Despite all the foregoing difficulties, there is fairly general agreement that if interest rates were pushed high enough, the demand for credit could be curtailed. There is less agreement, however, on how far interest rates would have to be pushed and on whether such increases would be politically and socially acceptable.

Sales of public sector debt to the non-bank private sector

In order to persuade the non-bank public to lend more to the public sector, public sector debt must be made more attractive. This can be done in a number of ways, such as offering a wider range of debt with different characteristics. Thus in the 1970s several new kinds of government debt were introduced in the UK. Probably the most important way of increasing sales of public sector debt is to increase its relative price attractiveness, i.e. to offer higher interest rates. This can be achieved by appropriate open-market operations.

This method, like all the others, is not without problems. If the non-bank public are persuaded to lend more to the public sector, then this may well be at the expense of lending less to the private sector, i.e. there may be 'crowding-out'. The real problem for the authorities is not the resulting fall in private expenditure (after all that is one of the purposes of reducing the money supply) but the fact that it would probably be the investment rather than the consumption component of private expenditure which would fall.

To some extent the purpose of the increased sales of public sector debt may be frustrated if the debt sold is so short-dated that its substitution for money in the portfolios of wealth-holders leaves their liquidity positions virtually unchanged and with it their economic behaviour.

Finally the policy may be difficult to implement if it means forcing securities onto an unwilling market. The question of how best to sell government securities has long been of concern to the authorities and has generated a variety of proposals. In the 1970s the authorities developed the so-called Duke of York tactic for creating the conditions that would enable large-scale sales of government securities (see pp. 278–279).

Net external flows

There are several market controls that may be used to influence the net external flows into or out of the country. Tariffs are one possibility but interest rates are more likely to be effective. Lowering interest rates would be expected to increase the outflows of capital thereby contracting the money supply. However, lower interest rates are, as we have seen, apt to expand the domestic component of the money supply (i.e. DCE) and therefore would be working in two opposite directions.

Another possibility would be to influence net external flows through changes in the exchange rate. With a freely floating exchange rate, the external value of a country's currency adjusts so as to maintain the supply and demand for the currency in equilibrium, with a zero net inflow/outflow of money.[1] If the authorities intervene in the foreign exchange market in order to keep the external value of the currency below its equilibrium level then there will be a net inflow of money into the country. The authorities cannot control both the exchange rate and the supply of money. If they decide that the net inflow of money must be reduced or removed, then the authorities must play a more passive role in terms of non-intervention in the foreign exchange market, and allow the exchange rate to move to levels that they might otherwise resist. In principle, the authorities could also influence the external currency flow by actively intervening in the foreign exchange market and deliberately forcing up the external value of the country's currency above its equilibrium level. Such action would be expected to cause a net outflow of money, in contrast to the passive approach of allowing the exchange to float up towards its equilibrium level, where the consequence will be a reduced inflow of money.

Controlling the PSBR

The PSBR can be influenced either by acting upon government outlays and/or by acting upon government revenues. The outlays may be classified into (i) expenditure on goods and services; (ii) transfer payments both to persons and businesses; (iii) interest payments; (iv) loans. Revenues come from three main sources: (i) taxes; (ii) charges on goods and services; and (iii) the sale of assets. To reduce the PSBR, therefore, the authorities must try to reduce one or more of the categories of expenditure and/or increase the size of one or more of the categories of revenue.

There are a number of difficulties associated with attempts to change the PSBR. To begin with, cuts in public expenditure may be politically unpopular both because of social welfare and electoral implications. Likewise, attempts to increase taxes would be 'electorally' unpopular.

Secondly, government outlays and revenues are administratively very difficult to vary in the short run. Even in the long run they cannot be controlled precisely. For example, the authorities cannot fix what their total tax revenue will be, they can only fix tax rates and allowances. Similarly while the authorities can fix rates for unemployment benefits and other transfers, they cannot fix the number of recipients and cannot therefore fix the total outlay. Even for categories of expenditure more obviously under the control of the authorities it is still virtually impossible to guarantee that targets will be met.

In any case, changes in the PSBR may well have effects on other supply side counterparts which cannot be accurately quantified. For example, a reduction in public sector loans to the private sector may well increase the demand for bank credit.

On the 'plus' side however control of the PSBR has the advantage that it avoids the major problems associated with the other techniques, and would, if pushed far enough, achieve its goal of influencing the money supply. It is not a technique to be used for achieving short-run control over the money supply, but is much more a weapon for medium and longer-run control.

Notes

1. Under freely floating exchange rates, an inflow will result in an appreciation of the exchange rate, producing a matching outflow: the exchange rate moves to clear the foreign exchange market. A freely floating exchange rate will not however completely isolate £M3 from external flows because it can be affected by changes in the composition of the flows. Suppose, for example, there is an improvement in the current account, resulting in an inflow to the private sector and an increase in domestic residents' deposits, and this is matched by a fall in non-residents' holdings of sterling bank deposits. The net effect of these flows is a direct increase in £M3, since non-residents' sterling deposits are excluded from the £M3 definition (see Lomax and Mowl 1978 and Bank of England 1978b).

13

Monetary policy in the UK since the Second World War

Since the Second World War, monetary policy has undergone several re-appraisals, which has meant that the targets of policy have changed over time, and a large number of instruments have been employed. The start of each decade for example has witnessed a major change in the methods and/or role of monetary policy, while the 1970s alone saw three significant changes.

1945–7: cheap money

From 1945 to 1947 monetary policy was directed towards a 'cheap money' policy. There were several possible reasons for this. Firstly, the war effort had been financed at low rates of interest and it was thought desirable and possible to continue this for the transitional years of adjustment from a wartime to a peacetime economy. The Chancellor, Dr Dalton, was particularly concerned with the re-distribution effects of cheap money.

> First and foremost comes the relief to the taxpayer, on whom falls the burden of servicing the National Debt ... But cheap money benefits not only the Central Government. It benefits the local authorities: it benefits private industry at large: and indeed it benefits other members of the British Commonwealth of Nations. (Dalton 1947).

Secondly, there was general scepticism about the interest-elasticity of aggregate expenditure, particular investment expenditure. This scepticism reflected both *a priori* reasoning and the evidence of business attitude surveys. Moreover the authorities believed that 'High interest rates are more effective in preventing excessive investment in periods of prosperity than are lower interest rates in encouraging investment in periods of depression.' (White Paper on Employment Policy 1944). Thirdly, it was the possibility of recession and not a boom which was the fear of the authorities for the post-transition period.

Bank Rate was kept at 2% where it had been since 1932 (apart from a very brief period at the start of the war), and open-market operations were undertaken to force other interest rates down to artificially low levels. However, the policy became increasingly difficult to enforce as the gilt-edge market came under pressure following such diverse events as a 'fuel crisis', a 'dollar crisis' and a 'sterling convertability crisis', and it was abandoned in late 1947.

1948–51: 'neutral' policy

From the collapse of the cheap money policy until the end of 1951 monetary policy was 'neutral' or dormant. Dow (1964 p. 227) noted that

> for a year or two in the middle of the period there is scarcely a sentence in any official statement which mentions credit or interest rates,

while *The Banker* of February 1951 commented

> the authorities have never given any sign of intent to use control over the volume of money as a positive instrument of economic discipline.

1951–60: the 'new' monetary policy

A number of factors contributed towards the re-emergence of monetary policy in the early 1950s. The Conservative government which took office in November 1951 was committed to removing direct controls and relying more on market forces. At the same time inflation was reaching what was then, historically high levels. The ranking of priorities also changed, with the new administration placing greater importance on the strength of sterling and the balance of payments.

Bank Rate was raised in November 1951, and the 'new' monetary policy had begun. Several aspects of this policy need to be distinguished. Let us start by looking at the role of interest rates. Short-term rates were used primarily to influence the external situation. An increase in Bank Rate was both a symbol of the government's attitude and intentions and a guide to the way policy was going. An upward movement in short-term rates would be used to attract an inflow on the capital account of the balance of payments.

As far as long-term rates were concerned there was still fairly general scepticism about their effect on the incentive to invest. There was however a new view emerging in the early 1950s which was based on the so-called 'locking-in effect.' Essentially what this said was that a fall in the market price of government securities would discourage holders of these securities from selling them in order to raise funds to finance an expenditure or make another loan. Such lendable or spendable funds would be 'locked-in'. Thus interest rates were seen as playing a role in influencing the availability of funds to finance expenditure, rather than influencing the incentive to spend. In fact the locking-in effect was never really put to the test because of the authorities' concern for the management of the National Debt.

The Second World War had seen an enormous increase in the size of the National Debt, and the authorities became increasingly concerned that the gilt-edged market should be 'orderly'. This was considered necessary if new borrowing by the government was to be made on favourable terms. Consequently the authorities developed a policy of 'leaning into the wind' whereby they would sell on a bullish market and buy on a bearish one. In this way they reduced the fluctuations in interest rates. This conflict in the objectives of the authorities as managers of the National Debt and as operators of monetary policy has been an important feature of monetary policy for much of the post-war period.

The early 1950s saw a change in the way by which authorities tried to control the commercial banks. Prior to 1951 the 'old orthodox' method of control, as it was called, focused on the banks' cash ratio. After the war however the banks found themselves holding large quantities of Treasury bills which they could readily sell to replenish any cash deficiency. This led to the 'new orthodox' method of control, whereby the banks were required to observe a 30% liquid assets ratio as well as a cash to deposits ratio. The authorities could then act on the availability of liquid assets to the banks, so that it was the liquid assets ratio that was the fulcrum of policy. This view of how the authorities controlled the banks was clearly stated by the Radcliffe Committee (1959, para. 376).

> It [the Bank of England] readily varies its own holding of Treasury bills in order to secure reasonable stability of the Treasury bill rate. Treasury bills can therefore always be turned into cash without much disturbance of the market rates of discount on them. It follows that the Bank cannot restrain the lending operations of the clearing banks by limiting the creation of cash without losing its assurance of the stability of the rate on Treasury bills. It is because of this circumstance that the effective base of bank credit has become the liquid assets (based on the availability of Treasury bills) instead of the supply of cash.

Such control over the banks was aimed not at their deposits and the supply of money, but at bank advances and the supply of credit.

Monetary policy during the 50s was characterized by the so-called 'package deal', whereby

> a collective of measures, intended to have a deflationary impact, ... [were] ... imposed amid some publicity, all together at one date; and then ... [were] ... folowed by piecemeal, gradual and unpublicized relaxation (Dow 1964, p. 252).

Included in the package deal were:

(1) Variations in Bank Rate (changed 17 times between November 1951 and the end of 1960). Bank Rate was the 'symbol' of government policy and probably had some psychological effect. Additionally it caused other short-term rates to move in the same direction and thereby affected the net inflow of capital.
(2) Variation of HP regulations. These were probably successful in influencing aggregate demand, but the effects were concentrated on consumer durable goods industries.
(3) Direct quantitative control of bank advances. At first used fairly loosely, they had by 1957 become clearly quantitative controls.

The 1960s

The monetary policy of the 1960s was heralded by the first call for special deposits. In fact they had been introduced into the armoury of monetary policy in 1958, but were not actually used until April 1960.

Special deposits are called by, and placed with, the Bank of England, where they remain 'frozen' till such time as the Bank releases them. In the 1960s calls for special deposits were made only on the clearing banks. They were expressed as a percentage of a bank's total deposits and earned interest for the bank, usually at a rate close to that on Treasury bills. The effect on the banks was initially to reduce their liquidity; this necessitated adjustments elsewhere in their balance sheets in order to maintain their required liquidity ratio. The intention of the authorities in making a call for special deposits appears to have been that the adjustment in bank portfolios would take the form of reduced bank advances to the private sector. The particular advantage of the special deposits scheme to the authorities was that it appeared to enable them to achieve a reduction in bank liquidity and bank advances without the need to push up interest rates by as much as would be required by the use of other techniques.

In fact the banks did not have to adjust to a call for special deposits by reducing their advances. It was just as possible that they would re-build their liquid assets by purchasing Treasury bills and pay for them by selling bonds to the authorities. Given the authorities' concern for the stability of interest rates, they stood prepared to take up the bonds being offered for sale. As a call for special deposits had a similar effect to increasing the banks' liquid assets ratio, it might have been expected that the banks would re-adjust their holdings of other assets, switching from investments to the more profitable advances.

It has been argued that the aim of special deposits was not so much to bring about the absolute reduction in bank advances as to remove excess liquidity in the banking system, liquidity which might otherwise be used as the basis for an expansion of bank lending. The alternative way of removing the excess liquidity was funding which would have brought about an unacceptable increase in interest rates.

The monetary policy of the 1960s broadly followed the approach that had been laid down in the previous decade. Bank advances and credit flows generally remained the major target of policy. Primary reliance for influencing such flows was placed on direct controls. Quantitative controls over bank advances became increasingly formal and specific and were extended to hire purchase companies. Regulation of hire purchase terms (initial deposit and repayment period), although not strictly a weapon of monetary control (being under the regulation of the Department of Trade and Industry rather than the Bank of England), remained an important element in the authorities' policy of credit regulation. Finally, variations in Bank Rate continued to be used for its psychological effect and to influence the balance of payments through capital flows.

Direct controls were not popular either with the banks or with the authorities. Over the period as a whole the operation of the controls generated all the side-effects that elementary theory predicts (see Chapter 12, pp. 255–258). The banks themselves found some ways of evading the controls, but perhaps more importantly the banks lost business as new kinds of credit and new channels for its provision grew up outside of the controls.

Moreover the banks had no incentive to compete amongst themselves, and the whole banking system was widely criticized for its lack of competition and efficiency (see National Board for Prices and Incomes 1967; Monopolies Commission 1968). The major symptoms of this lack of competition included (i) the collective agreement (i.e. cartel arrangement) among the banks to fix interest rates on deposits and minimum charges on advances to customers; (ii) the agreement among the discount houses to take up, at a common price, that part of the weekly issue of Treasury bills not sold to higher bidders.

The late 1960s witnessed the first tentative steps towards targeting the money supply. The decade had seen the increasing influence of monetarists and monetarism on both sides of the Atlantic, though the greater emphasis attached to monetary aggregates by the UK authorities in the late 1960s was attributable less to their acceptance of monetarist principles than to the need to borrow from the IMF. In response to pressure from that institution the UK government agreed in a first Letter of Intent (November 1967) to reduce the rate of growth of the money supply. In a second Letter, the authorities agreed to set a target for the increase of DCE in 1969–70. An important implication of the setting of such targets was that the authorities would hence forth be prepared to see greater flexibility in interest rates. This change in the attitude of the authorities towards the gilt-edged market was made explicit in the Competition and Credit Control arrangements introduced in 1971.

Competition and credit control

The new arrangements for the regulation of the monetary system, which were introduced in September 1971 and which were known as Competition and Credit Control, represented a major change in the thinking of the monetary authorities.

It had become clear that the methods of control which had evolved during the previous two decades were not only incapable of achieving their objectives but had also inhibited competition, promoted inefficiency and caused a maldistribution of financial resources.

The new arrangements consequently were intended and designed to achieve two main objectives. The first was to remove the obstacles to, and generally stimulate, competition among the various institutions involved in the provision of credit. The second was to provide a more effective means of controlling credit flows and the supply of money. The new package of regulations would

> involve less reliance on particular methods of influencing bank and finance house lending and more reliance on changes in interest rates, supported by calls for special deposits on the basis of a reserve ratio across the whole of the banking system (Bank of England 1971a, p. 189).

Essentially the authorities had decided to abandon direct controls and instead to use market controls to influence certain of the supply side counterparts of the money supply. This was clearly stated by the Governor of the Bank of England:

> Basically what we have in mind is a system under which the allocation of credit is primarily determined by its cost ... we expect to achieve our objectives through market means ... the resulting change in relative rates of return will then induce shifts in the asset portfolios of both the public and the banks (Bank of England 1971b, p. 196).

The main features of the new scheme were:

(1) All banks to hold a uniform minimum reserve ratio of 12½% of their sterling deposit liabilities in certain specified reserve assets.
(2) These reserve assets to comprise balances with the Bank of England (other than special deposits), British and Northern Ireland Treasury bills, company tax reserve certificates, money at call with the London money market, British government stocks with one year or less to run to maturity, local authority bills eligible for rediscount at the Bank of England, and (up to a maximum of 2% of deposits) commercial bills eligible for rediscount at the Bank of England.
(3) All banks required to deposit with the Bank of England such special deposits as the Bank may from time to time call for. Such calls to be expressed as a percentage of each bank's deposit liabilities and to be a uniform percentage across the banking system.
(4) The London and Scottish clearing banks to abandon their collective agreement on interest rates.
(5) To support these changes, the extent of the Bank of England's activities in the gilt-edged market was restricted from the time of the proposals (May). It was decided that from that date the Bank would no longer stand prepared to buy stock outright, unless the stock had one year or less to run to maturity; longer-dated stock would only be bought at the Bank's discretion and initiative. Provided it did not unduly shorten the life of the debt the Bank would still be prepared to meet any bids for 'tap' or other stocks held by them and which they wished to sell.
(6) The discount houses would no longer tender at an agreed price for Treasury bills, but would continue to bid in sufficient amount to cover the tender.

(7) Arrangements similar to those made with the banks were agreed with the finance houses. They were requested to observe a minimum reserve asset ratio of 10% and the Bank could, under certain circumstances, call special deposits from them at a higher rate than from the banks, though the total of the finance houses' reserve assets and special deposits would not represent a higher ratio of their liabilities than that for the banks.

We ought perhaps to add as an eighth point that the authorities 'hedged their bet' by including two clauses which were inconsistent with the spirit of the new approach. The first of these was that 'the authorities would continue to provide the banks with such qualitative guidance as may be appropriate'. The second was that the Bank would have the right to impose a ceiling on the interest that the banks could pay on small (i.e. retail) deposits. The intention of this 'Regulation Q' was allegedly to protect the building societies and savings banks.

The target(s) of the policy was never made clear. Some commentators saw it targeting on the money supply (M3), others saw it targeting on credit flows, with the money supply acting more as an indicator.

One thing the authorities did make clear was that the inclusion of a reserve asset ratio did not mean that the policy was going to use manipulation of the reserves available to the banks as the basis for a multiple contraction/expansion of bank deposits. This was clearly stated by the Governor of the Bank of England (Bank of England 1971b, p. 197).

> It is not to be expected that the mechanism of minimum reserve ratio and special deposits can be used to achieve some precise multiple contraction or expansion of bank assets. Rather the intention is to use our control over liquidity, which these instruments will reinforce, to influence the structure of interest rates. The resulting change in relative rates of return will then induce shifts in the current portfolios of both the public and the banks.

CCC came into being against a background of high and rising unemployment and a slow growth of output. The stance of government demand management policy was clearly expansionary. In the last quarter of 1971 there was a significant increase in the rate of growth of the money supply, and the Barber budget of 1972 was very expansionary. Further 'dramatic' increases in M3 occurred in the first and second quarters of 1972 (nearly 5% and 8% respectively). A chronic deterioration of the balance of payments and the threat of industrial action by trade unions combined to trigger off a run on sterling which culminated in the crisis of June 1972. The UK government's response was to float the pound and quit the Common Market 'snake'.

The sterling outflow of late June seriously deteriorated the liquidity position of the banks, and the authorities had to support them by an agreement for the sale and repurchase of gilts, an agreement which was seen by some commentators as being contrary to the spirit of CCC.

From the middle of 1972 the expansionary stance of the authorities changed to one of trying to restrain the rate of growth of the money supply. In August the Bank requested the banks to restrict their lending for property and financial transactions.

In October 1972 Bank Rate was replaced by Minimum Lending Rate. This new rate was to be determined by the average rate of discount for Treasury bills plus 0.5% rounded up to the nearest 0.25%. Thus the minimum lending rate would normally follow market rates, but should the authorities wish to give a definite lead to rates, then the operation of the formula could be temporarily suspended and the

Bank's minimum lending rate fixed independently of it. The new rate was originally fixed at 1¼% above the Bank Rate it replaced, and by the end of the year had risen to 9%. In fact the second half of 1972 saw an increase in interest rates generally, and there were calls for special deposits in early November and late December. This tightening of monetary conditions however may be aptly described as 'too little, too late'.

Bank lending to the private sector and M3 continued to rise at a very considerable rate during the first half of 1973, yet interest rates were allowed to fall. Another sterling crisis in early July marked, if not caused, the start of a more restrictive policy, for in the second half of the year interest rates were pushed up significantly. MLR, for example, which had been at 7½% at the end of June had risen to 13% by the middle of November, while bank base rates rose by 3% between the beginning of July and the end of August. But the money supply continued its explosive path upwards.

In September the banks and finance houses were reminded by the Bank of England of the need to exercise significant restraint in the provision of personal credit for uses other than house purchase. 'Regulation Q' was invoked at the same time, the banks being requested not to pay more than 9½% on deposits under £10,000. November saw the Bank making a 2% call for special deposits and directing the banks to raise their base lending rates.

But still the money supply continued to rise dramatically. Thus in the two years from December 1971, M3 had risen by 60%. CCC appeared to have failed and the authorities were forced to introduce a new technique of control.

What had gone wrong? One view is that the underlying situation was not as bad as it appeared. The statistics, it is argued, were misleading with M3 overstating both the increase in the 'money supply' and the increase in the supply of credit. The removal of the quantitative controls over bank lending enabled the banks to compete with the other financial intermediaries on a normal basis. Consequently there was a significant amount of re-intermediation with the clearing banks attracting back business that had been lost to the non-clearing banks during the period of direct controls. The extent to which this occurred however is far from clear. Moreover, the significance of the re-intermediation depends on the extent to which bank credit and bank liabilities have the same impacts on the flows of expenditure as do the credit and liabilities of non-clearing banks. The view taken of this depends on which transmission mechanism one believes in, and how one regards the liquidity of money compared with other assets.

A further reason for the alleged inadequacy of the M3 statistics was the 'round-tripping' which occurred. For a variety of reasons the banks bid down the rates of interest charged on overdrafts to such an extent that it became profitable for some borrowers to draw on their overdraft facilities and re-deposit the funds obtained in the money markets. To the extent that these deposits were taken up by the banks the M3 figures were distorted. In similar fashion, and quantitatively probably more important, a loophole in the tax system made it profitable to borrow from banks and re-deposit with them via the purchase of a certificate of deposit.

A rather different reason for arguing that the situation was not as bad as it appeared was that the increase in the money supply simply kept pace with the demand for it. However a demand-determined money supply can still be excessive with regard to its inflationary effects. It has in any case been strongly argued that the increase in the money supply during this period was largely in excess of the demand for it (Artis and Lewis 1976, 1981).

The rapid growth in the supply of money (i.e. M3) has been attributed to several factors, some of which we have already mentioned. One approach emphasizes the removal of the lending ceilings, which resulted not only in reintermediation but also in the satisfying of a previously frustrated demand for credit. An alternative approach has been to emphasize that CCC increased the reserve assets available to the banks and made them more aggressive in their lending activities. Related to this view is the argument that the authorities were impeded in their attempts to control the banks because of the 'excess' reserves that the banks held, and also because of the banks' ability to obtain additional reserves as required.

It was, however, through interest rates that CCC was supposed to work, and its 'failure' has been attributed to the unwillingness and/or inability of the authorities actively to control interest rates. Trying to avoid the use of direct controls over bank advances, the authorities operated on the assumption that market activities that pushed up the rate of interest on funds available to the banks would force the banks to raise their lending rates. Unfortunately for the authorities this was not an inevitable linkage. In fact, as we have already seen, in November 1973 the authorities had to resort to ordering the banks to raise their base lending rates.

Quite apart from the question of the ability of the authorities to raise interest rates, there was the separate question of whether they were prepared to accept the consequences of doing so. With inflationary expectations rising, an increase in real interest rates requires larger and larger increases in nominal rates. The political implications of very high nominal interest rates may well have loomed large in the thinking of the authorities, for clearly they were not prepared to countenance the interest rate levels that would have been necessary to achieve any significant effect on the demand for bank credit.

December 1973–9

The authorities' response was to introduce in December 1973 a new form of quantitative control known as supplementary special deposits (or more usually 'the corset'). There is some disagreement as to whether this represented a complete break with CCC or whether it was reconcilable with it. Thus the Bank claimed that:

> As far as possible the supplementary scheme is intended to maintain the main structural benefits to the banking system of the reforms introduced in 1971. (Bank of England March 1974, p. 37).

Similarly Coghlan (1981, p. 75) has argued

> SSDs did not represent a change in emphasis from the CCC regime introduced in 1971, but rather an expedient to maintain control of the money supply while preserving the main characteristics of the existing system.

On the other hand, Gowland says that the introduction of SSDs was the first step of a new 'new approach':

> the authorities replaced the new approach (CCC) with a totally different method of monetary control … . There were also a number of volte-face which meant the total abandonment of the principles of competition and credit control. (Gowland 1982, p. 144).

Supplementary special deposits and IBELs (Bank of England 1982b)

The SSDs scheme was essentially a quantitative regulation. But unlike those quantitative controls that had been employed in earlier periods the SSDs scheme was aimed at bank liabilities rather than bank assets. Moreover it was a particular category of bank liabilities that was being aimed at; specifically their interest-bearing deposits from the non-bank private sector (their interest-bearing eligible liabilities, IBELs). Non-interest-bearing eligible liabilities were excluded because it was felt that they were not within the banks' ability to control.

Under the scheme a maximum rate of growth of IBELs was set by the authorities. If this were exceeded by the banks, they were obliged to place a proportion of the excess with the Bank of England in the form of non-interest-earning supplementary special deposits. The required proportion increased as the size of the excess IBELs increased. Initially the figures were: for an excess up to 1%, then 5% must go in SSDs; an excess between 1% and 3% required an SSD of 25%; an excess over 3% meant a 50% SSD. Subsequently (April 1974) the band ranges to which these SSD rates applied were altered to 0–3%, 3–5% and over 5% respectively.

The basic objective of the scheme was clearly stated by the Bank of England (1974, p. 37) It was to

> restrain the pace of monetary expansion, including the pace at which banks extend new facilities for bank lending, without requiring rises in short-term interest rates and bank lending rates to unacceptable hights.

The scheme was clearly open to all the problems associated with quantitative controls which were discussed in Chapter 12. Numerous opportunities existed for evasion, and to the extent that they were used there would be increased inefficiency and inequity. It would, for example, have been possible for the banks to have engaged in 'switching' within their overall balance sheets. An obvious possibility would have been to switch deposits from the controlled interest-bearing category to the uncontrolled one. One possible way of doing this would have been to reduce interest rates on deposits and also reduce bank charges on non-interest-bearing accounts. Such action would result in a fall in IBELs but not a fall in M3.

Similarly, one might have expected an increase in disintermediation and the growth of parallel markets. In this case there would be a reduction both in IBELs and M3, but the reduction would have been more cosmetic than real. In other words the corset distorted the money supply statistics and in so doing complicated the conduct of monetary policy by altering the relationship between the money stock and the goals of policy.

The use of such evasive techniques is partly a function of the duration of the quantitative control. They are not costless, and consequently may be unprofitable to develop and use for short periods of time. It would seem that quantitative controls are more likely to be effective if they are used for only short periods of time.

Thus the SSDs scheme was probably more effective when it was first introduced, but became less so as evasive techniques were developed in response to its fairly prolonged use. The scheme was eventually dropped in 1980.

Monetary targets

It was during this period that monetary targets were first explicitly stated by the authorities. We have already seen that the money supply had started to appear in official statements about the aims of monetary policy in the late 1960s. It was not until 1976 however that the first quantitative target was set for any measure of the money supply. In the budget of that year, the Chancellor (Mr Healey) said

I aim to see that the growth of the money supply is consistent with my plans for the growth of demand expressed in current prices ... . After two years in which M3 has grown a good deal more slowly than money GDP, I would expect their respective growth rates to come more into line in the coming financial year. (*Hansard*, 6 April 1976, col 237).

The quantitative implications of this were set out in July of that year, when a M3 growth target of about 12% was set for the financial year 1976/7. For the financial year 1977/8 a target was set in terms of £M3 rather than M3; this was for growth in the range 9–13%. The target for 1978/9 was again £M3 and set at 8–12%, on a rolling basis. A rolling target is one which is reassessed regularly, which in the case of the UK means every six months. Thus a target may be set in April to run to the next April, but be reassessed in October and (possibly) a new target set to run to the next October.

The authorities were not very successful in achieving these targets. In 1976/7 the increase in M3 was some 1.3% below target, while in 1977/9 the upper boundary of the target range was exceeded by some 3½%. The target set in April 1978 for the period until April 1979 was in fact met, while the target set in October 1979 for the ensuing year (still 8–12%) was exceeded by just over 1%.

This period also brought into sharp focus the inevitable conflict arising from attempts to control both the exchange rate and the money supply. Large scale capital inflows during 1977 resulted in considerable upward pressure on the exchange rate, and the authorities, concerned about industrial competitiveness, intervened heavily in the foreign exchange market to try and keep the exchange rate down. It became clear, however, that the intervention policy was undermining the domestic money supply objectives and intervention was abandoned in the Autumn of 1977.

We must now consider the reasons why the authorities adopted monetary targets in the second half of the 1970s. Several have been suggested.

First of all the widespread adoption of floating exchange rates made the use of monetary targets more feasible, though in no way guaranteeing that national authorities would be successful in achieving their targets. National money supplies and inflation rates were brought within the potential control of national authorities in a way they had not been under the old fixed exchange rate system. This, together with some of the other reasons considered below, helps to explain why the UK was not alone in adopting monetary targets during this period.

It may be argued that monetary targets were adopted not out of any positive belief in monetarism, but because of disillusionment with the other policy instruments. The 1970s had seen inflation accelerate at an alarming rate, not only in the UK but worldwide and its control had come to command a greater priority in the thinking of governments. Incomes policies had been tried and found wanting, and in any case they had become something of a political 'hot potato'. Thus it could be argued that monetary targets were adopted almost as a last resort.

Alternatively, it could be argued that there were clear signs that the government had come to accept the view that in the fight against inflation, control of the money supply was necessary though not sufficient. In the budget speech of April 1976 for example, the Chancellor, Mr Healey, said '... it remains my aim that the growth of the money supply should not be allowed to fuel inflation as it did under my predecessor'.

Another suggested reason for the authorities' adoption of monetary targets is because of the discipline which they impose and the effect they have on inflationary expectations. Those involved in wage bargaining for example might be expected to recognize that excessive wage increases would no longer be facilitated by a passive expansion of the money supply, and consequently be prepared to settle for smaller increases. Thus the Governor of the Bank of England said

> One purpose of announcing monetary targets is to serve notice that excessive increases in domestic costs will come up against resistance. If people believe that the money supply will be expanded to accommodate any rise in costs and prices, however fast, inflationary fears are likely to be increased. If, on the other hand, people are convinced that the rate of growth of the money supply will be held within well-defined limits, this should help to reduce inflationary expectations. (Bank of England 1977a, p. 49).

Moreover monetary targets could act as a discipline on public expenditure, for they impose a restriction on the financing of that expenditure.

Monetary targets were also chosen, at least partly, because in the inflationary context of the 1970s, they were considered a more reliable guide to the thrust of policy than were interest rates. As the Governor of the Bank said:

> What swung the argument in favour of choosing a quantity rather than a price as the best indicator of the thrust of monetary policy was the acceleration of inflation .... We can, if we like, think of the nominal interest rate as having an 'expected inflation' component and a 'real' interest element. But we can never observe expectations, which are in any case likely both to differ from person to person, and to be volatile. The real rate of interest is an abstract construct. This has made it very difficult to frame the objectives of policy in terms of nominal interest rates.' (Bank of England 1978a, p. 32).

Finally we refer to the argument that monetary targets were adopted because although the government itself was not 'monetarist' it believed that the financial community was, and the government therefore saw the adoption of monetary targets as a way of generating confidence in financial markets.

Debt management policy and the role of the PSBR

The first half of the 1970s saw a huge expansion of government borrowing. In 1975 for example the PSBR was over £10½ b (10¼% of GDP), whereas in the eight years up to 1970 it had averaged a little over £¾ b (2% of GDP at current market prices). During the same period the rate of inflation, as well as its variability, increased markedly, causing an increase in the level and variability of nominal interest rates. This increased uncertainty aggravated the problems of debt management policy. Moreover there was still the difficulty of reconciling management of the gilt-edged market for monetary control purposes with the need to maintain a healthy market which would maximize the official longer-run sales of bonds.

> And this tension became more marked during the 1970s as the emphasis on control of the broader money supply increased. (Bank of England June 1979, p. 138).

The response of the authorities was to develop the so-called Duke of York tactic, whereby interest rates are marched up to a peak and then allowed gradually to fall. This tactic is thought to secure the conditions most suitable to large bond sales by the authorities. These conditions are

(1) Interest rates are high (i.e. prices are low).
(2) Interest rates are falling: the idea is that the market will expect interest rates to continue falling and therefore buy in anticipation of making a capital gain.
(3) An increased margin between short and long rates in favour of long.

The Duke of York tactic involves the authorities in driving up both short and long rates and then lowering short rates. Thus conditions (1) and (3) are satisfied and the demand for gilts rises. This pushes up gilt prices (i.e. pushes down long-term rates) and therefore satisfies condition (2). The authorities are then able to sell large quantities of gilts, and repeat the tactic whenever it is desired to sell more bonds.

The tactic was employed by the authorities on several occasions during the period under consideration. It is not, however, without its problems and its critics. It is argued that the gilt sales are 'variable and difficult to predict' (Artis and Lewis, 1981). It is also argued that the 'lumpiness' of gilt-edged sales, which the technique gave rise to, sometimes deprive the banks of liquidity which was made good by the authorities, with the result that there were undesirable short run fluctuations in the money supply. The volatility of interest rates are considered damaging to the real economy. Moreover this volatility *vis-à-vis* the relatively sticky rates on building society liabilities reduced the flow of funds into those institutions. The tactic is also regarded as increasing the interest cost of the National Debt.

In view of these difficulties there was much discussion in the late 1970s about alternatives. In fact the authorities themselves tried to increase the attractiveness of government debt by introducing three new kinds of security during the 1970s (Bank of England 1979). Two of the more widely discussed proposals were for a tender system for new stock issues and the introduction of index-linked securities.

The tender (or auction) system was advocated as a replacement for the 'tap' system of making new issues, which was the usual method used during the period. With the 'tap' system, the new issue is offered at a fixed price, and any stock unsold at that price is taken up by the Bank of England to be sold later. With this method new stock is more or less continuously available at fixed prices from the Bank of England 'tap'. In contrast the tender system would see the whole of any new issue being sold on one day at whatever price is necessary to 'clear the market'. Advocates of the tender system see it as forcing the authorities to abandon discretionary control of interest rates, and believe it would facilitate control of the money supply (Griffiths 1979). This latter argument is not necessarily true however (Bank of England 1979), as much will depend on who takes up the debt and on what is happening to the other credit components of the money supply. Opponents of the scheme emphasize that the greater volatility of interest rates would be harmful to the longer run health of the gilt-edged market, that it would not necessarily increase the demand for gilts in the short run, and it would shorten the maturity structure of the debt.

Index-linked securities would be attractive to investors during periods of rising inflation, but have been opposed on the grounds that they would feed the inflation through their adverse effects on inflation expectations. In periods of falling inflation, index-linked bonds loose their attractiveness to investors, but become more attractive to the authorities by reducing the real interest payments on such bonds.

One of the major developments of this period was the acknowledgement by the authorities that fiscal policy had important monetary effects, and could be used to influence the rate of growth of the money supply. The PSBR was recognized as one of the supply side counterparts of £M3, and its manipulation was seen as one instrument amongst several which could be used to control that monetary aggregate. To this end a system of 'cash limits' was introduced, restricting the level of certain kinds of public expenditure measured at current prices. This did not of course ensure precise control over the PSBR because some kinds of public expenditure could not be controlled in that way (or indeed in any other way) and were virtually impossible to predict. Similarly, tax revenue cannot be 'fixed'. In addition to introducing the 'cash limits' system of control, the Government cut public expenditure on several occasions. Clearly the PSBR had become part of monetary policy.

The period from the introduction of the corset to the beginning of the new decade had therefore seen some notable developments in the conduct of monetary policy. Amongst the more important of these were the adoption of monetary targets and the integration of the PSBR into monetary policy. On the other hand, it may be argued that although new types of government debt had been introduced and a new tactic for debt management adopted, and though a new kind of direct control had been introduced, monetary policy still operated through interest rates and direct controls. According to Griffiths (1981, p. 27).

> ... the important point is that the general framework within which [monetary] control was exercised was very similar in both design and practice to that of the previous system [i.e. pre CCC] which it replaced.

Before moving on to consider the changes to policy that were introduced at the start of the new decade, it will be useful if we conclude this section by briefly summarizing the way monetary policy was being conducted in the late 1970s.

(1) The major concern of policy was with monetary aggregates.
(2) Control over the money supply was exercised via the supply side counterparts. As the Governor of the Bank put it:

> Thus we look separately at the main items which statistically speaking are the components of the money supply on a broad definition – such as the PSBR, sales to the public of government debt, the volume of bank lending to the private sector and external flows to the private sector. ... The essence of monetary management, as I see it, is to act to offset divergences from forecast in these sources of monetary expansion – difficult to predict and control – as soon as it becomes reasonably clear that inaction is likely to undermine achievement of the monetary target. (Bank of England 1978a, p. 36).

(3) The major instruments of control were
    (a) Interest rates (to influence bank credit).
    (b) Fiscal policy (to influence the PSBR).
    (c) Debt management policy (Duke of York tactic).
    (d) Direct controls (SSDs).

The early 1980s

In May 1979 a new Government came into office more fully committed to the principles and policies of monetarism. In line with this commitment, the Government rejected Keynesian short-run stabilization policy and concentrated on a medium-term strategy of reducing the rate of inflation by means of monetary restraint.

This policy approach was made more explicit in the budget of 1980 by the introduction of a medium-term financial strategy which set out a four year path for a reduction in the growth of sterling M3 and a progressive reduction in PSBR as a proportion of national income. Considerable importance was attached to reducing PSBR to avoid excessive reliance on interest rates to restrain monetary growth.

During this period a wide ranging debate was taking place on methods of monetary control. Monetarists, in particular, were critical of the authorities approach and strongly advocated a move to monetary base control (see Chapter 12). As a result of this debate and the authorities concern to improve short-term control of monetary growth, the Government decided to publish a Green Paper (1980) on monetary control, as a basis for public discussion and consultation. In the event no decision was taken by the authorities to introduce a system of monetary base control, but certain changes were, however, made in methods of official intervention in the money (discount) market. The new monetary control arrangements were formally introduced in August 1981 (Bank of England, 1981), although the Bank had been modifying its operations in the market in stages from October 1980. The changes had the two-fold aim of giving the authorities greater flexibility in the administration of very short-term interest rates and allowing market forces a greater influence on the structure of short-term rates.

Prior to these changes, the Bank, in order to maintain control over short-term rates, aimed to keep the money market short of cash by deliberately over-issuing Treasury bills at the weekly tender, thereby 'forcing the market into the Bank'. Shortages were relieved by either direct lending to the discount houses at MLR ('lender of last resort' lending), or by purchasing of bills at pre-determined rates. It became apparent to the authorities that, given a background of increased volatility of interest rates, these arrangements did not give the authorities sufficient flexibility in the adjustment of short-term rates. It was therefore decided in 1981 to cease direct lending to the market at MLR and instead, to seek to influence short-term interest rates chiefly by open market operations, buying and selling bills at dealing rates determined on a daily basis, instead of at pre-determined rates. With these new arrangements, if the discount houses are short of cash, they offer bills to the Bank at rates of their own choosing. If the Bank is satisfied with the pattern of interest rates implied by the offers, it will purchase the bills and relieve the cash shortage in the market. If, however, the rates offered conflict with the authorities' interest rate objectives, the Bank may refuse to purchase the bills and the discount houses will have to come back with a more acceptable offer. For example, if the Bank wishes to resist a downward trend in interest rates, it may reject offers from the discount houses to purchase bills at lower rates, forcing them to come back with a higher rate offer more in line with official interest rate objectives. (For a more detailed account of the Bank's money market dealing arrangements, see Bank of England, 1982c).

A list of the main 1981 changes is given in the Appendix to this chapter. These alterations clearly did not represent a significant change in the overall approach to monetary control. The authorities continued to seek to influence the main counterparts of the money stock, using short-term interest rate policy to influence the demand for bank loans, debt management policy to ensure sufficient sales of gilt-edged stocks to the non-bank public, and taxation and expenditure policy to influence the medium term path of the PSBR.

Although the incoming Government in 1979 was more fully committed to a policy of money supply control, actual monetary growth over the period 1979–81 was at times considerably in excess of sterling M3 targets. In order to restrain monetary growth, MLR was raised in November 1979 to a record level of 17 per cent, and exchange controls were abolished, partly to encourage outflows of capital and hopefully offset, to some degree, the strong upward pressure on the exchange rate, due in part to the rapid rise in world oil prices during the year and the UK's position as an oil producer.

By the start of the new decade it was clear that the authorities were struggling to keep the rate of monetary growth down to acceptable levels. Over the financial year 1980–81 sterling M3 increased by around 20 per cent, compared with the target range for the period of 7–11 per cent. A number of factors contributed to the rapid monetary expansion.

First, the severe recession was a major expansionary influence on the money supply. A major feature of the 1979–81 recession, the heavy destocking in the company sector, highlighted the severe financial pressure on companies in this period and created a high corporate demand for bank credit. The rapid rise in unemployment also increased the PSBR as a result of an expansion in demand-determined public expenditure.

In addition, the growth of the sterling M3 measure was distorted by the abolition of the corset scheme in June 1980, which created a once and for all upward shift in the money supply as a result of a return of business to the banks (reintermediation). An additional factor that distorted sterling M3 growth was the rapid structural changes that took place in the financial system; for example, the banks' move into the mortgage market. There was also considerable concern about the response of sterling M3 to interest rate changes over this period. It was possible that high interest rates served to *increase* the growth of sterling M3 in the short-term with savers increasing the proportion of their savings held in interest bearing deposits.

Given these developments, it became increasingly apparent that the sterling M3 measure gave a misleading guide to the stance of monetary policy in this period. The rapid growth in this aggregate seemed to indicate a very lax monetary policy, but other indicators, the exchange rate, interest rates and the growth of narrow money measures, suggested that monetary conditions were very tight.

Although there was considerable concern about the behaviour of sterling M3, the authorities continued to target this aggregate for 1981–82, but greater importance was paid to other measures of monetary growth in assessing monetary conditions. The increased emphasis on a range of monetary measures was made more explicit in the March 1982 budget when a single target range of 8–12% for 1982–83 was set for three monetary aggregates, M1, sterling M3 and PSL_2. In addition to these targets, the authorities were monitoring the movement of other monetary indicators, such as the wide monetary base (MO), non-interest-bearing M1, PSL_1, and the exchange rate (see Chapter 1, pp. 18–21, for definitions of these aggregates). The growth of three targeted aggregates over 1982–83 was within the somewhat more relaxed target range, and in the 1983 budget, a target range of 7–11% was set for the three measures.

The principle reason for setting a target for the narrow money measure, M1, was the increased concern about the sensitivity of the wider money supply measures to interest rate movements. As a result of this problem, more attention was paid to money balances held for current spending reasons – transactions balances, rather than on balances held as savings – investment balances. It was considered that the narrow money measure might be subject to less distortion as a result of financial innovation and provide a better indicator of monetary conditions. With, however, the recent rapid development of interest-bearing sight deposits, it became clear to the authorities that the M1 measure had become an increasingly poor measure of money held for transactions purposes. In a speech at the Mansion House in the City in October 1983, the Chancellor of the Exchequer revealed that, in view of this development, the authorities were giving greater weight to the growth of the wide monetary base measure, MO, in their assessment of monetary conditions. He also pointed out that the narrow money measures were much better indicators of inflation in recent years than the wider money supply measures, '...it was the surge in the narrow aggregates in 1977 which was followed by the surge in inflation in 1979. And the deceleration in the growth of narrow money in 1979 and 1980 preceded the recent decline in inflation' (quotation cited in Barclays UK Financial Survey, 1983).

Figure 13.1, in which changes in MO and inflation (with MO advanced two years) are plotted, shows that MO has been in recent years a useful leading indicator of the path of inflation, with the slow growth in MO over 1980–81 predicting well the downturn in the rate of inflation in 1982–83. This is in sharp contrast with the sterling M3 measure, the high growth of which in 1980–81 proved to be totally misleading as a guide to subsequent inflation.

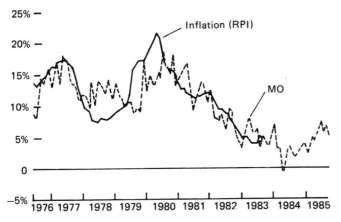

Figure 13.1 Changes in MO and inflation (percentage change on previous 12 months) – with MO advanced 2 years (from *Barclays UK Financial Survey 1983*)

The greater emphasis on the narrow monetary aggregate was confirmed in the 1984 budget with the introduction of an explicit target for the growth of MO. A target range for 1984–85 was set at 4–8 per cent for MO and 6–10 per cent for sterling M3. Different target ranges were set in view of the tendency for MO to grow more slowly in the longer term than the wider monetary aggregate. The Chancellor stated in his budget speech (March 1984) that the two target aggregates will have equal importance for the conduct of policy and also stressed that the adoption of a target for MO did not represent any change in the authorities overall approach to monetary control.

With the authorities at present reluctant to move to a full monetary base control system and control base money directly, it does raise the question of whether MO will continue to be used as just an indicator of monetary conditions, or whether, as implied by the introduction of an MO target, measures will be taken to control its growth. MO mainly consists of currency in circulation which would normally be considered to be demand-determined and mainly a function of the volume of transactions in the economy. Attempts to control MO by altering short-term interest rates would therefore presumably only influence MO by acting on the level of economic activity in the economy. Recent evidence, however, does indicate that, at least for recent years, the response of MO to interest rates is reasonably stable and significiant (Johnston, 1984). Johnston's results suggest that a one percentage point rise in nominal interest rates reduces MO by 1.7 per cent (with a mean response lag of 11 months).

This evidence does provide some support for a policy of controlling MO by operating on interest rates. However, previously seemingly stable relationships between monetary aggregates and macroeconomic variables have proved to be highly fragile when used for policy purposes and it is not unlikely that 'Goodharts Law' (see p. 240) will apply also to this MO relationship if the authorities do actively seek to control MO growth. It would also probably have the unfortunate effect of destroying the usefulness of MO as an advance indicator of the course of inflation.

We end this section and the chapter with a few observations about the recent conduct of monetary policy.

(1) As a result of targeting a defective indicator, monetary conditions were far too tight during much of 1979–81, given the state of the economy, and exacerbated the deep recession.

(2) There are at present *eight* different official measures of monetary aggregates (see Chapter 1, pp. 18–21); two currently being targeted and the rest as far as can be ascertained, being monitored by the authorities. It could be argued that this bewildering array of money measures indicates the high degree of confusion and uncertainty in the minds of the authorities about the conduct of monetary policy. It is a a situation to further increase the scepticism of non-monetarists about the wisdom of money supply control.

(3) On the other hand, the recent changes in monetary control techniques could be interpreted as a gradual and painful move by the authorities in the direction of a full monetary base control system. Monetarists, who consider the present system of indirect control via interest rates as highly unsatisfactory, might therefore see in the recent changes some hope that the authorities have reached the final stages in an evolution towards the monetary base control approach. Certainly the changes in the early 1980s provide a framework for a move to this system of control.

Appendix: summary of the new monetary control arrangements introduced in 1981

The new monetary control measures included:

(1) A newly defined monetary sector which was wider than the pre-existing banking sector and included all recognized banks and licensed deposit-taking institutions.

(2) The abandonment of MLR and direct lending to the money market. The Bank however reserved the right, in exceptional circumstances, to lend directly to the market at an interest rate of its own choosing.

(3) The Bank abandoned the practice of quoting prices at which it would buy and sell bills in the money market. The Bank also discontinued the practice of deliberately over-issuing Treasury bills at the weekly tender.

(4) The Bank will seek to influence very short-term interest rates chiefly by open market operations in the money market. The purpose of the Bank's money market operations is to keep very-short-term interest rates within an unpublished band determined by the requirements of money supply control.

(5) The Reserve Assets Ratio was abolished. As outlined earlier in this chapter, this ratio had only been intended for use as a means of regulating bank liquidity in order to influence short-term interest rates, and not for the purpose of achieving a multiple change in bank deposits. The authorities had come to the conclusion that this ratio had little to contribute to the new monetary control arrangements (Green Paper, 1980).

(6) Each institution in the new monetary sector which had eligible liabilities of £10 m or more was required to keep a balance of ½ per cent of its eligible liabilities in a non-operational, non-interest-bearing account with the Bank of England. This was not a monetary control ratio and its purpose was simply to provide income and resources to the Bank. This ratio replaced the previous 1½ per cent cash ratio.

(7) The Special Deposits scheme was retained.

(8) The list of institutions whose acceptances are eligible for discount at the Bank of England was widened, and now includes non-Commonwealth banks.

(9) Eligible banks were required to keep an average of 6 per cent and a minimum of 4 per cent of their eligible liabilities in the form of secured loans with the discount houses and/or gilt-edged jobbers. In this way funds are provided to the relevant dealers in the bill and gilt-edged markets and the efficient functioning of these markets is protected.

References

ALEXANDER, S. S. (1952), The effects of devaluation on a trade balance, *International Monetary Fund Staff Papers*, **2**, April, 263–278

ANDERSON, L. C. and CARLSON, K. M. (1970), A monetarist model for economic stabilization, *Federal Reserve Bank of St. Louis Review*, **52**, April, 7–25

ANDERSON, L. C. and JORDAN, J. L. (1968), Monetary and fiscal actions: a test of their relative importance in economic stabilization, *Federal Reserve Bank of St. Louis Review*, **50**, November, 11–24

ANDO, A. and MODLIGLIANI, P. (1965), The relative stability of velocity and the investment multiplier, *American Economic Review*, **55**, September, 695–728

ARCHIBALD, G. C. and LIPSEY, R. G. (1958), Value and monetary theory: a critique of Lange and Patinkin, *Review of Economic Studies*, **25**, 1–22

ARGY, V. (1969), The impact of monetary policy on expenditure with particular reference to the UK, *International Monetary Fund Staff Papers*, **16**, November, 436–487

ARGY, V. (1970), The role of money in economic activity: some results for seventeen developed countries, *IMF Staff Papers*, **17**, November

ARTIS, M. J. (1980), in *Treasury and Civil Service Committee on Monetary Policy: Memoranda*, Vol II, HMSO, London

ARTIS, M. J. and LEWIS, M. K. (1976), The demand for money in the UK 1963–73, *Manchester School*, **44**, June, 147–181

ARTIS, M. J. and LEWIS, M. K. (1981), *Monetary Control in the United Kingdom*, Phillip Allan, Oxford

ARTIS, M. J. and NOBAY, A. R. (1969), Two aspects of the monetary debate, *National Institute Economic Review*, **49**, August, 33–51

BANK OF ENGLAND (1969), Domestic Credit Expansion, *Bank of England Quarterly Bulletin*, **9**, September, 363–382

BANK OF ENGLAND (1971a), Competition and Credit Control, *Bank of England Quarterly Bulletin*, **11**, June, 189–193

BANK OF ENGLAND (1971b), Key issues in monetary and credit policy, *Bank of England Quarterly Bulletin*, **11**, June, 195–198

BANK OF ENGLAND (1974), Credit control: a supplementary scheme, *Bank of England Quarterly Bulletin*, **14**, March, 37–39

BANK OF ENGLAND (1977a), The Governor's speech at the biennial dinner of the Institute of Bankers in Scotland, 17 January 1977, reprinted in *Bank of England Quarterly Bulletin*, **17**, March, 48–50

BANK OF ENGLAND (1977b), Economic commentary, *Bank of England Quarterly Bulletin*, **17**, December, 415–433

BANK OF ENGLAND (1978a), Reflections on the conduct of monetary policy, *Bank of England Quarterly Bulletin*, **18**, March, 31–37

BANK OF ENGLAND (1978b), External and foreign currency flows and money supply, *Bank of England Quarterly Bulletin*, **18**, December, 523–529

BANK OF ENGLAND (1979), The gilt-edged market, *Bank of England Quarterly Bulletin*, **19**, June, 137–148

BANK OF ENGLAND (1981), Monetary control provisions, *Bank of England Quarterly Bulletin*, **21**, September, 347–350

BANK OF ENGLAND (1982a), Transactions balances – a new monetary aggregate, *Bank of England Quarterly Bulletin*, **22**, June, 24–25

BANK OF ENGLAND (1982b), The supplementary special deposits scheme, *Bank of England Quarterly Bulletin*, **22**, March, 74–85

BANK OF ENGLAND (1982c), The role of the Bank of England in the money market, *Bank of England Quarterly Bulletin*, **22**, March, 86–94

BANK OF ENGLAND (1982d) Composition of monetary and liquidity aggregates, and associated statistics, *Bank of England Quarterly Bulletin*, **22**, November, 530–538

BANK OF ENGLAND (1984), Changes to monetary aggregates and the analysis of bank lending, *Bank of England Quarterly Bulletin*, **24**, March 78–83

BARRETT, C. R. and WALTERS, A. A. (1966), The stability of Keynesian and monetary multipliers in the UK, *Review of Economics and Statistics*, **48**, November, 395–405

BARRO, R. J. (1974), Are government bonds net wealth?, *Journal of Political Economy*, **82**, 1095–1117

BAUMOL, W. J. (1952) The transactions demand for cash in an inventory theoretic approach, *Quarterly Journal of Economics*, **66**, November 545–556

BLACK, H. (1975), The relative importance of determinants of the money supply – the British case, *Journal of Monetary Economics*, **1**, 257–264

BOUGHTON, J. M. (1979), Demand for money in major OECD countries, *OECD Economic Outlook Occasional Studies*, January

BRAINARD, W. C. and TOBIN, J. (1968), Pitfalls in financial model building, *American Economic Review, Papers and Proceedings*, **58**, May, 99–122

BRANSON, W. H. (1975), Monetarist and Keynesian models of the transmission of inflation, *American Economic Review, Papers and Proceedings*, **58**, May, 99–122

BROWN, A. J. (1939), Interest, prices and the demand for idle money, *Oxford Economic Papers*, **2**, May, 46–69

BRUNNER, K. and MELTZER, A. H. (1967), Economies of scale in cash balances reconsidered, *Quarterly Journal of Economics*, **81**, August, 422–436

BRUNNER, K. and MELTZER, A. H. (1969), The nature of the policy problem, in *Targets and Indicators of Monetary Policy*, ed. K. Brunner, Chandler, California

BRUNNER, K. and MELTZER, A. H. (1971), The uses of money: money in the theory of an exchange economy, *American Economic Review*, **61**, December, 784–805

BRUNNER, K. and MELTZER, A. H. (1972), Friedman's monetary theory, *Journal of Political Economy*, **80**, September/October, 837–851

CAGAN, P. (1958), *The Demand for Currency Relative to the Total Money Supply*, National Bureau of Economic Research, Occasional Papers, 62

CARLSON, J. A. and PARKIN, J. M. (1975), Inflation expectations, *Economica*, **42**, May, 123–138

CHICK, V. (1977), *The Theory of Monetary Policy*, Gray-Mills, London

CLAYTON, G., DODDS, J. C., FORD, J. L. and GHOSH, D. (1974), An econometric model of the UK financial sector: some preliminary findings, in *Issues in Monetary Economices*, eds. H. G. Johnson and A. R. Nobay, University Press, Oxford

CLOWER, R. (1965), The Keynesian counter revolution: a theoretical appraisal, in *The Theory of Interest Rates*, eds. F. H. Hahn and P. P. R. Breckling, St. Martins, New York

CLOWER, R. W. (1969), 'Introduction', in *Monetary Theory*, ed. R. CLower, Penguin, Harmondsworth

CLOWER, R. L. (1971) 'Theoretical foundations of monetary policy', in *Monetary Theory and Monetary Policy in the 1970s*, eds., G. Clayton, J. C. Gilbert and R. Sedgewick, Oxford University Press, London

COGHLAN, R. T. (1978), A transactions demand for money, *Bank of England Quarterly Bulletin*, **18**, March, 48–60

COGHLAN, R. (1980), *The Theory of Money and Finance*, Macmillan, London

COGHLAN, R. (1981), *Money, Credit and the Economy*, Allen & Unwin, London

COURAKIS, A. S. (1978), Serial correlation and a Bank of England study of the demand for money: an exercise in measurement without theory, *Economic Journal*, **88**, September, 537–548

CROCKETT, A. D. (1970), Timing relationships between movements of monetary and national income variables, *Bank of England Quarterly Bulletin*, **10**, December, 459–472

CROSS, R. and LAIDLER, D. (1976) Inflation, excess demand and expectations in fixed exchange rate open economies: some preliminary empirical results, in *Inflation in the World Economy*, eds., M. Parkin and G. Zis, Manchester University Press, Manchester

CROUCH, R. L. (1967), A model of the UK monetary sector, *Econometrica*, **35**, July–October, 398–418

CROUCH, R. L. (1968), Money supply theory and the UK monetary contraction 1954–56, *Bulletin of the Oxford University Institute of Economics and Statistics*, **30**, May, 143–152

CUKIERMAN, A. (1974), A test of the 'no trade-off in the long run' hypothesis, *Econometrica*, **42**, 1069–1080

CURRIE, D. A. (1976), Some criticisms of the monetary analysis of balance of payments correction, *Economic Journal*, **86**, September, 508–522

DALTON, H. (1947), Budget speech, April 1947, quoted in *The Management of the British Economy 1945–60*, J. C. R. Dow, 1964, p. 224, Cambridge University Press, Cambridge

DAVIS, R. G. (1969), How much does money matter? A look at some recent evidence, *Federal Reserve Bank of New York Monthly Review*, **51**, June, 119–131

DE LEEUW, P. and KALCHBRENNER, J. (1969), 'Monetary and fiscal actions: a test of their relative importance in economic stabilization', *Federal Reserve Bank of St. Louis*, **51**, April, 6–11

DENNIS, G. E. J. (1981), *Monetary Economics*, Longman, London

DE PRANO, M. and MAYER, T. (1965), Tests of the relative importance of autonomous expenditure and money, *American Economic Review*, **55**, September, 729–752

DORNBUSCH, R. (1976a), Expectations and exchange rate dynamics', *Journal of Political Economy*, **84**, December, 116–176

DORNBUSCH, R. (1976b), Devaluation, money and non-traded goods, in *The Monetary Approach to the Balance of Payments*, eds., J. A. Frenkel and R. G. Johnson, Allen and Unwin, London

DORNBUSCH, R. (1980), Monetary policy under exchange rate flexibility, in *The Functioning of Floating Exchange Rates*, eds., D. Bigman and T. Taya, Ballinger Publishing Co., Cambridge, Massachusetts

DOW, J. C. R. (1964), *The Management of the British Economy 1945–60*, Cambridge University Press, Cambridge

DUCK, N., PARKIN, J. M., ROSE, D. and ZIS, G. (1976), The determination of the rate of change of wages and prices in a fixed exchange rate world economy, 1956–71, in *Inflation in the World Economy*, eds., J. M. Parkin and G. Zis, Manchester University Press, Manchester

FISHER, D. (1968), The demand for money in Britain: quarterly results 1951 to 1967, *Manchester School*, **36**, December, 329–344

FLEMING, J. M. (1962), Domestic financial policies under fixed and under floating exchange rates, *International Monetary Fund Staff Paper*, **9**, November, 369–379

FOOT, M. D. K. W., GOODHART, C. A. E. and HOTSON, A. C. (1979), Monetary base control, *Bank of England Quarterly Bulletin*, **19**, June, 149–159

FRIEDMAN, B. M. (1977), Even the St. Louis model now believes in fiscal policy, *Journal of Monetary, Credit and Banking*, **9**, May, 365–367

FRIEDMAN, M. (1956), The quantity theory of money – a restatement, in *Studies in the Quantity Theory of Money*, ed., M. Friedman, University of Chicago Press, Chicago

FRIEDMAN, M. (1964), Post-War trends in monetary theory and policy, *National Banking Review*, **2**, September, 1–9

FRIEDMAN, M. (1968), The role of monetary policy, *American Economic Review*, **58**, March, 1–17

FRIEDMAN, M. (1969), *The Optimum Quantity of Money*, Macmillan, London

FRIEDMAN, M. (1970a), A theoretical framework for monetary analysis, *Journal of Political Economy*, **78**, March/April, 325–337

FRIEDMAN, M. (1970b), The counter-revolution in monetary theory, *Institute of Economic Affairs, Occasional Paper*, **22**

FRIEDMAN, M. (1971), A monetary theory of nominal income, *Journal of Political Economy*, **79**, March/April, 323–337

FRIEDMAN, M. (1977), *Inflation and Unemployment: the New Dimension of Politics*, Institute of Economic Affairs, Occasional Paper, No. 51

FRIEDMAN, M. (1980), in *Treasury and Civil Service Committee on Monetary Policy: Memoranda*, Vol. I, 55–61, HMSO, London

FRIEDMAN, M. and MEISELMAN, D. (1963), The relative stability of monetary velocity and the investment multiplier in the US 1897–1958, in *Stabilization Policies*, Commission on Money and Credit, Prentice-Hall, Englewoods Cliffs

FRIEDMAN, M. and SCHWARTZ, A. J. (1963a), *The Monetary History of the USA*, National Bureau of Economic, Washington DC

FRIEDMAN, M. and SCHWARTZ, A. J. (1963b), Money and business cycles, *Review of Economics and Statistics*, **45**, (Suppl.), February, 32–64

FRIEDMAN, M. and SCHWARTZ, A. J. (1969), The definition of money: net wealth and neutrality as criteria, *Journal of Money, Credit and Banking*, **1**, February, 1–14

GENBERG, H. and SWOBODA, A. K. (1975), *Causes and Origins of the Current Worldwide Inflation*, Discussion Paper, Ford Foundation International Monetary Research Project, Graduate Institute of International Studies, Geneva

GOODHART, C. A. E. (1970), The importance of money, *Bank of England Quarterly Bulletin*, **10**, June, 159–198

GOODHART, C. A. E. (1973), Analysis of the determination of the stock of money, in *Essays in Modern Economics*, ed. M. Parkin, Longmans, London

GOODHART, C. A. E. (1975a), *Money, Information and Uncertainty*, Macmillan, London

GOODHART, C. A. E. (1975b), *Problems of Monetary Management: the UK Experience*, Discussion paper for Reserve Bank of Australia Conference in Monetary Economics, July 1975

GOODHART, C. A. E. and CROCKETT, A. D. (1970), The importance of money, *Bank of England Quarterly Bulletin*, **10**, June, 159–198

GOWLAND, D. (1982), *Controlling the Money Supply*, Croom Helm, London

GRAMLICH, E. M. (1969), The role of money in economic activity: complicated or simple?, *Journal of Business Economics*, **4**, September, 21–26

GRANGER, C. W. J. (1969), Investigating causal relations by econometric models and cross-spectral methods, *Econometrica*, **37**, July, 24–38

GRAY, M. R., WARD, R. and ZIS, G. (1976), The world demand for money function: some preliminary results, in *Inflation of the World Economy*, eds., M. Parkin and G. Zis, Manchester University Press, Manchester

GREEN PAPER (1980), *Monetary Control*, Cmnd 7858, HMSO, London

GRIFFITHS, B. (1979), The reform of monetary control in the United Kingdom, *The City University Annual Monetary Review*, **I**, October, 29–41

GRIFFITHS, B. (1981), The new monetary control procedures in the UK, *The City University Annual Monetary Review*, **3**, December, 25–30

GROSSMAN, H. I. (1980), Rational expectations, business cycles, and government behaviour, in *Rational Expectations and Economic Policy*, ed. S. Fischer, University of Chicago Press, Chicago

GURLEY, J. G. and SHAW, E. S. (1960), *Money in a Theory of Finance*, Brookings Institution, Washington

HACCHE, G. (1974), The demand for money in the UK: experience since 1971, *Bank of England Quarterly Bulletin*, **14**, September, 284–306

HAMBURGER, M. J. (1977), The demand for money in open economies: Germany and the UK, *Journal of Monetary Economics*, **3**, January, 25–40

HARRIS, L. (1981), *Monetary Theory*, McGraw-Hill, New York

HELLER, H. R. (1976), *International Reserves and Worldwide Inflation*, International Monetary Fund Staff Papers 23, March, 61–87

HELLIWELL, J. F. (1978), The balance of payments: a survey of Harry Johnson's contributions, *Canadian Journal of Economics Supplement*, November

HOLLY, S. and LONGBOTTOM, J. A. (1982), The empirical relationship between the money stock and the price level in the UK: a test of causality, *Bulletin of Economic Research*, May, 17–42

JACKMAN, R., MULVEY, C. and TREVITHICK, J. (1981), *The Economics of Inflation*, Martin Robertson, Oxford

JACOBS, R. L., LERNER, E. E. and WARD, M. P. (1979), Difficulties with testing for causation, *Economic Inquiry*, July

JOHNSON, H. G. (1958), Towards a general theory of the balance of payments, in *International Trade and Economic Growth*, ed. H. G. Johnston, Allen and Unwin, London

JOHNSON, H. G. (1962), Monetary theory and policy, *American Economic Review*, **52**, June, 335–384

JOHNSON, H. G. (1970), Recent developments in monetary theory – a commentary, in *Money in Britain 1959–1969*, eds., D. R. Croome and H. G. Johnson, Oxford University Press, London

JOHNSON, H. G. (1971), *Macroeconomics and Monetary Theory*, Gray-Mills, London

JOHNSON, H. G. (1976), The monetary theory of balance of payments policies, in *The Monetary Approach to the Balance of Payments*, eds., J. A. Frenkel and H. G. Johnson, Allen and Unwin, London

JOHNSON, H. G. (1977), The monetary approach to the balance of payments. A non-technical international guide, *Journal of Economics*, **7**, 251–268

JOHNSON, H. G. (1978), Comment on Mayer on monetarism, in *The Structure of Monetarism*, ed. T. Mayer, Norton, New York

JOHNSTON, R. B. (1984), The demand for non-interest-bearing money in the United Kingdom, *Treasury Working Paper No 28*, February, HM Treasury

JONSON, P. D. (1976), Money and economic activity in the open economy: the United Kingdom, 1880–1970, *Journal of Political Economy*, **84**, October, 979–1012

KAHN, F. H. (1976), Thoughts on the behaviour of wages and monetarism, *Lloyds Bank Review*, **119**, 1–11

KALDOR, N. (1970), The new monetarism, *Lloyds Bank Review*, **97**, July, 1–18

KALDOR, N. and TREVITHICK, J. (1981), A Keynesian prespective on money, *Lloyds Bank Review*, **139**, January, 1–19

KAREKEN, J. and SOLOW, R. (1963), Monetary policy. Lags versus simultaneity, in *Stabilization Policies*, Commission on Money and Credit, Prentice-Hall, Englewood Cliffs

KAVANAGH, N. J. and WALTERS, A. A. (1966), The demand for money in the UK 1877 to 1961: some preliminary findings, *Bulletin of the Oxford University Institute of Economics and Statistics*, **28**, May, 93–116

KERAN, M. W. (1970), Monetary and fiscal influences on economic activity: the foreign experience, *Federal Reserve Bank of St. Louis Review*, **52**, February, 10–28

KEYNES, J. M. (1936), *The General Theory of Employment, Interest and Money*, Macmillan, London

KHUSRO, A. M. (1952), An investigation of liquidity preference, *Yorkshire Bulletin of Economic and Social Research*, **4**, January, 1–20

KOURI, P. (1980), Monetary policy, the balance of payments, and the exchange rate, in *The Functioning of Floating Exchange Rates*, eds , D. Bigman and T. Taya, Ballinger Publishing Co., Cambridge, Mass

KRAUSE, L. B. (1975), 'Comment' on M. V. N. Whitman, Global monetarism and the monetary approach to the balance of payments, *Brookings Papers on Economic Activity*, **3**, 491–555

LAIDLER, D. E. W. (1969), The definition of money: theoretical and empirical problems, *Journal of Money, Credit and Banking*, **1**, August, 509–525

LAIDLER, D. E. W. (1971), The influence of money on economic activity: a survey of some current problems, in *Monetary Theory and Policy in the 1970s*, eds., G. Clayton, J. C. Gilbert and R. Sedgewick, Oxford University Press, London

LAIDLER, D. E. W. (1974), Information, money and the macro-economics of inflation, *Swedish Journal of Economics*, 1974, 26–41

LAIDLER, D. E. W. (1978a), Money and money income: an essay on the transmission mechanism, *Journal of Monetary Economics*, 4, April, 157–191

LAIDLER, D. E. W. (1978b), A monetarist viewpoint, in *Demand Management*, ed. M. Posner, Heinemann, London

LAIDLER, D. E. W. (1981a), 'Evidence' to *Treasury and Civil Service Committee on Monetary Policy*, Vol. II, Minutes of Evidence, HMSO, London

LAIDLER, D. E. W. (1981b), Monetarism: an interpretation and an assessment, *Economic Journal*, **91**, March, 1–28

LAIDLER, D. E. W. (1982), *Monetarist Perspectives*, Philip Allan, Oxford

LAIDLER, D. E. W. and PARKIN, J. M. (1970), The demand for money in the UK, 1955–67 some preliminary estimates, *Manchester*, **38**, 187–208

LANGE, O. (1942), Say's law: a restatement and criticism, in *Mathematical Economics and Econometrics*, eds., F. McIntyre and T. O. Yutema, University of Chicago Press, Chicago

LAUMAS, G. S. (1978), A test of the stability of the demand for money, *Scottish Journal of Political Economy*, **25**, November, 239–251

LAURY, J. S. E., LEWIS, G. R. and ORMEROD, P. A. (1978), Properties of macroeconomic models of the UK economy. A comparative study, *National Institute Economic Review*, **85**, February, 52–72

LEIJONHUFVUD, A. (1968), *On Keynesian Economics and the Economics of Keynes*, Oxford University Press, Oxford

LEIJONHUFVUD, A. (1969), *Keynes and the Classics*, Institute of Economic Affairs, Occasional Paper No, 30

LIPSEY, R. G. (1960), The relationship between unemployment and the rate of change of money wage-rates in the UK, 1862–1957: A further analysis, *Economica*, **27**, February, 1–31

LLEWELLYN, D. T. (1979), Do building societies take deposits away from banks?, *Lloyds Bank Review*, **131**, January, 21–34

LLOYD, C. L. (1962), The real balance effect: sine qua what?, *Oxford Economic Papers*, **14**, October, 267–274

LOMAX, R. and MOWL, C. (1978), Balance of Payments Flows and Monetary Aggregates in the UK, HM Treasury Working Paper No. 5

MACKAY, D. I. and HART, R. A. (1974), Wage inflation and the Phillips relationship, *Manchester School*, **42**, June, 136–61

MARSHALL, A. (1924), *Money, Credit and Commerce*, Macmillan, London

MATTHEWS, K. G. P. and ORMEROD, P. A. (1978), St. Louis models of the UK economy, *National Institute Economic Review*, **84**, May, 65–69

MAYER, T. (1978), *The Structure of Monetarism*, Norton, New York

MEADE, J. E. (1951), *The Balance of Payments*, Oxford University Press, Oxford

MIDDLETON, P. E, MOWL, C. J., ODLING-SMEE, J. C. and RILEY, C. J. (1981), Monetary targets and the public sector borrowing requirement, in *Monetary Targets*, eds., B. Griffiths and G. E. Wood, Macmillan, London

MILLS, T. C. (1978), The functional form of the demand for money, *Applied Statistics*, **27**, February, 52–57

MILLS, T. C. (1980), Money, income and causality in the UK – a look at the recent evidence, *Bulletin of Economic Research*, **32**, 18–28

MINFORD, P. (1981), 'Comment' on M. D. K. W. Foot, Monetary targets: their nature and record in the major economies, in *Monetary Targets*, eds., B. G. Griffiths and G. E. Wood, Macmillan, London

MODIGLIANI, F. (1977), The monetarist controversy or, should we forsake stabilization policies, *American Economic Review*, **67**, March, 1–19

MONOPOLIES COMMISSION (1968), *Report on proposed merger–Barclays, Lloyds and Martins Banks*, No. 319, July, HMSO, London

MONTI, M. (1971), A theoretical model of bank behaviour and its implication for monetary policy, *L'Industria revista di Economia Politica*, **2**, 165–191

MORGAN, E. V. (1969), The essential qualities of money, *Manchester School*, **37**, September, 237–248

MUNDELL, R. A. (1963), Capital mobility and stablization policy under fixed and flexible exchange rates, *Canadian Journal of Economics and Political Science*, **29**, November, 475–485

MUNDELL, R. A. (1965), A fallacy in the interpretation of macroeconomic equilibrium, *Journal of Political Economy*, **73**, 61–66

MUSSA, M. (1977), Tariffs and the balance of payments: a monetary approach, in *The Monetary Approach to the Balance of Payments*, eds., J. A. Frenkel and H. G. Johnson, Allen and Unwin, London

NATIONAL BOARD FOR PRICES AND INCOMES (1967), *Bank charges*, Cmnd 3292, HMSO, London

NEWLYN, W. T. and BOOTLE, R. (1978), *The Theory of Money*, Clarendon Press, Oxford

NOBAY, A. R. and JOHNSON, H. G. (1977), Comment, on Some criticisms of the monetary analysis of balance of payments correction, D. A. Currie, *Economic Journal*, **87**, December, 769–770

ORR, D. (1970), *Cash Management and the Demand for Money*, Praeger, New York

PARKIN, J. M., SUMNER, M. and WARD, R. (1976), The effects of excess demand, generalized expectations and wage-price controls on inflation in the UK 1956–71, in *The Economics of Price and Wage Controls*, eds., H. Brunner and A. H. Meltzer, North Holland, Amsterdam

PATINKIN, D. (1965), *Money, Interest and Prices*, Harper and Row, New York

PESEK, B. and SAVING, T. (1967), *Money, Wealth and Economic Theory*, Collier MacMillan, New York

PESEK, B. and SAVING, T. (1968), *The Foundations of Money and Banking*, Collier Macmillan, New York

PHELPS, E. S. (1967), Phillips curves, expectations of inflation and optimal unemployment over time, *Economica*, **34**, August, 254–281

PHELPS, E. S. (ed.) (1971), *Microeconomic Foundations of Employment and Inflation Theory*, Macmillan, London

PHILLIPS, A. W. (1958), The relation between unemployment and the rate of change of money wage rates in the United Kingdom, 1861–1957, *Economica*, **25**, November, 283–299

PIGOU, A. C. (1943), The classical stationary state, *Economic Journal*, **53**, December 343–351

POOLE, W. (1970), Optional choice of monetary policy instruments in a simple stochastic macro-model, *Quarterly Journal of Economics*, **84**, May, 197–216

POOLE, W. and KORNBLITH, E. B. F. (1973), The Friedman–Meiselman CMC paper: new evidence on an old controversy, *American Economic Review*, **63**, December, 903–917

PURVIS, D. D. (1980), Monetarism: a review, *Canadian Journal of Economics*, **13**, February, 96–122

RADCLIFFE COMMITTEE (1959), *Report on the Working of the Monetary System* Cmnd 827, HMSO, London

RITTER, L. S. (1963), The role of money in Keynesian theory, in *Banking and Monetary Studies*, ed, D. Carson, Irwin, New York

ROBINSON, J. (1937), The foreign exchanges, in *Essays, in the Theory of Employment*, Allen and Unwin, London

ROWAN, D. C. and MILLER, J. (1979), The demand for money in the UK: 1965–77, University of Southampton Discussion Paper, No 7902, January

SAUNDERS, P. G. (1978), Inflation expectations and the natural rate of unemployment, *Applied Economics*, **10**, September, 187–193

SAVAGE, D. (1980), Some issues of monetary policy, *National Institute Economic Review*, **91**, February, 78–85

SAVING, T. R. (1967), Monetary-policy targets and indicators, *Journal of Political Economy*, **75**, August, 446–456

SHACKLE, G. L. S. (1967), *The Years of High Theory: Invention and Tradition in Economic Thought 1926–39*, Cambridge University Press, Cambridge

SHACKLE, G. L. S. (1971), Discussion Paper in *Monetary Theory and Monetary Policy in the 1970s*, eds. G. Clayton, J. C. Gilbert and R. Sedgewick, Oxford University Press, Oxford

SHAW, L. S. (1969), Money supply and stable economic growth, in *Readings in Economics*, ed. H. Kohler, Holt, Rinehart and Winston, London

SHEPPARD, D. K. (1971), *The Growth and Role of UK Financial Institutions 1880–1962*, Methuen, London

SIMS, C. A. (1972), Money, income and causality, *American Economic Review*, **62**, September, 540–552

SMITH, W. L. (1959), Financial intermediaries and monetary controls, *Quarterly Journal of Economics*, **73**, November

SOLOW, R. M. (1969), *Price Expectations and the Behaviour of the Price Level*, Manchester University Press, Manchester

SPENCER, P. and MOWL, C. (1978), The model of the domestic monetary system, part 1 of *A Financial Sector for the Treasury Model*, Government Economic Service Working Papers No. 17 (Treasury Working Paper No. 8), December

SPRINKEL, B. W. (1959), Monetary growth as a cyclical predictor, *Journal of Finance*, September, 333–346

TARLING, R. and WILKINSON, F. (1977), Inflation and the money supply, *Economic Policy Review*, **3**, March, 56–60

TOBIN, J. (1956), The interest-elasticity of the transactions demand for cash, *Review of Economics and Statistics*, **38**, August, 241–247

TOBIN, J. (1958), Liquidity preference as behaviour towards risk, *Review of Economic Studies*, **25**, February, 65–86

TOBIN, J. (1961), Money, capital and other stores of value, *American Economic Association Papers and Proceedings*, **61**, May, 26–37

TOBIN, J. (1963), Commercial banks as creators of money, in *Banking and Monetary Studies*, ed. D. Carson, Irwin, Homewood, Illinois

TOBIN, J. (1965), The theory of portfolio section, in *The Theory of Interest Rates*, eds., P. H. Hahn and F. P. R. Breckling, Macmillan, London

TOBIN, J. (1969a), Monetary semantics, in *Targets and Indicators of Monetary Policy*, ed. K. Brunner, Chandler, California

TOBIN, J. (1969b), A general equilibrium approach to monetary theory, *Journal of Money, Credit and Banking,*, **1**, February, 15–29

TOBIN, J. (1970), Money and income: post hoc ergo propter hoc, *Quarterly Journal of Economics*, **84**, May, 301–317

TOBIN, J. (1980), *Asset Accumulation and Economic Activity: Reflections on Contemporary Macroeconomic Theory*, Blackwell, Oxford

TOBIN, J. and HESTER, D. D. (1967), Introduction, in *Risk Aversion and Portfolio Choice*, Cowles Foundation for Research in Economics at Yale University, Wiley, New York

TURNOVSKY, S. J. and WACHTER, W. L. (1972), A test of the 'expectations hypothesis' using directly observed wage and price expectations, *Review of Economics and Statistics*, **54**, February, 47–54

WALTERS, A. A. (1971), Money in boom and slump, Institute of Economic Affairs, Hobart Paper No. 44

WHITE PAPER (1944), *Employment Policy*, Cmnd 6527, HMSO, London

WHITMAN, M. V. (1975), Global monetarism and the monetary approach to the balance of payments, *Brookings Papers on Economic Activity*, **3**, 491–536

WILLIAMS, D., GOODHART, C. A. E. and GOWLAND, D. (1976), Money, income and causality: the UK experience, *American Economic Review*, **66**, June, 417–423

WILSON, T., Effective devaluation and inflation, *Oxford Economic Papers*, **28**, March, 1–24

WREN-LEWIS, S. (1981), The role of money in determining prices: a reduced form approach, Government Economic Service Working Paper No. 42, HM Treasury, London

YEAGER, L. B. (1968), Essential properties of the medium of exchange, *Kyklos*, **21**, 45–69

ZELLNER, A. (1979), Causality and econometrics, in *Three Aspects of Policymaking: Knowledge, Data and Institutions*, North-Holland, Amsterdam

Index